Managing Diversity

Managing Diversity

A Complete Desk Reference
& Planning Guide

THIRD EDITION

Lee Gardenswartz and Anita Rowe

Society for Human Resource Management
Alexandria, Virginia | www.shrm.org

Society for Human Resource Management
Haidian District Beijing, China | www.shrm.org/cn

Strategic Human Resource Management India
Mumbai, India | www.shrmindia.org

The Society for Human Resource Management (SHRM) is the world's largest association devoted to human resource management. Representing more than 250,000 members in over 140 countries, the Society serves the needs of HR professionals and advances the interests of the HR profession. Founded in 1948, SHRM has more than 575 affiliated chapters within the United States and subsidiary offices in China and India. Visit SHRM Online at www.shrm.org.

Interior and Cover Design: Shirley E.M. Raybuck

Library of Congress Cataloging-in-Publication Data

Gardenswartz, Lee.
  Managing diversity : a complete desk reference & planning guide / Lee Gardenswartz and Anita Rowe.–3rd ed.
      p. cm.
  Includes bibliographical references and index.
  ISBN 978-1-58644-156-2
  1. Personnel management. 2. Supervision of employees. 3. Minorities–Employment. 4. Psychology, Industrial. 5. Diversity in the workplace. I. Rowe, Anita, 1946- II. Title.
  HF5549.5.M5G37 2010
  658.3008–dc22
                                    2009053862

09-0473

Brief Table of Contents

Detailed Table of Contents

• •

Activities, Checklists, Figures, and Tables

• •

SECTION 1
Making Diversity Work:
The What and How for
Managers and Trainers

CHAPTER 1.

Making This Book Work for You

· ·

This chapter will provide you with:

- An overview of *Managing Diversity*:
  - » Who it is for
  - » What is in it
  - » How to use it
- A road map for using each of the sections
- A brief explanation of each of the chapters

The pure and simple truth is rarely
pure and never simple.

—OSCAR WILDE

Why Managing Diversity Is Still Relevant

The identity of U.S. Americans—as a collective nation and as individuals—is in a state of constant flux. Our bedrock values (mostly inherited through historical documents written more than 200 years ago) might articulate beliefs most of us willingly subscribe to, but complexity rears its head the minute we try to determine what these beliefs (articulated in the late 1700s) mean at the beginning of the 21st century. Hence the wisdom of Oscar Wilde's quote about the illusion of simplicity. We can no longer pretend to think of ourselves as a homogeneous and predominantly white, Anglo Saxon, Protestant nation, where subscribing to a creed and adhering to these principles is done in unison.

The field of diversity has evolved in a similar fashion to the identity of our nation, which has been evolving and transforming demographically for centuries. We have been in this field long enough to remember when the phrase "melting pot" was common and acculturation was a worthy goal. Over time, the salad-bowl metaphor seemed more apt and implied that people wanted, and indeed needed, to retain their uniqueness. Acculturation was too high a price because it suggested that fitting into the existing culture was the prize and the cost of that fit was one's roots and initial identity. Now in 2010, the focus is on inclusion and globalization, whether we look at differences inside our own borders or work with people all over the world, many on their own soil. This is not your father's concept of diversity. Individuals from diverse groups are less willing to shed their rich cultural identities as the price for belonging. Rather, they seek an America that will accommodate the cultures of their disparate roots while they simultaneously adopt and integrate norms of mainstream culture.

This change from traditional assimilation to multicultural juggling has significantly impacted U.S. business. Individuals who know and feel the value added in their own uniqueness are less willing to adapt to the traditional white-male model of behavior in order to succeed, and that single or dominant model has less hold on the imagination of organizations and its employees today. There is far too much evidence, statistically and anecdotally, that indicates how much better off both organizations and individuals are where views and ideas can benefit from cross-pollination.

Knowing that diversity brings benefits and advantages does not necessarily mean organizations are embracing the changes. The rich mix does not always lead to harmony. The blend of cultures, genders, lifestyles, and values often becomes a source of misunderstanding and conflict. Many enlightened leaders and managers, from CEOs in the executive suite to supervisors on the shop floor, want to create an environment where differences are valued and where people who look, talk, and think differently can work productively together. However, most managers' do not have the knowledge or experience to orchestrate such harmonious change. Like explorers in a new land, they are entering uncharted areas. Old methods fall short, and new ones are just in the beginning of the development process. Existing mind sets are limiting, yet new paradigms have not come into focus. Long-held assumptions are no longer in sync with today's reality, and new truths are yet to be determined.

The task is daunting, the challenge is formidable, and the stakes are enormous. Something new is being attempted in human history. Milton J. Bennett, a cross cultural specialist, states, "Intercultural sensitivity is not natural. It is not part of our primate past, nor has it characterized most of human history. Cross cultural contact often has been accompanied by bloodshed, oppression, or genocide. Clearly this pattern cannot continue. Today, the failure to exercise intercultural sensitivity is not simply bad business or bad morality—it is self-destructive. So we face a choice: overcome the legacy of our history, or lose history itself for all time."[1] If Bennett's quote was not enough of a wake-up call, we are also trying to accomplish this harmony in an unforgiving economic and political climate. Those who work in the diverse environment of American business today, and those who travel the world over, readily see the truth of Bennett's challenge.

Whom This Book Is For

This book is designed for those of you who spend much of your lives in organizations across this country and around the world and who are willing to move beyond the painful legacy of human history, thus creating humane, prosperous, positive, and productive organizations. *Managing Diversity* can help you if you have any one of the following job titles or responsibilities:

- A **diversity director or coordinator** who is charged with implementing an organization-wide diversity initiative. If you are tasked with diversity implementation, this book is a gold mine, an endlessly useful tool that combines the systemic, strategic-level possibilities with a continuous array of both practical and tactical charts, tools, grids, assessments, models, and checklists. Suggestions, questions about, and considerations regarding the actions an organization needs or wants to take regarding culture change are sprinkled throughout the book. This is an A-to-Z reference and resource for a person charged with the full scope of diversity implementation.
- Diversity councils—advocates for communication and change regarding diversity. Knowing how to effect change and get commitment is critical, but it is not easy. Diversity councils need this book for the same reason. It is full of strategic information that will enable councils to function as leaders of change, and it also provides rich, plentiful team-building tools for any diversity council that needs to shape its own cohesion and interpersonal understanding.
- A **manager** who sees the effects of diversity from the trenches. It has never been easy to deal with motivation, productivity, and morale, but the challenges facing the manager of today's diverse workforce are monumental. With Facebook, texting, and Twitter, even racial, ethnic, and gender issues can take a back seat to the immediacy of the moment and the ubiquity of technology. Dealing with workgroup issues and conflicts that are rooted in a variety of cultures, values, and languages, as well as new global business

realities, means that new skills, knowledge, and techniques are required. *Managing Diversity* can help you gain knowledge and insight, and also help you develop the skills for building a cohesive group as personal and cultural differences show their constant presence.

- A **human resource (HR) professional** charged with the responsibility of managing the changing workforce, recruiting staff to achieve a more diverse employee base, or opening up the promotional system to increase diversity at the top. Beyond managing change and attracting unique, unquestionable talent among the rich diversity that is everywhere, this book is helpful to HR professionals concerned with system-wide strategies regarding career development, performance review, and accountability systems. It can also be an aid in discovering how diversity may be at the core of grievances, feelings of isolation, and repeated bouts of frustration that some employees experience because the organization seems unyielding, unwelcoming, inflexible, and exclusionary.

- A **trainer** who conducts seminars or workshops that offer knowledge, awareness, and skills regarding managing a diverse workforce. This book presents content information for lectures about changing demographics and different cultural norms, as well as guidelines for dealing with specific diversity-related issues such as how to deal with language differences in the workplace or celebrate holidays that not everyone subscribes to. In addition, training activities, worksheets, and inventories are given in a ready-to-use format. Directions for how to use them can be found on the accompanying disk. Finally, the book offers information that can help the trainer design sessions that are effective with trainees from different backgrounds. Training tools foster interactive learning and open dialogue. They can be adapted, used in part or whole, combined and used in very different ways with any number of groups across such differences as years in the organization, job function, language differences, and fluency, or lack of it in English. The *Suggestions for Using* portions of this book will help you think through the best use of the tools for each situation and group.

- An **internal** or **external consultant** leading an organization, division, or workgroup through the change process from monocultural to multicultural. Conducting a diversity audit may help determine where the problem areas and opportunities for growth might be. However, all the work might not be diagnostic. If a survey indicates a need for training to increase awareness, information, or skill building, this book offers the consultant that information as well. Whether the consultant teaches managers how to build more cohesive work teams or how to better develop personnel, the necessary information and tools are there for immediate use.

- A **facilitator** who works with groups to help them identify and solve diversity-related problems and build individual and group skills. A facilitator can make use of the tools offered in any chapter because they can all be adapted, but if, for example, better teamwork is the goal, our suggestion is to start with Chapter 8.

- An **affirmative action officer** looking for tools and information to help managers create a more open and diversity-friendly climate.

- A **CEO** or **president** who understands that effectively leveraging the changing workforce is part of the equation in being a profitable, successful organization. This is for the organizational leader who sees himself or herself as the person setting strategy, leading the change process, holding others accountable, and determining how to use the workforce effectively. This role also involves paying attention to what policies and practices pose barriers to the goal of creating a more inclusive organization and ensuring that real and necessary changes occur. Finally, this book is for the CEO who knows the value of winning in the marketplace by attracting extraordinary talent, and by creating an organizational culture that is welcoming to both employees and consumers. The leadership of the CEO in capitalizing on diversity is paramount and will impact employee productivity, creativity, commitment, and, ultimately, profitability. This book serves as a tool that focused and committed leaders can offer to staff members who have the responsibility of implementing a CEO's vision.

How To Use This Book

This book can be useful in a number of ways. It gives both a macro and a micro view of diversity. Which view you choose to focus on at any given time depends upon the objectives and needs of your organization. While the book is written from a U.S. American diversity perspective, it also has a global reach and framework. We encourage you to adapt any tool in this book to your global or virtual team's reality or circumstance. Sometimes we specifically call out adaptations and applications for global use but even when we don't, the possibilities are there for you and we encourage you to make them. By previewing the three sections and becoming familiar with the distinct contributions each makes before you actually read the whole book, you will get a sense of the scope of *Managing Diversity*'s content.

Section I is intended for practitioners who are dealing with the nitty-gritty issues that emerge when people from different places, backgrounds, ages, and religions come together in the workplace. This section is full of ready-to-use tools that can be used as is or adapted by managers and trainers for use with individuals, workgroups, or training session participants. All training tools and inventories are accompanied by a guide in the previously referenced disk with directions on how to use them. In addition to hands-on materials, you will also find suggestions for dealing with specific diversity-related problems you may be encountering, such as when to use an interpreter, how to solve culture-related conflicts, or what techniques to use in implementing effective performance reviews amidst group members with different cultural practices and values.

The information in Section I will be most helpful if you start with Chapter 2, which gives you a context regarding changes and trends, and then proceed to Chapter 3, which explains the dimensions of diversity, then continue to read the remaining chapters in Section I in sequence—that is, if you need all of the background and basic information to begin doing the work in your organization. If you don't need all the basic information, use the chapters in real time as needed. For example, while you may want to find out how to get more employee participation in performance reviews, it is important to first understand the diversity dimensions, cultural variables, and communication techniques that impact working with diverse employees. If you have a fragmented work team, we suggest you understand the diversity dimensions and cultural influences operating on those teams and possible explanations for how or why team members react to one another before trying to build a more cohesive group. Again, reading Chapters 2, 3, 5, and 6 before you dive into team-building activities would provide that important background. This section is designed to be used often and we hope you will make repeated visits to the specific information you seek on an as-need basis. Even for those of you who have been in the field for a while, those chapters can remind the reader of some of the subtle complexities of diversity that one loses track of over time. Reviews *are* helpful.

Section II provides the macro view for change agents and those in charge of strategic planning. The information in this section can help you modify existing organizational systems to remove the barriers that prevent your organization from capitalizing on diversity. Chapter 11 gives guidance in planning a strategic diversity implementation process, and Chapter 15 helps you measure and evaluate your initiative. Chapter 12 presents audit tools that can pinpoint the organizational Achilles' heels, while other chapters can offer suggestions about redesigning systems to be more inclusive. For example, if your recruiting efforts for women and people of color are good but your retention isn't, the information on mentoring and career development in Chapter 14 will be useful. While you're looking at retention issues, you may also decide that the organizational climate needs a little scrutiny. Chapter 10 on corporate culture will give you tools to assess how inclusive and inviting your organization's climate is to all employees. Inclusion conversations are being taken to a deeper and more practical level now than when we wrote and revised the first two editions of this book in the early and late 1990s. Look for important questions that are raised about inclusion. Examples of organizations that are successfully adapting to change offer both food for thought and hope. If you're not the major power wielder in your company and you lack the clout to be the major catalyst in changing the systems, Section II can give you information to make your case and build support among those who do have the influence to make the necessary changes.

Section III offers information that clarifies the difference between managing diversity and previous anti-discriminatory policies. It also gives you a host of other resources that can provide more information for further learning and research. In the Appendix, books, videos, web sites, and training materials, simulations, and questionnaires are annotated and listed with information that tells you how to obtain the material you are seeking. Chapter 16 looks at the opportunities organizations are creating to make diversity sustainable and to truly be a good corporate citizen. It delves into the notion of corporate responsibility and how both sustainability and being socially responsible connect to diversity.

What's in This Book

The following information will give you a chapter-by-chapter overview. Additionally, specific objectives are listed at the beginning of each chapter.

Section I: Making Diversity Work: The What and How for Managers and Trainers

Chapter 1: Making This Book Work for You functions as a guide that tells you how to use *Managing Diversity*. It explains the three-part structure of the book, details the content you can expect to find in each chapter, and describes how to maximize the learning while finding easy access to the specific material you need or want.

Chapter 2: Diversity Then and Now: Changes and Trends provides information about the current context, both in the workplace and society in general. Changes such as electing our first bi-racial president and having some states recognize gay and lesbian marriages are only two examples.

Chapter 3: Diversity: What It Is in a Complex World answers the question of what diversity is by presenting a model of diversity that delineates the multiple dimensions and creates a paradigm for inclusion. Each dimension is explained with examples and an assessment/analysis tool is provided to apply the model to your organization. The model is a starting point for you. As you read it, do so with an eye toward what needs to be added and adapted for your own organization, and also with the idea that the more inclusive and broad the definition, the less resistance you'll have to the whole conversation about diversity.

Chapter 4: Dealing with Diversity in a Global Context expands the domestic model of diversity by explaining additional dimensions of diversity that need to be understood in global organizations. It provides tools for applying the model to your organization and analyzing information and actions needed to build inclusion globally.

Chapter 5: Increasing Cultural Competence explains the 10 specific ways in which culture programs behavior and impacts workplace relationships and performance. You will see, for example, how such programming shapes everything from perceptions about the role of women in the workplace to how directly or indirectly to communicate or resolve conflicts. You will also get suggestions about how to deal with cultural differences that are obstacles to workgroup harmony and productivity.

Chapter 6: Learning the Cultural Etiquette of Communication gives critical information about communication across cultures. It is designed to help you decode the behavior of others, whether from different parts of the world, regions of your own country or departments in your organization. From understanding the different nonverbal aspects of interactions and communicating with limited-English-speaking individuals to giving feedback and resolving conflicts, it offers techniques and strategies for effective interactions in a multicultural environment. Language issues such as using interpreters and translators, dealing with accents, and teaching English are also discussed.

Chapter 7: Managing Stereotypes and Prejudice in the Workplace provides an explanation of how stereotypes and prejudice influence assumptions, interactions, and decisions in the workplace. It also gives tools to help others manage these phenomena to reduce their negative impact.

Chapter 8: Building Multicultural Work Teams identifies cross-cultural factors that impact team building among groups of individuals whose norms, practices, and values are different. It helps to see examples of expected norms and what is behind them. For example, how is consensus achieved in different cultures? Global and virtual teams are part of this conversation. While the dimensions of cross-cultural team building illustrate differences, areas of common ground are also highlighted. Strategies are given for helping a team meet universal human needs such as self-esteem, belonging, and trust.

Chapter 9: Performance Evaluation in a Diverse Organization explains aspects of diversity that affects the performance evaluation process and gives methods and techniques for making effective use of performance appraisal with a diverse staff. Specific how-tos, guidelines, and skills are shared.

Section II: Integrating Diversity Into Your Organization: Modifying Systems to Capitalize on the Benefits of a Pluralistic Workforce

Chapter 10: Creating an Inclusive Culture That Leverages the Strength and Power of Diversity deals with the issue of creating a welcoming, open organizational environment. It provides assessment tools for measuring how open the climate is and explains the resistance to change which is so often a factor in an organization's cultural rigidity. This chapter also shows ways to make inclusion more than a catch phrase and leverage it as a retention strategy.

Chapter 11: Diversity and Inclusion as an Organization Development Intervention: Culture Change That Works presents guidelines for implementing diversity initiatives. Seven steps, followed by examples at each stage, are given. Specific systems change practices are highlighted along with saboteurs and pitfalls, as well as ways to avoid them.

Chapter 12: Conducting a Diversity Audit: Taking an Organizational Snapshot compares three fundamental assessment methods: questionnaires, interviews, and focus groups. Suggestions are given for using each appropriately. The chapter also offers a myriad of assessment tools that measure individual attitudes, awareness, and knowledge, as well as management skills and organizational progress in managing diversity.

Chapter 13: Recruiting and Hiring a Diverse Workforce presents numerous tools for finding ways to create the reputation for being a top-notch place to work. It looks at the practices an organization employs to get people and create the reputation that attracts top talent. Cross-cultural networking tips are presented as a way to increase contact with a diverse employee base. In addition, suggestions for asking questions and gathering information in culturally sensitive ways are provided to make the entire recruiting process more compatible with a pluralistic population.

Chapter 14: Promoting, Coaching, and Career Development To Engage the Talent of Everyone focuses on what qualities and characteristics are rewarded and promoted in your organization. It outlines the qualities needed for global leadership. In addition, suggestions are given for using coaching and mentoring techniques to develop high-potential employees, and the chapter concludes by explaining the impact of culture on career development.

Chapter 15: Evaluation and Measurement: Tracking the Effects of Diversity Initiatives gives guidelines and steps for designing measurement systems that evaluate the effect of diversity interventions. Measurement data sources are listed and methods of evaluating are presented. In addition, a five-level model of evaluation that can help focus the process is provided.

Section III: An External Focus for Diversity
Chapter 16: Corporate Social Responsibility, Sustainability, and Diversity: A Strategic Partnership presents the visionary paradigm of long-term diversity work, highlighting the intersection of corporate social responsibility, sustainability, and diversity. It looks at multiple ways organizations can help and invest in small, local communities, as well as those on a wider scale. Relevant questions are posed that highlight both the challenges and opportunities of making choices that help human and natural ecosystems.

Chapter 17: Diversity and Inclusion Means More Than Equal Employment Opportunity helps place diversity and inclusion in an historical context as part of a long evolution within American society and business. Specific differences between affirmative action, valuing differences, managing diversity, and inclusion are delineated. A tool for assessing your organization's progress in its evolution is also presented.

Chapter 18: Making Diversity Work: Summing It Up looks at essential attitudes that need to be fostered in a diversity-friendly organization and identifies the organizational imperatives that must be in place if diversity and inclusion are to work and become a corporate asset.

Appendix: Diversity Resources provides lists of resources for reading, research, and training about various aspects of diversity. Relevant books, periodicals, newsletters, audiovisual materials, and web sites are included along with a short description of each.

What Makes This Book Different

Managing Diversity (now in its third edition) continues to provide hands-on activities for any member of the organization accountable to the CEO, a board of directors, or manager who wants to have a better team or task force. It gives guidelines for implementing diversity initiatives from a strategic perspective, including a range of suggestions about measurement and evaluation. It is essentially a one-stop shop diversity primer full of information, context, examples, user-friendly tools, provocative questions for your organization, and a lot of practicality. It has been reinvigorated to suit our fast-paced technological world full of global teams. Opportunities for adaptation abound.

While the book aims to fill many functions, the feedback we have gotten over 16 years is that the book's most unique and valuable contribution is the plethora of tools and activities it offers managers, trainers, coordinators, consultants, and facilitators. The inventories and worksheets are relevant, easily reproducible, and ready to use. They provoke rich conversations and provide methods for dealing with significant and sometimes tough issues. Each activity comes complete with objectives, a description of the activity, processing questions, and notes about special caveats or considerations. The training materials, audits, instruments, questionnaires, and tools are user-friendly and provide variety in purpose and complexity. All will enable individuals and workgroups first to look inside themselves, then to look outside the personal domain to the organizational arena, and, finally, to move beyond insight and awareness toward change.

The combination of individual assessments, management training tools, systems audits, and clear models make this a ready-to-use resource. Separate lists of charts, models, and reproducible training tools are given with page numbers to make them easily accessible. The comprehensive resource guide at the end, which delineates training materials, simulations, books, videos, and other resources, gives you a road map for future learning.

Visionary organizations that want to be leaders in their respective fields will take the reality of diversity and make it a corporate asset. The wisdom in and of diversity can truly be realized by using all this book has to offer. We frequently chuckle that if we lived 1,000 years we could not exhaust all these tools. They are numerous, engaging, nonpolarizing, and they have the capacity to get you where you need to go. We wish you our best on your journey.

CHAPTER 2.

Diversity Then and Now: Changes and Trends

• •

This chapter will provide you with:

- A look at recent history

- A reflection on future trends

- A sense of what is the same, and where the changes are

This chapter is designed to provide some history and context on the subject of diversity. As we write this in late 2009, major changes are leaving a big impact on how diversity is defined, resourced, and practiced. It is impossible to discuss the future of diversity without acknowledging the impact of a severe recession in the United States and around the globe. Meeting basic needs, such as keeping employees in their current jobs, sometimes trumps an interest in forward-looking systemic investments which would bode well for economic and communal sustainability over time. And the economic crisis, however severe, is only one of many catalysts that are triggering significant changes. Globalization and the proliferation of new technology are among other factors that diversity practitioners have to deal with and adapt to.

We will highlight past shapers of diversity implementation and direction, but our largest emphasis is on what remains the same through the years and also what has changed. Dealing with the latter will require taking a look at the implications for diversity practitioners and organizations today.

What's Old and Evolving News

Over the last 20 years, there have been some strong themes that populated the focus of diversity in organizations. Here are some that stand out:

Diversity: What Is the Definition and How Wide Are the Parameters?

In the early days of this work, visible differences and an emphasis on making room in organizations for people from groups previously excluded was the rallying cry. To some, it felt like it was all about affirmative action, and in some cases, it was. There were many conversations where people strongly advocated as the top priority opening the systems to those previously excluded, while others talked about an affirmative action mind-set as exclusionary for white males and bad for business. Other conversations went beyond the traditional boundaries. For example, an employee didn't have to be black or lesbian to need the benefits of a more open culture. If she were a mother with young children who got overlooked repeatedly and automatically for more challenging jobs due to presumed parental obligations, that was a legitimate diversity issue to some segment of people involved in the early days of this work. Over time, the definition has almost universally expanded for numerous reasons. Being inclusive is good business. It gets more commitment and engagement, which also makes it very practical.

Any parameter that automatically excludes white males, for example, because of their gender, skin color, and perceived opportunities, turns out to be not only unfair and unethical, it also engenders divisions and resistance in organizations, especially among white-male hourly workers who often feel very powerless and don't relate to the idea that their skin color gives them privilege. Over time, the evolution from counting those who were visibly different to creating a culture more hospitable for everyone became the norm. However, it was not uncommon to hear black employees talk about never getting their own historic issues front and center before a broad definition put them at the back of the line again, and record numbers of Hispanic employees (some documented, some not; some U.S. born, some not) began to be part of a rapidly changing demographic that also left some blacks feeling alienated. The huge increase in Hispanics called attention to politics, as well as language policy in the workplace and in U.S. schools. The definition of diversity involved politics, a sense of power and belonging, and the very practical implications of hiring and retaining good people.

Affirmative Action

The phrase "affirmative action" usually kicks up emotions, both positive and negative. As globalization has increased, so has the experience of seeing a wide variety of very talented, competent people in many organizations looking for opportunity. Coming in contact with so many good people from different backgrounds has lessened resistance to those who are different. Also, the truth is that most people at the top of organizations are still white and male, so fears of losing all opportunity have not been realized. There have been two other important dimensions to affirmative action, one of which involves white females: They have been the biggest beneficiaries of affirmative action policy, so while affirmative action is necessary to expanding the talent pool and providing much needed and earned opportunity, it is not sufficient to creating diversity in the fullest sense. If doors are to really open, more work remains.

Another barrier regarding affirmative action has to do with a subtle and subconscious but still present assumption that goes like this: Anyone who is an affirmative action hire or appointment only got that promotion or job because of gender, race, and so on. This involves the subtle assumption of substandardness. It is a false assumption. We have both excellence and mediocrity that comes in all backgrounds, sizes, shapes, colors, and languages, but the perception, though subtle, still exists that through merit alone, affirmative action candidates could not get hired or promoted.

It seems that the globalization of the marketplace and world demographics have stolen some thunder from this debate. A legally driven affirmative action position is not much of a driver in corporate diversity today, though it still does hold sway in government contracts. When the Board of the University of California did away with affirmative action in admissions, there was conversation with many of our clients in California. We asked what difference it would make to them if there was no affirmative action requirement and virtually every single person we talked with from every organization said, "None." They want the variety of background, talent, experience. The driver for them had long stopped being a legal one. While executives and boards of directors may see the business reason for affirmative action at strategic levels, the challenge for diversity practitioners at the tactical level with the rank and file is they have to implement initiatives in an often emotionally charged and volatile environment. One strategy for overcoming this potential volatility and resistance has been to craft a broad definition of diversity which is inclusive and avoids pitting group against group. Regarding the replacement of affirmative action with a different strategy or policy due to the fact that lack of equal opportunity still exists, the question centers around having the will to tackle the hard job of coming up with other options. It remains to be seen whether or not that will exists.

The Business Case

Making the business case has been a prominent part of diversity conversations over the last 20 years. Two things stand out about the business-case conversation. The first is that when we did this work in the 1980s, organizations that hired us asked us to make their case for them. At first we accepted what we saw as a legitimate challenge in doing this work. Over time, we saw that when we made the case for any particular organization, they would refute it. When they didn't work on it, own it, or have to think about the rationale for leveraging diversity, they could and would easily reject doing anything. No investment in making the case resulted in zero investment in doing the work. We no longer even attempt to make the case. We will facilitate their doing it, but the case must be their own.

Finally, on the topic of the business case, we thought we had moved past that. In the spring of 2008, SHRM brought together approximately 100 thought leaders for a conversation on diversity to determine the current status of the field. The need to make the business case was still at the top of that list. At a session filled with rich conversation and talented people who have seen and done a lot of this work, it was sobering to learn that so many organizations were still grappling with this issue. In the context of the economic downturn, stressing the importance of diversity is certainly smart and probably even more necessary.

Increasing Globalization

"At its core, globalization is about broadening markets to include more participants."[1] Changes in technology, communication, and transportation have made cross-border transactions for goods and services much more common. Current newspaper and magazine articles tout the global era, but the Hudson Institute's *Workforce 2020* gives concreteness and specificity to this sometimes abstract notion. Note the following facts, which reveal an increasingly borderless world where distance is often meaningless.[2]

- The cost of a transatlantic call between New York and London dropped sixfold from 1940 to 1970, and it dropped another tenfold between 1970 and the beginning of the 1990s. If you are on the Internet today, you can communicate virtually free of charge by using SkypeExpansion in the volume of goods and services continues. To get a sense of how much, note the following: Between 1980 and 1995, total world output grew by approximately 60 percent but international trade grew by 120 percent.

- In 1970, annual world trade output was about 25 percent. In 2000, that figure was about 50 percent, and, by 2020, it is not inconceivable that world output may be 67 percent. The estimate of 2020 predates the global recession of 2009. That recession will slow imports and exports down, but the slowdown is a specific change due to economic factors, not structural ones. When the economics of the world improve, so will trade numbers.

Proof of globalization can be seen everywhere. Few people dispute its growing importance. The question posed to those responsible for diversity initiatives then is, "How does increasing globalization impact the work of practitioners, both internal and external?" The answer to that question requires a look at the openness of the attitudes that accompany changes required for effectiveness in cross-border norms, languages, policies, values, and a host of other variables. Beyond attitudes being more flexible, globalization requires examining the relationship between home-country ethics and doing business abroad. And, finally, at a very practical level, globalization calls into question training methodology, format, and a host of other issues that need to be taken into account in a world where borders are so permeable.

Diversity Evolution Continued: Present to Future

A Change in the Executive Suite

Any discussion of potential changes in the climate and the composition of the executive suite must start with the election of Senator Barack Obama, our first bi-racial president. The election was historic and so was the campaign. At 72 years of age, Senator John McCain was the oldest candidate we've ever had. Barack Obama's primary Democrat opposition was Senator Hillary Clinton, but most of the energy was around Obama and Governor Sarah Palin. The campaign, and the ultimate election of Barack Obama, changes what is perceived to be possible for people growing up in the United States. The symbolic value of Obama's election and his subsequent wide-ranging cabinet selections is noteworthy. Perhaps most noteworthy of all is that people's backgrounds, gender, and ancestry did not have to be called out as extraordinary. Leadership at the top of the U.S. government is evolving into a wider palate.

The Evolution of Inclusion

When the broad definition of diversity was fully accepted as a matter of course, the conversation about inclusion alluded to the fact that those who sat at the table might look and be different from those who sat there in the past. Making certain that everyone in the organization felt both heard and represented was the centerpiece of early conversations about inclusion. Leaving people or groups out was not OK. What inclusion has evolved to over the years is more than representation. The question now is more about how these differences will be used. They have to count for and mean something. Real inclusion means differences in policies, practices, and procedures. A seat at the table was an important first step but it is not enough.

Diversity as Means to an End

In the early years of diversity work, much of the energy was on educating people about terminology, sensitivity, and language to use and avoid. Basic diversity training was one prominent way to have the dialogue and ask some good, hard questions around which that dialogue took place. This education, often referred to as Diversity Training 101, was seen as a valuable end in itself. Over time, people at every level of most organizations came to realize that diversity is a vehicle to a better, more productive and profitable organization. Smart organizations link or integrate diversity initiatives to other ongoing change efforts so it becomes more of an organization development (OD) effort than an end point. Diversity can be a catalyst for changing policies, practices, and systems, any or all of which can create a huge change in the organization.

Immigration: The Ongoing Issue

Immigration has been a hot, divisive issue for a long time, and emotions run high along the U.S./Mexican border. It is sometimes hard to have discussions that actually look at the complex economic interplay of businesses and families hiring cheaper labor against the use of services given to people who live in a particular place. It is volatile, indeed. Again, with economic slowdown and fewer jobs to be had, reasons to come north and cross the border, with all the dangers and disruptions inherent in that process, are fewer. When we wrote the first two editions of *Managing Diversity*, we did not have a wall between Mexico and the United States, But we have the beginnings of one now. How the immigration numbers and debate play out remain to be seen. Furthermore, Sept. 11 had an impact on immigration beyond our immediate borders. Change in visa policies and an ability to recruit talent from abroad testifies to these changes.

Technology and Online Training

One of the most massive changes in society at every level involves technology and how pervasive it is in every part of life. For people 40 and older, it is difficult (generally speaking) to remember a time without the Internet. For people younger, it is impossible. While texting may be a fairly recent phenomenon, there is hardly a person 30 or younger who doesn't have texting as a dominant mode of communication, and they have plenty of company from adults over 30 as well. But as teachers and facilitators, it is only in the last few years that we have had to fight BlackBerry devices in class to get attention from students. Cell phones are everywhere. It is very difficult to even find pay phones any more. In classes, we try to enforce no cell phones and pagers, but seeing people's eyes is tough when they are trying to hide a BlackBerry in their lap as they text away.

Social networking is pervasive: Facebook, My Space, LinkedIn, and Twitter create a whole new way to connect with others, and present a new reality in organizations. One impact is that as people text, Skype, and e-mail people from all over the globe, a global connection becomes more clear and constant. A world without the pervasiveness of technology is unimaginable. A primary consideration, from a diversity standpoint, is how to keep from having insiders and outsiders in an organization defined by degrees of "tech savviness" or "tech awkwardness." Age is probably an important dividing line here, but the insider/outsider issue is relevant nonetheless.

One more important diversity-related impact is the natural evolution in a highly technological world toward people wanting to take more classes or learning online. Webinars are a constant presence. For the HR practitioner, the question centers around what classes could legitimately be done online without sacrificing too much quality, and which ones warrant face-to-face interaction. There aren't any right or wrong answers; just very good questions that need thoughtful dialogue. As we write this book, we are sure of only one thing: By the time it comes out, a good part of today's technology will be obsolete and we will be on to the next thing. Luckily, diversity is above all else an exercise in change—managing it well should help us deal effectively with all the changes that face us.

Corporate Responsibilities and Supplier Diversity ... a Growing Emphasis

Finally, as we look at factors that continue to emerge, one topic is coming out of the shadows to gain increasing focus and attention: Better corporate social responsibility is becoming a stronger business imperative. When we worked in the United Kingdom in the mid-1990s, we saw organizations in Europe pay serious attention to their impact on communities, and they found ways to intentionally give back so that the people they served would benefit. Corporate brands got polished by assisting communities. Whether we're talking about Target investing huge money in education, or Revlon sponsoring *race for the cure* for breast cancer, the idea is that where a company invests time, energy, and resources in helping communities, they do so as a brand that wants their name associated with making life better for people in whatever geographic or service territory the organizer carves out for itself.

So What for Diversity Practitioners?

It is one thing to recognize trends, but it is an entirely different thing to respond in a way that maximizes an organization's output. For diversity practitioners, the questions are practical and concrete:

- How does globalization impact training content? For example, what are the implications and limitations if American-based multinationals want to do sexual harassment training?

- Beyond the training content, how is training design altered? In what languages are materials printed and in what language is training delivered? Does an organization use translators? If so, how much content gets eliminated? Regarding teaching and learning methodology, how will a U.S. American bent towards interactive learning be received in cultures that like and are used to didactic modalities? Are you teaching in Europe, where theory and abstractions are more valued than in pragmatic American culture? If so, what alterations need to be made?

- In sharing, giving or getting feedback, problem-solving and brainstorming, what adaptations must be made to teach the same concept across different cultures?

- What ethical considerations (e.g., issues around the definition of truth/honesty) need to be explored to help employees understand values of host countries?

While there is clearly no one answer (or even a right answer) to any of these questions, they do form the beginnings of some thinking that needs to be part of an expanded mindset for anyone practicing diversity and inclusion.

Looking Ahead: Changes in the Field

Bob Abramms and George F. Simons catalogued a number of trends they were seeing, some of which, from our perspective, have become current reality:

- The "victim vs. oppressor" paradigm and terminology gets mentioned or used less frequently. Diversity definitions tend to include everyone and are not designed to blame or point fingers at European Americans (or anyone else for that matter).

- The emphasis, conceptually and linguistically, focuses on culture, ethnicity, and organizations rather than affirmative action, law suits, or sexual harassment. Culture—in particular, ethnic culture as it relates to the packaging, marketing, selling, and delivery of services—is a convenient way to get people on board. It is a business case most can understand, and it removes some of the polarization that a legal bent almost guarantees.

- The affirmative action paradigm is much less frequently linked to cultural competence. Diversity seen as value added is driven differently than affirmative action considerations, and the two are kept separate by most practitioners we know.

- Some African Americans believed that the new discipline and paradigm of diversity would siphon off energy needed to complete the original justice agenda of blacks. There may, in fact, be African Americans who feel that way, and based on the discussion of President Bill Clinton's proposed race dialogue in the 1990s, how you see this last issue may depend to a great extent, on where you live. If you live on the West Coast, where, for example, Latin and Asian populations are growing in huge numbers, and 51 percent of the population in Southern California speaks a language other than English at home, your reality is that diversity is a multicultural phenomenon. East of the Mississippi, where demographics are different, a narrower black/white dialogue is more prevalent. However, this demographic is also in flux. Fewer immigrants from Mexico and Central America are coming to the United States because there is little opportunity for work, but even those who do come now make their way more to the Southeast. States such as Georgia and North Carolina, which have traditionally had a mostly black/white population, are experiencing a major influx of native Spanish speakers. All over the United States, populations are getting more pluralistic. As we look ahead, two things strike us:

1. Practitioners need to be sensitive to the perception and reality of blacks who feel that their agenda is incomplete.
2. The United States is not exclusively, or even predominately, a black/white country. As we write this book, the United States is becoming less of a black/white nation. In the 2008 election, for example, the Latin vote was chased vigorously across the board. The challenge for those of us trying tackle the work of diversity is to identify other future trends and the opportunities, dilemmas, consequences, and realities that result.

Measuring Results

To site an old cliché, the proof will be in the pudding. If we don't find a way to show the value added, funding will continue to be a tough sell. Never mind that other training or HR dollars don't get the same scrutiny or face the same demands as dollars spent on diversity. Once we understand the arena in which we work, it is incumbent upon practitioners to find meaningful ways to measure not just individual behavior change and skill enhancement, but also systems changes. We need the data. We need to know what works and what doesn't or hasn't worked. Frankly, we can cite a lot more efforts that have fallen short than we can those that have transformed people and organizations. Without credible measurement, diversity work will continue to be kept in the background. And while most people at all levels of any organization have an intuitive belief that it matters, we can adapt a line from the film *Jerry Maguire*—instead of "Show me the money," the battle cry is "Show me the results." We fail to do so at our peril.

Different results talk to different audiences, so do your homework. At one level in the organization, it may be all about market share or products sold. For a manager who has a team that has more conflict than productivity, getting people to solve problems more effectively and be more creative involves a different measure. Know your audiences and what measures talk to each, and then go about the business of tracking results.

Equate Diversity with a Change Process

If diversity continues to be seen as "a training intervention," it will continue to be a box that needs to be checked off on someone's performance appraisal. We go to conferences where we talk about diversity as a process, but we may be talking to those who are already converted. Perhaps people in organizations don't understand what real change around diversity implies. In other words, we hear lots of talk, and the right words are frequently espoused, but following through to make real culture change happen in an organization is very hard work. As a field, we have to get better at sharing what works, and where the pitfalls are. We understand why change does not occur after resources have been committed and lip service given. We will, in fact, spend time in Chapters 10 and 11 focusing on organizational culture. Recognizing the competitive world in which we live means that we can't ignore our inability to grab change and make it work. Change can be a tough sell for a lot of reasons. There is a great deal at stake in creating a culture that combines the magic of being humane, open, productive, and fun with the practice that produces results. Our life and experiences have taught us the following lessons:

- An organization changes priorities when it hits survival mode. Commitments made in more sanguine times can be easily parted with in a crisis.
- It takes tons of diligence and discipline to make changes happen. Many employees have so much going on and are so fragmented that giving the diversity effort what it requires in order to see real change take place is too demanding, and there is not sufficient reward in the organization to complete diversity work at the expense of other organizational priorities.

These are some of the reasons sustained change may not happen. But a diversity process that fails to create a more humane, inclusive and productive organizations is not worth the effort. Realizing more productivity and a better return on investment (ROI), while also evolving into a greater place to work that provides more respectful service to all of our customers (internal and external) is irrelevant, costly, and not worth the effort. A long-term diversity change effort that alters the way business is conducted and how people see and engage with the world is required. The consequence of starting down this road and not completing the effort is one that will breed increased cynicism and lack of trust.

CHAPTER 3

Diversity:
What It Is in a Complex World

· ·

This chapter will provide you with:

- A four-layer model of diversity that builds inclusion

- An explanation of internal, external, and organizational diversity dimensions

- A discussion of the impact of each dimension on the workplace

- An analysis/assessment tool for applying the model to your organization and engaging employees in the process

- A template for discussing differences in a respectful, constructive way

When asked what diversity means, people frequently respond with words such as "differences," "race," "gender," and "ethnicity." Some reveal a more skeptical viewpoint when they reply that they see it as "affirmative action with another coat of paint," "political correctness," or "the flavor of the month." In the evolving social, political, and business contexts in which diversity is discussed, it is critical to consider the implications of the diversity paradigm the organization uses. An inclusive definition, one that is broad enough to encompass a wide range of human dimensions, is a key element in reducing resistance to diversity because it positions it as everyone's issue. When narrowly defined, on the other hand, anything done in the name of diversity and inclusion is likely to be resisted because it is seen as benefiting others and excluding many of those whose support and commitment is needed.

What Is Diversity?

Diversity is not a liberal ideological movement. Rather, it is a reality in today's business environment. Put simply, diversity encompasses all the ways that human beings are both similar and different. While diversity itself is neutral, its impact rests on inclusion and exclusion, and the ways that those differences are used. Diversity involves variations in factors we control as well as those over which we have no choice. They give us areas of commonality through which we can connect with others, as well as aspects of difference from which we can learn. They also represent points of contention over which we can have conflict. In fact, diversity becomes an issue of concern to organizations when these differences impact the workplace. If assumptions and preconceived notions prevent talented employees from being hired or heard, if values differences block communication and teamwork, if new perspectives and points of view are ignored, or if lack of knowledge about cultural norms loses customers, diversity becomes a pragmatic focus for organizations. In order to capitalize on the benefits diversity can bring and deal with the challenges it presents, it is critical for all employees to understand its many dimensions and participate in sharing perceptions about their impact in the workplace. The following model of diversity is a beginning point for these discussions. The critical and pragmatic questions for organizations focus on inclusion and exclusion. Are there exclusions that hinder our effectiveness? Are there inclusions that could increase our ability to be successful?

The Four Layers of Diversity

While it is evident that there are a multitude of ways in which humans are both alike and unlike, all differences are not created equal. Some have profound effects on our opportunities and experiences while others have relatively little impact. Powerful assumptions may be held about some aspects of diversity while others may evoke little reaction. However, the combined patterns of diversity dimensions form a filter through which we see the world as well as a screen through which others view each of us. When we are aware of the many influences that have formed these filters, and when we realize how these influences play out in our organizations, we can make active choices about our behavior and reactions as well as our organizations' practices and policies.

Diversity can be seen as four concentric circles, at the center of which is personality, the innately unique aspect that gives us each our own particular style (see Figure 3.1). This core aspect permeates all other layers. Moving out from that center are the internal factors which Judy Rosener and Marilyn Loden[1] label primary dimensions of diversity. These are aspects over which we have little or no control, such as gender, age, sexual orientation, and race. The next layer of factors, most of which Rosener and Loden refer to as secondary dimensions, is made up of external influences, those brought to bear by society and one's experiences in the world. Whether you are married or have children, how your religious affiliation guides you, and the amount and type of education you have, are examples of these kinds of external differences. Finally, the fourth layer encompasses organizational influences related to factors such as seniority, the kind of work you do, your level within the company, or your work location. Let's take a look at each of these layers to see their impact on individuals and organizations.

FIGURE 3.1 | Four Layers of Diversity

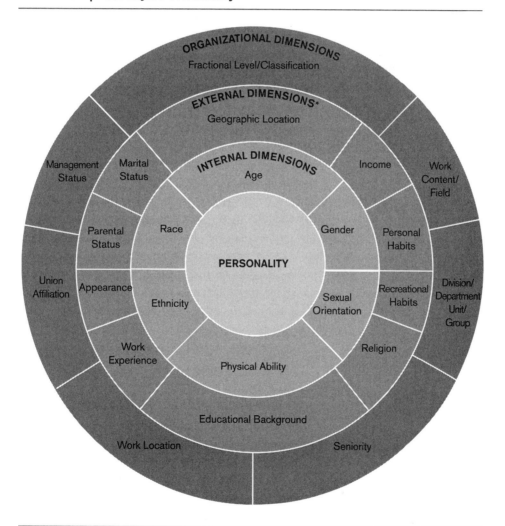

From *Diverse Teams at Work*, Lee Gardenswartz and Anita Rowe Alexandria, VA: SHRM, 2003
Internal Dimensions and External Dimensions are adapted from Marilyn Loden and Judy Rosener, *Workforce America!*
Homewood, IL: Business One Irwin, 1991.

Personality: The Unique Core

Why is it that you feel an immediate closeness with some individuals and an equally quick negative response to others? Why are there some co-workers and bosses you'd go miles out of your way for, while there others you'd go even more miles to avoid? The answer may have to do with the most basic factor about human beings—personality. Each of us has a unique way of interacting with others. Whether a person is seen as charming, irritating, fascinating, nondescript, approachable, or intimidating depends in part on personality, or what some might describe as style. This unique combination of personal characteristics forms each person's distinct personality.

In many organizations, style inventories such as the Meyers Briggs Type Indicator, the Strength Deployment Inventory, or the DISC model are used to help employees understand their own and their co-workers' motivational and interactional styles. Identifying and analyzing these characteristics and predispositions can help colleagues adjust to each others' styles, have more realistic expectations of each other, and avoid misinterpreting each others' behavior.

Internal Dimensions: Powerful Shapers of Opportunities, Access, and Expectations

Beyond the central core of personality, the six internal dimensions of diversity are, for the most part, out of our control, yet they have a powerful effect on behavior, attitudes, and opportunities in organizations. The impactful role they play can be seen in the Glass Ceiling Commission's report that claims that only 3 to 5 percent of CEOs of *Fortune* 1000 and 500 organizations are women and 3 percent are people of color.[2] These dimensions also impact perceptions about workplace conditions. A *Los Angeles Times* national poll of 987 working individuals indicated that 19 percent of whites surveyed believed more effort is needed to guarantee racial minorities fairness in the workplace while 66 percent of blacks did, and 87 percent of whites felt race relations at their workplace were good or excellent while 52 percent of blacks did. In addition, 11 percent of whites reported having been discriminated against, while 46 percent of blacks had. Finally, the poll reported that 38 percent of women believed more effort is needed to guarantee that women get fair treatment in the workplace while 26 percent of men did.[3] Such disparities can be seen among groups in most employee satisfaction surveys results, showing that we see the world through different eyes.

Age

With seniors, Gen Xers, Baby Boomers, Nexters, Echos, and Millennials working together, age is currently one of the most frequently cited diversity issues. The era in which each individual is reared leaves an indelible mark on values, norms, motivations, and expectations (see Table 3.1). Loyalty, security, work ethic, and flexibility are factors often seen very differently by 20-somethings and their 50- and 60-something co-workers. Generally raised with different expectations than their older co-workers, younger employees tend to place a greater value on work/life balance, such as time with family. They also tend to be more flexible in work style (working on laptops at coffee houses and home), and they don't assume that their tenure in the organization is permanent. Older employees, on the other hand, were raised with a more "signed on for life" expectation that the organization will repay their loyalty with job security. Employees from these different points of view may find it difficult to understand one another and may make negative judgments about each other, such as disparaging remarks about a declining work ethic or resistance to change. Younger employees often complain that their older co-workers don't take them seriously or listen to their ideas, while older staff members often feel displaced and discounted in the technological world of BlackBerry devices, text messaging, Twitter, and Facebook. In addition, both sides may experience difficulties when the boss is a generation or so younger than some of the employees in the department. While there are many variations within each group, the chart that follows gives an overview of the five generations and the values that they tend to hold.

TABLE 3.1 | Generations in the Workplace[1]

LABEL	YEARS OF BIRTH	VALUES
Silent Generation/Seniors/Veterans	1922 – 1945	Duty, loyalty to the organization, security, saving
Baby Boomers	1946 – 1964	Opportunity, individualism, anti-authority, meritocracy, spending
Generation X	1965 – 1976	Independence, resilience, pragmatic, fun, loyalty to team and boss rather than organization
Generation Y/Nexters/Baby Boom/Echo	1977 – 2000	Self-confident, goal-oriented, multi-tasking, technology, structure
Millennials	2000 +	Flexibility, technology, results rather than time clock

Source: Hankin, Harriet, *The New Workforce: Five Sweeping Trends That Will Shape Your Company's Future*, New York: Amacom, 2005.

Gender

Men and women grow up in and live in different worlds. They are socialized by parents, schools, and the media to see themselves, and to behave, differently. With different gender roles, even similar behavior is interpreted differently, as described in the following poem.

"Impressions from an Office"
  The family picture is on HIS desk.
    Ah, a solid, responsible family man.
  The family picture is on HER desk.
    Umm, her family will come before her career.
  HIS desk is cluttered.
    He's obviously a hard worker and a busy man.
  HER desk is cluttered.
    She's obviously a disorganized scatterbrain.
  HE is talking with his co-workers.
    He must be discussing the latest deal.
  SHE is talking with her co-workers.
    She must be gossiping.

HE's not at his desk.

He must be at a meeting.

SHE's not at her desk.

She must be in the ladies' room.

HE's not in the office.

He's meeting customers.

SHE's not in the office.

She must be out shopping.

HE's having lunch with the boss.

He's on his way up.

SHE's having lunch with the boss.

They must be having an affair.

The boss criticized HIM.

He'll improve his performance.

The boss criticized HER.

She'll be very upset.

HE got an unfair deal.

Did he get angry?

SHE got an unfair deal.

Did she cry?

HE'S getting married.

He'll get more settled.

SHE's getting married.

She'll get pregnant and leave.

HE's having a baby.

He'll need a raise.

SHE's having a baby.

She'll cost the company money in maternity benefits.

HE's going on a business trip.

It's good for his career.

SHE's going on a business trip.

What does her husband say?

HE's leaving for a better job.

He knows how to recognize a good opportunity.

SHE's leaving for a better job.

Women are not dependable.

—NATASHA JOSEFOWITZ[4]

In addition, men and women communicate differently. According to Deborah Tannen, in her book, *You Just Don't Understand,*[5] men communicate "vertically" while women do so "horizontally." Men use communication as a means of establishing a hierarchy of order or power and to solve problems. Women, on the other hand, interact to form relationships and share feelings and reactions. This difference can lead to subtle barriers in transmitting information and even subtler unconscious assumptions. She may be seen as wasting time;

he may be seen as cold and insensitive. Her comments may be taken as nagging or an attempt to control, while the solutions he offers may be rejected as proof that "He didn't hear what I was saying."

All groups and cultures have assigned appropriate and inappropriate roles and behaviors to each sex. Even with all the progress made in gender equity at work, Title IX legislation in the schools, and consciousness-raising in society, many people are often still surprised when the secretary or nurse is a man or when the mechanic or pilot is a woman. Women are still asked more often to take notes at meetings or to oversee the refreshments. Eyebrows still are raised in many organizations when men take parental leave to stay home with a newborn or change jobs because of a wife's career move.

Finally, another aspect of gender is the discussion of gender identity and the increase of transgendered individuals in the workplace. When an employee goes through the transition from one gender to the other, the reverberations are generally felt throughout the organization. Questions about restroom use are the tip of the iceberg and difficulties in dealing with this change can create barriers to teamwork and productivity. One manager responded in a humane and effective way to an employee who came to her with the news of his impending gender transition. He knew that his change would impact his workgroup and he wanted to let her know. At first she was blocked by her fear and feelings of inadequacy at dealing with this situation. However, once she calmed down she found a clear and effective way to deal with this change. She asked him if he was willing to talk openly with his co-workers about this. When he agreed, she called a staff meeting where he explained the transition he was going through and answered their questions. Not only did his colleagues give him emotional support through the transition, they became ambassadors throughout the organization, dispelling misconceptions and giving clear and honest information. Teamwork was strengthened, productivity was maintained, and dignity and respect were reinforced as norms in the organization.

Race

We do not live in a color-blind society as Cornell West's book, *Race Matters*, validated.[6] Generally associated with physical characteristics such as skin color, eye shape, and hair texture, race forms a powerful diversity dimension because it is so visible. While categorization according to race is unsupported by genetic research, which finds more genetic variation within a racial group than between groups, it remains a social construct. According to Janet Elsea's research, it is the first thing we notice about another person.[7] According to her, the nine factors, in the order in which we notice them are:

1. Skin color
2. Gender
3. Age
4. Appearance
5. Facial expressions
6. Eye contact
7. Movement
8. Personal space
9. Touch

We don't notice what doesn't matter, so the fact that race is first on the list indicates the salient role it plays in perceptions and interactions. From daily news stories of discrimination and unequal treatment to Farai Chideya's explanation of the role of media in stereotypes about African Americans, much continues to be written about the disparities between the races.[8] In addition, statistics from many parts of society tell us that race makes a difference. For example, a Federal Reserve Bank of Boston study reported that mortgage applications of nonwhites were rejected 60 percent more often than for whites with the same level of income and credit history.[9] *Occupational Medicine* reports that the mortality rate for African-American males is 50 percent higher than for white males and females, and that the life expectancy for African-American males and females is seven and five years less than for whites.[10] The Glass Ceiling Commission reports reveal that "African-American men with professional degrees earn 79 percent of the amount earned by white males who hold the same degrees and are in the same job categories."[11] A complex load of feelings, perceptions, and experiences about race that employees of all races bring to the workplace often forms an unacknowledged backdrop for work interactions and decisions about hiring and promotion.

Ethnicity

An individual's nationality or ethnic background is another difference. Some proudly identify themselves as hyphenated Americans, such as Mexican-American, Arab-American, or Polish-American, or sport buttons or bumper stickers heralding their heritage, such as "Viva la Raza" or "I'm Proud I'm Irish." And some bristle at the mention of hyphenated ethnicities; "We're all American and that's all that matters" might be their motto.

These ethnic differences can bring variations in cultural norms, holiday observances, language proficiency, and group affiliation. What happens when a staff begins to separate because one group speaks its own language in front of others? How can you build a cohesive workgroup if the team begins to splinter into isolated groups? What can you do when contrasting cultural norms have taught people to respond differently to conflict? These are difficulties that can arise in an organization when ethnicity becomes a divisive, rather than a unifying, force.

An even more subtle demonstration of ethnicity can be seen in culture, the "software" that forms the rules, norms, and assumptions that guide each person's behavior. In some cultures, not making eye contact is seen as deceitful or unassertive, while in others it is deemed a sign of respect shown to elders and authority figures. Some individuals may beam when complimented publicly at a staff meeting, while others would be embarrassed and demotivated by being singled out from the group. You may consider the person who stands too close as pushy or rude, the one who talks loudly as ill-mannered or aggressive, the one who nods and says "yes" when he means "no" as unassertive or deceitful. (You can find out more about cultural differences and their influence on the job in Chapters 5 and 6.)

Another impact of ethnicity is seen in language differences. When employees and customers literally don't speak the same language, bilingual materials and interpreters may be needed. Language differences often serve as a divider, splintering the staff into separate groups, and accents are frequently cited as communication inhibitors on both sides. Nonnative English speakers often report being discounted and assumed to be stupid because of their accents. On the other hand, employees and customers alike complain about the difficulty in understanding heavily accented speech, especially over the phone.

Beyond these tangible language issues is the less concrete but volatile impact of the power struggle and turf battles symbolized by language differences and immigration. Concessions to bilingualism or the need to communicate with non-English speaking customers, clients or patients can cause frustration and anger among staff. Speakers of languages other than English, on the other hand, may feel that they are handicapped when they are prevented from speaking their native languages on the job.

Physical Ability

About 43 million Americans have some type of physical disability.[12] These different physical-ability levels will also be present in most workplaces. Some employees will be able-bodied, while others may be physically challenged. Some will be able to bench press 250 pounds, while others will have much less physical strength. A staff member may need the help of a hearing aid, crutches, or wheelchair. Incorrect assumptions are sometimes made about the capabilities of employees with physical challenges: "We can't ask her to do that. She can't reach the high shelves from a wheelchair." Or expectations of ability can be based on gender or size: "Have Dave carry these boxes out. He looks like a defensive lineman." In addition, employees who have had little contact with anyone with a physical disability may, because of discomfort, avoid contact with staff members or customers who have some impairment.

Adaptations may be called for in order to enable a physically challenged employee to work at a particular job. A TDD line may need to be added or a rearrangement of work responsibilities may be required to accommodate an individual's special needs. A staff member may be asked to change work stations or schedules to fully utilize the contribution of an individual with a physical limitation. These changes can have varied effects, from quick acceptance and an "it's-no-big-deal" attitude to grudging resentment and irritation.

Sexual Orientation

Sexual orientation is still another dimension in which employees may differ. Some will be heterosexual, while others may be gay, lesbian, or bisexual. Some will openly discuss their sexual orientation and others will not. How an organization deals with this dimension can be a telling test of its openness to differences. What does it cost an organization when an employee feels, as a focus-group participant once shared, that he has to hide who he is to succeed in his company? What happens to workgroup camaraderie when a gay or lesbian individual does not feel free to bring a same-sex partner to company social events or even to talk about weekend activities or vacation plans? How do trust and teamwork suffer if individuals judge a co-worker's lifestyle as morally inferior? Do gay and lesbian staff members have equal access to benefits? Many organizations are now expanding health care and other benefits to same-sex partners and domestic partners of either gender, and states such as Iowa, Vermont, and Massachusetts have legalized same sex marriages.

External Dimensions: Additional Influencers of Assumptions and Behaviors

In addition to internal dimensions, external influences such as social factors and life experiences also have an impact on how people are treated at work. While individuals have more control over these factors, they, too, exert a significant impact on behavior and attitudes.

Religion

Once considered a Judeo-Christian country, the United States is rapidly becoming home to people of many other religions. The number of people in the United States who claim no religious affiliation is currently up to 15 percent, nearly double what it was in 1990, and the number of Christians has fallen from 86 percent to 76 percent. However, one third of U.S. Americans report that they consider themselves born-again Christians.[13] The populations of Muslims, Hindus, Buddhists, Bahais, and other faiths are growing in cities across the country as are the numbers of atheists. For believers, religion gives them a basic set of values and rules that guide their lives. The Ten Commandments, the Golden Rule, and the Noble Eight-Fold Path are examples of these teachings. In addition, many in today's workforce tend to bring religious beliefs on the job: symbols in offices, screensaver displays, and biblical e-mail messages, for example.

Religions also prescribe observances, rituals, and holidays that may be at variance with one another. Seventh Day Adventists and observant Jews, for whom Saturday is the Sabbath, would not work or go to company functions on that day. A Muslim employee who prays five times a day would not be available for lunch staff meetings because of noon prayers. Non-Christian employees might be less than enthusiastic about Christmas decorations in their work sites. In one client organization, a non-Christian Southeast Asian employee was uncomfortable when staff meetings were customarily opened with a Christian prayer. In another case, a supervisor, whose religion forbade celebrations, refused to allow her team to hold birthday parties, causing much resentment, conflict, and morale problems in her group. Because of this expanding range of religious adherence, organizations are more frequently called on to respond with greater flexibility in schedules and holidays and to remove inadvertent exclusions.

Marital Status

One seminar participant proudly proclaimed she never hired anyone who is single. When asked why, she responded with a laundry list of assumptions she had made about single peoples' lack of responsibility, commitment, work ethic, alcohol consumption, party-loving lifestyle, and dependability. Although her stereotyping is extreme and behavior illegal, nevertheless, marital status does connote different things to different people. For example, married people are often assumed to be less available for travel assignments or overtime. However, marital status is perceived differently for men and for women. Stereotypes tend to endure regarding this double standard. Married men are often seen as more stable and dependable, while married women, particularly in their childbearing years, are often thought to be more of a risk than their single counterparts. The stereotypic assumption is that women may go on leave because of pregnancy or may not be willing to transfer or take on projects that involve travel because of their spouses. More times than we can count, pregnant women have told us that they withheld news of pregnancy until it became absolutely unavoidable. All of them were fearful of the career consequences, and in many cases, their fears were justified. On the other hand, single individuals may complain about being overburdened with extra assignments and travel demands, and treated as though they had no life or responsibilities outside of work.

Educational Background

Educational requirements are generally prominent job qualifications, yet their role may have other impacts. One of the frequent complaints we hear in organizations has to do with preferences about educational levels. "They hire college interns rather than promoting experienced workers from within," and "All they care about is a college degree, not what you know," are commonly heard perceptions. Differences in education, either in level (a high school diploma or an MBA) or type (an engineering degree vs. a liberal arts education) can create divisions among staff. People with certain levels or types of education are sometimes excluded or preferred, and certain colleges and universities are targeted for recruitment. Comments made by an employee with a high school diploma are sometimes not given the same credence as suggestions made by a college graduate. On the other hand, those with more academic credentials can be discounted as too "ivory tower" or not "real world" enough. Finally, tuition reimbursement for taking technical courses rather than college courses is sometimes lacking.

Income

Much of an individual's esteem may come from the numbers on his or her paycheck. Disputes over existing salaries or small cost-of-living raises, resentments over job reclassifications, or rivalries among staff members concerning opportunities for overtime may have as much to do with the symbolic value of income as the actual dollars involved. These differences can play havoc with cohesion and cause time and energy to be spent on nonwork-related debates, especially in precarious economic times.

In addition, the income levels of individuals' families of birth may have provided or prevented opportunities, such as travel or education, that may give some staff members advantages over others. They can also influence employees' level of comfort with one another. In one manufacturing organization that was having a problem with a high rate of product defects, the lead man on the line was invited to a meeting with top management to discuss ways to solve the problem. This employee had never been to a meeting with "suits" before and was intimidated to be in a setting where others clearly had a different income level. Knowing he had information they needed to solve the problem, the "suits" paid full attention to his input and suggestions. What resulted was an identification of the cause of the problem and a solution that worked. None of this would have been possible if either side had allowed the difference in income to block their interaction.

Parental Status

Having children generally means that employees have outside responsibilities and time commitments that may affect their ability to adapt to work schedules. A staff member who coaches a Little League team may not want to put in overtime on a project. A colleague may be called away to pick up a sick child from school right in the middle of work on a project deadline. A single parent may be incorrectly assumed to have less flexibility for travel assignments. Finally, those employees who do not have children may also have unacknowledged outside responsibilities: caring for an ill parent, leading a scout team, or volunteering on the board of a nonprofit organization.

Many working parents, especially women, opt for a flextime or part-time position at some point early in their children's lives. One young professional with an MBA decided to switch to a half-time position after the birth of her first child. As a top-producing professional, she gave the organization more than the required 20 hours of work each week, getting excellent reviews from every direction. She was therefore shocked when, at performance-review time, she did not get the top rating. The reason was that, despite her exemplary performance, the unwritten rule held that no flextime employee could get top marks. She argued and lost. However, by the next year's review, the organization had changed its norm regarding part-time workers and, after much discussion, decided that performance was the only basis for evaluation. Not only did she get top marks, but the way was paved for future working parents and other flextime employees.

Appearance

We're taught not to judge a book by its cover, but we do. Beauty is definitely in the eye of the beholder, and preferences differ across cultures and generations. What is seen as appealing and appropriate in one group may not be in another. This diversity factor is often commented upon in training sessions, especially with regard to weight. It is no secret in the United States that many negative assumptions exist about people who are considered overweight. A consultant recently spoke of a bright, capable executive who stopped him in the hall one day to ask a painful question. Concerned that her plain face and stout body were obstacles to moving up, she asked if he really thought she could ever be considered for the post of CEO because of her looks. In other examples, a plant worker felt the need to remove his pierced earring before he entered the company parking lot each morning, and a manager made sure to wear long-sleeve shirts to cover his tattoos. They knew, as most of us do, that job opportunities are sometimes offered or withheld because of appearance.

Personal Habits

Differences in personal habits, such as smoking and drinking, can be the catalysts for relationship-building or exclusion in the workgroups. In today's smoke-free workplaces, smokers often become a cliquish group because of their shared experience in taking smoking breaks outside the building. Exercisers may do Pilates together after work or go to the same health club in the morning before coming to work. Beer drinkers may form close ties through get-togethers that leave out their nondrinking co-workers. Strong scents from heavy perfume or after shave can be difficult for co-workers with allergies. Finally, any substance-abuse problem can impact not only individual and team performance but safety as well.

Recreational Habits

The recreational preferences in your organization bring still another piece to the diversity puzzle. In one organization, most of the major decisions were made on fishing trips that only a few top leaders attended. In another, playing golf was an unstated but clearly understood requirement for promotion into the management team. In still others, camaraderie builds among those who share an activity week after week or who can talk together about a favorite sport or hobby. Again, these differences can form relationships, but they can also shut people out. One manufacturing organization inadvertently found that recreational activity could also bring together a polarized staff. Assembly-line workers had formed separate, warring camps because of their different ethnicities and educational backgrounds. While all were recent immigrants, some were from rural villages in Mexico and had little formal education. Others were refugees from Bosnia, most with university educations, who had worked in professions such as engineering, law, and medicine in their homeland. There was little respect or interaction between the groups, though they worked on the same line. A breakthrough came at their company picnic when one of them posted a sign-up sheet for a soccer game. Engaging in a sport they shared in common gave them the first opportunity to connect as equals, to build rapport, and begin bridging the differences that had kept them apart.

Geographic Location

Where employees grew up influences their perspectives, values, experiences, and awareness levels. Social norms and business practices also vary not just around the world, but across the country. In one national sales organization, for example, regional differences made for some interesting variations in attitudes about gender roles. Sales managers and directors from the U.S. South were more than surprised that there were many women serving in those roles in the western region. In their area, women had not been considered for such positions.

Work Experience

Staff members bring a wide range of levels and types of work experience. Old hands and neophytes, those that are computer literate as well as those who are technophobic, engineers and accountants, technicians and typists—employees with such disparate work histories will undoubtedly come together in your organization and all can make their unique contributions.

In some organizations, experience within the company or field is highly valued, while in others it is less important and outsiders are seen as adding value. Workgroups often prefer some kinds of work background over others. In one public utility, restructuring meant the redeployment of staff to different divisions in order to retain employees. However, former office workers were not warmly welcomed in the field, where construction workers were disdainful of their "soft" colleagues, who had a lot of computer know-how but no hard-hat experience.

Organizational Dimensions:
Job-Related Factors Making an Impact at Work

Beyond the personal and societal influences on employee's filters are the organizational dimensions which also make a difference in assumptions, expectations, and opportunities.

Functional Level or Classification Within the Organization

No matter how level-free organizations aim to be, nor how many attempts are made to flatten the hierarchy, there is always some structure that delineates functional levels or classifications. Functional levels may be signified by numbers, for example, with everyone knowing that a level 13 is executive management, while a level 7 is clerical support staff. Or they may be indicated by titles such as vice president, team leader, administrative assistant, customer service representative, or sales manager. Whatever the system, differences in level may serve as coveted signs of status, indications of pay differentials, or formal sources of power. They can even determine whether you get a call returned. The important thing to recognize is that these levels may impact employees' self-esteem, level of participation, communication, and workgroup interactions. One organization that regularly referred to its staff as either "professional" and "nonprofessional" (to signify the difference between those with college degrees and those without degrees) got an instructive piece of feedback: Clerical workers let management know that they resented being called nonprofessional since they considered themselves to be very professional in their commitment and behavior. In another company, water was a bone of contention. Bottled water was provided on the top floor where executive offices were located while all other floors had water fountains. Employee surveys often reveal differences between levels regarding satisfaction.

Management Status

Closely related to functional level is the dimension of management status. From supervisor to CEO, everyone who reviews another's performance and has accountability for other employees has some level of management status. There may be perceptions of inequality, lack of trust or fears of retribution. Newly promoted supervisors often complain of feeling alienated from former peers who treat them as though they've joined the enemy camp. There may also be different attitudes toward bosses because of cultural variations. For those from hierarchical backgrounds, respect for authority figures might inhibit them from sharing feedback with managers. However, having management included in groups can also help dissolve the "us vs. them" rift that often exists between management and nonmanagement personnel.

Division, Department, Unit, and Workgroup

What do the sales and marketing departments say about each other? How about customer service and manufacturing? Rare is the organization that doesn't have complaints about silos creating barriers between departments. It is not uncommon for there to be images, assumptions, and stereotypes about specific departments or units. Revenue-generating departments may be held in higher regard than those that are considered overhead. Some are well respected as high performers while others are known as troublemakers. Some are seen as stepping stones to advancement, while others are seen as career dead ends.

In today's re-engineered and restructured organizations, units that were at one time separate departments may now have to work together. Though they previously functioned independently, they may be expected to cross-train and collaborate.

Union Affiliation

Whether employees are union members or not can add another wrinkle to the diversity fabric in your organization. If the union and management are at odds, the distrust may spill over into work relationships. However, common interest can also build significant bridges. Bridge-building occurs in many companies as union and management work together to keep jobs. Their joint vested interests are creating new and important shared goals as they create alternatives to plant closings or outsourcing. And even without the critical issue of job salvation, having individuals from both sides of the fence work together can lead to improved communication and commitment, as well as increased understanding of sometimes unsympathetic positions. Many organizations include union representatives on their diversity planning team so that the union is a business partner in implementing diversity.

Work Location

"Headquarters gets all the good stuff." "They always forget about us out here in the regions." "We're treated as second-class citizens because we're not at corporate." These are the kinds of commonly heard gripes that indicate the impact of work location. Whether you are in the corner office, the executive suite, or the portable trailer in the parking lot can make a difference in your viewpoint and attitude, as well as in the perceptions other people have about you. Work location often influences communication and can be seen as a sign of importance or value.

Seniority

A bastion of the old order in businesses across the country is the value that has traditionally been placed on seniority. Although this is slowly changing in some places, an employee's length of time at the company generally does make a difference. Promotions, schedules, overtime, and other perks are often expected to be doled out on this basis.

Generally, the hierarchy of seniority is adhered to more by mature workers reared in a system where longevity was a plus and by employees from hierarchical cultures who see age as commanding respect and seniority as a sign of wisdom. In addition, union contracts and organizational policies have traditionally used seniority as a fair way to distribute advantages.

Work Content or Field

The type of work people do brings still another dimension. Plumbers and social workers probably see things differently. Lawyers and engineers would probably bring divergent views, as might secretaries and computer programmers. Each type of work has a subculture of its own, which tends to give people a methodology for working with problems. The accountant would most likely approach a situation in a different way than the assembly-line supervisor; the engineer might draw a diagram, while the marketer might start with focus groups. In one biotechnology organization, a manager revealed that her most difficult diversity barrier was one of work content. As a nontechnical HR professional, she found communicating with engineers to be her foremost challenge—sometimes they just didn't speak the same language. In addition, each type of work may have its own status within the organization.

Assessing the Impact of Diversity in Your Organization

While all the dimensions of diversity undoubtedly have some influence in your organization, some are more impactful than others. The following chart will give you an opportunity to assess that impact and identify issues which need attention. This analysis is best done in diverse groups so employees can share perceptions from a wide variety of perspectives. Not only does this diverse outlook give a more accurate picture of diversity in your organization, but it provides the opportunity for a healthy sharing and discussion of differences. A broad and all-encompassing definition of diversity moves beyond the limits of a race- and gender-based paradigm and includes everyone in the organization. It helps employees see that all of us are far too complex and interesting to be described by two or three dimensions. It gives voice to everyone's perceptions and concerns and enlists all staff in the identification of diversity issues. Finally, it helps staff see points of connection as well as of difference. This tool can also be used as an informal organizational assessment that gathers staff perceptions about diversity and its consequences.

In discussing responses, remember that there are no right and wrong answers, and that each person's perceptions are his or her reality. You will learn more if you make it your goal to listen for differences and to try to understand others' points of view. The discussion may bring to light additional dimensions that are significant in your organization. For example, social class and political affiliation have been brought up as critical differences in some organizations. Individuals have also suggested that mental ability be added to physical ability and that parental status be changed to family responsibilities to encompass a wider range of duties. The more that employees shape the definition of diversity, the more committed they will be to the initiative.

A Process for Engaging Employees in Discussion About Differences

As specific dimensions of diversity emerge, it is helpful to give employees a chance to talk about them, share their perceptions, and find productive ways to work together across lines of difference. Two of the most prominent dimensions that are the current focus of attention, discussion, and, sometimes, contention are age and religion.

Generational differences are particularly critical in many organizations now because a large group of employees are baby boomers who are currently retiring (or about to retire), taking much experience and institutional memory with them. There is often a generation or two between them and the next large age cohort. The need for succession planning and transmitting knowledge is great. On the other hand, there is a need for younger staff to have their input valued and to shape the culture. A lack of understanding between the two groups can inhibit the organization's ability to get the most from each.

Religion is another dimension emerging in importance in the workplace. Requests for prayer and meditation rooms and prayer groups at work are increasingly common, as are e-mail messages with religious content. Recent attempts at creating more inclusive holiday celebrations at the end of the year have been met with backlashes and insistence on calling them Christmas parties instead of holiday celebrations.

When diversity dimensions are at the root of strong emotions, there is a need to address them. Giving employees a safe and respectful way to discuss differences is critical to constructive dialogue. The following template is suggested for these kinds of discussions and can be applied to any dimension of diversity. Select a few of these open-ended statements from each section and have people share their responses to them to have a respectful and productive discussion.

ACTIVITY 3.1 | Assessing the Impact of Diversity in Your Organization

Directions: Think about each dimension of diversity and rate the degree of difference each makes in how people are treated in your organization by putting a check in the appropriate column. Then indicate in the last column whether this difference in treatment is a positive or negative one for your organization.

	1 Little difference	2	3	4	5 Great deal of difference	+ or −
Personality						
Different styles and characteristics						
Internal Dimensions						
Age						
Gender						
Sexual Orientation						
Physical Ability						
Ethnicity						
Race						
External Dimensions						
Geographic Location						
Income						
Personal Habits						
Recreational Habits						
Religion						
Educational Background						
Work Experience						
Appearance						
Parental Status						
Marital Status						
Organizational Dimensions						
Functional Level/Classification						
Work Content/Field						
Division/Department/Unit/Group						
Seniority						
Work Location						
Union Affiliation						
Management Status						

Source: Lee Gardenswartz and Anita Rowe. *Diverse Teams at Work.* Alexandria, VA: SHRM, 2003.

Suggestions for Using
"Assessing the Impact of Diversity in Your Organization"

Objectives:
- Increase understanding about the dimensions of diversity
- Raise awareness about the impact of these dimensions on organizational life
- Share perceptions about inclusion and exclusion in the organization

Intended Audience:
- Participants in a diversity awareness training session
- Diversity council members
- Members of a diverse workgroup
- Managers of diverse teams and departments
- Executives leading diverse organizations

Time: 45 minutes

Materials:
- Copies of *Assessing the Impact of Diversity in Your Organization* for all participants
- Enlargements (18" x 24") of the worksheet (one for each 5 participants)
- Colored markers

Processing the Activity:
- Facilitator gives a brief lecture on the Four Layers of Diversity, giving and soliciting examples.
- Facilitator distributes worksheets and asks participants to consider the impact of each dimension of diversity by responding to the worksheet. Participants rate the degree of difference in treatment (1 = Very little difference to 5 = A great deal of difference) resulting from each of the dimensions. Facilitator emphasizes that there are no "right" answers, but that each person's perceptions are important.
- Participants count off into groups of 5-6 and go to the enlargement posted on the wall with their number and put their responses on the chart.
- Participants discuss the responses on their chart, focusing on those dimensions that seem to make the most difference in how people are treated as well as on those dimensions where there are large variations in rating. They also discuss the consequences for the organization.
- Facilitator leads a total-group discussion of issues and insights.

Questions for Discussion
- Which dimensions seem to make the most difference in how people are treated?
- How are those differences in treatment shown?
- On what dimensions are there variations in ratings among group members?
- To what do you attribute these differences in perception?
- How might/do these differences in treatment impact performance? Morale? Teamwork? Productivity? Service?
- Which dimensions are priorities to be addressed to create an environment that gets the best from everyone?

An inclusive framework for diversity and an opportunity to share perceptions regarding inclusion and exclusion is a critical early step in any diversity process. The greater the involvement at this stage, the greater the engagement and support in the ensuing steps of the process.

ACTIVITY 3.2 | Discussing Differences Respectfully and Constructively

Increasing Understanding

- This dimension of diversity is important to me because …
- This dimension of diversity impacts me at work because …
- The ways my _____ (age, religion, sexual orientation, ethnicity, etc.) contributes to this team/workplace/organization are …
- What I'd like others to know about my _____ (age, religion, sexual orientation, ethnicity, etc.) is …
- What irritates/upsets/frustrates/hurts me about how people deal with me in regard to this dimension of diversity is …
- What I don't understand about differences in this dimension is …
- I feel excluded because of this dimension when …

Sharing Needs and Expectations

- What I'd like others to do in dealing with me with regard to this dimension is …
- When others don't understand why I'm doing something, I'd like them to …
- I would feel that my contributions are valued if …
- I'd feel more included around this dimension if …
- One way we could use the contributions of all _____ (generations, religions, etc.) is …
- The team/organization would benefit if we …

Suggestions for Using
"Discussing Differences Respectfully and Constructively"

Objectives:

- Enable employees to discuss emotionally-laden issues in a safe environment
- Give employees a way to share their perspectives and feelings
- Enable staff to learn from each other

Intended Audience:

- Staff members experiencing difficulties around a particular dimension of diversity
- Employees on a team with a range of differences in a particular dimension of diversity

Time:

30–60 minutes

Materials:

- Sheets with the open-ended statements to be used, or a slide or a chart with the statements on them

Processing the Activity:

- Explain the dimension to be focused on (e.g., generation, religion, gender, etc.) and the reason for the discussion (e.g., "There have been some comments or complaints, a suggestion, questions or some misunderstanding about ...").
- Show people the open-ended statements selected, or give them the full sheet and ask them to select two from each section.
- Allow time for people to think about their responses. Some may wish to jot down notes.
- Go around the group with each person sharing one response from the Increasing Understanding section.
- Lead a total group discussion of insights and questions.
- Go around the group again, having each person share one response from the Sharing Needs and Expectations section.
- Lead a total group discussion of insights, questions, and suggestions.
- Ask each person to share one action they will take to create more inclusion around the dimension.

Caveats, Considerations, and Variations:

- Participants group into pairs in which each is from a different generation or religion, and share responses.
- Participants can formulate ground rules or guidelines to follow for dealing with each other across differences in the particular dimension.

CHAPTER 4.

Dealing with Diversity in a Global Context

This chapter will provide you with:

- A model of the multiple dimensions of global diversity
- A tool for assessing the impact of diversity in your worldwide organization
- A guide to assess information needed to implement diversity and inclusion initiatives globally
- An understanding of the requirements for diversity and inclusion leaders in global organizations
- Suggested areas where diversity and inclusion leaders can assist HR staff

Globalization is on the rise as organizations around the world seek new markets, cheaper raw materials, specialized skills, reduced labor costs, and improved systems and technology. Crossing borders brings tremendous opportunity for increased creativity along with business expansion. However, it does not come without its challenges. When cultures, continents, civilizations, and time zones are crossed, there is a risk of conflict, misunderstanding, and decreased productivity. Managing a multinational, multilingual workforce across the world adds another layer of complexity to an organization's diversity process.

Diversity directors are often asked to:

- Expand a domestic diversity initiative to include operations around the world.
- Provide diversity training in multiple countries.
- Form a Global Diversity Council.
- Assist HR staff with expatriate preparation, cross-cultural training, globalizing promotion and performance review systems, and adapting HR policies to other countries.

When organizations attempt to "roll out" their domestic diversity initiatives in the larger global sphere, they are often met with unforeseen obstacles. Understanding the landscape and considering some of the pitfalls ahead of time can increase the effectiveness of your global inclusion process. Having a sensitivity to the privilege inherent in being from the corporate headquarters and the dominant culture is one key to your success. Another is having a clear model of global diversity to guide your process.

Five Layers of Global Diversity

While the dimensions of diversity outlined in the previous chapter also exist in global organizations, there is an additional layer of factors that impact individual employee behavior, team performance, and the organization's operations. While the first four layers of diversity, personality, internal, external, and organizational dimensions, exist and play a role in global organizations, their impact may take on a different form in a global context. For example, how much difference does it make if an individual is born and raised in the country of the headquarters of the organization? What is the impact of one's gender or religion in different countries? Does it matter whether an individual speaks the official language of the organization natively or as a second, third or fourth language? Can a person who values time with family get ahead in an organization that expects up-and-comers to participate in nightly bar socializing? In addition, beyond these four layers, there are differences in each country of operation that also impact inclusion in the organization.

FIGURE 4.1 | Five Layers of Global Diversity

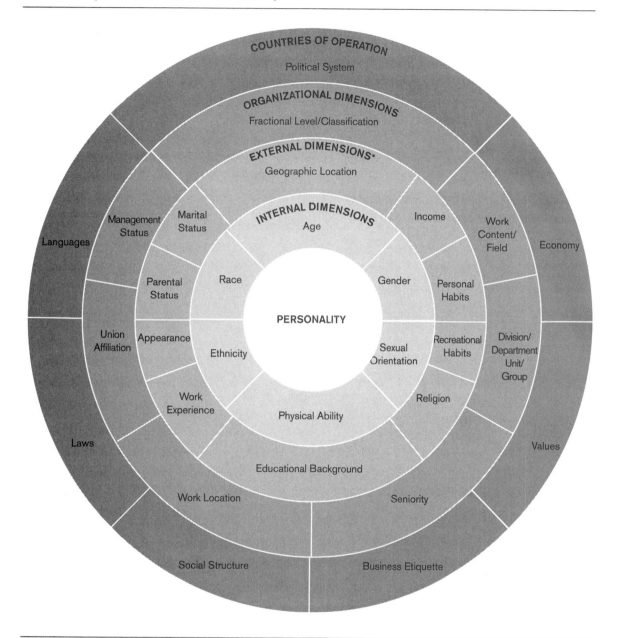

Adapted from *Diverse Teams at Work*, Second Edition, Lee Gardenswartz and Anita Rowe, Alexandria, VA: SHRM, 2003, and *The Global Diversity Desk Reference*, Lee Gardenswartz, Anita Rowe, Patricia Digh, Martin Bennett, San Francisco: Pfeiffer, 2003

Internal Dimensions and External Dimensions are adapted from Marilyn Loden and Judy Rosener. *Workplace America!*, Homewood, IL: Business One Irwin, 1991

Dimensions of Diversity in Countries of Operation

A fifth layer of diversity between countries around the world plays a role in business operations and inclusion. Among these are the political system and economic system, both historically and current, the national values, social structure, laws, languages spoken, and norms of business etiquette. Without understanding these differences, faux pas and costly mistakes can hinder productivity and relationships, as well as your ability to create an inclusive culture.

Political System

Whether a country is a representative democracy, federated republic, monarchy, theocracy, dictatorship, or communist state determines the power structure and the legal system and influences workers' expectations. Do employees expect Election Day to be a work holiday? Does EU membership of the country impact cross-border employment? Are practices different in various states or provinces? For example, the different political systems in East and West Germany from the post-WWII era to the fall of the Berlin Wall still play a challenging role in a united Germany where values differ on everything from proper child rearing to work ethic. Do religious leaders have a part in regulating workplace practices? Is vigorous political discussion and debate the accepted norm, or is it avoided at all costs? The political system within the country will determine much that affects your organization and how diversity is dealt with.

Economic System

How wealth is made, distributed, and used is determined by the country's economic system. A capitalist, socialist, communist, or hybrid economy may influence employees' compensation opportunities, benefits and rewards desired, as well as initiative and motivation. Do employees expect the government or unions to take care of their needs? How is income taxed? What role does the economic system play in employee incentives? How does income influence inclusion and exclusion within the organization?

Social Structure

How society is organized is another difference across countries and regions. How much of a social hierarchy exists and on what is it based? Is the distinction one of class, wealth, tribe or region? Is one's position based on individual achievement and merit through aspects such as education, skill or language acquisition, or is it based on family or tribe? How do newcomers such as expatriates and refugees fit in? These differences play a role in employee interactions, cooperation, and teamwork. Expecting members of warring tribal groups to work collaboratively on a project or creating a situation where an individual who has lower social status supervises someone on a higher level in the social structure would undoubtedly backfire. Knowing how the social structure works is critical to being able to get the best from employees.

Laws

It is important to understand the legal system and, specifically, the laws governing employment. What are the rules about employing immigrants and expatriates? What regulations pertain to workplace practices? Are there laws about gender equity, sexual harassment, or fair employment? What are the legal requirements regarding compensation, vacations, and benefits? For example, U.S. employees are often surprised at the questions that are permitted in hiring interviews in other countries. Inquiries about age, marital status, family background, and pictures on resumes, while not allowed in the United States, are common practices abroad. In another example, smoking, which is prohibited by law in most U.S. workplaces, is an accepted practice in many parts of the world.

National Values

Most U.S. corporations are based on values that are fundamental to U.S. culture. Among these are individualism, equality, fairness, and freedom. These values form the basis of beliefs about diversity and how differences among people should be managed, such as:

- Human rights should be universal.
- Equal opportunity and fairness should prevail in the workplace.
- Advancement should be based on achievement, not connections.
- Differences add value to the country, corporation or team.
- All people should be treated with equal dignity and respect.
- The needs of individuals, their perspectives, and their preferences are important.[1]

While other countries may also share these values, the danger for any organization is to assume that its value set is universal. Value sets in other countries within your organization's operation may be different. For example, the notion that a U.S. manager would change the team's meeting time to accommodate a Muslim team member's prayer time was perplexing to a Swiss banker. In his value system, the rules of the corporation took precedence over an individual's religious observance. While all individuals may be treated with respect in a Japanese firm, it would be unthinkable for an employee to leave before his or her boss does. Educational degrees are credibility and career builders in Germany, while in the U.S. achievement and a track record of accomplishment would generally have more weight. U.S. American's fast-paced, action-oriented, just-do-it approach might seem hasty, unplanned, and unrealistic to their European colleagues. Gaining an understanding of the basic values of the countries in which your organization operates is a key element of successfully leveraging your global talent pool.

Language(s)

While organizations generally have a designated official corporate language, multiple languages are usually spoken throughout the areas of operation and there is sometimes variation in how fluent employees are in the official language. Royal Dutch Shell, though headquartered in the Netherlands, has designated English and French as its corporate languages, though many of its employees speak Dutch as a first language. Also, even when all employees speak the same language, there are variations such as those between British, Australian, and U.S. English. For example, a proposal means a bid for a job to U.S. Americans while to a Brit, it would mean an agenda. According to intercultural consultant Melissa Lamson,[2] the word "recommendation" has different meanings in the United States and Europe. In Germany it means that you vouch for someone's competence and guarantee his performance. In the United States it is more a suggestion, and it is left for the individuals involved to see if the person is the right fit. Additionally, global organizations need to attend to the local sensitivities about language, including how many languages should be included on signs and corporate documents (e.g., Mandarin and/or Cantonese) and what alphabets or writing should be used (e.g., Latin and/or Cyrillic in Serbia, Katakana and/or Hiragana in Japan).

Business Etiquette

Who sits where at the meeting, how formal presentations are, how decisions are made, and how to use business cards are just a few of the questions that arise when working globally. The norms of business interactions and relationships are another way in which diversity manifests itself globally. Misinterpretations and misread cues can result in unintended offense, perceptions of disrespect, and even failure of a project. The *nemawashe* process of Japan requires you to do advance work with each person who will be in a decision-making session, giving them information and getting their input and buy-in beforehand. The actual meeting itself is more of a formality. Failure to do so would doom your project and cause you much frustration.

Even describing diversity can be a different experience in other countries. One of our colleagues, who conducts diversity training in India and the Philippines, got a cross-cultural lesson regarding how different cultures view the phenomenon. When she showed them the diagram of diversity with the concentric circles and multiple dimensions in separate sections, they gave her feedback. They said that while they agreed that all of those dimensions were aspects of diversity, they would not depict it that way. They preferred no separate circles or boxes but rather all the dimensions in one big circle. In their holistic view, these aspects were not separate but intertwined and overlapping. What is most important about her discussion with them is that they designed a model that described their reality and would then own it. However employees conceptualize about diversity, it is important to gain their input in how it impacts the operation of the organization.

Assessing the Impact of Global Diversity in Your Organization

As with domestic diversity, deciding how and where to focus your diversity process requires an assessment of the impact these differences have in the organization. That answer lies within the organization and soliciting input from staff with different locations and perspectives is critical. The following tool, *Assessing the Impact of Global Diversity in Your Organization,* gives you a method for getting that input.

ACTIVITY 4.1 | Assessing the Impact of Global Diversity in Your Organization

Directions: Think about each dimension of diversity and rate the degree of difference each makes in how people are treated in your global organization.

	1 Little difference	2	3	4	5 Great deal of difference
Personality					
Different styles and characteristics					
Internal Dimensions					
Age					
Gender					
Sexual Orientation					
Physical Ability					
Ethnicity					
Race					
External Dimensions					
Geographic Location					
Income					
Personal Habits					
Recreational Habits					
Religion					
Educational Background					
Work Experience					
Appearance					
Parental Status					
Marital Status					
Organizational Dimensions					
Functional Level/Classification					
Work Content/Field					
Division/Department/Unit/Group					
Seniority					
Work Location					
Union Affiliation					
Management Status					

(continued on next page)

ACTIVITY 4.1 | Assessing the Impact of Global Diversity in Your Organization (continued)

	1 Little difference	2	3	4	5 Great deal of difference
Countries of Operation					
Political System					
Laws					
Social Structure					
Economic System and Conditions					
Values					
Language(s)					

Adapted from *Diverse Teams at Work*, Lee Gardenswartz and Anita Rowe, Alexandria, VA: SHRM, 2003 and *Global Diversity Desk Reference: Managing an International Workforce*, San Francisco: Pfeiffer, 2003

Suggestions for Using
"Assessing the Impact of Global Diversity in Your Organization"

Objectives:

- To increase understanding about the dimensions of diversity operating in a global organization
- To raise awareness about the impact of these dimensions on inclusion in the organization
- To engage staff in discussing and giving input regarding their perceptions about the impact of the dimensions

Intended Audience:

- Participants in a global diversity awareness training session
- Members of a diverse workgroup
- Managers of diverse teams and departments
- Members of a Global Diversity Council

Time: 45 minutes

Materials:

- Copies of Assessing the *Impact of Global Diversity in Your Organization* for all participants
- Pens/pencils

Processing the Activity:

- Facilitator gives a brief lecture on the dimensions of global diversity giving and soliciting examples.
- Facilitator distributes worksheets and asks participants to consider the impact of each dimension of diversity on organizational life by responding to the worksheet. Participants rate the degree of difference in treatment (1 = Very little difference to 5 = A great deal of difference) resulting from each of the dimensions. Facilitator emphasizes that there are no "right" answers, but that each person's perceptions are important.
- Participants gather in small groups (4 to 6 people) and share their responses, focusing on those dimensions which seem to make the most difference in how people are treated as well as on those dimensions where there are large variations in rating.
- Facilitator leads a total-group discussion of issues and insights.

Questions for Discussion

- Which dimensions seem to make the most difference in how people are treated?
- How are those differences in treatment shown?
- On what dimensions are there variations in ratings among group members?
- To what do you attribute these differences in perception?
- How might/do these differences in treatment impact performance? Morale? Teamwork? Productivity? Service?

Caveats, Considerations, and Variations

- Enlargements of the worksheet (18" x 24") can be posted around the room. Participants, can each chart their responses and have a discussion in small groups about their responses.

Global Diversity Assessment

"Forewarned is forearmed," as the saying goes. Gaining information about the countries that are part of your organization's operation will help you determine how best to engage these areas in your global diversity process. The key is finding cultural informants within (and outside) the organization who can help you. Expatriates who have had experience working abroad can be a great source of information. In addition, you can make use of consultants with country-specific expertise and cross-cultural knowledge. Many helpful resources are also listed in the Appendix. Activity 4.2 can help you in gathering this data.

Global Issues Facing Diversity Officers

Globalization expands the role of the diversity officer as there are additional aspects that need to be addressed. The following chart from *Diversity Best Practices*[3] lists the primary issues facing those leading diversity initiatives in global organizations.

Core Global Issues Facing Diversity Officers

- Setting corporate-wide diversity policies that are consistent worldwide
- Diversity leadership and the role of the diversity officer and team
- Business and culture ties
- Negotiating the legal obstacles of implementing diversity initiatives throughout different countries
- Allocating the right staff and budget while building a talent pool within different cultures that will garner business results and community support; using a mix of local diversity councils and employee resource groups
- Developing the right tools, techniques, and training programs
- Building the base for communications and marketing support programs utilizing goals and solid measurements
- Ensuring that diversity awareness training classes are tailored for the business case in each country
- Translating domestic diversity programs for use globally and learning from global initiatives to enhance and strengthen the U.S. program
- Building community support
- Tying the program to philanthropy support
- Nurturing governmental ties with the local community to enhance global diversity efforts
- Measuring programs to ensure accountability
- Reviewing the tracking system and ROI, and adapting as warranted

While all of these are important, select the three that are most critical at this point in your process. Once you have decided these three areas, determine some steps you can take.

ACTIVITY 4.2 | Global Diversity Assessment

When dealing with diversity in a global organization, gaining information about the following criteria is critical. Use these questions to help you gain that information and consider its impact on your diversity-and-inclusion process.

	What Do I Need to Know?	Where Can I Find Information?	Impact on Diversity-and-Inclusion Process
Political System	What is the history of the country's political system? What kind of a political system currently exists?		
Economic System	What is the economic system? How does it operate? How is wealth acquired, distributed, and regulated?		
Social Structure	What is the social structure? How is social status determined? What are the salient social designations?		
Laws	What are the relevant laws regarding employment and the workplace? What are the different jurisdictions?		
Values	What are the core values of the culture? What are the values regarding diversity? How do they play out in business?		
Languages	What languages are spoken in the organization? Is there an official language in the organization? How important is language fluency in promotion and career success?		
Business Etiquette	What are the rules of business communication, relationships, and meetings? How are these different in the various regions of the country?		

Suggestions for Using
"Global Diversity Assessment"

Objectives:

- Assess information needs regarding global operations
- Recognize the impact of the seven aspects of diversity in each country of operation
- Develop a plan for obtaining needed information

Intended Audience:

- Global diversity director
- Global Diversity Council
- Trainers involved in predeparture training for expatriates
- Executives and managers preparing for global assignments or managing global teams

Materials:

- Copies of *Global Diversity Assessment* worksheet

Processing the Activity:

- Explain the multiple layers of diversity, placing special emphasis on the seven dimensions in the countries-of-operation layer.
- Ask participants what they have already learned about these aspects. Have participants jot responses in the middle column, places where they can find necessary information.
- In small groups, participants discuss where they can obtain the necessary information and how this may impact the diversity-and-inclusion process.
- Have participants take responsibility for gathering specific information.

Questions for Discussion:

- In which area do we need the most information?
- What are some ways this impacts the work of inclusion?
- What other aspects do we need to investigate?
- What are some sources of needed information?

Assisting HR Management with Global Challenges in Multiple Countries and Time Zones

Globalization brings additional tasks to the plates of both HR staff and diversity-and-inclusion leaders. These additional responsibilities offer an opportunity for partnership between the HR department and the diversity-and-inclusion staff. According to Jennifer Palthe, the following seven specific areas enlarge the job of HR staff in global organizations.[4] They offer prime areas where the diversity officer can assist the HR department in creating inclusion, sharing contacts, information, and resources. Determine how you can help your HR department in each of these areas.

1. Expanded scope of HR activities, which includes providing translation and relocation services, taxation counseling, housing and education, and other help for expatriates and their families

2. A broader perspective regarding HR practices and the legal system in the countries of operation as well as knowledge about the history, culture, political, and social issues that affect HR management

3. More personal involvement in the lives of employees, especially with regard to aspects such as travel arrangements and resettlement, including housing and education for expatriates and their families

4. Management of the workforce mix, which tends to change over time from a reliance on more parent-country nationals to host-country nationals

5. Coping with additional risks and difficulties such as the financial cost of failed international assignments, terrorism, derailed careers, and dissatisfied expatriates

6. Greater external influences—such as political and economic systems, changes in host countries, as well as governmental challenges

7. Managing cross-cultural diversity as the cultures of the headquarters, the corporation, and the local areas meet multiple interpretations, expectations, and norms

Diversity initiatives need to cope with these challenges in creating inclusion throughout the organization in all locations. The cross-cultural orientation and knowledge of diversity staff can be of great help to HR departments in meeting these challenges.

Managing diversity and inclusion in a global organization takes the process one step further. It requires an understanding of the global landscape and the differences operating in each part of the world. It also requires that you allow the staff from around the world to describe their reality and define their needs so that you walk the talk of inclusion. You can obtain more in-depth information about managing global diversity in our book, *The Global Diversity Desk Reference*.[5]

CHAPTER 5

Increasing Cultural Competence

. . . .

This chapter will provide you with:

- An explanation of culture and how it influences behavior

- Information about different cultural norms and underlying behaviors

- Suggestions for managers in dealing with cultural differences on the job

- Exercises to increase cultural sensitivity and knowledge

- Tips for learning about other cultures and helping diverse employees learn your organization's culture

- A manager promotes a top-performing Latino employee to a supervisory position and is perplexed when the employee refuses to accept the promotion.
- An African-American female accountant is shocked and upset by her performance review. Her boss tells her she did not get the highest rating because she's not perceived to be a "team player" by the rest of the staff, especially during the stress of tax season.
- A physician gives directions to a Filipino nurse. When he asks if she understands the procedure, she nods her head and says "yes." Later, the physician notices her doing the procedure incorrectly. In exasperation he asks, "Why didn't you tell me if you didn't understand?"
- A manager is frustrated by mistakes made by one of her best employees, a newcomer from Indonesia. At the end of the shift, she asks the employee to stop by her office. She points out the mistakes that were made and tries to explain what needs to be done to avoid these errors in the future. The employee never returns to work.
- A supervisor is angry because one of his immigrant employees takes the day off each time his wife needs to go to a doctor's appointment. The boss cannot understand the need for the employee to do this, as the wife drives and takes care of shopping and other errands on her own.

Traditionally, these kinds of difficulties have been called performance or motivation problems; however, they are not that simple. The cultural differences at the heart of each of these situations will become clear to you as you read this chapter. If you have had experiences such as these, you have probably already become aware of the differences among us due to our cultural backgrounds.

Culture: Behavioral "Software" That Programs Us All

All of us are programmed by culture, what intercultural researcher Geert Hofstede terms "software of the mind."[1] It determines our behavior and attitudes, from whom to make eye contact with and when to smile, to how to deal with conflict or talk to a boss. Cultural programming guides our behavior and attitudes. Without it, we would be as useless as a computer without software. Culture teaches us how to interact with each other, how to solve life's daily problems, and, in effect, how to control our world. No society exists without these rules, and no individual is free from culture. Culture is more than manners—it directs the most subtle aspects of behavior, such as how long to wait between sentences, when it is OK to interrupt someone, and how to interpret the look on someone's face. Though most cultural rules are never written, they are all the more powerful because they are absorbed unconsciously as we watch others and their reactions to us.

It is easy for us to accept and understand that while we may eat cereal and juice for breakfast, someone else is having tortillas, rice, grits, or black coffee and cigarettes. However, when it comes to interpreting each other's behavior, cultural differences make understanding more difficult. To make matters worse, when we interpret another person's behavior through our own cultural software, we often make mistakes. We take the nodding head to mean "I understand," rather than "Yes, I heard you," as in the case of the Filipino nurse (above). We think the quick smile means the person is friendly and affable, rather than that he or she is uncomfortable and perhaps embarrassed by our behavior or his or her own confusion. Or we assume that the employee who does not speak out in staff meetings is not a go-getter, not assertive, or worse yet, stupid, when in fact she may be showing you respect by keeping her ideas to herself.

How does this misinterpretation happen? According to Adler and Kiggunder,[2] when we encounter another's behavior, we need to make sense of it, so we follow a three-step process. First, we describe what we see, as in the case of the Latino employee (above): "This employee has refused a promotion to a management position." Second, we interpret the behavior: "He is not interested in getting ahead and is missing a wonderful opportunity." Third, we make an evaluation: "He is lacking in initiative, ungrateful for this opportunity, underconfident," or any combination of these. Steps two and three are the ones that get us into trouble in our intercultural interactions. A critical step in bridging the gap is learning more about others' cultural programming so that we can avoid making incorrect assumptions about someone's behavior. For example, when asked, the young Mexican immigrant explained that he refused the promotion because, in his culture, being part of a group was more important than advancement. What's more it would put him in a supervisory position over older men from his same village. Since by his norms, elders are respected, and promotions are made by age, he said he would be very uncomfortable being forced to embarrass himself and his older compatriots by giving them orders.

We Are All Bound by Culture

In dealing with a culturally diverse workforce, one of the myths is that an individual needs to speak with an accent, have different skin color, or wear exotic clothes to have a culture. Even those who can trace their ancestors back to the Mayflower are culturally programmed. Just as a fish doesn't know it is in water until it is taken out, we only begin to become aware of our own programming when we come in contact with different cultural norms.

Edward Hall, the famous anthropologist who writes about culture, tells us we are all "captives of culture." Try this activity to see how much of your behavior is culturally directed. Imagine you wake up tomorrow morning as a member of a different cultural group in this society. Using the worksheet, *Culture and You*, check which aspects of your life would be the same and which would be different.

ACTIVITY 5.1 | Culture and You

If you woke up tomorrow morning and found that you belonged to another culture or ethnic group, how would your life be the same and how would it be different?

	Same	Different
1. The friends you associate with		
2. The social activities you enjoy		
3. The food you prefer		
4. The religion you practice		
5. The way you dress		
6. The community where you live		
7. The home you live in		
8. The job/position you hold		
9. The car you drive		
10. The music you enjoy listening to		
11. The language(s) you speak		
12. The political party you belong to		

Suggestions for Using
"Culture and You"

Objectives:
- Help individuals see the pervasiveness of cultural programming
- Increase awareness about the interplay between culture and individual personality in influencing life situations
- Empathize with individuals of other cultural backgrounds

Intended Audience:
- Individuals seeking to increase their own awareness about cultural differences
- Participants in diversity training sessions
- Workgroup members coping with issues related to diversity

Materials:
- Copies of the worksheet, *Culture and You*

Processing the Activity:
- Ask participants to imagine themselves suddenly becoming members of another cultural or ethnic group in this society. Stress that they are to imagine being born into and socialized by that other culture. As a variation, individuals may be asked also to imagine themselves of a different gender, sexual orientation, or physical-ability level.
- Individuals discuss reactions and insights in pairs, triads, or small groups.
- Smaller groupings share discussion highlights with a total group in a wrap-up discussion.

Questions for Discussion:
- Which parts of your life would remain the same? Which would be different?
- On what did you base your decisions about where to place your checks?
- What surprises did you have? What reactions?
- What questions or issues do these raise for you?
- What did you learn from this activity?

Caveats, Considerations, and Variations:
- Some individuals may balk at being asked to make choices based on assumptions or stereotypes. This activity can lead to a discussion of such issues.
- When giving directions, be sure to emphasize that the purpose of the activity is not to reinforce stereotypes, but to see how culture influences our lives.
- Issues beyond culture, such as income or education level, will undoubtedly be brought up as influences. This serves to broaden the scope of the discussion to other dimensions of diversity.

It may come as a surprise to those of us brought up in the United States, and schooled in the doctrines of individual freedom, personal choice, and free will, to find that our choices and life paths are culturally influenced. An African-American man in this society would undoubtedly have much different life experiences from an American-born daughter of immigrants from Mexico or a recently resettled Southeast Asian refugee family. What is your reaction? Are you surprised at how many checks you have in the "different" column? Were you stumped because you didn't know enough about the other culture to know if aspects of your life would be different? Perhaps you were irritated because this activity forces you to make assumptions about that other culture. Yet that is how we make sense of our world when there is an information gap. When we don't know or understand, we fill in the void with assumptions; that is, our own explanations for the events or situations that perplex us. And, often, our assumptions based on our own cultural software are incorrect.

Why Treating Everyone as You Want To Be Treated Doesn't Work

It is said that the Golden Rule is a universal principle underlying the foundations of most religions and moral codes. While "Do unto others as you would have them do unto you" is in spirit a wonderful rule, in practice it may create problems. As Sondra Thiederman, an intercultural communication expert, says, "We all have the same basic needs for dignity, survival and social contact. What is different between groups is the way in which these needs are satisfied."[3] Stop for a moment to consider how you like being treated.

ACTIVITY 5.2 | How I Like To Be Treated

Check off any of these statements that are true for you. Feel free to add more of your own as well.

☐ "I want to be told when I make a mistake so I don't make it again."

☐ "I want you to tell me if you disagree with me."

☐ "I like being told when I'm doing well so I know I'm on the right track."

☐ "I want the boss to ask for my input and to listen to my concerns."

☐ "I want the freedom to do things my own way."

☐ "I want my boss to roll up his or her sleeves and help out when we're busy."

☐ "I don't want to have to ask for directions and approval every step of the way."

☐ "I like it when others tell me what's on their minds."

☐ "I like it when people call me by my first name."

☐ "I want my staff to see me as their partner rather than as their boss."

☐ "It feels good when I am noticed and singled out for praise."

☐ "I like to be seen as an individual, not just considered one of the group."

☐ "I like being treated as an equal."

☐ "I like people to look me in the eyes when they talk to me."

☐ "I like_____."

☐ "It feels good when _____."

☐ _____

☐ _____

☐ _____

☐ _____

· ·

Suggestions for Using
"How I Like To Be Treated"

Objectives:

- Identify one's own behavioral preferences and expectations of others
- Increase awareness of the cultural influences on those preferences
- Empathize with those who hold different expectations

Intended Audience:

- Individuals wanting to increase their own sensitivity to cultural differences
- Trainees in diversity seminars
- Managers desiring better communication and relationships with diverse employees
- Workgroup members attempting to overcome cultural obstacles with co-workers and customers/clients

Materials:

- Copies of the worksheet, *How I Like To Be Treated*

Processing the Activity:

- Ask individuals to check their own preferences, adding others if desired.
- Have them also jot down their typical reactions to not being treated as desired.
- Discuss, in small groups or together as a whole group, how culture influences these preferences.
- Ask individuals to share "war stories" about examples of differences in preferences.
- Lead group discussion of the consequences for individuals and work relationships when individuals do not give or get the desired treatment.

Questions for Discussion:

- Which did you check? Which did you not check?
- What preferences did you add to the list?
- How/where did you acquire these preferences?
- Which preferences pertain to the mainstream culture of your organization?
- What happens if you don't get the behavior you want? How do you feel? How do you react?
- What does this tell you about dealing with and managing diverse individuals?

Caveats, Considerations, and Variations:

- To avoid arguments and polarization over which of these behaviors are *right* or *better*, explain that they are individual preferences, each with upsides and downsides.

· ·

How many of these statements did you check off? Did you realize that many were typically U.S. American cultural preferences that are not shared by many other groups? In each case, if you treated individuals from other cultures as you wanted to be treated, you might not be treating them as they would want. In fact, you might be embarrassing them and/or treating them rudely by their cultural standards. For example, the dominant U.S. American preference for directness ("Tell it like it is," "Don't beat around the bush," and "Put your cards on the table") is not universally shared. In many other cultures, such as those in Asia and the Middle East, communication is much more indirect and subtle. The direct, no-frills approach is seen as harsh or rude, and may lead to loss of face. Another cultural difference can be seen in the expectations employees have of bosses. In most other places in the world, there is a more hierarchical structure, and workers feel more security when they are told rather than asked what to do. Pay attention to your staff, colleagues, and customers, and to their reactions. If they seem uncomfortable, incommunicative, or evasive, it may be because they are confronted by behavior that breaks their cultural rules. Once you are aware of this barrier, you are in a position to do something different to change the interaction.

A friend of ours spent a number of years working in Vietnam. She recounted an incident that demonstrates how differently people want to be treated. Patti had worked at her new office job in Saigon for about a month. Being new to the country and not having family or friends around, she felt the need to get to know her Vietnamese colleagues better, so she invited the whole office staff over for dinner the following Sunday. They all nodded and indicated to her they accepted her invitation. She spent all weekend cleaning, shopping, and preparing an elaborate dinner for her co-workers. Then she waited. She was devastated when she realized no one was going to show up. The next morning at the office when she asked why no one came, she was at first given a polite runaround. No one wanted to discuss it. Finally, they began to explain that after only a month, they did not know her well enough to go to her home for dinner. In exasperation she asked, "Why didn't you tell me?" One of her co-workers served as her cultural interpreter and told her they knew the invitation was a honor to them, however, they did know her well enough to come to her home and they could not hurt or embarrass her by refusing the invitation. In Patti's culture, not showing up was the biggest sin; in theirs, it was saying no to an invitation. Patti realized how much more she needed to learn about her co-workers' culture so that she could avoid putting them in such an awkward position. So much for the Golden Rule: Treating others with consideration and respect for who they are may be a more insightful mind-set.

Sources of Cultural Programming: Where We Learn the Rules

We learn the rules of our culture from the first sounds and sights we experience as babies. The smiles and frowns of our parents are usually our first teachers. When we behave in socially accepted ways, we are praised, smiled at, and rewarded. When we don't, we are scolded, punished, or ignored. We soon learn the rules, from table and bathroom etiquette to how to talk to adults to get what we want. When we venture beyond our family of origin, to school, we continue the process. In his gem of a book, *All I Really Need To Know I Learned In*

Kindergarten, Robert Fulghum talks about how the instruction one receives at age five has implications for all of life.[4] We go on to learn from the larger culture in our neighborhoods and cities, and from radio, television, movies, and music. Additional rules come from the religions we practice or are taught. We continue to be enculturated by the colleges and universities we attend, and the professions, industries, and organizations in which we work. Each individual is like the proverbial onion, with layer upon layer of cultural teaching. Each of us has a unique culture, which is an amalgam of what has been absorbed from these various influences and experiences. An individual's cultural identity is shaped strongly by the following:

- *Ethnicity*—the ethnic group with which the individual identifies, including the native language the person speaks.
- *Race*—the racial group(s) with which the individual identifies.
- *Religion*—the organized religion, denomination, or sect to which the person adheres, has been taught, or rejects.
- *Education*—the level and type of education the person has experienced.
- *Profession/field of work*—the type of work the person is trained to do.
- *Organizations*—groups and associations, to which the individual belongs or has belonged; for example, the military, the Girl or Boy Scouts, a labor union or a fraternal organization.
- *Parents*—the messages, both verbal and nonverbal, given by parents about ethnicity, religion, values, cultural identity, prejudices, and so on.

While the above are powerful cultural influences, one's gender, family, peers, place of birth, and many other life experiences also significantly impact cultural identity.

Each Individual as a Culturally Diverse Entity

Because we receive our cultural teachings from a variety of sources, none of us has exactly the same program. If you have been married or have lived with another person, you've surely disagreed over the rules of conduct because you each got your rules from different places. The next activity gives you a chance to examine your own cultural influences so that you can better understand other people's programs. In each circle, write one of the sources of your programming. Parents or family of origin would undoubtedly go in one (although some individuals in our seminars put each parent in a different circle, saying they learned very different rules from each). Religion might go in another; for example, Catholicism, Islam, or Orthodox Judaism. The dominant national culture of the country in which you grew up—for example, the United States, Mexico, or Iran—might be in another circle. In another you might put the community in which you were reared: a small town or a big city; a rural, an urban, or a suburban setting. Continue filling in each circle, and add more circles if you need to. Then write down the most important things you learned from each of these sources of your programming. For example, if you grew up in the United States, you might have learned that individual freedom and independence are to be treasured, while you might have learned to respect and honor elders if your parents were of Asian or European ancestry. If your family emigrated from the Philippines, you might have learned to place importance on harmonious relationships, while if your parents came from Iran, you might have learned to have a deep loyalty to extended family members.

ACTIVITY 5.3 | You as a Culturally Diverse Entity

Directions: In each circle, write one of the sources of your cultural programming. Then, next to each circle, write the most important rules, norms, and values you learned from that source.

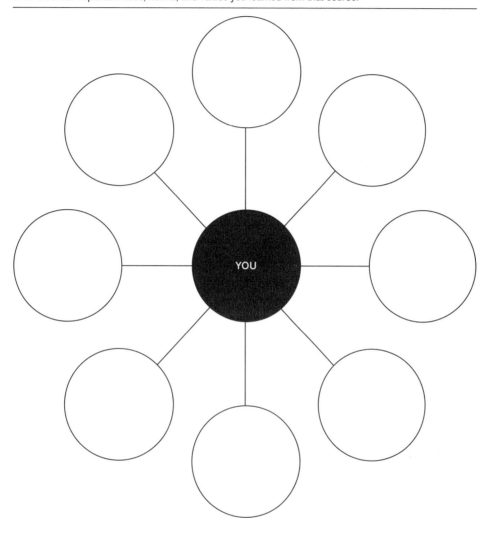

1. How do these aspects of your programming influence your behavior on the job?

2. How much do you know about the cultural programming of your co-workers, boss, or staff?

Suggestions for Using
"You as a Culturally Diverse Entity"

Objectives:

- Identify the sources of one's own cultural programming
- See oneself as a microcosm of the societal dynamic of intercultural contact
- Increase awareness about the complexity of each individual's cultural programming, which, in turn, affects behavior
- Raise awareness about the need to find out more about the backgrounds of others in the workplace
- Understand that everyone has a culture
- Learn more about others with whom one works in order to increase understanding

Intended Audience:

- Individuals wanting to increase their understanding and awareness about cultural influences and intercultural interactions on the job
- Trainees in diversity seminars
- Members of work teams wanting to understand each other better
- Managers wanting to learn more about employees

Materials:

- Copies of the worksheet, *You as a Culturally Diverse Entity*
- Easel, flipchart, and markers

Processing the Activity:

- Have the group brainstorm sources of cultural programming and chart responses on an easel or a board. You might get them going by asking them how they learned the rules of behavior they now live by.
- Individuals write one source of their own cultural programming in each circle on the diagram. Under each, they write the most important rules, norms, and values they learned.
- Individuals, in pairs or small groups, share information from their circles. They then discuss their reactions and the implications of the information.
- Lead a total-group discussion of reactions, insights, and learning.

Questions for Discussion:

- Which were the most important sources of your programming?
- Where do they come in conflict?
- Under what circumstances does one take priority over another?
- How are these differences resolved?
- What similarities and differences did you find with your partner(s) in your discussion group?
- What do you know about the programming of your colleagues, staff members, bosses, and so on? How can you find out more?
- What insight did you get?
- What does this say about dealing with others who are different from you?
- What is one way you can learn more about the software of others with whom you work?

Caveats, Considerations, and Variations:

- This activity causes participants to look back to childhood, which can be a painful or emotional experience for some. It is not surprising to see eyes filled with tears as individuals share their experiences and memories with others in the room.
- Tell people at the beginning of the activity that they will be sharing their responses with another person or a small group. In this way individuals can control the degree of disclosure.

When you analyze your programming, you may see places where different parts of your programming come into conflict. For example, perhaps your upbringing has taught you to be modest about your accomplishments, yet the culture of your organization has shown you that you don't get ahead unless you toot your own horn a bit.

How do you resolve conflicts between aspects of your own programming when they come up? While these internal conflicts can cause some pain, most of the time you make your peace with them. In the same way, conflicts related to culture between individuals can be resolved if they are acknowledged and dealt with. In addition, working through this activity, you probably came to realize how complex we all are and that no one can be pigeonholed into a particular pattern. ("All Filipinos do . . . " or "Mexicans never . . ."). Finally, ask yourself how much you know about the cultural programming of your staff. What influences are in their backgrounds, and what rules were they taught? Consider discussing these ideas or even doing this activity with them at a staff meeting. You might be surprised at what you learn about them. There will undoubtedly also be a team-building spin-off, giving staff a greater understanding of one another, a greater appreciation of their common areas, and an increased cohesiveness.

Ten Aspects of Culture: Understanding Culture's Influence

How frequently you bathe, how close you stand to someone with whom you are talking, how you address a boss, how you solve a problem, and how you respond to stress are all determined by your cultural programming. For example, the African-American accountant mentioned at the beginning of this chapter was not regarded as a team player because she demonstrated and dealt with her stress differently from her colleagues. Her response to pressure was to get very quiet, close her office door, and hunker down to work. Her co-workers, on the other hand, went around complaining about being overworked and pressured, getting sympathy and support from one another. It was only when the accountant's boss uncovered the reasons for the conflict that he could correct his own and his staff's misinterpretation of her behavior and then take steps to resolve the conflict.

To understand the aspects of cultural teachings, it is helpful to contrast different cultural rules within the 10 areas of cultural programming described by Harris and Moran.[5] However, the risk in doing so is that new stereotypes will develop. The cultural norms described in the following section are generalizations that do not take into account individual personalities or the degree of acculturation to the larger U.S. American culture. For example, while U.S. culture teaches individuals to make direct eye contact and speak their minds, many U.S. Americans are shy, avert their eyes, and keep their opinions to themselves. In addition, there is much variation within any group. The term Latino can mean a third-generation Mexican American, a recent immigrant from El Salvador, a Cuban exile, or a Puerto Rican businessman.

1. Sense of Self and Space

Have you ever felt uncomfortable because someone stood too close when talking with you? Have you ever felt put off when your warm hug was received with a stiff, statue-like response? Or have you reacted to what you consider the pretension of someone addressing others by their titles instead of their first names? Chances are these rubs have their roots in cultural norms.

"Too close for comfort" and "Get out of my space" are common expressions that deal with the issue of space. U.S. American culture teaches us to stay about 1 1/2 to 3 feet, or an arm's length, from people with whom we are talking in a business or friendship relationship. Any closer is reserved for more intimate contact with family, romantic relationships, or very close friends. Maintaining greater distance signifies a desire to stay aloof or protect oneself. When someone steps into your space, you'll probably move back to maintain a comfortable distance. Other cultures have different norms. According to Edward Hall, in the Middle East, people stand close enough to be able to feel your breath on their face and to be able to catch your scent.[6] As for greeting, in Japan, it's a bow; in North America, it's a hearty handshake; in Mexico and South America, it's a warmer, softer handshake sometimes accompanied by a hug; and in the Middle East it's a hug and a ritualistic kiss on each cheek.

These physical aspects of the way we respect an individual's sense of self and space also have a less tangible counterpart in the degree of formality we expect in relationships. Many languages (Spanish, German, Tagalog, etc.) have two forms of the word "you"—the formal and the familiar. In these cultures, the familiar form is reserved for children, family members, close friends, and those below you in the social hierarchy. English has long since dropped the familiar "thee" and "thou," so we are left with one pronoun, "you," for all relationships, whether we are talking with the president, a boss, or a spouse.

"Let's not stand on ceremony" is the culture's response to what most U.S. Americans consider stuffy formality. New acquaintances, bosses, and older individuals are commonly called by their first names. In other cultures, formal introductions using Mr., Mrs., and titles are expected as a sign of respect for both parties.

Since most other cultures are more formal, you are safest if you err on the side of formality. Trying to be buddy-buddy with a staff of people from other cultures that expect more formal behavior from a boss is apt to make workers uncomfortable and embarrassed. In business relationships and discussions, keeping a more reserved tone also tends to send the message that you respect the individuals with whom you are meeting. An American employee of a Japanese company doing business in the United States learned the hard way. Well schooled in both Japanese language and culture, she made a presentation at a meeting. Because the company had succeeded in achieving its goal, she couldn't contain her excitement and she ended her recounting of the success statistics with a "Yeah!" Her Japanese boss told her later that her show of emotion was inappropriate for a formal business presentation.

Suggestions for Managers
- Make sure you say good morning and good-bye to each employee every day.
- Introduce new employees to their co-workers formally, taking the individual around to meet each new colleague.
- Be careful in using first names, especially with older workers and customers.
- Ask people how they prefer being addressed.
- Guard against being overly familiar with employees.

- Learn to listen and create an atmosphere of trust where you can learn about each other's needs.

2. Communication and Language

It is clear that language differences often accompany cultural differences. However, more is involved than just the specific language an individual speaks. By some estimates, more than half of our communication is nonverbal, which indicates the significance of gestures, facial expression, tone of voice, and intonation patterns.

The most obvious of the nonverbal signals is eye contact. All cultures use it to send signals, but the difficulty comes when the signals are misinterpreted. When being reprimanded as children, many of us were told the following by our parents: "Look at me when I'm talking to you." We break eye contact when we want to end the conversation with the bore who has cornered us at a party. We catch the eye of the waiter to let him know we want the check in a restaurant. Not making eye contact in U.S. culture is generally taken as a sign of deceitfulness, nonassertion, or disinterest. However, in Asian and Latin cultures, averting one's eyes is a sign of respect and the proper behavior when in the presence of an older person or authority figure.

Gestures are another nonverbal communicator, one we often depend on when there is a language barrier. Yet gestures can get us into trouble in multicultural groups. The OK sign, for example, made with the thumb and index finger, is an obscene gesture in Greece and some parts of South America. Smiling, often considered an international gesture, is another nonverbal cue that can be misinterpreted. The following examples are cases in point:

- A bank's customer service representative assists a limited-English-speaking customer in filling out a form. In an attempt to put the customer at ease, he smiles and speaks in a lighthearted manner. He is shocked when the customer calls from home a few minutes later to complain about being laughed at and treated disrespectfully.
- An engineering manager asks why the Asian engineers whom he supervises smile so much. "I feel like they are snickering and laughing at me," he says.

A smile is seen as a welcoming, friendly gesture in the United States. In many Asian cultures, it may be a sign of embarrassment, confusion, or discomfort. In the Middle East, a smile from a woman to a man can be construed as a sexual come-on. In Germany, smiling is reserved for friends and family.

Nodding the head is yet another nonverbal cue that causes problems. Saying "no" is considered rude, impudent behavior in many cultures because it upsets the harmony of relationships. A nod often means, "Yes, I heard you," not "Yes, I understand" or "Yes, I agree."

Perhaps the difference that causes the most difficulty in communication is the subtlest. It has to do with the degree of directness or indirectness, or the amount of information that is stated rather than implied. In Japanese culture, for example, communication is very indirect, depending on subtle contextual cues. An individual would not tell someone to turn the heat on but would instead hug herself. If that did not get a response, she might mention that it was a bit chilly. The other party would immediately pick up the cue and turn the heat on. A manager wanting to tell an employee about some errors on a report might suggest the employee look it over again. If both manager and employee are Japanese, the employee would understand that this subtle suggestion meant something was wrong with the report. This implied direction would be missed by most U.S. American employees, who would probably be perplexed by the suggestion.

Contrast this approach with the "Don't beat around the bush" dictum of U.S. culture, which favors a very explicitly stated message. When these two approaches collide, problems can result. The Japanese, for example, are often exasperated at what they see as Americans' "rudeness" when they say "no" directly or demand a clear, direct answer. On the other hand, U.S. Americans are just as frustrated when they miss the unstated clues that their Japanese counterparts automatically pick up: "How was I supposed to know I had to wait until the boss left? Why don't they just tell me?"

Suggestions for Managers

- When there is a language barrier, assume confusion. Don't take the nod or "yes" to mean the individual understands or agrees. Watch for tangible signs of understanding such as immediately beginning the task and doing it correctly.
- Consider that smiles and laughter may indicate discomfort or embarrassment. See if you can identify what is causing the difficulty.
- Avoid smiling when giving directions or when having serious work-related discussions with employees, especially when giving feedback or when conducting performance reviews.
- Be careful not to think out loud. Employees hearing you may take your off-the-cuff comments literally and may even act on them.
- Watch for subtle clues that may be speaking volumes. A comment about another worker's frustrations may be telling you about a work-group complaint. Hints about family members moving in might be an indirect way to express a desire for more overtime.

3. Dress and Appearance

Though we may be taught not to judge a book by its cover, we often do. The problem is that each culture has different rules about what is appropriate. Not only does "dressing for success" mean different things in different cultures, but rules also differ within a society, especially across the age range. In addition, dress codes, tattoos, and piercings get different reactions depending on generation. In some groups and cultures, clothing is a sign of social class; hence, much money and attention are spent on dressing expensively. In others, clothing offers a chance to express one's personality and creativity, so the brighter and more decorative, the better. In still others, clothing is just a necessity of life, neither a status symbol nor an individual statement.

Take a look at the different workplace implications of dress. One client almost discounted a qualified job applicant because of these differences. The selection committee was interviewing applicants for a community outreach position in which the individual would be developing business with minority-owned firms. When the interviewee arrived dressed in a bright silk dress, lots of jewelry, and long painted nails, the committee collectively gulped. However, when they stopped to think, they realized she was dressing very appropriately as her appearance might be right in sync with the community members with whom she would be working. In another example, one government agency dealing with the management of state vehicles found that the rift between male and female mechanics was made less of a problem when all wore unisex uniforms that minimized the differences between genders and became a badge of their profession.

Hair can also be an appearance hot spot. Turbans, dreadlocks, corn rows, ponytails on men, and fluorescent stripes are just a few of the different hairstyles that raise eyebrows across cultures and generations. Hindus believe that the hair should never be cut, and the men wrap their heads in turbans. Many Orthodox Jewish men wear forelocks, while their wives cover their hair in public. In many cultures, hair is a symbol of virility for men, femininity for women, and individual dignity for all. Prisoners, for example, are often shorn, thereby stripping them of their individuality and humanness.

Probably one of the most uncomfortable areas to deal with regarding grooming is body odor. U.S. American culture has a near fetish on the topic. There is a deodorant for almost every part of the body. In polite society, people react negatively to the smell of another human being. Not so in other parts of the world. According to Edward T. Hall, in the Middle East, marriage go-betweens often ask to smell the girl before they recommend her as a prospective bride.[7] Also, as mentioned, it is considered a normal part of communication in the Middle East to be able to feel and smell another's breath when talking. Body odor, whether from a lack of deodorant use or from diet (as in the garlic-laden kimchi eaten by many Koreans), can cause real problems in work teams when people find each other's odors offensive.

Suggestions for Managers:

- Before reacting to another's appearance, stop to consider the meaning attached to appearance by the individual.
- When making assessments about job applicants, consider their cultural norms regarding dress.
- When determining appropriate dress, consider the job the individual will be doing and the people with whom he or she will be interacting.
- Teach individuals the cultural rules required in your organization regarding dress and grooming.
- Remember that body scent is not necessarily a sign of bad hygiene.
- Consider uniforms as a way to eliminate differences and build credibility and common ground.

4. Food and Eating Habits

While you may know that what we eat, when we eat, and how we eat are culturally directed, you may wonder what food and eating habits have to do with work. When asked about the benefits of living and working in a multicultural environment, food is almost always mentioned high on the list. Most of us enjoy the potlucks with exotic and enticing dishes that result from having a diverse staff. Yet in the workplace, differences can cause conflict, as in the following examples:

- At a catered lunch at a management meeting, the entrée is Quiche Lorraine made with ham. Two managers never touch their plates.

- Employees at a manufacturing plant complain about the smell of the fish lunches being heated and eaten by their Vietnamese co-workers.
- Bosnian immigrants avoid taking most of the food being served by executives at the annual holiday buffet. Not being familiar with much of what was offered, and not knowing if it contained pork, they abstained.

Understanding food restrictions and taboos is a starting point. Prohibitions against certain foods are often associated with religious rules. Among the Kosher food laws adhered to by some Jews is the prohibition against eating pork and shellfish. Devout Muslims also refuse pork and alcoholic beverages. Hindu religious beliefs prohibit the eating of meat of any kind. In addition, many individuals choose to eat a vegetarian diet because of ethical considerations, medical reasons, or personal preferences. Beyond restrictions, cultural norms influence our food preferences. Animals that are pets in one culture may be a food source in another. The U.S. American repugnance and outrage at the eating of dog, horse, or cat meat are probably akin to a devout Hindu's feelings about Americans eating beef.

Do you eat with chopsticks or a fork and knife? In which hand do you hold your fork and knife? What do you think about eating with your hands? Chopsticks are the utensils of choice in most of Asia, while holding the knife in the right hand and the fork in the left is proper for Europeans. In parts of the Middle East, eating with the right hand from a communal bowl is the accepted practice.

Smacking one's lips, burping, and picking one's teeth at the table are considered breaches of etiquette in the United States, yet these behaviors may be entirely acceptable elsewhere. In fact, belching is seen as a compliment to the cook in Asia. Europeans eat with both hands on the table, while Americans are admonished to keep the left hand in the lap unless cutting food. Before you judge others' table manners, stop and think about what might be proper by their standards. Also consider that others may be just as appalled by your table manners.

Suggestions for Managers:
- When planning catered meals or snacks for meetings and group gatherings, include a variety of foods so there will be something edible and acceptable for all.
- Avoid serving food that might be offensive to some staff members.
- Have alternate dishes available (e.g., a vegetarian plate or fruit salad).
- When choosing restaurants for business meetings, keep individual dietary restrictions and preferences in mind.
- Provide well-ventilated (or outdoor) eating areas for staff where odors can be more easily dissipated.

5. Time and Time Consciousness

When asked about the hardest adjustments they've had to make, U.S. Americans who work abroad invariably talk about the differences in time consciousness. The so-called mañana attitude in Mexico and the *Inshallah* of the Arab world clash with the "Time is money" and "The early bird gets the worm" U.S. views of time. In that view, time is seen as a commodity to be used, divided, spent, and saved. It is linear and finite: The meeting starts at 2 p.m. and ends at 4 p.m., as stated in the memo. However, in other parts of the world, such as Latin America and the Middle East, time is considered more elastic and more relative. The meeting starts when the necessary people are there and ends when what needs to be done is done. Time is used not just to accomplish tasks but also to develop relationships and enjoy oneself. When things happen depends not on just a schedule, but also on other events, priorities, and the will of God. So, mañana does not necessarily mean "tomorrow," but sometime in the future. *Inshallah* may mean "whenever it comes to pass."

A U.S. American concerned with deadlines is understandably frustrated by what may appear to be a lack of motivation, efficiency, or honesty when encountering such a response. That same person, on the other hand, may be seen as always in a hurry and more concerned with tasks than with people.

Suggestions for Managers:
- Recognize that differences in time consciousness are cultural and are not a sign of laziness.
- Allow time in your schedule for the development of relationships.
- Make it a point to spend some time each week with each employee.
- Explain the reasons for deadlines and schedules.
- Explain the part promptness plays in assessment of performance and work habits.

6. Relationships
Generally, in U.S. American culture, hiring relatives is considered nepotism and is, in fact, prohibited in many organizations. Yet in most other parts of the world, hiring kin is not only common, but also expected. Not to do so would be considered abdicating one's responsibility to family. Furthermore, while family in the United States usually means the nuclear group of parents and siblings, in other cultures it involves a large network of extended family members: cousins, aunts, uncles, nieces, nephews, and in-laws. Loyalty is expected toward kin, and obedience and respect are paid to older family members. Organizational rules or directions that require employees to go against these norms will be circumvented or disobeyed. You might experience an employee who hides the fact that his "friend" is really a relative, for example, or an employee who takes extended leaves to go back to his home village during the holidays.

In most other cultures, families are not egalitarian democracies. There is a definite hierarchy of status, with age being the determiner of power and respect. A definite pecking order exists, for example, with an older brother having authority over a younger one or a grandmother having matriarch status. An employee from such a family would not think of making a work-related decision, such as seeking a promotion or accepting a transfer, without talking it over with the "head of the family." This same sense of respect may transfer to the work unit, where employees apply a similar hierarchy within the group.

A seminar participant related how she learned about this kinship hierarchy on the job. As a nursing manager, she was in charge of running her unit, which included dealing with family members and visitors. A problem arose one evening when one of her patients, a Roma, had the entire extended family (more than 20 people) visiting. There were complaints from staff and other patients, so the manager went in to deal with the problem.

Luckily, a security guard accompanied her. Before she could say anything, the guard formally introduced her to the head of the family, explaining that she was the manager in charge. She then explained the situation to the head of the family and asked for his cooperation. She got it. However, she was certain that without the cultural sensitivity and savvy of the security guard, she would not have paid attention to the family hierarchy and probably would not have gotten the quick cooperation she did by respecting the group's cultural norms.

Suggestions for Managers:
- Recognize that family responsibility and loyalty to kin will be a prime value of many workers. Take this into consideration when identifying rewards and motivators for staff (e.g., hiring relatives and giving time off for funerals, vacations, and holidays).
- Allow employees time to discuss important decisions with family members before they give you a final answer.
- Recognize the informal leadership older members may hold in the work unit. Consult with them and seek their cooperation.
- Show respect to older employees by addressing them first and giving them formal authority when appropriate.
- Recognize that, as the boss, you may be seen as the "head of the work family."
- Employees may come to seek your advice and counsel about problems in and out of work.

7. Values and Norms

One of the cornerstones of U.S. society is the doctrine of individual freedom. A revolution was fought to attain independence and the inalienable rights of life, liberty, and the pursuit of happiness. The Bill of Rights goes further in specifying the extent of individual freedoms. The promise of freedom has attracted immigrants to these shores for centuries. In recent times, the idea of personal entitlement has pushed the ideas of individual freedom even further. But this isn't the case in many other cultures, where conformity to the group, family, and larger society is the norm. To most U.S. Americans, the need to conform, to subjugate one's individual needs to the those of the group, would feel confining and stifling. On the other hand, in many collectivist cultures, such as in Asia, the priority of the group over the individual assures harmony and order, and brings a feeling of stability to life. In an interesting experiment, a group of bilingual Japanese women were given a series of open-ended statements to complete in both Japanese and English.[8] When asked, in English, to complete the statement, "When my wishes conflict with my family's," one woman responded, "I do what I want." When asked to complete the same statement in Japanese, the response was "It is a time of great unhappiness." In the workplace this difference may show itself in employees' discomfort with individual praise, especially in public; with staff members' reluctance to break rank and blow the whistle; or with workers' difficulty in openly seeking advancement.

Competition vs. Cooperation is another difference, which is related to group orientation. The competitive spirit is an underpinning of U.S. life and the capitalist economic system. However, competition upsets the balance and harmony valued by cultures that prefer cooperation and collaboration. A high-tech Japanese firm doing business in the United States discovered this difference in attempting to correct a problem. Dismayed to learn of the theft of some expensive equipment, top management assembled a group of middle managers to come up with a solution. The U.S. managers concluded that offering a reward to the individual who reported the thief was the best solution. The lone dissenting voice came from a Japanese manager, whose suggestion that the team that did not have any theft be rewarded. His suggestion was laughed at. Each solution, however, was culturally appropriate.

Another cultural difference that emerges in the workplace regards privacy. To many newcomers, U.S. Americans seem naively open: Discussing personal matters outside the family is seen as embarrassing, and opening up to someone outside of one's own cultural group is rare. Thoughts, feelings, and problems are kept to oneself in most groups outside the United States. Off-the-cuff thinking, shooting from the hip, and giving an immediate response to a question from the boss would be difficult for someone raised with this cultural norm.

On the other hand, when it comes to privacy with regards to personal space, as opposed to thoughts and feelings, U.S. Americans are not so open. Perhaps because the United States has had the luxury of vast open spaces, we have a culture that fences off each person's area: children have their own rooms, backyards are fenced, and office spaces are partitioned into cubicles. In much of the rest of the world, such "fencing off" is not the case: Families may sleep in the same room, and the work spaces are communal. In Japanese offices, the boss generally does not have a separate office but rather shares a portion of the work space with employees. Likewise, in public areas, a new passenger on a bus or train would generally take a seat next to someone rather than sit in an unoccupied section. That would be considered odd behavior at best, and dangerously threatening at worst, in the United States.

Loyalty is another value that is displayed differently across cultures. Most U.S. Americans are taught to be loyal to such abstract principles as "truth, justice, and the American way" and believe no one is above the law. Mexicans, Filipinos, and Middle Easterners, on the other hand, are generally loyal to individuals rather than to abstractions. That personal allegiance might mean breaking a rule to help a friend or covering up for a relative's infraction. Employees who feel this personal attachment also tend to give their allegiance to the boss rather than to the organization.

Finally, we get to an issue critical to all human beings: respect. While all of us want to be treated with dignity and respect, we define and demonstrate respect differently. Loss of face is important to avoid in all cultures. In Asia, in the Middle East, and to some extent in Latin America, one's face is to be preserved at all costs. In fact, death is preferred to loss of face in traditional Japanese culture, hence the ritualized suicide, as a final way to restore honor. Any embarrassment can lead to loss of face, even in the United States. To be criticized in front of others, to be publicly snubbed, or to be fired would be hard to swallow in any culture. However, inadvertent slights or unconscious faux pas can cause serious repercussions in intercultural relationships.

In Mexico, the Middle East, and parts of Asia, for example, the separation of the individual from the behavior is not so clear. "I am my behavior and my behavior is me" might be the motto. Criticism of performance may be taken as a personal insult, hence the case of the Indonesian worker who quit because of the loss of face he experienced in being corrected by his boss. In another example, the owner of a large travel agency had decided to reorganize her company, streamlining in the face of an economic slump. In doing her assessing, she noticed that one supervisor's group had slowly dwindled so that there was no one left for the supervisor to manage. The owner, an immigrant from the Philippines herself, called in her Chinese-born supervisor to discuss reorganization plans. While the employee understood the need for the changes, she begged the boss not to take away her title of supervisor and demote her. "I would lose face in my community if I lost my title," she said. The boss, understanding that "face" in this case took priority over a logical organization chart, complied. "What difference does it make to me what her title is? I just care that she is a satisfied and committed employee. If letting her be called supervisor accomplishes that, why not?" she thought.

Suggestions for Managers:
- Consider giving rewards and feedback to the whole workgroup rather than to individuals.
- Structure tasks to require teamwork rather than individual action.
- Give workers time to think about and formulate responses to input requests.
- Consider the face-losing potential of any actions you are planning. Seek out ways to achieve your objectives while avoiding diminishing employees.

8. Beliefs and Attitudes

Religion probably comes to mind when you think of beliefs and attitudes with regard to cultural programming. Whether we practice them or not, religion is a powerful influence of beliefs and attitudes. While the doctrine of separation of church and state is set down in the U.S. Constitution, there is a strong Judeo-Christian foundation in this country, with an emphasis on the Christian part. If you don't think so, look at legal holidays and school vacations.

Given today's pluralistic workforce and a trend toward bringing religion into the public sphere, it is important to realize that everyone does not practice the same religions, celebrate the same holidays, or want the same days off. An observant Orthodox Jew, for example, would not work during the Sabbath, from sundown Friday to sundown Saturday, so holding important staff meetings on Friday afternoons or scheduling a teambuilding retreat on a Saturday would exclude this person, as it would a Seventh-Day Adventist. Among Muslim religious observances is the month of Ramadan, during which devout Muslims can have nothing to eat or drink each day from sunup to sundown. If you have Muslims on your staff, this might be a month to avoid holding heavy duty negotiations or employee recognition luncheons. One manager reported that since one of his Muslim employees reserved the noon hour for midday prayers, the manager made sure he never scheduled meetings during lunch.

Holiday celebrations are often times when religious differences are inadvertently ignored. In one client organization, management was surprised to find that not all employees appreciated the red poinsettia plants that were purchased to decorate all office cubicles at Christmastime. Finding ways to acknowledge the range of holidays, such as Hanukkah and Kwanza, celebrated during the season helps create an environment of inclusion.

In addition to religious views, beliefs about the position of women in society differ among cultures. In some groups, it is accepted that women work outside the home. In other groups, it is seen as a deficiency on the part of the male head of the house if any of the women from his family work. In other cases, while women may work outside the home, they cannot be in a position of authority over men. For a man to take orders from a woman would cause loss of face. This difference may cause problems between bosses and subordinates or between female staff and male clients/customers. Beyond ethical principles, with today's laws regarding equal employment opportunity (EEO) and affirmative action, organizations need to educate employees about the legal risks involved in discriminating because of gender.

Still another area of cultural programming regards attitudes about social order and authority. In Asia, it is rare for students to question teachers, employees to confront bosses, and children to talk back to parents. But this isn't the case in many parts of the U.S., where the culture tends to be more egalitarian than in cultures that have more traditional and hierarchical attitudes about authority. While no society is truly classless, there is a wide range in views about social class, from the social mobility suggested in the "It's not who you are but what you are that counts" motto popular in the United States to India's more rigid social caste system. Once you understand this difference, you can interpret others' behavior more accurately. You will see differently the housekeeper who calls you Miss/Mr./Mrs. before your first name, the employee who will not participate in group decision making at meetings, or the staff member who will not take direction from a countryman who is younger or on a lower social scale than he.

Suggestions for Managers:
- Find out what religious holidays staff members celebrate. Keep those in mind when planning workgroup activities, holiday celebrations, and individual schedules.
- Avoid scheduling meetings and training programs on any religious holidays.
- Take advantage of the fact that employees want different holidays, days off, and vacation times (e.g., some people would be willing to work on Sundays or on Christmas day).
- Help newcomers understand the reasons for shared decision-making and the need for suggestions and input from employees.
- Educate employees about EEO and discrimination. Explain the legal liabilities as well as the principles of equality that, though not always adhered to, are foundations of this country.

9. Mental Processes and Learning

Do you prefer getting directions in words or with a map? Do you learn best by listening and taking notes; by being involved in experiential activities; by seeing models, diagrams, and graphs; or by taking part in lively discussions? Do you attribute your successes to your hard work and tenacity, or to luck and fate?

We all have preferences in learning and thinking styles, and some of these preferences are cultural. The columnist George Will once quipped, that in contrasting the United States and the former USSR, the game that best represents the thinking style of the

United States is poker, while that of the USSR is chess. These two games represent very different styles of problem-solving and thinking. Such different approaches may show up on your staff.

Perhaps the most obvious difference in problem-solving has to do with the perception of human control. U.S. American culture professes a "fix it" approach to problems, one that assumes that we have the power to control our world. Problems are seen as obstacles to overcome, and success in doing so depends on our actions. Progress and change are often seen as ends in and of themselves. In most of the rest of the world, the view is different: Problems are viewed as situations to which one must adapt, and the changes required by problem-solving are seen as a threat to order and harmony. In addition, fate and luck play a great part in determining the outcome of ventures. Cause-and-effect relationships are less emphasized in this kind of thinking. U.S. culture also has a preference for logical analysis, while other cultures may bring more intuition and holistic thinking to a problem.

Another difference is in learning style. Teaching and learning are generally much more didactic, formal, and one-way (from teacher to student) in most of the rest of the world. There is also more dependence on written information. Therefore, staff from other cultures might feel lost in a typical American training seminar that emphasizes experiential activities and role playing, which require the learner to draw his or her own conclusions. Staff might also want copies of all information charted at the board or easel, or they may ask for notes or outlines from a meeting.

Suggestions for Managers:
- Explain cause-and-effect relationships when getting staff members involved in problem-solving.
- Ask staff members what they suggest be done about the problems and complaints they express.
- Use nonlinear problem-solving methods such as brainstorming that capitalize on lateral thinking and intuition rather than logical analysis.
- Ask troubleshooting questions such as "What would happen if...?" in order to get staff to think about possible consequences.

10. Work Habits and Practices

"The devil makes work for idle hands" exemplifies the Protestant work ethic, a cornerstone of U.S. society. In this view, work is seen as more than a means to survival; it is a divine calling, a "vocation." In today's vernacular, we talk about job satisfaction and creating a career that brings joy, esteem, and achievement. Work is not always held in such high regard in other cultures. In fact, it may be seen as a necessary evil.

The type of work one does may also be seen as a sign of status. In the United States, we make distinctions between blue-collar and white-collar work, manual labor and professional work, and exempt and nonexempt employees. In other cultures, such as in India and the Arab world, for example, working with one's hands has lower status than doing professional work. This may explain why workers balk at certain tasks or prefer one kind of work over another. A physicist who managed an international staff at a premier space and technology research organization noticed that some loved to tinker, work with their hands, and build models, while others disdained working with their hands and found it beneath their dignity to have to input their own data into the computer.

If you are trying to get motivation and commitment from staff, the reward structure is a critical area to understand. What an employee considers rewarding is in the eye of the beholder, and that eye is cultural. A promotion to management might be considered a reward to one individual and a punishment to another; a bonus for a job well done might feel like a pat on the back to one employee and an insult to another. Paying attention to what individuals consider rewarding is important in any workgroup, but, in a diverse group, it may be more difficult to figure out. If you know that an employee has family responsibilities outside of work, allowing a more flexible schedule with staggered hours might be more of a motivator than a promotion. If an employee is trying to save money to send a child to college or to bring other family members to this country, giving overtime assignments as tangible reinforcers might be appreciated.

Taking initiative and being self-directed are other work habits not universally taught. In most other cultures, workers are not expected to exercise independent judgment, make decisions, or initiate tasks without being directed to do so. When you notice employees waiting for direction, do not immediately assume these employees are unmotivated or lazy; they may be waiting for you to exercise your leadership role.

Suggestions for Managers:
- Get to know your employees and find out what place work plays in their lives. Find out what gives them satisfaction on the job.
- Be sensitive to employees' perceptions about the status of certain kinds of work. Explain the reasons for each assignment and its importance in the whole scheme of things.
- Talk to employees and find out what is rewarding to them.
- Understand that taking initiative and making independent decisions may be difficult for some employees. Take time to coach them in this direction.

Table 5.1 gives a brief recap of the major differences between mainstream U.S. American and other cultures relative to the 10 aspects of culture discussed. The three tools that follow offer activities that can help individuals learn about cultural differences and apply that knowledge to their own situations. Activity 5.4 gives you a format to record information about different cultural norms. Activity 5.5 helps you apply that knowledge to specific work relationships. Finally, Activity 5.6 enables you to gain a better understanding of your own intercultural button-pushers.

TABLE 5.1 | Comparing Cultural Norms and Values

Aspects of Culture	U.S. American Culture	Other Cultures
Sense of self and space	Informal: handshake	Formal: hugs, bows, handshakes
Communication and language	Explicit, direct communication Emphasis on content—meaning found in words	Implicit, indirect communication Emphasis on context—meaning found around words
Dress and appearance	"Dress for success" ideal Wide range in accepted dress	Dress seen as a sign of position, wealth, prestige Religious rules
Food and eating habits	Eating as a necessity—fast food	Dining as a social experience Religious rules
Time and time consciousness	Linear and exact time consciousness Value on promptness, time = money	Elastic and relative time consciousness Time spent on enjoyment of relationships
Relationships, family, friends	Focus on nuclear family Responsibility for self Value on youth, age seen as handicap	Focus on extended family Loyalty and responsibility to family Age given status and respect
Values and norms	Individual orientation Independence Preference for direct confrontation of conflict	Group orientation Conformity Preference for harmony
Beliefs and attitudes	Egalitarian Challenging of authority Individuals control their destiny Gender equity	Hierarchical Respect for authority and social order Individuals accept their destiny Different roles for men and women
Mental processes and learning style	Linear, logical, sequential Problem-solving focus	Lateral, holistic, simultaneous Accepting of life's difficulties
Work habits and practices	Emphasis on task Reward based on individual achievement Work has intrinsic value	Emphasis on relationships Rewards based on seniority, relationships Work is a necessity of life

ACTIVITY 5.4 | Dimensions of Culture*

This table gives you an opportunity to make some notes about cultural differences you have encountered in each of these 10 areas of cultural programming.

ASPECTS OF CULTURE	EXAMPLES OF DIFFERENCES
1. Sense of Self and Space • Distance • Touch • Formal/Informal • Open/Closed	
2. Communication and Language • Language/Dialect • Gestures/Expressions/Tone • Direct/Indirect	
3. Dress and Appearance • Clothing • Hair • Grooming	
4. Food and Eating Habits • Food Restrictions/Taboos • Utensils/Hands • Manners	
5. Time and Time Consciousness • Promptness • Age/Status • Pace	
6. Relationships • Family • Age/Gender/Kindred • Status	
7. Values and Norms • Group vs. Individual • Independence vs. Conformity • Privacy • Respect • Competition vs. Cooperation	
8. Beliefs and Attitudes • Religion • Position of Women • Social Order/Authority	
9. Mental Processes and Learning • Left/Right Brain Emphasis • Logic/Illogic	
10. Work Habits and Practices • Work Ethic • Rewards/Promotions • Status of Type of Work • Division of Labor/Organization	

Suggestions for Using
"Dimensions of Culture"

Objectives:

- Identify both U.S. American and other cultural norms
- Recognize the cultural roots of behaviors encountered at work
- Expand understanding and knowledge of different cultural norms

Intended Audience:

- Individuals wanting to increase their knowledge about different cultural norms
- Trainees in a diversity seminar
- Employees wanting to understand and deal more effectively with staff, customers, or clients from other cultures

Materials:

- Copies of the worksheet *Dimensions of Culture*

Processing the Activity:

- Give a lecture on the information on the preceding pages regarding different cultural norms in the 10 areas of programming. Give and solicit examples. Individuals make notes on the chart.
- Divide group into smaller groups, with each discussing one or two of the areas of programming and sharing differences and their impact in the workplace. Information is charted on a flip chart or board.
- Small groups report to the larger group, giving a recap of the points made in their discussion.

Questions for Discussion:

- What are mainstream norms in each area? Norms of other cultures?
- What are the norms in your organization?
- Which differences cause problems or misunderstanding?

Caveats, Considerations, and Variations:

- It may be difficult for individuals to see the cultural influence beneath the behaviors. You may need to help by giving additional examples or asking participants from other cultures to share examples.
- It is important to avoid giving the impression that people from other cultures are so different, and that other norms are so strange, that we cannot understand them. One way is to present sets of differences as a continuum, for example, conformity and individualism. Peer pressure and group solidarity are powerful shapers of behaviors in the United States, and in cultures that value conformity, individuals do have their own opinions and may want the freedom to do things their own way.

(continued on next page)

Suggestions for Using
"Dimensions of Culture" (continued)

- It is also important to avoid creating new stereotypes about different cultural groups. It can be insightful to have individuals from the same culture discuss how differently they interpret their own culture's norms. The group then sees that all those of a particular group (African Americans, Cambodians, Russians, Israelis, etc.) are not the same and that there are as many differences within a group as from group to group.

- This activity can also be expanded by having the group identify U.S. norms using popular sayings and aphorisms that express cultural values which express cultural values such as:

  » *Better late than never, but better never late.*

  » *A penny saved is a penny earned.*

  » *You are your brother's keeper.*

ACTIVITY 5.5 | Analyzing Cultural Differences[9]

Apply what you just read about different cultural programming to your own situation. Choose one of your employees whose cultural programming is different from yours. (You'll get more from this analysis if you choose an individual with whom you are experiencing difficulties.) Analyze your own programming first, in each of the 10 areas; then analyze what you think your employee's programming has been.

Aspects of Culture	You	Employee
1. Sense of self and space		
2. Communication and language		
3. Dress and appearance		
4. Food and eating habits		
5. Time and time consciousness		
6. Relationships, family, friends		
7. Values and norms		
8. Beliefs and attitudes		
9. Mental processes and learning style		
10. Work habits and practices		

See if you can identify any of the areas where differences in programming and expectations may be causing friction. How can you use this information to help you overcome some of these cultural barriers? Perhaps you will see and interpret this employee's behavior differently now, so it will not irritate you quite as much. Or maybe you can explain your own behavior to the employee to clear up misunderstandings and erroneous assumptions. Better still, can you negotiate a resolution by each of you giving a little and creating a new norm you both can live with?

Suggestions for Using
"Analyzing Cultural Differences"

Objectives:
- Apply information about cultural programming to specific work relationships
- Identify cultural differences that may be at the root of performance problems or communication barriers
- Gain more information and a new perspective that can help in resolving interpersonal issues on the job

Intended Audience:
- Managers wanting to improve their relationship with, resolve a conflict with, or increase commitment from a specific employee or a group of employees from a similar background
- Managers participating in a managing diversity seminar
- Employees needing to increase effectiveness with customers/clients from other cultures
- Employees wanting to resolve a conflict with someone from another cultural background

Materials:
- Copies of the worksheet *Analyzing Cultural Differences*

Processing the Activity:
- Ask individuals to jot down information about their own cultural programming in each of the 10 areas, then about the programming of one of their employees (or customers/clients or co-workers).
- Individuals analyze differences at the heart of the problem.
- Individuals share their analyses in pairs or small groups, getting input from their partner(s) and responding to the discussion questions.
- Lead a discussion where insights can be shared.

Questions for Discussion:
- What are the most irritating differences?
- What are the advantages and disadvantages of your norms, rules, and values? The other individuals?
- What does this analysis tell you that can help you resolve this problem?
- What are you willing to do or expect differently in order to resolve this? What do you need to ask the other individual to do or expect differently?

Caveats, Considerations, and Variations:
- Occasionally, individuals are so emotionally involved in an interpersonal impasse that it is difficult for them to stand back and analyze it more objectively. You can help them by offering some examples of differences that may be operating.
- You can also tailor this to the organization by having participants identify the rules of the culture of the organization and compare those to their own.

Another way to help get beyond irritations you may feel when encountering cultural differences is to identify the specific behaviors that bother you and then look deeper to understand the cultural programming that underlies them. Using the following cross-cultural hook activity will help you do that.

ACTIVITY 5.6 | Cross-Cultural Hooks

Put a check by any of the cross-cultural hooks that could result in frustration or negative interactions between you and another individual. Then, next to any you've checked, jot down your reaction when you encounter this hook.

_____ Speaking in a language other than English.

_____ Bringing whole family/children to appointments.

_____ Refusal to shake hands with women.

_____ No nonverbal feedback (lack of facial expression).

_____ No eye contact.

_____ Soft, "dead fish" handshake.

_____ Standing too close when talking.

_____ Heavy accent or limited English facility.

_____ Coming late to appointments.

_____ Withholding or not volunteering necessary information.

_____ Not taking initiative to ask questions.

_____ Calling/not calling you by your first name.

_____ Emphasizing formal titles in addressing people.

_____ Discounting or refusing to deal with women.

_____ Other: _____

What aspects of cultural programming might be at the root of this behavior?

Suggestions for Using
"Cross-Cultural Hooks"

Objectives:

- Identify personal cross-cultural button pushers
- Recognize the cultural sources of irritating behaviors
- Take a first step in getting beyond culturally connected blocks to productive relationships

Intended Audience:

- Individuals seeking to increase cross-cultural understanding
- Trainees in a diversity seminar
- Managers who are finding difficulties in dealing with their diverse staff members
- Employees who are experiencing negative interactions with employees and/or customers/ clients of other cultures

Materials:

- Copies of the worksheet *Cross-cultural Hooks*

Processing the Activity:

- Individuals check those behaviors they find irritating, then they jot down their typical reaction to each behavior checked.
- After a lecture or explanation of the 10 dimensions of culture, individuals discuss (in small groups or the total group) the dimensions of culture that may be at the source of each behavior checked.
- Individuals discuss insights or new perspectives gained.

Questions for Discussion:

- What are your typical reactions when you get hooked?
- How does this affect how you deal with the situation?
- Which areas of cultural programming come into play?
- What are you willing to do to adapt to a particular norm?
- What are you willing to do to teach others to adapt to a particular norm?

Ten Ways To Learn More About Other Cultures

If this analysis shows you what you don't know and leaves you with a desire to learn more, here are some ways to become better informed.

1. Ask the Employee

Sometimes the best way to find out about another culture's norms is to ask employees from that culture to teach you about it. You'll get a better response if you make your request a real search for information, not an accusation. Also, choose someone who has some degree of acculturation and ask specific questions, such as the following:

- What are the biggest differences between Philippine and U.S. American cultures?
- What are some of the most difficult adjustments you have made in living here?
- What do you wish your co-workers understood about your culture?
- What does it mean in your culture when a person...?

2. Ask Colleagues from Other Cultures

If you don't get enough information from your employees, ask fellow managers who are from the cultures you are trying to learn about. These colleagues can be invaluable *cultural informants* who can teach you about subtle but often powerful cultural norms that may be causing misunderstandings. From their management perspective, they're apt to be able to see things biculturally and so give you some interesting insights into the areas of friction you may be trying to resolve.

3. Tap Community Resources

Another rich source of information about cultures are community organizations such as the Anti-Defamation League that have been dealing with these differences for a long time. Ethnic associations (e.g., the Korean Business Association) and social service, and refugee resettlement agencies, are good sources of information about the cultures they represent or serve. They may provide publications with concrete answers to your questions, as well as speakers. In addition, school districts—both through their English as a Second Language (ESL) departments and their staff development units—have long been teaching about multiculturalism. A call to your local school district headquarters could give you some of the information you are looking for. Finally, community relations groups make it their business to help various segments of society understand one another. The Los Angeles County Commission on Human Relations, for example, has published a booklet entitled, *How to Communicate Better with Clients, Customers and Workers Whose English Is Limited*.[10]

4. Read About Different Cultures

Reading nonfiction books, such as *Communicating with the Mexicans* or *Considering Filipinos*, is one way to get information directly. Another is to read nonfiction books such as *Three Cups of Tea* or fiction such as *The Namesake* or *The Kite Runner* that teach about other cultures. A list of resources is provided in the Appendix.

5. Observe Without Judgment

Pay attention to how people behave without judging the behavior (e.g., avoid thinking "Oh, that's poor taste,'" "'It's low class," or "How ignorant"). One of the most enlightening learning experiences in our doctoral program was an assignment to observe parent-child interactions in two cultures—U.S. American and Mexican. Watching parents and their children communicate in Los Angeles, California, and Tecate, Mexico, was an instructive way to see culture in action. Among the many differences, one stood out: U.S.-American parents were much more verbal, giving directions by telling their children what they wanted them to do. Mexican parents, on the other hand, were less verbal and more physical, walking over, taking the child's hand, and leading him or her. This kind of detached observation may help you understand your workgroup.

6. Share in Staff Meetings What You Have Learned

Talk about cultural differences at staff meetings and at management meetings. Share insights about cultural norms and how to deal with them. Dr. Jorge Cherbosque suggests that you can even form a peer support group with a multicultural configuration. You can then serve as resources to one another, giving and getting consultation and advice.

7. Conduct Focus Groups

If you still want to find out more, you might want to organize some culture-specific focus groups to get information through group discussions. Questions such as those mentioned in tip 1 above might be used. Additional information about using focus groups is given in Chapter 12.

8. Use Employee or Customer Survey Information

Pick up the clues from what people tell you or complain about. If they make comments that people always seem in a hurry or that they feel rushed, they may be talking about differences in time consciousness. If they complain about the performance review process, they may be surfacing issues related to loss of face. If they feel the boss doesn't take an interest in them, they may be reacting to an emphasis on task at the expense of relationship.

9. Experiment with New Methods

When we interview managers who are dealing effectively with their diverse staffs and ask how they learned what to do, they invariably say, "Trial and error." If you are experiencing a culture-related block, try a new behavior or a different approach, then watch to see how it works.

10. Spend Time in Other Cultures

Immersion in other cultures is a less traditional but very effective way to learn about different norms. This doesn't mean you need to take a leave of absence and live in Mexico, the Israel, or Korea, though that experience would undoubtedly be enlightening for anyone. You can immerse yourself by watching foreign films, tuning in to the Spanish-language channels on TV, reading literature from and about another culture, and spending time in ethnic communities such as Little India, Chinatown, or Koreatown, for example.

Cultural Humility

In dealing with cultural differences, people often throw up their hands in frustration and complain that they can never learn the rules of all the cultures they deal with. What's more, the rules are generalizations that don't apply to all members of a cultural group. A more recent approach used in health care takes a different tack: "Cultural Humility"[11] goes beyond lists and generalization and is based on the concept that each individual is the expert on his or her cultural software. It advocates a focus on the other person and on the relationship between the individuals involved. It also requires honest self-evaluation to avoid an ethnocentric or paternalistic approach in dealing with those from different cultural backgrounds. It begins with an assessment of one's own multicultural identities and backgrounds, an examination of reactions to others' cultural norms that are different, and a commitment to removing power imbalances to create mutually respectful relationships.

Helping Others Acculturate to U.S. Norms

Learning about cultures is a two-way street. There is also a need for you to help others learn the norms of their adopted land.

1. Explain the Reasons

Telling employees the reasons for the preferred behavior helps them understand and accept it. For example, you could say, "It is important to let people know when you don't understand so they can explain it another way. That way they can help you."

2. Show Employees the Benefits

You might position the desire for more open requests by saying, "There is a saying in the United States that the squeaky wheel gets the grease." This means that you won't get any help unless you let people know you need it. That help makes the whole team's performance better. In teaching employees to take more responsibility for their careers, you could say, "You might be overlooked for a project or promotion if you don't let people know you are seeking it."

3. Suggest Resources

Books and movies are great cultural resources. Considering the interests and education level of the individual, you might suggest appropriate material. A book such as *American Ways: A Guide for Foreigners in the United States*, by Gary Althen, hits the issues head on.[12] Valuable insights into American values can also be gained by reading such classics as *To Kill a Mockingbird*, and movies such as *All the President's Men*.

4. Spend Nonwork Time Together

Eating lunch together, going bowling after work, or inviting an employee over to your home gives them a chance to experience this culture outside of work. One friend of ours invited an Armenian immigrant colleague and her family over for Sunday dinner. Both the host and the hostess were taken aback when the colleague's husband thanked them as they sat down to eat: "You know, we have been in this country for 12 years and this is the first

American home we have been invited to." It's difficult to learn all the cultural rules on the shop floor, in the office, or at the supermarket.

5. Talk about Differences Openly

When you see surprise, confusion, or hesitancy, stop and discuss the cultural differences at play: "I'll bet this is different from the way this is done in your country. How do bosses let you know how you're doing in your culture?" Or, "This may be awkward at first because I believe people are a little more direct here. They don't mean to be rude. It is considered helpful to tell people when they make a mistake."

How Ethnocentrism Sabotages Valuing and Managing Diversity

When we look at other cultural norms, it is easy (and human) to make judgments about rules different from our own. The feeling that one's own cultural rules are superior or more right than the rules of other cultures is the essence of ethnocentrism. Cultural comparisons are natural. The problem isn't the comparison, but rather the universal tendency to see those other norms in a less favorable light. Those who have a different time consciousness might be judged lazy and undependable. People from cultures that respect authority and stress harmony might be considered unassertive and lacking in initiative. Those from cultures with an exacting dependence on promptness and an irritation at wasting time might be seen as cold and robotic. Those whose cultures depend on less direct communication might be seen as devious and sneaky. We are both targets and perpetrators of such ethnocentric judgments, which create some of the biggest barriers to intercultural harmony.

One way to overcome this "Our way is the best way" attitude and to see things in a more neutral light is to recognize that each cultural norm has advantages and disadvantages (see Activity 5.7). See if you can recognize the two sides of the following U.S.-American cultural norms. Then see if you can find both the upside and the downside of the foreign cultural norms.

How did you do? Was it hard for you to see the downside of American norms and the upside of foreign cultural norms? Seeing that all cultural norms cut two ways makes it easier to be patient with and less judgmental of others.

Since ethnocentrism is a normal, predictable human response, you might wonder what's wrong with it. When we approach others from different cultures with this "My way is better than yours" attitude, we trigger a defensive, protective, ethnocentric response from them in return. On the other hand, when we approach different norms less judgmentally, with an understanding that all cultural rules have advantages and disadvantages, we have a better chance of making everyone feel valued and wanted. What's more, when people feel accepted, they are more open to learning your way.

Culture is a powerful factor in all human behavior. Understanding its pervasiveness and its various rules is a critical step in managing your multicultural staff more effectively. There is a relevant Chinese saying that advises, "We see what is behind our eyes." Likewise, you have just taken an important step in expanding your vision.

ACTIVITY 5.7 | Decreasing Ethnocentrism

U.S.-American Cultural Norms	Disadvantages	Advantages
1. Emphasis on promptness and time	_____ _____	_____ _____
2. Direct, explicit communication	_____ _____	_____ _____
3. Competitive spirit	_____ _____	_____ _____
4. Rugged individualism	_____ _____	_____ _____
5. Informality in relationships	_____ _____	_____ _____

Other Cultural Norms	Advantages	Disadvantages
1. Emphasis on harmony and order	_____ _____	_____ _____
2. Respect for authority	_____ _____	_____ _____
3. Precedence of group over the individual	_____ _____	_____ _____
4. Focus on relationship-building	_____ _____	_____ _____
5. Emphasis on saving face	_____ _____	_____ _____

Suggestions for Using
"Decreasing Ethnocentrism"

Objectives:

- See cultural norms in a less ethnocentric, more neutral light
- Increase understanding about different norms

Intended Audience:

- Individuals seeking increased cultural sensitivity
- Managers frustrated with behaviors arising from different cultural norms
- Employees frustrated with behaviors of co-workers or clients/customers that arise from different cultural norms
- Trainees in diversity seminars

Materials:

- Copies of the worksheet *Decreasing Ethnocentrism*

Processing the Activity:

- Individually or in groups, participants list the advantages of both mainstream U.S. American and other cultures' norms.
- Lead a discussion of reactions, surprises, and insights gained.
- As a personal application, ask individuals to identify a particular norm they find difficult. They then follow the same process, listing advantages and disadvantages of that norm.

Questions for Discussion:

- Which norms were hard to find either advantages or disadvantages for?
- Which norms do you feel strongest about?
- What surprises did you have? What insights?
- How can this help you in dealing with differences on the job?

Caveats, Considerations, and Variations:

- Individuals may want to get into discussions about the rightness and/or wrongness of particular norms. Avoid polarization by reminding them that while they may have preferences, all cultural norms have a purpose and cut two ways, and that working with others who have different norms is made much easier when we approach them without the judgments that their ways are wrong or inferior.
- As a variation, groups may make their own lists of favorite American norms and irritating foreign norms.

CHAPTER 6.

Learning the Cultural Etiquette of Communication

● ●

This chapter will give you:

- Information about cross-cultural communication barriers that go beyond language
- Tips for communicating with non- and limited-English-speaking individuals
- Ways to deal with other languages on the job
- Guidelines for when and how to use interpreters and translators
- Strategies for getting employees to improve and learn English skills
- Ways to deal with accents that block communication
- Exercises for improving feedback skills
- Ways to resolve conflict related to culture

"If they'd just learn English, everything would be okay," is a commonly heard refrain in organizations with multicultural staffs or clientele. If it were only that simple; effective communication requires a shared base of experience and a common set of rules about the meaning of not just words, but intonation patterns, word order, volume, pauses, facial expressions, and gestures.

Consider how differently we say, "I'm going to get you," as we teasingly tickle a baby under the chin as opposed to the same sentence uttered threateningly in anger to someone who has wronged us. Someone may say, "Sure, I'm OK," but his rolling eyes and sarcastic tone tell you he's not really OK at all. In addition, the word we stress in any sentence can drastically alter its meaning. Try the following sentence, stressing a different word each time:

I am going to do this for you tomorrow.

I **am** going to do this for you tomorrow.

I am **going** to do this for you tomorrow.

I am going to do **this** for you tomorrow.

I am going to do this for **you** tomorrow.

I am going to do this for you **tomorrow**.

It's More than Language: Cultural Sources of Misunderstanding

Communication is definitely more than just words. In addition to language differences, cultures have varied norms about the nonverbal aspects of getting the message across. Newcomers who learn English may still be operating according to the nonverbal rules of their native languages, and herein lies the confusion and chance for misinterpretations. Some examples include:

- The Arab who speaks louder and stands closer is seen as pushy.
- The Latina who drops her eyes when speaking with a boss is seen as unassertive.
- The Chinese who has an impassive facial expression is seen as inscrutable and deceptive.
- The Filipina who confuses the pronouns "he" and "she" is thought to be uneducated.
- The Middle Easterner who takes time to chitchat before getting down to business is seen as inefficient.
- The African American who makes direct eye contact is seen as challenging and aggressive.

Let's take a look at the differences in nonverbal rules that are at the source of miscommunications.

Degree of Directness

Even the purpose of communication is culturally defined. U.S. Americans and Northern Europeans see communication pragmatically, as a means of getting information across and accomplishing tasks; much of the rest of the world sees it as a means of building relationships. In the Middle East, for example, business is not transacted until there has been a cup of tea and a period of chitchat, inconsequential conversation that eases both parties into the relationship. This ritual of small talk may seem like a time-wasting block to efficiency by U.S. standards, yet it is an expected and necessary part of business for Middle Easterners. Americans' direct, "Let's get to the point" approach, on the other hand, may seem rude, cold, and offensive to a Latin American or an Arab expecting a more subtle approach.

Appropriate Subjects

Still another difference is apparent in the subjects that are considered appropriate. Many Asian groups regard feelings as too private to be shared. Latinos generally appreciate inquiries about family members, while Arabs and Asians find this topic far too personal to discuss with work associates. Most Filipinos and Arabs think nothing of asking the price you've paid for something, while U.S. Americans would usually see such behavior as rude.

Facial Expressions and Eye Contact

What makes facial expressions and eye contact such stumbling blocks in communication is that these behaviors are learned at an early age and are generally unconscious. The widened eyes that show a U.S. American's anger have their counterpart in a Chinese person's narrowed eyes. A smile may not signify affability and friendliness, but may be a sign of embarrassment and confusion on the part of your Asian employees. A direct stare by an African American or Arab is not meant as a challenge to your authority, and dropped eyes may be a sign of respect from your Latino and Asian employees. A smile and nod from many Asians may mean they are trying to preserve harmony and save face. Differences in eye contact during listening have caused misunderstandings between African Americans and Caucasian Americans. According to communication expert Dr. Bob Mezoff, whites generally look away while speaking but make eye contact when listening. Because blacks do just the opposite, the impression is often made that they are not paying attention when listening or that they are challenging the listener when they are speaking.[1]

Touch

One of the most powerful nonverbal communicators is human touch. Yet whom and how we touch is culturally prescribed. Devout Muslim and Orthodox Jewish men never touch a woman outside of their families, even to shake hands. A soft, warm handshake, which is seen as welcoming and friendly in Mexican culture, might be viewed as weak and wimpy by U.S.-American standards. In addition, in some cultures, people are sensitive to being touched in certain places. The Chinese, for example, never want to be touched on the head. It has been suggested that the culture clashes between Koreans and African Americans in both Los Angeles and New York may have had roots in different cultural rules about touch. Korean store owners, feeling it is rude to touch anyone they do not know, place change on the counter. Their African-American customers, on the other hand, expecting to have the change placed in their hands, are offended at what they perceive as the Koreans' repulsion at touching them.

Loudness and Pitch

U.S. Americans are often viewed as noisy and rude by the English and other Europeans who speak more softly, while Arabs and southern Europeans generally speak more loudly.

Many Asian languages make use of higher pitch levels, which may be grating to the ears of those who are used to lower pitches.

Silence

Even not talking is culturally prescribed. While in the mainstream U.S. culture there is a recognition of the "pregnant pause," silence is generally something to be avoided. Because of this discomfort with silence, someone will usually jump in and start talking. In Japanese culture, silence is considered an important part of communication, a chance for serious consideration of what has been said and a gesture of respect for the speaker. It is no wonder that the Japanese are often irritated by the American's constant barrage of words while the listener is trying to think. Japanese also find the American habit of finishing a person's sentences disconcerting, rude, and even arrogant. Even when individuals learn English, many of their native-language rules will stay with them, influencing both how they send and receive messages.

Dealing with the Frustration of Not Understanding or Being Understood

Whenever we ask seminar participants what they do when they are attempting to communicate with someone who does not speak English, they invariably reply, "Speak louder and slower." It is common to continue to repeat unsuccessful behavior, getting more and more frustrated all the time. An experience with a Korean store clerk showed the pointlessness of this approach.

It was December 23, and Anita ran into her local minimarket to get a few lottery tickets as last-minute stocking stuffers. Because she was in a rush and harried by holiday season pressures, she blurted out in her usual rapid-fire speaking style to the unsuspecting Korean clerk behind the counter, "I'd like five rub-off lottery tickets." She couldn't understand what the clerk said, but she could read the confusion on the clerk's face, so she repeated her original request, only this time louder and slower: "I'd like five rub-off lottery tickets." Again, the clerk said something unintelligible, this time looking even more bewildered. For the third time, louder and with even more exaggerated mouth movements, Anita repeated her request. In exasperation, the clerk went to the computerized ticket machine and punched out a ticket with five quick picks. By this time Anita's slow burn had turned to a boil, and she said between clenched teeth, "This is not what I asked for. I want five rub-off tickets!" At this point, another clerk came to the rescue, saying a few words in their native language. The no longer frantic clerk turned to Anita with a smile of relief on her face. "Scratch-off, scratch-off," the clerk kept repeating.

This incident points up some of the difficulties and frustrations experienced on both sides of the language barriers we face regularly in our multicultural society. It also clearly shows the mistakes we often make in communicating with people with a limited command of English.

What Doesn't Help

The biggest stumbling block in situations like these is the anger that often comes from the frustration of not understanding or being understood. That anger becomes a powerful saboteur of communication in two ways. First, a message that comes out of anger threatens the receiver, making him or her less able to use the little English he or she may know. Anger also blocks the thinking of the sender, preventing that person from finding creative solutions to the impasse. So, the sender keeps repeating the same unsuccessful behavior, each time louder, slower, and with more irritation.

What Does Help

Understanding the source of your anger is a step in getting beyond it. Language is more than just a means of communicating—the language we speak gives us our identity and defines our nationality. Although the Pilgrims had found freedom from religious persecution in Holland, they felt compelled to leave to come to America because their children were growing up speaking Dutch. Fast forward to present day and the battles about bilingual education rage on in school districts all over our country.

But language is more than identity. It also represents turf. My territory, my barrio, or my country is defined by the dominant language spoken there, hence the fights in many communities over English-only laws or the heated debates about bilingual ballots and driver's tests. The emotional content of these arguments signals much deeper issues than the rule or regulation being debated; power and esteem are at stake.

Finally, being able to communicate gives us one of our most powerful means of control in the world. It is our prime vehicle for influencing events and people. We see its impact daily when we explain procedures to a subordinate, order food in a restaurant, or get directions when we're lost. When we can't communicate and find it difficult to get our message across, we feel our control slipping away. The less control we feel, the greater the frustration and stress. And that frustration is generally directed toward those whom we don't understand.

Dealing with Other Languages on the Job

One of the most divisive issues in multicultural workplaces involves the speaking of other languages on the job; tempers flare, and employees polarize into warring camps, building resentment and animosity toward one another. Let's take a look at the issue from a different perspective: Imagine that you've just been transferred to a division in one of your company's manufacturing plants in Brazil. Images of carnivals, Ipanema, Sugar Loaf, and the Amazon flash through your mind. When reality sets in, you realize you don't speak Portuguese. But you think there must be people there who speak English—there are always people who speak English.

You take a crash course in Portuguese, enough to get the basics, though you're still far from comfortable. When you get there you find that there are many bilingual supervisors and a few U.S. transplants working at your new location. You breathe a sigh of relief. Ask yourself what language you would use when:

- Talking with your bilingual supervisors?
- Having a meeting with other American managers?
- Eating lunch with another U.S.-born manager?
- Conferencing with British, Australian, or Canadian business associates?
- Phoning home to talk with your spouse and/or children?

Wouldn't it feel awkward not to use English in these situations? Yet people take offense when others speak their native languages around us, especially at work. A first place to start in dealing with the language issue is to examine and question the almost automatic assumptions staff make when confronted with languages other than English.

Assumptions That Get Us into Trouble

1. They're Talking About Me

When you hear a group of staff members speaking a language other than English, you may jump to the conclusion that you are the topic of conversation. In fact, they may be talking about their families, a work problem, or the weather. If you knew that they were speaking English but couldn't overhear what they were saying, would you still assume that they were talking about you?

2. They Don't Want To Learn English

Huge enrollments and long waiting lists at adult education English classes in cities with large immigrant populations tell us that newcomers to this society do want to learn English. Evans Adult School in downtown Los Angeles, one of 27 adult schools in that city, offers English classes from 5:30 a.m. to 2:30 a.m., and still has a waiting list of more than 15,000 would-be students. However, making a living and taking care of family may take up all the waking hours some employees have. At a subsistence level, spending two to three hours in the evening at school may be a lower priority than taking a second job. It is clear to everyone in this society that English is the language of power and that to advance in this culture, one must learn English. How long that takes (a few months, a few years, or a generation) depends a great deal on economic circumstances.

3. They Know English, They Just Don't Want To Use It

Even when someone is learning a new language, he or she may be hesitant to use it until he or she feels more proficient. How easy is it for you to use your high school Spanish or French when traveling? Most people feel self-conscious and unsure of themselves when beginning to use a new language. In a diversity seminar, one Filipino nurse manager expressed her feelings about the stress of having to speak a second language all day. She explained that while she does speak English on the job and requires her native-Tagalog-speaking nurses to do the same, she understands their stress level and the comfort they feel in lapsing into their first language. Imagine the pressure of having to think, speak, and perform in a second language all day.

Finally, there is another factor operating. Many newcomers to the United States come from cultures where social class distinctions make it difficult to initiate conversations or converse at all with someone whom they believe to be above them in society's pecking order. To do so in a language in which they are not confident is doubly difficult.

Rethinking your assumptions and walking in the other person's shoes can help you arrive at a more neutral position about some of the language clashes you experience. Resolving this issue is a two-way street: Every nation needs a common language as a unifying element, and newcomers do need to make an attempt to learn English. On the other hand, those who are native-born or longtime residents can help the process of acculturation by showing understanding and openness to those who haven't yet acquired proficiency in English.

One way to do this is to team-build around language differences. Use these differences as an opportunity to strengthen your workgroup's feeling of being on a team. Have employees share perceptions, as well as their needs, in relation to language differences. Speakers of other languages need to hear the reactions of co-workers who may be feeling left out or talked about, while English-only speakers need to understand the comfort that others find in speaking their native tongues. Open-ended statements are often helpful in getting the discussion started and in keeping it focused:

- When I hear employees speaking another language, I ....
- When I don't understand someone who speaks with an accent, I ....
- When someone doesn't understand me, I wish they would ....
- I speak my native language to others at work because ....
- When someone doesn't understand me, I ....
- One thing that is frustrating for me is ....

These discussions can lessen tension by helping staff members understand each other's difficulties. Insights gained improve relationships and can lead to creative problem-solving.

It is also important to clarify the language policy at work. Let people know the rules about language—what's permitted and what's off limits. Some legal precedents have been set recently regarding this issue, so be careful about respecting the rights of employees when they are on their own time at breaks and lunch. When all is said (or not said) and done, remember, there is a form of communication that supersedes all tongues: the language of attitudes. As we approach one another in our multicultural world, our attitude speaks volumes. As a participant once quipped, "Attitude is more important than aptitude."

Communicating with Limited-English-Speaking Staff

In the meantime, you still need to find a way to communicate effectively. Here are 10 techniques that could work in your organization.

1. Make It Visual

As the saying goes, a picture is worth a thousand words. Using pictures, signs, diagrams, and symbols gives you another dimension beyond words with which to make yourself clear. In Anita's lottery-ticket-buying impasse, had she pointed to one or shown a sample, she could have quickly overcome her difficulty. A veteran army instructor who regularly taught courses to allied military personnel from many countries advised that diagrams, charts, and graphs were critical aids in teaching his classes, where most students had limited command of English. International symbols on road signs have long been used in Europe, where there are many languages spoken in a relatively small area, and where there is much travel between countries. Be wary, however, of overkill with visuals. One organization, attempting to explain its new 401(k) plan to Spanish speaking employees, used an elaborate slide presentation full of graphics and diagrams. Most of the assembly-line workers in the audience had no experience reading bar graphs and pie charts and were totally confused by the presentation.

2. Show-and-Tell

Kindergarten isn't the only place where show-and-tell is useful. Demonstrating what you are explaining can often get the message across faster than words in any language. Many individuals would rather have someone show them how to do something than have to figure it out from written instructions in a manual. For example, Anita could have taken a coin and made scratching motions to show the clerk what kind of lottery ticket she wanted. In on-the-job situations, this works best when you first show the person how to do a task, then do it together, and finally observe the individual in action so you can be sure he or she has understood.

3. Use Their Language

If getting your message or information across is more important than showing your displeasure at someone's limited English, then using the other person's language may be your best bet. Don't panic—this doesn't mean you need to speak the other person's language. Emergency instructions, school district letters to parents, and signs in airports are common uses of bilingual or multilingual communication. However, there are more forms of bilingual or multilingual communication. For example, a local nursing home was temporarily stumped when its elderly residents kept complaining about not being able to communicate their needs to the mainly Spanish-speaking aides. The solution: bilingually printed sheets with the 20 or so most-used requests written in English in the left column and Spanish in the right. Now when residents need something, they just point to the request on the English column and the aide reads it on the corresponding line in the Spanish column. Another example of bilingualism in action is the Teatro Para Los Niños (Children's Theater), which performs Spanish/English musicals for elementary school children. One of their performances focused on changing role stereotypes, showing that it is OK for boys to cook and for girls to play basketball. Without the use of both languages, many students would not have understood the message.

4. Take It Easy

When a language is not one's mother tongue, processing information in it takes longer. Not only is the vocabulary often unfamiliar, but grammar and intonation patterns are sometimes new. It is helpful to slow down and pause between sentences so the listener has time to let each segment of your message sink in, then summarize at the end, pulling all the pieces together.

5. Keep It Simple

"Take the ball and run with it," "go the extra mile," "a tough row to hoe," "a thumbnail sketch," and "beyond the call of duty" are examples of idiomatic expressions common in everyday speech. Most of us probably use many of these expressions throughout the course of a day. Yet, for a non-native speaker who tries to translate them literally, they make no sense at all. In addition, jargon, that is, words that are specific to a particular business or industry, may also be confusing. In construction, for example, calling mortar "mud" or talking about "roughing in the plumbing" would be difficult for anyone outside the profession to understand, let alone someone struggling with English. Finally, it helps to use simple words that are commonly heard; for example, "problem" rather than "glitch" or "snafu."

6. Say It Again

When you're having difficulty making yourself understood, it does help to repeat if you use different words. But tread carefully in doing this, however: When looking for another way to say something, beware of cognates, or words in other languages that look and sound similar to English words. The most common mistakes occur between Spanish and English. While *largo* in Spanish looks like *large*, it means "long." And if you're embarrassed, don't say you're *embarazada* because that means "pregnant."

7. Assume Confusion

Whatever you do, don't ask people if they understand and then take their "yes" to mean they do. In many other cultures, saying "no" is the height of rudeness. Besides, even in the mainstream American culture, we often say we understand even when we're a little fuzzy because saying we don't understand makes us feel inadequate. Instead of asking, watch the person's face for nonverbal signs of confusion to see if they are following your directions correctly. Also watch behavior as the individual begins to act on what you've said. Often the look on the face of the person with whom you are communicating lets you know if you've gotten your message across.

8. Get Help

When you've done steps 1 through 7 and you still are having trouble, get help. A bilingual friend or colleague can often get you out of a bind. In many organizations, staff who speak other languages are listed and called on a rotating basis to translate in interchanges between staff and customers or clients. Just make sure the person who is doing the interpreting is fluent enough in both languages to be able to make things clear to all parties. Also make sure the interpreter understands the concepts you are communicating.

9. Walk in Their Shoes

To help reduce your frustration and anger when you get blocked by a language barrier, try to put yourself in the other person's place. Have you ever been somewhere where no one spoke English? How did it feel? What would have helped you? Remembering these times gives you some empathy for the bewilderment that the individual might be feeling.

10. Smile, but Don't Laugh

A smile helps others relax, and the reduction of tension increases your chances for effective communication. However, be careful not to appear to be laughing at the individual. The Los Angeles County Commission on Human Relations reports that immigrants' most common request is that people not laugh at them when they try to speak English. When we're not confident of our ability in an area, we're particularly vulnerable and sensitive to slights. While you may not be laughing at the person's poor English, your joking manner or teasing banter may seem like ridicule. No matter what languages we do or don't speak, all of us need to be treated with dignity and respect. Communication that has these elements at the base will go a long way toward overcoming language and cultural differences.[2]

Speaking of Accents

"I couldn't understand a thing they said!" is a common response to accented English. While we may think accents are charming, all too often, native English speakers tune out the minute they hear an accent. Instead of trying to understand the speaker, attention is focused on finding a pause to interject an irritated "What?"

All accents are not created equal in our perceptions. A British accent, for example, calls up images of an Oxford scholar or a Shakespearean actor, and a continental accent might be a prized qualification for a maitre d'. But this isn't the case with many other accents, though. There is often an assumption that the person speaking with an accent is less competent or knowledgeable.

The "Fax Solution"

A clever manager in a large insurance company found a unique solution to the accent barrier. Many of the company's claims processors in the San Francisco home office were Filipinos with strong accents. There were continual complaints from the French-Creole employees in Louisiana, who regularly phoned in claims to the home office, that they couldn't understand the claims processors. To deal with this impasse, the boss designed a form that was sent via fax to the claims department. It contained all the information previously obtained through phone conversation and avoided the interpersonal rub. It worked to smooth out the procedure, reducing claims response time from 72 hours to 24-48 hours. But an even bigger miracle took place: The fax exchange brought these two groups of employees together. When the claims reporters saw how efficiently the claims were processed by people they had previously discounted, they gained new respect for their accented home-office colleagues. Employees from the two groups began talking with each other and developing more productive relationships. The frequency of phone conversations increased, problems were solved more quickly, and complaints about accents disappeared.

In communicating with people who speak with accents, it is helpful to remind yourself that an accent tells you an individual is attempting to learn and use English. Second, have a little empathy. How perfectly do you speak Spanish, French, or some other language? Third, recognize that no matter how well someone learns English, he or she will almost never be able to sound like a native speaker because of a number of language differences.

Sounds

It is believed that all human babies are capable of making all the sounds of every language in the world. By the age of 5, however, children are only able to reproduce the sounds of their native language. Hence, some sounds may be impossible for a non-native speaker of a language to learn to articulate as an adult. English has 26 letters, yet 44 sounds. Many of these sounds do not exist in other languages. The *sh* sound is as difficult for many non-native speakers as the rolled *r* is for Americans. In Spanish, for example, there is no *sh* sound, hence the substitution of the *ch* as in chave for "shave" and chure for "sure." In addition, b and v have the same sound in Spanish and are used interchangeably, so there is generally a difficulty in distinguishing between the two in English. In Tagalog, there is no *sh* or *f* sound, so *s* is often substituted for *sh* (*see* for "she") and *p* for *f* (*pun* for "fun"). Japanese speakers often confuse the *l* and *r* sounds. It helps to pay attention to the sound patterns of the accents you deal with most frequently and learn the most common substitutions people make.

Structure

Languages differ in more than just vocabulary; they have different systems of syntax (word order), grammar, and parts of speech. When someone attempts to translate into English vocabulary using another language's syntax and grammar, meanings may become distorted, resulting in confusion. In Spanish, as in many European languages, for example, adjectives follow the nouns they modify rather than preceding them as they do in English ("the house white" versus "the white house"). Some Slavic languages have no articles (the, a, an), so figuring out when and how to use these words in English may be difficult. A native speaker of Serbo-Croatian, for example, may leave out the article when needed, as in "I go to store," or add it when not appropriate, as in Czechoslovakian-born Ivana Trump's "the Donald." In Tagalog, there is no distinction between the masculine and feminine pronouns *he/she* and *him/her*, so it is not uncommon to hear Filipinos using the wrong pronoun when speaking English.

Accent Reduction Training for Presenters and Customer Contact Staff

While you may be open to taking the time to develop the extra patience and skill to get across the accent barrier, your customers and clients may not. Employees whose responsibilities involve customer/client contact or those who make presentations need to communicate as clearly as possible. In many cases that calls for accent reduction training. Not only does this improve relations with those using your organization's services or products, but it often serves as an aid in the employee's career mobility. Generally, this type of training is conducted by a communication consultant with expertise in accent reduction and focuses on the following:

- American pronunciation of vowels, especially the *schwa* sound (the *uh* sound of a vowel in any unaccented syllable) and consonants, especially *r*, *ch*, *sh*, *th*, *l*, *n*, *s*, and *d*
- Intonation and stress patterns
- Linking rules to create smoother-sounding statements
- Presentation skills for staff involved with this responsibility

Judith Weidman, a Los Angeles-based communications consultant who teaches ESL (English as a Second Language) and American pronunciation classes, offers advice to organizations about this type of training. First, she cautions them to bill the course as effective communication rather than finger-pointing at the immigrant employee. She suggests advertising the training in company newsletters, on bulletin boards, and through managers and supervisors at staff meetings. Once the first course is completed, she says, graduates then become the best promoters.

Weidman goes on to say that the consultant needs to understand both the organization and the students in order to tailor the training appropriately. For example, simulations of meetings and presentations that give participants a chance to practice are important vehicles for learning, and they need to fit the organizational reality. Rewards such as certificates and newsletter mention are important as well. Finally, supervisors and managers need to be encouraged to reinforce the use of new learning by employees on the job.

Weidman, a former Peace Corps volunteer who taught English in the Philippines, coaches her students to become "pronunciation detectives" so they can continue learning on their own. She gives them tips, such as the following:

- Find a mentor/model, such as a favorite television announcer, and tape that person speaking. Listen to the tape in the car or on your iPod whenever there is time.
- Record yourself speaking English on the phone at work or at home. Listen to your pronunciation. What do you need to work on?
- Record radio talk shows and put them on your iPod. Not only does this help with pronunciation but it also teaches the art of asking questions, something many non-native English speakers find difficult.

It is also important to put the shoe on the other foot when it comes to accents. One government agency offers a course on "Listening with a Multicultural Ear" to help employees understand accented English.

Teaching English: How To Set Up Classes and Recruit Students

Helping employees learn English benefits both the employee and the organization. Workers' confidence and career options increase when they have greater facility with English. Employees' appreciation of the organization's investment in them results in lower turnover for the company. In addition, the greater ease of communication that English skills bring means higher productivity from fewer mistakes and higher morale from decreased frustration on the part of English-only speakers. One of the challenges is getting employees to participate in ESL programs. Older workers who are comfortable with their limited English-language skills may have a difficult time overcoming inertia; others may be embarrassed about their poor English and may not want to call attention to themselves. Finally, workers who have not had much education or who have had bad experiences with school may not have the confidence in their own ability to succeed in a class.

Beyond the personal blocks, the most formidable obstacles to getting employees to learn English are the perennial time and money limits. Clever organizations have found some creative ways to deal with these obstacles.

1. On-Site Classes

Many organizations have brought English classes to employees by hiring instructors who teach classes after hours, on-site. Both the organization and employee invest; the organization pays for the instruction, while the employees give their time. Employers like Memorial Medical Center in Las Cruces, New Mexico, make use of U.S. Department of Education National Workplace Literacy Project grants to help fund on-site classes in their Step Ahead comprehensive literacy program. Employees attend during work hours, and classes are paid for by the employer.

Transamerica Occidental Life Insurance Company used a similar approach in providing ESL classes for its data-processing department. Instruction was provided at the request of managers who wanted help for their non-native speakers of English. Complaints were registered from internal customers who reported having difficulties in communicating with the heavily accented speech of data-processing staff members, most of whom were Asian, with the largest group being native Chinese speakers. The first ESL course was given to a group from a variety of native-language backgrounds. The second time around, the model was refined and the course was offered to native Chinese speakers only, enabling the course content to be tailored to the specific language acquisition and accent-reduction needs of the group. Courses were arranged through UCLA's American Language Center and provided on-site, with Transamerica paying tuition and workers giving the time, and included four one-hour sessions per week for eight weeks. Managers were included in planning and debriefing sessions. In planning future classes, Dr. Joan Klubnik, coordinator, says she would recommend more support for managers in helping them reinforce the learning on the job; more emphasis on the "buddy system" of reinforcement for participants; and the use of Visipitch, a device that helps language learners see pitch ranges and thereby modify their speech.

Care needs to be taken in how classes are set up, however. Another organization decided to provide ESL classes for its mainly Spanish-speaking housekeeping staff. Classes were held on site immediately after shift at 3 p.m. As the department had no budget for education, employees were asked to pay a nominal fee for the 10-week course, approximately $50-$60. Because they were happy with the convenience of the time and location, workers were willing to pay their own tuition. Once classes began, another group of limited-English-speaking employees joined. These, however, were researchers with Ph.D.s. Since they worked until 5 p.m., classes were held during their regular work hours. In addition, since their boss had sent them, they requested that their department pay for their tuition. Because this department had money in its education budget, the department head complied. Both groups were learning and enjoying the experience. However, when the housekeeping staff found out about the differences in arrangements, they felt they had been unfairly treated. Although they still wanted the class to continue, because of the discriminatory nature of the arrangement, the organization canceled the class.

2. Joining Forces with Community Colleges and Adult Schools

If your organization has a potential group of ESL students, you may be able to team up with a local community college or adult school. Since these schools are generally reimbursed by the state based on the number of students they have and the instructional hours they provide, they may be willing to hold classes for your employees on-site if you provide the classroom space. Even if classes are held in school facilities, fees are minimal.

3. Paying for Students' Tuition

Some organizations pay the tuition for private English instruction for key employees or for accent-reduction classes for those who need it. Generally, independent consultants who specialize in this area are contracted with to provide this tutoring.

4. Rewarding English Acquisition

In other organizations, employees are given pay increases as they pass into higher levels of English proficiency. Promotions and pay upgrades may depend on these skills.

5. Teaching Supervisors the Language of Employees

Teaching supervisors the language of employees may sound counterproductive. If you are attempting to teach employees English, why teach their language to supervisors? A Southern California discount retail chain found this approach very effective. Their initial objective in presenting Spanish-language classes for supervisors on company time was to enable them to communicate more easily with their Spanish-speaking workers, but they got more than they bargained for. When workers saw their supervisors trying out their fledgling Spanish, they felt that the organization was trying to meet them halfway. This effort gave them the motivation to use the English they were learning. And as they heard supervisors make mistakes in Spanish, they were less self-conscious about doing so in English. What had been a language barrier now became a cooperative venture, with each asking the other for help: "How do you say *shelf* in Spanish?" "Como se dice *caja* en Inglés?" ("How do you say *box* in English?").

Using Computer-Assisted Instruction

One cost-effective way to teach English to employees is to make use of computer-assisted instruction. Weber Metals, a manufacturer of aluminum and titanium forgings for aerospace, had a problem: Most of its 200 employees were Latino workers whose native language was Spanish and who had a low level of formal education. In addition to communication difficulties, the company was concerned about their employees' ability to deal with planned-for changes such as computer-assisted design and manufacturing (CAD/CAM) and an expanded management information system (MIS). Enter Sinclair Hugh, a personnel consultant who engineered a partnership with the Paramount Unified School District to deal with the challenge. Knowing how difficult it was to get workers to go to the school, Ed Quesada, director of the district's adult school and co-creator of this partnership, helped bring the school to the workers. With a $50,000 federal grant, the school district set up four computers at Weber Metals, which were hooked to the adult school's system. The Computer Assisted Instruction Centers, in a pilot project with Computer Curriculum Corporation of Sunnyvale, California, offered 24 courses in 1,800 hours of instruction to Weber employees. Programs feature self-paced learning and interactive instruction, with the computers asking the students questions and telling them if their answers are correct. The ESL program even has a digital speech system that gives the learner audio information through headphones so he can hear digitized pronunciation of English words and sentences. In addition to ESL, programs in reading, math, communication skills, and GED preparation have been added, and a Spanish-language program is in the works.

Though employees are not given time off to spend at the learning center, more than 50 percent of the factory workforce have enrolled, and ESL is the most popular course. What motivates these hourly employees to come in before work, stay after their shifts, or eat lunch on a morning break so they can spend their half-hour lunch period on the computer? Weber entices employees with lottery tickets and a gift program in which they receive a $15 gift for each five hours of instruction. However, the greatest motivators seem to be the increased promotional opportunities and self-esteem gained by employees who take advantage of this opportunity. One ESL participant's increased bilingual skills, for example, helped him get promoted to supervisor. Another center student commented that what he gained in knowledge was worth the $20 a day he lost in overtime by coming to the center.

Solving the Interpreter and Bilingual Dilemmas

If your organization decides that communication in an additional language is necessary, it's important to set up a mechanism for doing so. One of the biggest complaints by bilingual staff who are asked to interpret is that this extra duty takes time away from their regular work and leaves them continuously backlogged. Another complaint is that they are sometimes asked to interpret when the message sender does not want to give bad news; for example, calling to collect on an overdue bill or telling a family member that a loved one has died in the emergency room. A third complaint is that the organization wants them to use their second language with clients and customers who speak that language, but punishes them for using it with co-workers. To avoid some of these problems and to assure that interpreters are available, organizations have devised the following methods.

1. Rotating Interpreter Bank

In one organization, all bilingual staff members are listed by language on a master list. When an interpreter is needed, the next person on the list is called so that no one is unduly burdened.

2. Full-Time Interpreter

One organization with a large Spanish-speaking clientele employs a full-time interpreter who is on call at all times. Since she is a trained interpreter who understands the culture and language of the receivers of the information and a professional who understands the content of the messages she is relaying, the organization can be assured that the correct information is getting through. In another company, which has targeted a small but lucrative Japanese clientele, there is a Japanese interpreter on duty 24 hours a day.

3. Pay for Bilingual Skills

Many organizations pay additional bonuses to those who have and use their bilingual skills on the job. One such employer allows managers to make a request for this bonus by documenting the need for the use of the second language by one of their staff members. In others, employees applying for the bilingual pay differential must pass written and oral tests in the second language to be certified.

4. Hire or Train Bilingual Supervisors

When hiring supervisors, bilingual ability can be a job requirement, or existing supervisors can be taught a second language. A third option is to target bilingual employees with managerial potential and teach them supervisory skills.

5. Informal Interpreter Network

The informal interpreter network method, using bilingual employees, is probably the most common. This system only works if these employees have a good command of both languages and if they understand the content of the information that needs to be communicated.

Avoiding the Common Pitfalls in Translation

In communicating in a multilingual environment, you may find the need to put information in writing in other languages. Monica Moreno, an intercultural communications expert and translator, explains that organizations may unknowingly subvert their goals by not making use of professional translators. She sees the mistakes and the problems caused when translations are not professionally done, such as the case of the poorly translated employee benefit program that led to workers' disappointment when they didn't get the "prize" (*premio*) they were mistakenly promised. To make her point, Monica asks executives if they would be comfortable having the receptionist make a presentation on a complex company policy or program. She then explains that is often what they do when they assign a translation to any employee who happens to speak the second language. What often results are the most common translation pitfalls:

- Poorly written translations due to incorrect grammar and misspelling, which insult readers
- Inadequate translations due to lack of understanding on the part of the translator
- Inaccurate translations due to lack of vocabulary and understanding on the part of the translator
- Inappropriate translations due to the translator's inability to write to the level of the reader

Monica, a native of Argentina, gives the following suggestions to assure accurate and appropriate translations that achieve the organization's objectives:

1. The translator should be a native speaker of the language he or she is writing in. While Monica is fluent in English, Italian, and French, she writes only the Spanish translations because Spanish is her native language. A native speaker generally has the most complete grasp of a language.
2. A translation should be edited by a native speaker from a different country than the original translator's. This is especially important in the Spanish-speaking world, where regional and national differences in vocabulary and idiomatic expressions can cause confusion.
3. Use a professional translator. While interpreters in the United States are certified, there is no official U.S. certification for translators as there is in many other countries.

A professional understands the nuances of communication and has the ability to grasp different levels of content. Information may be more credible coming from an objective outsider who has no vested interest in the communication or previous relationship with staff. He or she is also able to adjust the translation to suit the target group. Checking references and having a native speaker read a sample might be ways to verify the translator's skill.

4. Augment the translated message with Q-and-A sessions in the language used by staff. An employee newsletter is generally understandable to all who can read; however, if the document being translated has to do with policies, procedures, or programs, there is a need for employees to discuss implications, get clarification, and verify their understanding. This can best be done in an explanation session held in the employees' native language.

5. Think ahead, and budget for translation services. To have a document that is written by an executive vice president and checked by the legal department translated by a bilingual employee with a sixth-grade education is asking for trouble. Include the cost of translation in the budget when planning for any program that needs to be communicated to non-English-speaking employees.

6. If you use internal bilingual staff to translate, verify the translation. Having the document translated back into English by another bilingual employee is a way to check for accuracy.

7. Provide the option of translation in a nondiscriminatory way. If you ask employees if they want a translation of a document or a session in their native language, workers are apt to say "no"; most don't want to burden the organization or expose their lack of English skills. It is more helpful to make the option available in a practical way, by providing two stacks of documents, one in each language, or two discussion groups: Spanish in room A and English in room B.

From the Organization's Point of View: Formal Communication That Everyone Understands

Getting information to employees is a critical link in any organization, and one that is not easily accomplished anywhere. When employees don't understand English, the task is even more difficult. Consider the following:

• A group of Spanish-speaking new hires in a large metropolitan hospital sit through four hours of new employee orientation, not understanding a word of what's being said. Many take the written materials home and have their children explain it to them in Spanish.

• A manufacturing firm introduced a new employee stock option plan (ESOP) program to employees. Knowing that many production-line workers did not speak English, the firm had the program translated into Spanish. After the extensive Spanish-language presentation was made, the first question that was timidly asked was, "What is stock?"

• A firm that is attempting to reach its limited-English-speaking staff has its newsletter printed bilingually. The Spanish portion, however, is so poorly written, with grammatical and spelling errors, that the Spanish-speaking readers are insulted.

In working through these communication mazes, an important question needs to be answered: What is the objective of the communication and who is the end receiver? If the goal is to get information to a particular group of employees, all of whom do not understand English, then sending the message in English probably won't meet your objective.

English-Only vs. Bilingual Communication

Many organizations have policies that proclaim English as the official language of the organization. Other companies routinely communicate in more than one language. Rather than polarize opinions between these two extremes, let's take a look at the advantages and disadvantages of each, as well as the range of alternatives between them.

It is said that India, with its myriad native languages, would not have become a nation without the English language as a unifying force. Using one language throughout the organization can be a common base for all staff. It also has the advantage of not showing preference for any one second-language group. In addition, having documents translated into many different languages or having a session in 10 different languages may be unwieldy and costly. Waving an "English Only" banner, on the other hand, can alienate workers who are non-English speaking, making them feel less valued. A policy of all-English communication may also keep you from getting your message across; it may lead to a distortion of the message because you do not control how the English is being informally translated. We've all played the game of telephone and seen how even in the same language, a message gets altered as it is passed from person to person. When employees are left to figure it out for themselves, the translations of their bilingual children or co-workers can produce the same misinterpretations. When misunderstandings can be dangerous, as in safety procedures and labels on hazardous chemicals, you may be legally required to make sure you convey necessary information to workers.

Bilingual or multilingual communication is common among utility companies, law enforcement, school districts, and other agencies that need to get information to users of their services in the community. The main difficulty seems to be in determining when a group has enough people to warrant the use of its language. For example, if you have 150 Spanish-speaking employees and only 10 Vietnamese workers, are the 10 any less important than the 150? Once begun, the practice sets a precedent that needs to be followed with each succeeding group.

There are some beneficial alternatives. One is to have all written communication in English but hold bilingual explanation sessions where employees can comfortably ask questions and get clarifications and additional explanations in their native languages. Another is to set up multilingual discussion groups where employees can discuss the information in their own languages and have the one employee in the group who is most proficient in English present the group's questions to the presenter or panel.

Suggestions for Managers and HR Professionals

In communicating formally with employees, it will be helpful to consider the following points:

1. Adjust the level of the communication to the education level of the employees to whom it is aimed. The legalese of a new 401(k) plan would be unintelligible to most

employees regardless of language. New employee orientation materials written at the 12th-grade level may be over the heads of many entry-level new hires. Complicated graphs and charts may only confuse someone with little formal education.

2. Pictures that show what you are describing in words are helpful. Visual depictions are especially helpful in explaining safety procedures. For example, the international symbol ⊖ is generally understood cross-culturally. The correct and incorrect ways to lift a box can be shown more clearly in pictures than in many pages of text.

3. Demonstrations that show right and wrong ways overcome language barriers. Showing the group the wrong, then the right, way to climb a ladder, for example, will get the message across faster and more effectively than pages of written explanations.

4. Using video presentations to augment written material gives the receiver more information. It also makes the material come alive. A welcome from the CEO, for example, becomes a little more human when it comes through video than from a short written statement at the front of the employee handbook. Using a few words of the native language of employees can work wonders, too.

5. Leave employees with written information they can take away to go over later. This gives them the option of asking for an explanation from a bilingual friend and rereading it slowly at home.

Giving Directions That Are Clear and Comprehensible

In a multilingual environment, frustration and confusion can result when directions are given. Employees who do not understand are often reluctant to ask questions or indicate they are confused. They may fear upsetting the boss or the individual giving directions, not want to imply that the directions were not given clearly, or not want to call attention to their own lack of language facility. To preserve harmony, avoid hurt feelings, and not appear incompetent, they pretend to understand. It may become apparent only after mistakes are made that the directions were not understood. Many of the same points apply that were mentioned in communicating with limited-English-speaking staff members. Several more points can be added:

1. Hire or Train Bilingual Supervisors

The most frequent direction-giving interface is between the supervisor or lead person and the first-line worker. Communication consultant Monica Moreno advises that if the demographics of the labor market indicate that first-line workers are going to continue to be non-English or limited-English speakers, a very immediate solution is to have those who supervise them have bilingual ability. Taking this step not only helps in overcoming communication barriers but also helps workers feel more comfortable and accepted.

2. Print Basic Instructions Bilingually or Multilingually

When health and safety are concerned, and when the priority is to get the message across as quickly as possible, print instructions in the necessary languages. Using a two-column approach, matching English and the other language(s) line for line, serves three purposes: It enables the non-English speaker to immediately grasp the information; it allows an English speaker to communicate by pointing to corresponding lines; and it helps the employee learn English.

3. Be Specific and Explicit

Misunderstandings occur even in monolingual situations because "that report," "the same room," or "a longer board" may mean different things to the speaker and the listener. Pointing to the report in question, identifying the room as the second-floor conference room, and specifying that the board needs to be 38 inches, not 36, would be clearer. Holding up an example; giving exact measurements, dates, or numbers; and using descriptive words and examples help clarify directions. See if you can make these directions more specific:

Vague and Confusing	Explicit and Clear
a. "Take this downstairs and get it fixed." (Where is downstairs and what needs to be done?)	
b. "All special requests must be turned in by morning." (Which requests are special, and when is morning?)	
c. "Drop these off down the hall on your way out." (Where down the hall and to whom?)	

4. Give the Reason

When workers understand the reason for a direction, they are much more willing to accept it, figure it out, and make it work. Explain simply the reason why a certain process is followed, why a procedure should be done a certain way, and what happens if it is not.

5. Use as Many of the Learning Modalities as You Can—Visual, Auditory, and Kinesthetic

There is an old Chinese saying, "I hear and I forget, I see and I remember, I do and I understand." If you give directions both orally and visually, in writing, diagrams, or pictures, and then have the employee try it out him- or herself, you will have generally ensured success.

Calling People What They Want To Be Called: Preferred Diversity Language

Generally, people want to be dealt with as individuals, not categories or labels. Juan probably wants to be seen as an excellent mechanic, not the Mexican new hire, and Corazon wants to be regarded as a skilled nurse, not a Filipina recruited because of a nurse shortage. Nancy expects her colleagues to think of her as an excellent data processor, not the quadriplegic down in data processing. However, there are times when we need to talk about a group by name.

We have seen the labels shift over time, for example, from "colored" to "Negro" to "black" to "African American." Preferences among members of any group vary. It is not uncommon to hear people disagree over what they want to be called: Hispanic, Latino, Mexican American, or Chicano; disabled, handicapped, or differently abled. Fortunately, today's society has evolved to a point where derogatory racial epithets are not acceptable.

Here are some tips to help determine the most appropriate label to use when identifying a particular group:

- Ask the people involved about their preferred term: "Do you think of yourself as black or African American?" "Do you prefer the term Latino or Hispanic?" Not only can they tell you about their preference, but they can teach you as well.
- Pay attention to how people identify their own group—a feminist organization, the Latino Employee Support Group, or the Asian Pacific Staff Association, for example.
- Remember that all group members will not necessarily have the same preference.
- Realize that just as fashions change, so do the terms used to describe groups.
- Understand that terms used within a group may not be acceptable when coming from an outsider. The danger is that when overheard by outsiders in a public space, assumptions may be made that these terms are acceptable.

Finally, remember that, generally speaking, people care more about how they are being treated than whether they are called by today's correct term.

Ten Ways To Provide Constructive Feedback Without Losing of Face

Feedback is essential in any work environment; employees need to know when they are on track and when they are not. However, feedback is difficult enough to take in mainstream American culture, which values directness, let alone in cultures that value more subtle communication, harmony, and the saving of face. Before giving feedback, it is important to examine your motives. What is your reason for giving it? Is it really a chance to help the employee learn, or is it a way to assert your authority or to get the person back for something? Feedback that comes out of benevolent motives is more apt to be accepted positively. Once you're clear that your feedback is truly constructive, the following are some tips that will help.

1. Position the Feedback as a Benefit to the Receiver

Feedback can be helpful, as in being told by a dinner partner that we've got spinach on a tooth. A few seconds of discomfort prevent long-term embarrassment when we find out once we get home that we've spent all evening talking and laughing with a green tooth. When an individual sees how the information can help improve performance or the chances for a raise, he or she might be more receptive. You may say, for example, "You know, I was thinking about your frustration the other day with the long wait for materials. There is a way it might be avoided." Think about some feedback you want to give. See if you can find two or three benefits that will "hook" the receiver into being open to it.

2. Build a Relationship First

Feedback is most effective when it occurs in the context of a supportive and caring relationship. You probably have noticed in your own life that you can accept some of the most difficult and painful feedback from people who you know have your best interests at heart. Spending time building relationships with employees will pay off when you need to give constructive criticism. When asked how feedback is given in his country, a Japanese manager explained that the employee and boss have a relationship developed over time by socializing after work and spending time together. When feedback is necessary, the boss has already built rapport with the staff member.

3. Go from Subtle to More Direct Communication

The same Japanese manager mentioned above explained that if he were giving a subordinate feedback on a report that had an error, in order to save face he would never directly point this out. He would merely suggest that the employee look over the report again. This would be enough to alert the staff member that something was wrong. As long as both are Japanese, this works because both pick up the subtle cues. However, an American employee might be confused about the need to reread the report and would expect the boss to save time by pointing out problems.

Along the same lines, in Arab cultures, more circuitous communication is also used to save face. If, for example, a report had a problem area, the boss might praise one part of the report, emphasizing its excellence. The employee would then infer that the part not mentioned was weaker and needed work. The message is clear: If you are working with an employee who is particularly concerned with saving face, the subtler the better. You can always move toward more explicitness, but it is difficult to retreat once you have "let the cat out of the bag."

4. Make Observations About Behaviors and Conditions, Not Judgments About the Person

In any culture, defensiveness is apt to be the reaction when judgments are made. You can prevent this response and help the employee understand more clearly what is expected when you comment on behaviors and conditions. For example, you can say, "This carton had three defective units in it," rather than "This is careless work." Try improving each of the following pieces of feedback by focusing on behaviors and conditions rather than judgments:

Judgment/Evaluation	Behavior/Situation
a. This report is incomplete.	I'd like to see a table of contents and summary added.
b. Your tardiness has become a problem.	
c. Your work area is sloppy.	
d. I'd like more professional behavior from office staff.	
e. I've heard complaints about your attitude.	

5. Use the Passive Rather Than the Active Voice

By saying, "The switchboard was left uncovered for 15 minutes this morning," rather than "You were late," you avoid accusing the person and causing humiliation. The employee then can make the inference that it was his or her responsibility to be there and that the absence was noticed. In Spanish and Arabic, the passive and reflexive forms are very common so that actions are not attributed to individuals. In Spanish, for example, one does not say "I forgot my notebook," but rather "My notebook was forgotten to me" (*Se me olvidó el cuaderno*).

This may take practice since English favors the use of active verbs. Try transforming the following typical feedback statements from the active to the passive form:

Active	Passive
a. You forgot to turn off the air conditioner.	The air conditioner was left on all night.
b. You made some errors in these computations.	
c. You are late from lunch again.	
d. The night shift left these charts incomplete.	
e. Your department is slow in returning these forms.	

6. Be Positive, Telling What You Do Want, Not What You Don't

"Stop that!" sounds like a reprimand whether you are 2 years old or 52. When you tell the employee how you do want something done, you avoid the wrist-slapping emphasis on the mistake. Try changing the following statements from negative to positive:

Negative	Positive
a. That's not the way to do that.	Try it this way.
b. Don't be late to the meeting.	
c. Don't forget that your time cards are due on Thursdays now.	
d. There's not enough initiative on this staff.	
e. You are not following procedures.	

7. Give Feedback to the Group Rather Than to Individuals

Giving feedback to the whole group dilutes the sting and makes the information something the whole staff deals with rather than a personal affront to an individual. This may be difficult for you if it goes against your individualistic American reaction to making the whole group suffer for one person. However, if you have a group of employees from a culture that emphasizes the group over the individual, peer pressure may be able to influence the individual to get with the program. It also has the advantage of sending a more subtle, roundabout message that can get the point across without "nailing" the offender.

8. Make It Low-Key

Speak in a gentle, low tone of voice. While you may be using your normal tone of voice, to someone used to lower sounds you may sound like you are yelling or upset. The tension felt by the receiver of the feedback may make that person extra sensitive to the sound of your voice. Remind yourself to adjust your tone to a softer level that will not add to the already emotionally charged environment. Remember also to make it private, not public. That may mean going into your office; taking a walk; finding a conference room or a quiet, out of the way corner; waiting until you catch the person alone; or going out to lunch. Try to be unobtrusive in setting up the appointment as well. Announcing loudly that you want to talk with the person in your office has the same effect as giving the feedback in public.

9. Use an Intermediary

Much embarrassment can be avoided and acceptance gained if you use a third person to act as a go-between. Making a comment to a trusted friend of the employee such as, "I wish Nino would consider taking that CAD course. I think it would help him improve his drawings," might be a way to communicate feedback without loss of face. Be careful, though, that you are not perceived as talking about the person behind his or her back. Another way to use a go-between is to ask the intermediary for help: "I'd like to find a way to help Laura with her phone skills but I don't want to offend her. What would you suggest?" A third way is to ask the go-between to show the person what to do: "Oscar, could you help Hector in redesigning the work flow so it is more efficient?"

10. Assure the Individual of Your Respect for Him or Her

Above all, let the employee know you value him or her as a person and that you appreciate what he or she brings to the workgroup. Telling is one way, but, many times, actions speak louder than words. Spending time with an individual can be one of the most powerful communicators of respect. Another is asking for advice or sending others to the person for help. Finally, including yourself as part of the solution shows respect to the employee because you are demonstrating that you are both on the same team. "Let's see how we can solve this" is an approach that reinforces mutual respect because it concedes that no one person has all the answers and that you value the employee's views.

Using the *Intercultural Feedback Skills* worksheet will give you a chance to practice the three verbal skills discussed earlier. In addition, the *Intercultural Feedback Checklist for Managers* can help you integrate these techniques into your repertoire and increase your effectiveness on giving feedback to your diverse employees.

ACTIVITY 6.1 | Intercultural Feedback Skills

1. Make observations about behaviors and conditions, not judgments about the person.

Judgment/Evaluation	Behavior/Situation
a. This report is incomplete.	I'd like to see a table of contents and summary added.
b. Your tardiness has become a problem.	
c. Your work area is sloppy.	
d. I'd like more professional behavior from office staff.	
e I've heard complaints about your attitude.	

2. Use the passive rather than the active voice.

Active	Passive
a. You forgot to turn off the air conditioner.	The air conditioner was left on all night.
b. You made some errors in these computations.	
c. You are late from lunch again.	
d. The night shift left these charts incomplete	
e. Your department is slow in returning these forms.	

3. Be positive, telling what you do want, not what you don't.

Negative	Positive
a. That's not the way to do that.	Try it this way.
b. Don't be late to the meeting.	
c. Don't forget that your time cards are due on Thursdays now.	
d. There's not enough initiative on this staff.	
e. You're not following procedures.	

Suggestions for Using
Intercultural Feedback Skills

Objectives:

- Practice three specific feedback skills that can prevent loss of face

Intended Audience:

- Managers wanting to gain additional skill in giving feedback to diverse employees
- Trainees in a managing diversity seminar
- Trainers wanting to gain additional skill in giving feedback to diverse trainees

Processing the Activity:

- After reading the section *Ten Ways to Provide Feedback without Loss of Face* or hearing a lecturette on the topic, individuals write their own feedback statements for each of the three techniques.
- Then, if in a group, they can form smaller groups to share their statements, giving each other feedback on them. If working individually, compare statements to the suggestions at the end of the chapter.
- The total group then discusses difficulties encountered and specific items learned from this activity.
- To apply the learning, individuals using situations from their own experience write three feedback statements, one for each technique, which they would give in their real-life situation.

Questions for Discussion:

- Which techniques were easiest? Most difficult?
- Where could you use these?

Caveats, Considerations, and Variations:

- Some individuals may feel disgruntled because techniques 1 and 3 are standard feedback skills suggested in many supervisory and management development programs. Acknowledging their previous training in these areas up front may help circumvent this potential resistance. Stress that while it is an old technique, it has value with this new issue.
- Technique 2, using passive language, is apt to be difficult for native English speakers. There may be resistance from those who see it as vague, beating around the bush, and avoiding the issue. Help individuals see that it is an additional technique they may choose to use (or not to use) when and if appropriate.

CHECKLIST 6.1 | Intercultural Feedback Checklist for Managers

Think of a recent feedback situation in which you gave feedback to an employee from a different background. Check each of the techniques you used in that process.

_____ 1. I positioned the feedback as a benefit to the receiver.

_____ 2. I built a relationship first.

_____ 3. I went from subtle to more direct communication.

_____ 4. I made observations about behaviors and conditions, not judgments about the person.

_____ 5. I used the passive rather than the active voice.

_____ 6. I was positive, telling what I wanted, not what I didn't want.

_____ 7. I gave the feedback to the group rather than to individuals.

_____ 8. I gave feedback in a low-key and private manner.

_____ 9. I used an intermediary.

_____ 10. I assured the individual of my respect for him or her.

Suggestions for Using the
"Intercultural Feedback Checklist for Managers"

Objectives:

- Become aware of additional feedback techniques that could be employed
- Identify feedback techniques used
- Help managers plan more effective approaches for giving feedback in the future

Intended Audience:

- Managers wanting to overcome cultural barriers in giving feedback to employees
- Trainees in a managing diversity seminar
- Trainers wanting to overcome cultural barriers in giving feedback to trainees

Processing the Activity:

- Individuals analyze recent feedback-giving experience by checking which of the 10 techniques they used.
- In pairs or small groups, they discuss their satisfaction with their feedback session, which techniques were used, and which could have been used to make the feedback even more effective. (If working alone, these same issues can be considered.)
- Lead a large-group discussion of insights, learning, and application.

Questions for Discussion:

- How satisfied were you with effectiveness of your feedback-giving?
- Which techniques did you use? Which did you not use?
- Which might have helped make the feedback-giving more effective?
- What would you do differently the next time you give feedback to diverse employees?

Caveats, Considerations, and Variations:

- This activity can also be used as a planning guide for giving feedback in the future.

Reinforcing Positive Results:
Rewards That Enhance Rather than Insult

Positive reinforcement, which can be a powerful modifier of behavior and can help you get the desired performance from your staff, is based on three premises. First, a behavior that is reinforced will continue: as long as individuals get what they want by performing in a particular way, they'll keep doing it. Second, a behavior that is not reinforced will be extinguished: When they don't get what they want by behaving in a certain way, they'll quit. Third, a behavior that is negatively reinforced will not be extinguished, but rather will be masked: That means they will do it more covertly.

The key to using this method is to figure out what the reinforcers are for those you manage. What is considered rewarding depends first on individual preferences; for example, one person may want overtime while another may want time off. Culture influences the rewards as well. Time off for religious holidays or family celebrations may be important motivators. A reward that is not desired is no reward at all and will have no positive effect on behavior.

It has been said that we never really grow up—we just get older. Praise, whether it's the "good boy/girl" of childhood or the "great job" of adulthood, always feels good. As social creatures, human beings have basic needs for approval, belonging, and esteem. One of the most powerful reinforcers of behavior is sincere praise. Cultures differ, however, in their preferences about praise and how it should be given. Arabs tend to be pleased by praise; the more glowing and flowery the better. In cultures that prefer cooperation to competition, emphasize the importance of the group rather than the individual, and respect a social hierarchy; being singled out for praise is embarrassing, not rewarding. Giving a compliment at a staff meeting or publicly praising the accomplishments of one of your Asian or Native American employees might have the opposite effect of what you desire. In the case of employees from these groups, a private conversation, where you pay a low-key compliment, or a letter put in the person's file might be a more effective way to give praise. Traditional methods such as posting a picture of employee of the month or giving a preferred parking space might draw too much attention to the individual in his or her eyes, causing disruption in harmony, and hence would be counterproductive.

In cultures, such as that of Mexico, that value formality and outward symbols, the reward value of a spoken compliment would be greater if it were accompanied by an official certificate commending the individual. Business cards and titles have a similar effect among individuals from hierarchical cultures such as the Chinese and Mexican.

Reinforcement can be used with groups as well as with individuals, avoiding the singling out of particular workers. Paying the group a compliment is one way: "You guys did a great job on that rush order yesterday. Thanks." Another might be to host a group celebration to reward staff. Springing for pizza to thank a shift for coming through or having a staff picnic to show appreciation for a job well done might work more effectively than individual praise with group-oriented employees.

Suggestions for Managers

In rewarding employees appropriately and effectively, remember the following points:
1. Consider the individual's culture in choosing the reward, and watch the person's reactions. Do you get a beam or a frown? Does the reward seem to produce more effective behavior or not?

2. Reward effort and initiative, not just accomplishment. Let the person know you appreciate a try, a risk, an attempt, even if the result is less than perfect. Reinforcing small steps may be the best way to get employees to achieve your objectives.

3. Be careful not to over-praise. Heaping on compliments may backfire by making the individual feel patronized. The Japanese or Germans, for example, generally do not expect to be complimented for doing a good job. That performance is taken for granted. Overenthusiastic praise may also send the subtle message that you are surprised at the person's accomplishment, that the level of performance was unexpected.

4. Consider the employee's life situation in choosing rewards to reinforce behavior. A single parent may appreciate a more flexible schedule so she can attend parent conferences at her child's school, while a recent immigrant may find the extra overtime a boon to his savings to bring his wife and children here.

5. Be clear and specific about what you are reinforcing. Make sure there is a clear connection in the mind of the employee between the reward and the behavior it is reinforcing. For example, you can say, "That was very smart of you to stop the production line when you saw the defects. I'm glad you called me." Or, "All of you who volunteered to work extra hours on that project will have first choice for future overtime assignments."

6. Practice what you preach; employees will learn from what you do more than what you say. There is a wonderful scene in the movie *Starman* where the character from another galaxy shows what he has learned about the culture of driving on Earth. Through a series of mishaps, he is forced to drive his Earth hostess's car for the first time. Riding with him, she is horrified when he approaches a yellow signal and accelerates. When she reprimands him for not following the rules, he assures her he knows the rules: red means stop, green means go, and yellow means go faster! If you tell people you want them to take initiative, then punish them when they make their first mistake, they'll continue to avoid taking initiative. If you tell staff you want them to let you know when things go wrong, yet blame them for the first problem they announce, they'll soon learn to hide mistakes.

Communicating Your Expectations: Letting Staff Know What You Want

Every employee spends part of his or her time figuring out what the boss wants. Job security, as well as satisfaction, depends in good measure on getting along with one's boss and doing what the boss expects. This is not always easy even when both boss and subordinate are from similar cultural backgrounds. Much of the communication about expectations is left unstated, and the we'll-figure-it-out-as-we-go-along mentality prevails. When there are differences in cultures, employees may never clearly understand what is expected, and both boss and employees get increasingly frustrated. Even in monocultural groups, it is essential for a boss to let staff know what is expected, as each manager has a distinct style and preferences (see Activity 6.2). However, this is more critical when cultural barriers may make (the figuring out of and coming through on) expectations next to impossible.

ACTIVITY 6.2 | Expected Employee Behaviors

Place a check mark next to those behaviors you expect of your staff. Then go back and place an X next to those behaviors you have a difficult time getting.

I expect employees to:

Time

_____ Be on time for work, meetings, and appointments.

_____ Be prompt in returning from breaks.

_____ Be responsible for their own time, taking breaks and lunch when needed.

_____ Give early notification of absences due to illness.

_____ Stick to assigned break and lunch times.

_____ Give requests for vacation time in advance.

_____ Meet deadlines on projects and tasks.

_____ Give advance notification of deadlines that can't be met.

_____ Other: _____

_____

_____

Taking Initiative and Solving Problems

_____ Suggest improvements and solutions.

_____ Participate in staff meetings by discussing and sharing.

_____ Work together to find solutions to problems.

_____ Take independent action to deal with problems, then tell me about it.

_____ Use good judgment about when to ask me before they take independent action.

_____ When carrying out delegated tasks, check in with me as planned.

_____ Other: _____

_____

_____

Announcing Problems and Giving "Bad News"

_____ Let me know when there's a problem so we can fix it.

_____ Tell me when they disagree.

_____ Let me know when they are having difficulty.

_____ Tell me about complaints from clients/customers.

_____ Let me know when a mistake has been made.

_____ Other: _____

_____

_____

Communication

_____ Let me know when something is unclear or confusing.

_____ Ask if they don't understand.

_____ Speak English on the job.

_____ Make no derogatory remarks about another group.

_____ Not speak another language around others who do not understand.

_____ Other: _____

_____

_____

Suggestions for Using
"Expected Employee Behaviors"

Objectives:
- Identify behaviors expected of employees
- Pinpoint those that are forthcoming and those that are not

Intended Audience:
- Managers wanting to increase productivity, follow-through, and commitment of staff
- Trainees in a managing diversity seminar

Processing the Activity:
- Individuals check those behaviors they expect of employees, then go back and place an X next to those they have difficulty getting.
- In groups, individuals share their checklists and discuss those behaviors that are most difficult to get from staff. They then discuss ways to get the desired behaviors from staff.
- Individuals make a commitment to take specific action to get the desired behavior(s).

Questions for Discussion:
- Which behaviors are hardest to get from employees?
- What might be the cultural norms influencing employees' behavior?
- How can you communicate these expectations to employees?
- What can you do to get more of the desired behaviors?

Caveats, Considerations, and Variations:
- This tool can be used by HR professionals or employee relations specialists in coaching managers to more effective behavior.
- This tool can also be used in general supervisory/management training courses.

Once you have identified which behaviors you want, as well as those you are and are not getting, you need to figure out how you can teach these American cultural expectations to your staff. Explaining the reason for the behavior's desirability is important in this process. For example, you may say,

- "It may sound odd, but I like 'bad news.' I want to know when something goes wrong so we can fix it as soon as possible. If no one tells me, I'm not able to do my job, which is to solve problems that get in the way of productivity."
- "When you participate in staff meetings and make suggestions about improvements, that shows me you take your job seriously and are a committed employee."
- "Being on time for meetings shows you to respect others' time."
- "Speaking a language that others do not understand makes them feel left out. It may also make them angry and resentful."

By simply clarifying expectations, conflicts can sometimes be avoided. However, even with the best of communication, when human beings work together, there will be times when there is friction, anger, and disagreement.

Resolving Conflict in Culturally Sensitive Ways

Disagreements, disruptions, and tension in relationships are not relished in any environment. Most of us would prefer not to have to deal with the out-of-control feelings and potential loss of approval we risk in conflict. Even in the dominant U.S.-American culture, with its preference for direct confrontation, most people tend to play the ostrich, avoiding dealing with the situation until there is no other alternative. Hoping the problem will go away is generally wishful thinking, though. Conflicts that are not dealt with usually continue to fester, escalating into more serious situations. In addition, unresolved conflict is a significant source of stress, causing morale and productivity declines for the organization and illness for the individuals involved. Dealing with conflict is necessary, though often less than pleasant. Dealing with it in a diverse environment can be even more daunting.

Cultural Norms Affecting Conflict in a Diverse Environment

1. Conflict Is Seen as Disruptive to Harmony

In cultures such as the Thai, Vietnamese, and Filipino, which put a premium on harmony and smooth interpersonal relations, the potential for disruption makes conflict something to be avoided at almost all costs. Employees may deny, ignore, and avoid talking about or confronting the differences.

2. Conflict Presents a Risk of Loss of Face

Because confrontation sometimes leads to accusations, blaming, and arguments, there is a great risk of embarrassment. Employees from cultures such as those mentioned above, as well as Latino and Middle Eastern groups, will be very reluctant to participate in any interactions that could lead to someone losing face. When loss-of-face occurs, drastic measures may be required to restore lost honor. It is critical to reduce the potential of loss-of-face

3. Cultural Communication Style Differences Can Make Resolution More Difficult

Consider the following case in point. In a disagreement between two employees, one African American and the other Filipino, a few heated words were exchanged. Wanting to avoid further disruption, the Filipino employee walked away. The African American employee, on the other hand, coming from a background and upbringing that valued directly confronting conflict and wanting to settle the problem, followed her co-worker, trying to talk to her. This only caused more anxiety and panic for the Filipino, whose culture undoubtedly taught her to value harmony and smooth interpersonal relationships, so she continued to refuse to discuss it. When the African American persisted, the Filipino turned and threatened her co-worker, telling her if she came any closer, she would hit her. What resulted was a grievance where both employees reported being physically threatened by the other.

While individual personalities vary, there are culture- and gender-based tendencies in conflict styles: women sometimes cry, while men pound desks; and African Americans tend to confront verbally, while Filipinos get silent. Differences such as these can present barriers to resolution.

4. There Exists the Risk for Interpretation of the Conflict as Discrimination and Prejudice

Among groups with a history of discrimination—for example, African Americans, Mexican Americans, gays and lesbians, or Puerto Ricans—there may be a heightened sensitivity to prejudice and a tendency to perceive unwanted feedback or confrontation as discriminatory: "They're only doing this because I'm ...."

Understanding the cultural dynamics influencing the conflict arena is an important first step. Next, you need to work to resolve the impasse. Nancy Adler suggests a three-step process in resolving conflicts that are rooted in cultural differences.[3]

Nancy Adler's Model of Cultural Synergy

1. Define the Problem from Both Points of View

Let's consider the case of the supervisor whose immigrant employee takes the whole day off each time he takes his wife to the doctor, even though she can drive. The first step is to identify the points of view of each party. How does each view the conflict? What does each think is wrong? The boss in this situation is irritated and upset that the employee is not there when he needs him. In fact, the boss described the employee as "irresponsible" for taking time off work. The employee undoubtedly feels his boss is being insensitive and punitive.

2. Uncover the Cultural Interpretations

The second step is to uncover the cultural interpretations. What assumptions is each making about the other, based on his own cultural programming? In doing this, the boss might realize that, in the employee's culture, his role of head of the family required that he take his wife on such important appointments and that he was being very responsible. The employee might realize that in his boss's programming, work commitments take precedence over nonemergency family matters and that family members take care of such responsibilities on their own. The issue is not who loves his family more, who is a better spouse, or who is a more committed worker, but how can this be worked out.

3. Create Cultural Synergy.

Now, devise a solution that works for both. They might, for example, decide that the employee can use his sick days for such family responsibilities, that he might only take a few hours off for the appointment, or use comp time. What is important in this process is the recognition and acceptance of others' cultural values and the working out of mutually acceptable alternatives that honors the culture and needs of each.

Suggestions for Managers:

1. *Use the Indirect Approach.* Use a go-between, a third party who can give you suggestions for resolution and find out the other party's desires. This avoids direct confrontation, and, like the paper walls in Japanese homes which create the illusion of privacy, it allows both parties to save face by never having to confront the issue face-to-face.

2. *Emphasize Harmony.* In attempting a resolution, talk about the cooperative spirit and harmony that would result if the disagreement were settled. You can say, "This problem is upsetting for all of us and is causing remarks from other departments."

3. *Clarify the Cultural Influences Operating.* Help each party understand the cultural programming of the other. For example, talking privately with the African American and Filipino employees about the differences in cultural styles of communicating could help each see the other's behavior in a better light. It may also help to encourage each party to avoid relying on stereotypes. For example, you can ask, "What is one thing about [name] that does not fit the stereotype of [group]?"

4. *Work with Informal Leaders.* Get help from the most respected member of each party's culture or group, and ask for their advice and assistance in bringing the two individuals or groups together. This is especially helpful in conflict between groups.

5. *Get Specific.* Have each party spell out their issues with one another and their needs in specific behaviors and situations. It helps to give people time to think these through first. Open-ended statements, such as the following, are a good way to get the individuals involved to think constructively about the situation:
    - "I get most irritated when …."
    - "When this happens, I feel …."
    - "What I'd like from you is …."
    - "I'd be willing to resolve this if …"
    - "If this conflict were resolved, I'd …."
    - "If this disagreement continues, …."

6. *Get Honest with Yourself.* Recognize your own reactions and preferences. You, too, are culturally programmed. You may have a preference for one person's style or one group's position over another. If you are a party to the conflict, you may find the

behavior or values of the other party's culture distasteful. Dealing with your own reaction, feelings, and ethnocentrism before you get involved in attempting resolution will help you remain more objective and more helpful in the negotiation.

7. *Find Out How Conflicts Are Resolved in the Culture of the Other Party.* Knowing that a go-between is always used, for example, can help you choose an appropriate strategy. Seek help from a cultural informant, someone familiar with practices and norms in the other culture. Get that person's perceptions and explanations of the situation, as well as suggestions for resolution strategies.

8. *Keep Out of Corners.* In any conflict situation, avoid cornering someone in a losing position. Just as animals attack when cornered, human beings of any culture are apt to strike back in unpredictable and irrational ways when they feel they have no recourse. Always leave room for both parties to get something; either/or ultimatums produce losers who can become powerful saboteurs of any resolution.

9. *Capitalize on the Relationship.* If you have developed a relationship with the individual, use it to help you in working out a solution. You can say, "We've always had a cooperative working relationship. I'd like for that to continue. Having this tension between us is bothering me, and I care enough about you to want to work it through."

10. *Respect, Respect, Respect.* If an individual is treated with dignity and respect, he or she will be much more likely to work with you. If this universal law of human relations is broken, you may have created an enemy for life. You can show respect by dealing with the other party (or parties) privately and as discreetly as possible; by listening and not discounting what they have to say; by owning your part of the problem and being willing to give as well as take in the negotiation; by apologizing; and by showing sincere appreciation for this person's contribution to the work unit.

When all is said and done, effective cross-cultural communication depends on understanding and managing one's own reactions, learning about the cultural factors that may be operating and, when there is an impasse, problem-solving in ways that seek solutions that work for all. Most important, it requires an approach that honors the humanity in others no matter what language they speak.

ACTIVITY 6.3 | Intercultural Feedback Skills: Sample Responses for Exercises

Giving Directions

Be specific and explicit

a. Take this to environmental engineering in 8-36 and tell them to fix the broken switch.

b. Requests for vacations and time off during November and December must be turned in by 9 a.m.. tomorrow.

c. Drop these off at the mailroom slot on your way out.

Giving Feedback

Make observations about behaviors and conditions, not judgments about the person

a. You need to be at your work station by 8 a.m. each day.

b. I'd like the work area clear of food and coffee cups.

c. I'd like the phones answered by the third ring with "Good morning/afternoon, data processing, this is Teresa."

d. I'd like customers greeted with a smile and treated like a guest in your home.

Use the passive rather than the active voice

a. There are a few errors in these computations.

b. The desk was uncovered for a half hour this afternoon.

c. These charts were found incomplete this morning.

d. These forms have been turned in late for the last three weeks.

Be positive, telling what you do want, not what you don't

a. I'd like to start the meeting promptly at 9 a.m.

b. Please remember to turn in time cards on Thursdays now.

c. I'd like to see people offering to help each other when their own work is done.

d. I'd like you to follow the steps outlined in the personnel manual when calling in sick.

CHAPTER 7

Managing Stereotypes and Prejudice in the Workplace

• •

This chapter will provide you with:

- An understanding about stereotypes and prejudice and the role they play

- Activities that raise awareness about stereotypes and prejudice

- Tips for dealing with stereotypical behavior and comments

"I'm not prejudiced."

"I'm color and gender blind."

"I treat everyone the same, whether they're green, blue or purple."

You've undoubtedly heard these kinds of comments in your organization from well-meaning individuals. Yet, none of us escapes being both perpetrator and victim, and we are all impacted by the "second hand smoke" effect of these preconceived notions about other groups. One of the most powerful messages about this universal phenomenon can be experienced at the Museum of Tolerance in Los Angeles, California. The museum, dedicated to building more tolerance by showing the negative and limiting impact of intolerance, uses engaging interactive exhibits to teach visitors. The first experience of this is at the entrance where there are two sets of double doors, one labeled "Prejudiced" and the other labeled "Not Prejudiced." When visitors try to open the doors they find that only the "Prejudiced" doors open and all have to walk through them under that designation.

Prejudice: Recognizing the Archie Bunker in All of Us

Archie Bunker became an American anti-hero in the 1960s, an everyman whose exaggerated bigotry we could all laugh at. Perhaps the reason we laughed so hard at him was that there is a bit of Archie in all of us. Prejudice, acting on preconceived and often erroneous views about other groups, is a common, human response to a complex world. Stereotypes, generalizations that are at the base of prejudice, help us organize our thinking and manage massive amounts of information. Since none of us can know every individual in every group, we make categories to simplify our worlds and then slot people into those pigeonholes. In turn, our world then becomes more ordered and more stable. Generalizations sometimes serve a useful purpose, as in the case of lifeguards who know to watch certain groups at the beach more carefully because more individuals from these groups are involved in near drownings. However, stereotypes also serve to limit perceptions about individuals and their capabilities and hinder effectiveness. The lifeguards, for example, may be less vigilant of the behavior of other groups on the beach, assuming they are safe in the water.

Gordon Allport, the foremost writer and thinker on the topic of prejudice, illustrates this resistance of stereotypes to facts in the following dialogue in *The Nature of Prejudice.*[1]

> **Mr. X:** *The trouble with the Jews is that they only take care of their own group.*

> **Mr. Y:** *But the record of the Community Chest campaign shows that they give more generously, in proportion to their numbers, to the general charities of the community, than do non-Jews.*

> **Mr. X:** *That shows they are always trying to buy favor and intrude into Christian affairs. They think of nothing but money; that is why there are so many Jewish bankers.*
>
> **Mr. Y:** *But a recent study shows that the percentage of Jews in the banking business is negligible, far smaller than the percentage of non-Jews.*
>
> **Mr. X:** *That's just it; they don't go in for respectable business; they are only in the movie business or run night clubs.*

In addition, stereotypes provoke strong emotional reactions both in the victims and the perpetrators. Those who hold prejudices often do so with a vehemence that literally and figuratively defies reason. Those who are the objects of the prejudiced belief can find themselves hurt, angry, resentful, or depressed by the inaccurate and dehumanizing assumption, its inherent insult, and the limits it may impose.

The Realities of Stereotypes

Stereotypes do not develop out of thin air. They are built on some experience that produced information about a group. That information may be due to misinterpretation of other cultural norms. For example, it may be they are not lazy, but place a higher priority on relationships than time. Or it may indeed be based on accurate information, for example, if you have found that three people you've hired from a particular group have left without giving you advance warning. However, even when based on "facts," stereotypes are overgeneralizations that do not fit everyone in that category.

No one group has the corner on the market when it comes to prejudice, and no one is exempt from being the target of these preconceived notions. We hold them, not just about other racial and ethnic groups, but about people from other parts of this country, those of the opposite sex, alumni of certain schools, and members of other political parties or professions. One professional, a teacher from South Carolina, stunned us by saying, "I bet you think I'm stupid, don't you?" When we asked her why she thought that she said Northerners often reacted that way to her strong Southern drawl.

Assumptions Become Self-Fulfilling Prophecies

Like the hypochondriac who had "See, I told you so" carved on his tombstone, what we think often becomes reality. We look for behavior that validates our preconception and disregard what does not fit. We continue to collect evidence to prove our prejudices right and ignore that which shows us another picture. If, for example, you think a particular group sticks together and doesn't want to assimilate, you will notice every time employees from this group are together, talking on breaks, eating lunch, or exchanging information on the job. What you won't notice is when they are talking with people of different groups. You will probably operate according to your assumptions, ignoring people from this group, not including or inviting them to join your interactions because you believe they want to be separate. And so it goes, each time you get "proof" that your assumption is accurate, you add another brick in the barrier that separates you from them.

There is clear evidence from the many Pygmalion experiments that people perform to the level of expectation that is held for them. The expectations held by those who have a dominant or authority position within a relationship are the most influential and formative: parents over children, teachers over students, and managers over employees. If you see employees from another group as lazy, though you may never say it, your behavior will broadcast your feeling: you may continually hover or nag and prod; you might ignore them when more interesting work comes along or discount their complaints; and you will, in subtle ways, teach them to live down to your expectations.

One manufacturing organization refused to get hooked by these sabotaging assumptions. The managers noticed a problem on the assembly line that packaged restaurant condiments. Production was slow, and there were too many defective packets. The typical response in cases like these was to blame the immigrant workers, assuming that "They're slacking off," "They're not paying attention," or "They don't care." However, in this case, the managers went to the lead man and asked what was wrong. While not totally fluent in English, he explained that the new packaging film was the problem. They listened, but more important, they got others to listen. They set up a meeting with executives from both their own company and their film supplier. They invited the lead man to explain, with the help of an interpreter, the problem directly to the supplier. The supplier responded with a potential solution; however, the lead man explained why there would still be a problem. The good news is that he had management's support throughout. The even better news is that the meeting did not end until the supplier agreed to provide the quality of film necessary for proper packaging. By getting beyond inaccurate assumptions, this organization was able to get the best from this immigrant workforce and solve a production problem. They expected top-level performance, they believed these employees would give it, and they were right.

Admitting Stereotypes: The First Step

As painful as it may be, the first step in getting beyond our preconceived notions about others is admitting that we hold stereotypes; we all have them about some other groups. Stop for a moment and try this little brain teaser:

> *Just before the nurse died of the effects of an attack, she said, "He did it, the villain!", referring to one of the three doctors in the room. She didn't glance or point in his direction. The doctors were named Dr. Green, Dr. Brown, and Dr. White. Why was Dr. Brown immediately suspected?*

The answer is that Dr. Green and Dr. White were both women. Did you get hooked by your own stereotypes about the roles of women and men? If so, take heart—you're human.

CHECKLIST 7.1 | Stereotypes

As you read the following list, check any of the assumptions and beliefs you have held about other cultural, ethnic, professional, or geographic groups. Also check any you have heard, though not thought yourself. Think about the group they are associated with. Finally, identify an individual who disproves the stereotype.

		Group	Disprove
☐ 1.	Are smart and work hard		
☐ 2.	Are very good at sports		
☐ 3.	Tend to keep to themselves		
☐ 4.	Are usually good dancers		
☐ 5.	Are lazy, don't work hard, and aren't reliable		
☐ 6.	Usually become rich by cheating others		
☐ 7.	Are sneaky and not trustworthy		
☐ 8.	Are uninsured and don't have driver's licenses		
☐ 9.	Are dirty and smell bad		
☐ 10.	Are uneducated and not very intelligent		
☐ 11.	Are associated with organized crime		
☐ 12.	Think they are better than others		
☐ 13.	Don't want to become American		
☐ 14.	Are aggressive and pushy		
☐ 15.	Talk and think only about making money		
☐ 16.	Are happy-go-lucky and easygoing		
☐ 17.	Laugh and smile a lot		
☐ 18.	Don't want to learn English		
☐ 19.	Have illegitimate children		
☐ 20.	Can't hold their liquor and drink too much		
☐ 21.	Do well in school and get advanced degrees		
☐ 22.	Make good gardeners		
☐ 23.	Make the neighborhood go downhill		
☐ 24.	Are bigoted, prejudiced, and biased		
☐ 25.	Are miserly and ungenerous		

What do your responses tell you about how you have been impacted by the second-hand smoke effect of stereotypes? Consider the following ways you can challenge yourself and others when these thoughts and judgments arise.

Stereotype Busting: Getting Beyond Limiting Assumptions

Managing your stereotypes and assumptions is critical because if you don't, they'll manage you and your decisions. The first step in breaking free of limiting assumptions is to admit them, then you can begin taking action to deal with them.

1. **Challenge yourself to find exceptions to stereotypes.** Think of individuals you know or have read about who don't fit the generalization. This may be difficult because of a phenomenon called "cognitive dissonance"[2] by theorist Leon Festinger: We have mental pictures of how certain groups are, and when we meet those who do not fit the picture, we experience dissonance. At this point, the tendency is to make the person the exception and hang on to the stereotype. Comments such as "You're different. You're not like the rest of those …" demonstrate this phenomenon in action. When you find exceptions, work on changing your mental picture.

2. **Build relationships with people in other groups.** Once you know people as individuals, rather than labels, you will be less likely to hold on to a "They're all like that" attitude. You'll see the variations among individuals within the group and you'll also see the shared humanity between you. As Liz Winfeld, author of *Straight Talk About Gays in the Workplace,* says, "The individual is the enemy of the stereotype."[3]

3. **Confront yourself and others when you hear words or phrases such as "those people" or "they" in describing other groups.** Whether or not these words or phrases are about executives, immigrants, those on welfare, Wall Street financiers, or the homeless doesn't matter, because the bottom line is that they represent stereotypic views that are dehumanizing and often inaccurate.

4. **Take a walk in their shoes.** Spend time in a place where you are the outsider, the different one, and see how it feels. What is your reaction to being the target of stereotyping? How does it feel to have someone's incorrect assumptions impact you?

Because generational differences trigger stereotypical assumptions in many organizations, they offer a prime opportunity to practice stereotype busting. The following activity gives you a chance to confront your assumptions about different age groupings and consider the impact of those preconceived notions.

ACTIVITY 7.1 | Stereotype Busting

Jot down the assumptions you've had or heard about each age group, then consider the limits and impact of those assumptions.

Age Group	Assumption Generalization	Limits/Impact
Silent Generation/ Seniors/Veterans		
Baby Boomers		
Generation X		
Generation Y/Nexters/ Baby Boomer/Echo		
Millennials		

Suggestions for Using
"Stereotype Busting"

Objectives:

- Discover and confront assumptions about generational differences
- Learn a process for confronting preconceived notions about other groups
- Consider the limiting effects of stereotyping

Intended Audience:

- Participants in diversity training
- Employees working in multi-generational teams
- Managers of multi-generational work groups

Materials

- Copies of the worksheet *Stereotype Busting*

Processing the Activity:

- Give a short lecture on stereotypes and how they operate.
- Ask participants to jot down assumptions they have heard or held about different generational groups and to also indicate the limits or impact those assumptions have for both perpetrator and target.
- Have participants form small groups to discuss their responses.
- Lead a total-group discussion of reactions and insights.
- Ask participants to make a commitment to one specific action they will take to learn more about a different generational group.

Questions for Discussion:

- What reactions did you have to the assumptions about each age group?
- Which assumptions were most impactful? Limiting? Widespread?
- How do they play out in our organization?
- What can you do to manage these assumptions?
- What is one action you can take to learn more about a different generation?

Understanding Prejudice and Its Impact

Gordon Allport, in his book, *The Nature of Prejudice*,[4] describes the continuum of reactions to those who are different, the "other." Behavior ranges from the mildest form, avoidance, to the most horrendous, genocide. While these extremes are very different in the severity of their impact, they share a common denominator: dehumanization. When we see others as labels, rather than human beings like ourselves, we are capable of destructive behaviors.

Stereotypes are preconceived generalizations about groups, while prejudice involves taking actions based on those assumptions. If you hold the view that Asians are better at math, you may give preference to a Korean applicant over others for an accounting position. However, you may discount that same job seeker when it comes to a management or sales position. If you believe African Americans are recipients of affirmative action placements, you may discount an African-American applicant's educational achievements or employment history. If you believe that women are more nurturing than men, you may prefer the female nurse over the equally (or better) qualified male nurse or physician. These kinds of assumptions and behaviors play out in workplace decisions daily, impacting careers, motivation, and effectiveness.

How Stereotypes Are Perpetuated

Leslie Aguilar, in her practical book, *Ouch! That Stereotype Hurts*, describes the most common ways stereotypes show themselves and are perpetuated in organizations.[5]

1. Jokes (*What do they call a ...*)
2. Name-calling and labels (*Geriatrics, Nerds, Welfare Moms, Trailer Trash*)
3. Oversimplified statements applied to all people in a group. (*You know how _____ are; What can you expect from a_____?*)
4. Stereotypical descriptors (*Out-of-touch executives; Technophobic senior citizen; Typical politician*)
5. Personal assumptions about individuals based on a stereotype about a group. (*She won't want a promotion that involves relocation because of her husband's career; I wouldn't put him in a management position because his culture discourages self-assertion and confronting conflict.*)
6. Spokesperson syndrome (*Jose, what do union members think about this?; Tran, how would Vietnamese employees react to this change?*)
7. Descriptors that evoke stereotypes because they are a contradiction to an existing stereotype (*He's an articulate black leader; I finally found a qualified minority candidate; She's a logical, unemotional manager.*)
8. "Statistical" stereotyping (*A recent report that most immigrants ...; Statistics show that the majority of _____ vote for ....*")

These overt and subtle comments and thoughts embed stereotypic assumptions and undermine a climate of equity and inclusion. Recognizing them is a start. Then, not using them, and educating others when they use them, are next steps. Use the following activity to help you in that process.

ACTIVITY 7.2 | Common Ways Stereotypes Surface and Are Perpetuated

Directions: Circle the item numbers of any of these behaviors you have engaged in or experienced, and then write a more productive comment, behavior, or response. For example, if you've asked someone to speak for an entire group, you may find it more effective to ask, "What do you think, Jose? Who else can I speak to in your group to hear other views?"

Behavior	Productive Comment, Behavior, or Response
1. Jokes	
2. Name calling/Labels	
3. Oversimplified statements applied to all people in a group	
4. Stereotypical descriptions	
5. Personal assumptions about individuals based on stereotypes about a group	
6. Spokesperson syndrome	
7. Descriptors that evoke stereotypes because they contradict an existing stereotype	
8. "Statistical" stereotyping	

Suggestions for Using
"Common Ways Stereotypes Surface and Are Perpetuated"

Objectives:

- Raise awareness about the specific behaviors that perpetuate stereotypes
- Assess the degree of stereotyping in a work environment
- Generate ways to stop the perpetuation of stereotypes

Intended Audience:

- Managers of diverse staff
- Members of hiring and promotion panels
- Staff who work with diverse customers and co-workers

Processing the Activity:

- Give a short explanation of the eight ways stereotypes are perpetuated, giving and soliciting examples from the group.
- Ask participants to circle the number of any of the behaviors they have engaged in, experienced, or observed in the past year.
- Next, ask them to write more productive comments or responses for those they've checked.
- Take a total-group tally, charting the number of hands raised for each.
- Have participants share responses in small groups, generating more productive behaviors.
- Lead a total-group discussion of the experience focusing on insights gained.

Questions for Discussion:

- What questions does this raise?
- What is the impact of these behaviors in the workplace?
- What feelings do they elicit?
- What are some productive ways to respond or change this dynamic?
- What is one action you can take to address these comments?

Caveats, Considerations, and Variations:

- Comments illustrating each of the eight behaviors can be written on index cards and distributed to groups. Each group determines which of the eight kinds of behaviors the comment typifies, then, on the back, they write a more productive comment or response.
- In small groups, participants can respond to these comments using role play.

Responding to Prejudicial and Stereotypic Comments

One of the most frequently asked questions by employers and managers of diverse groups centers around how to respond to tough situations involving stereotyping. Whether the difficulty comes in the form of a prejudicial remark, an inappropriate joke, a stereotypic judgment or a frustrated outburst about "them," it's often a showstopper. Situations like these give you an opportunity to set the tone, teach about diversity, and demonstrate your commitment to creating a truly inclusive, respectful work environment.

One of our colleagues showed how this could be done when he responded to a potentially hurtful comment. During an open dialogue about race and discrimination, one of his colleagues said, "I bet you wish you weren't black." He did not respond in anger; rather, he made the encounter a chance to reframe the issue and to educate. "No, I don't wish I wasn't black, I wish there wasn't racism."

While effective responses are as varied as the comments and the personalities of both speakers and responders. there are a few guidelines that may help you frame your responses without coming across as the "PC police" that squelches dialogue.

Inquire

Ask questions to understand, clarify, or get more information. Dig deeper to find out what the person means and what reasoning is behind the comment or question.
- "What makes you say that?"
- "Is that a problem you're faced with?"
- "Can you tell me more about that?"
- "How does this impact your interactions with customers?"

Show Empathy

When powerful emotions are present, acknowledge and respond to the feelings expressed. This means listening not just to the words, but to the underlying feelings. Undoubtedly you've faced similar frustrations, and demonstrating understanding can help calm the upset individual so that further communication can take place.
- "It is frustrating when you can't understand someone."
- "It's difficult to help when you don't know if you're being understood."
- "That is irritating for me, too."
- "Dealing with situations like that is often stressful."

Educate

Once the emotional cloud has dissipated, you have a "teachable moment," a chance to debunk myths, give facts, and explain.
- "Did you know that the first civil rights law was passed right after the Civil War, over 130 years ago?"
- "The term 'gypped' comes from Gypsy."
- "Minorities are the majority in six of the eight largest urban areas in the United States."
- "'Sexual orientation' is generally preferred over 'sexual preference' as it expresses the sense that one's sexuality is not a choice but how someone is born."

- "Many women dislike being called a 'lady' in work situation as it is a social rather than a professional term, much like gentleman."

Express Your Feelings

Use nonblaming "I" statements to give your reactions. When it's your feelings that are involved, you have a right to let the other person know the impact of the comment.

- "I feel diminished when I'm referred to as a gal."
- "I get upset with jokes about other religions or cultures."
- "I'm uncomfortable when we make generalizations like that about other groups."
- "Ouch! That comment stings."

State Your Needs or Expectations

- If it's different behavior you desire, let people know what you do and don't want.
- "Jokes about religions or cultural groups are off limits with me."
- "Let's focus on creating an approach we can both agree on."
- "Let's spend time figuring out what we can do about the issue rather than rehashing what's wrong."
- "Let's use the names of the individuals involved and avoid labels about groups."

Avoid Polarization

Getting stuck in either-or choices is a deadly trap. You can help people avoid this by generating other options and points of view.

- "What might be other reasons for this behavior?"
- "What is another way to respond?"
- "How might someone of a different background see this?"
- "What other strategies might work?"

Silence

While silence can be interpreted as tacit approval, there are times when the silence of no response is deafening and sends a powerful message of disapproval. Not laughing at a joke or walking away from a sarcastic quip may communicate all that's needed.

Avoid Arguing and Defending

Curb the impulse to debate, persuade, argue, or defend your point of view; doing so generally only strengthens the resistance and drives entrenched opinions deeper. One of the most difficult diversities of all to deal with may be that of differences in values. Acknowledging that we can have differences of opinion yet respect one another also demonstrates your ability to "walk the talk" of diversity.

ACTIVITY 7.3 | Responding to Prejudicial and Stereotypic Comments

Think of times when you have encountered prejudicial or stereotypic comments. Check which of the responses you used, and, in the column on the right, jot down the impact your response had on the situation.

Response	Impact on Situation
Inquire	
Show empathy	
Educate	
Express your feelings	
State your needs or expectations	
Avoid polarization	
Silence	
Avoid arguing and defending	
Other	

CHAPTER 8

Building Multicultural Work Teams

• •

This chapter will give you:

- A look at cross-cultural values and norms, and their impact on team functioning

- Ways to adapt traditional team-building tools and theory to cross-cultural and virtual teams

- Ready-made assessments that indicate when team building is necessary

- Training materials and other assessment inventories that define team strengths and weaknesses

- Ten dimensions by which to gauge growth on a cross-cultural team

- Suggestions for increasing a sense of belonging, esteem, and trust among team members

"Team building," "cross-cultural synergy," "workgroup cohesion"—to paraphrase Shakespeare, a rose by any other name is still a rose, and team-building at the beginning of the 21st century, no matter what it's called, still requires that people who are fundamentally interdependent in a workgroup perform their tasks in some systematic, effective way, regardless of what time zone they are in, where they live, or how frequently they have face-to-face contact. This goal is more complicated when working in a culturally diverse environment where the norms, values, expectations, traditions, and priorities of team members from different backgrounds and parts of the world may seem to be (or literally are) foreign and out of sync with one another. Often, building effective teams is accomplished by using intentional processes and conscious design. At other times, teams get built by informal, indirect means through emphasizing strong relationships that enable a workgroup to persist through any obstacle. This chapter will help you understand the cultural influences that impact any team—whether it is virtual, global, somewhat homogenous or obviously cross-cultural—as you attempt to build harmonious and productive work units. By creating an environment where all employees are valued for their unique contributions, you can create a staff whose interconnectedness resembles a brilliantly colored kaleidoscope rather than a collection of shattered glass.

Team Building: Is the Whole Idea Culturally Biased?

When a colleague of ours was called to facilitate intergroup problem-solving between a U.S.-American group and a Latino group, the leader of the Latino group didn't want to participate. He saw team building as one more Western invention that he didn't want or need. Was he right? The answer to this question is both yes and no. His perception that team building is a culturally biased intervention is accurate in three significant ways:

1. **It is a linear, American intervention, designed to "fix" dysfunctional workgroups or teams.** It is reflective of the mainstream American culture's need to problem solve whatever ails it and, in so doing, make it better.

2. **The directness of the team-building method reflects the directness of U.S. mainstream culture.** If the issues are interpersonal, we design processes that enable staff members to articulate what they need from one another in order to smooth out relationship glitches. Then, in productive one-on-one negotiations, participants clarify their expectations and resolve their differences. Some other cultures communicate in more contextual and less direct ways. John C. Condon, in his book, *With Respect to the Japanese*, says that in Japan, "the shortest distance between two points is a curve."[1] People are expected to observe nonverbal cues or pay attention to facial expressions as a way to determine conflict in relationships. In most of the world, where harmony is a prime value, American team-building directness is difficult and counterproductive. In Asia, the Middle East, Mexico, or Central America, the traditional American team-building directness would cause discomfort.

3. **Team-building priorities differ.** Mainstream American business values both task accomplishment and satisfying relationships, but having good relationships is not viewed as an end in itself; they help grease the wheels of business. In most of the world, relationships have intrinsic merit: How people are treated is often more important than how, or even whether, the job gets done.

Beyond these examples of cultural bias in team building, symptoms of teamwork are culturally demonstrated. Trust, for example, is prized and valued worldwide. Team members in any workgroup would say that, for maximum productivity, they must be able to trust their co-workers, but how you demonstrate and build that trust is cultural. In mainstream America, trust is frequently expressed by looking someone in the eye. The opposite is true in Asia. Also, in U.S. culture, trust is built on someone's integrity and predictability. The thought goes something like this: If you are perceived to be honest or believable, and over time you validate that perception by coming through on your commitments, trust increases. However, in many cultures, to disappoint the boss is unthinkable. An employee who can't meet a deadline or complete a task would rather "lie" to protect you from hurt and disappointment than to speak the objective truth, which very well may be, "I didn't know how to do this job, and I was afraid to ask for directions, so I didn't get it done." In the United States, protecting someone from this unpleasant truth, especially in an era that talks about transparency, can erode trust but not necessarily so in other places.

In spite of these examples of American-style team building a part of the answer to the question "Is team building culturally biased?" is still no, in the sense that every culture wants workgroups to function productively, profitably, collaboratively, and harmoniously. The goal of developing productive work teams is universal, but it is the process of how to achieve this goal that has many cultural variations.

Team Building: When Is the Effort Justified?

There are many good reasons to engage in team building. The umbrella under which most reasons fall includes the belief that effective teams enable an organization to accomplish its goals and objectives in a timely and effective manner. The following five reasons are frequently cited as justifications for team building. As you read them, see if any seem appropriate for your group.

1. Form a New Team, Committee, or Task Force

Responsive, adaptive organizations frequently create groups or task forces for the purpose of accomplishing specific goals. These groups usually have a short "shelf life." Nevertheless, in order to function efficiently, members operate with an eye toward defining a clear purpose, creating group norms that foster productivity, establishing operating rules that get the job done, and building smooth working relationships so that work is conducted in a comfortable and creative environment. If a norm that values and uses heterogeneity for better results is not intentionally cultivated, differences can be irritating and pose obstacles, though cooperation is not necessarily a picnic on monocultural teams, either. Having different priorities can cause problems even with people who look and act alike. Cultural differences just complicate the issue. Look at the role of values, for example. Middle Eastern culture places extensive emphasis on hospitality and socializing before getting down to business. Reconciling this hospitality and socialization with the U.S. culture's strict time consciousness and get-down-to-business approach is a challenging task. The need to transact business and accomplish goals has to be balanced against various cross-cultural norms or else teams will be less productive, and their efforts could be sabotaged.

2. Improve the Functioning of the Existing Team

When dealing with permanent workgroups, team building can act as a self-cleaning oven, an important ongoing process that helps a group look at itself and how it operates. As a team increases its diversity, questions such as "What makes us effective and what gets in our way?" or "What norms and procedures do we need to change in order to be even more effective?" are timely and relevant. However, the way such questions are asked needs to take into account the backgrounds of employees. For example, in a group with Middle Easterners, you'll get better answers to your questions if you avoid using the first or second person pronoun in a group discussion of that nature. But you could say something to this effect: "Our workgroup does a lot of things well. It meets its production goals and improves its performance every month. But if we were to operate differently for the betterment of all, what changes would we need to make? How might these changes be brought about?" Focusing on the task as opposed to comments that are personal and potentially hurtful allows the groups to proceed without offense.

Another tool that can improve the functioning of a team is brainstorming. However, this takes some cross-cultural adaptation. In the case of Latinos, initiating discussions and being free to brainstorm is contradictory to what is expected from a loyal employee. It takes time and education to invite employees to offer their suggestions. You may increase a group's willingness to do so if you help its members understand that loyalty, a prime value in Latin culture, is partially defined by offering one's ideas. To improve the way your group functions, first look at and better understand its membership, then see what accommodations need to be made in both the process of how you build the team and also how you operate.

3. Develop a Strategic Plan

Effective teams plan carefully. In fact, strategic planning can be a very effective team-building tool, directly and indirectly. But long-term strategic thinking is something that U.S.-American business has not traditionally done very well; its planning has been more immediate and short-term. However, there is an increasing awareness that American business needs to look beyond the next quarter when it measures profitability. Think about your group. Is this a time for your cross-cultural team to define its values, mission, goals, and objectives? Should it spend time considering where it wants to be three or five years down the road? Given the pace of change, if that seems too far away, what does make sense? By defining some measurable goals in a particular time frame, your group is indirectly building its team as it plans.

4. Conduct Valuing Diversity Training and Skill Development Sessions

Training and skill development on a variety of topics are legitimate uses of team-building sessions. Having employees look at their reactions to change, or having them face their fears and prejudices, can be constructive. Some training may center on skills such as how managers conduct performance appraisals in culturally sensitive ways. Others may help solve intercultural conflict or design career paths that enable all employees to achieve career satisfaction, regardless of how comfortable or uncomfortable they feel being an advocate for themselves based on cultural orientation.

5. Solve Group Problems or Make Decisions

In U.S.-American organizations, one of the most frequent reasons for team building is to engage in and improve shoulder-to-shoulder problem-solving and increase productivity. Being in the trenches together can build strong bonds and take care of business at the same time. A workgroup can even use a problem-solving mechanism to deal with diversity-related issues such as what kind of language policy might work well on your team. The following are other sample questions that might be addressed: "How do we get a wider representation of people in the promotional pipeline?" "How do we keep them once we bring them on board?" "How do we create a diversity-friendly culture in our company or department?"

Though team building may not be directly cultivated through group problem-solving and decision-making, the process a team uses can enhance work-group cohesion. The facilitator/consultant needs to conduct this kind of team building in a way that is comfortable for people who differ from the dominant power structure. For example, employees from cultures where harmonious relationships are primary would be reluctant to engage in a direct, Western model of analyzing relationships, then prescribing solutions to make them better. Regardless of the intent, it would probably feel harsh and graceless. On the other hand, problem-solving related to a task can be a very relevant intervention; doing so would be appropriate and can indirectly shape and improve relationships. To see if your team is in need of a tune-up, use the *Team-Effectiveness Checklist.*

Directions for Scoring the Team-Effectiveness Checklist

Count your "yes" checks first, then your "no" checks. The more "yes" checks you have, the less your group needs team building. However, even if you have one or two "no" answers, the content embedded in the questions should raise some interesting issues for your group's consideration. Look at item number 2, for example. If you have a group of newly arrived immigrants, there is a good possibility that their cultural programming indicates a preference for a tight structure and clear hierarchy. They would probably feel most comfortable with preset expectations determined by the boss. Someone who answers "no" to that question because expectations were not collectively determined may still be a highly satisfied team member when you consider the cultural programming. Consider your own team's cultural variations as you apply these questions to your particular group.

It is one thing to determine there is a benefit to formal team building, but it is another thing to go about the task of conducting productive and constructive team-building sessions. Once you have determined that team building is necessary, it is important to consider the cultural lenses of team building.

ACTIVITY 8.1 | Team-Effectiveness Checklist

There are 15 questions, and all you need to do is respond by putting a check in the appropriate column.

Symptoms	Yes	No
1. Our team (or task force) has clearly defined objectives.		
2. Expectations of how we are going to operate have been collectively determined.		
3. An effective mechanism exists for dealing with interpersonal and/or intercultural conflict.		
4. Group trust builds in part because people come through on their commitments.		
5. Group members help each other out when needed.		
6. Team members can talk easily about joys and frustrations on the job, including team experiences on this team.		
7. There is usually an absence of competition between members of our team.		
8. Effective processes exist for solving both system and interpersonal problems.		
9. Cultural differences such as time consciousness are acknowledged and dealt with.		
10. Our mission statement has been discussed and jointly agreed upon.		
11. The values we preach are the values we practice.		
12. There is a strong belief in our mutual purpose and interdependence.		
13. Each person on the team is clear about everyone's job.		
14. Nonjudgmental is a word that accurately describes the attitude toward differences on this team.		
15. Official communication is more reliable than the grapevine.		

Suggestions for Using the
"Team-Effectiveness Checklist"

Objectives:

- Enable team members to assess their collective effectiveness
- Determine areas where the team needs strengthening.
- Gain awareness about what team members think the team does well, and also where it can improve

Intended Audience:

- Managers, for use with their own workgroups
- Internal and external training professionals or facilitators who conduct team-building sessions
- HR professionals who teach their managers how to team build
- Any workgroup that has a facilitator or rotating leadership

Processing the Activity:

- Distribute the questionnaire. Ask participants to focus on a specific team as they put a check in the appropriate column. This can be done virtually with enough lead time to let people fill out the assessment and send their responses back.
- Put people in pairs or small groups so they can discuss their responses. This can also be done as a group in a video conference.
- Identify "No" answers on which there is consensus.
- Discuss results and perceptions among the whole group.
- Make two lists on the easel and flip chart. One label is "Greatest Strengths," and the other is "Need to Improve." Get responses from the group about which items go where.
- Discuss where the biggest weaknesses lie and what you want to do about them.

Questions for Discussion:

- What are your/the team's greatest strengths? Areas ripe for improvement?
- What happens if we/you do nothing?
- If we/you decided to select one area for improvement right now, which one would have the largest impact on our performance?
- The next time you give feedback to diverse team members, how would you approach the conversation? How might you deliver the feedback in a different way?

Caveats, Considerations, and Variations:

- If you have many different cultures represented, some people who are less acculturated to the mainstream may have a hard time speaking up about the group's weaknesses.
- Put people in small groups with those they trust and with whom they feel comfortable. That will produce the most involvement and best data. If done virtually, collect these suggestions ahead of time and keep them anonymous.
- Respect people's reluctance. Work with them quietly and slowly to build trust. Over time, you will get more participation and openness.
- Get the cooperation of informal group leaders and you will increase chances of getting the data and participation you want.

Recognizing How Cultural Lenses Impact Teamwork

Cultural software influences how you and other people in your organization view team participation. The U.S.-American culture has traditionally focused on two areas in regard to team-building: task and relationship. Depending on what ills happen to plague a team, one of the two might be more important than the other at a given time. However, in cultures with higher relationship quotient, the interpersonal dimension takes priority over task accomplishment. This does not mean that completing the task is not important. It means that work will get done better and more efficiently if relationships are attended to in culturally appropriate ways. The cross-cultural lens on team building shows that nurtured relationships lead to accomplished tasks. In other words, taking care of people is the best way to take care of business—and that can be successfully accomplished with an understanding of how other cultural values impact team building.

1. Desire for Harmony

People who work in the U.S.-American business culture do not necessarily love conflict, but for the sake of getting the job done, they will participate in conflict resolution sessions, even if at times they have to be dragged to it kicking and screaming. For the almost 30 years that we have been conducting team-building sessions, we have seen people routinely reluctant to pinpoint differences due to a fear of discomfort or rejection, whether giving or receiving it. Conflict doesn't have to blow up or be difficult, but fear of it is common. We recently worked with a homogeneous group where several frightened people called us ahead of time to ask how volatile the sessions were going to be. Before our meeting, one person was suffering from insomnia, and one other person was experiencing irritability and anxiety. In fact, at the end of the second meeting with the group, when Lee asked, "What was the best thing that came out of the session?," one woman said, "I lived through it." Mainstream U.S. Americans don't relish having to deal with conflict, but solving problems from these differences is a higher priority than harmony.

Part of the difference in U.S.-American culture and much of today's immigrant workforce can be seen in what is called American pragmatism. There is the realization that limited resources balanced against different priorities and objectives will inevitably result in some level of conflict. U.S. business sees team-building sessions as a legitimate place to deal with these different priorities and perceptions, particularly as they relate to productivity. The pragmatic American doesn't necessarily expect harmony—it's a bonus when it occurs, but life isn't structured around creating it. However, in the Middle East, Asia, Central America, and Mexico, harmony is central. The value placed on smooth interpersonal relationships would make it very difficult and highly unlikely to surface conflicts and deal with them straightforwardly in a team-building session. Differences will get dealt with and problems will get solved through the informal network, which is powerful in maintaining harmony and dealing with conflict simultaneously. For example, the after-hours drinking for which Japan is so famous serves a legitimate business purpose: It is in these informal settings that many of the differences are dealt with and resolved. The same would be true, minus the drinking, in the Middle East.

2. A Sense of Place and Culture as They Influence Social Status Based on Family, Hierarchy or Connections

The gifted writer, Malcolm Gladwell, in his latest book *Outliers* exposes the myth, clearly illustrated through wonderful stories and examples, that achieving success in life is due to one's own talent and hard work.[2] Gladwell shoots holes in the theory that merit and personal competence are what count, not your bloodline. Many things count, and in Gladwell's view, family, where you are reared, and the culture of place matter in significant ways.

This concept of place, in particular the geography and culture of where you grow up, has relevance in team-building. In North America, Canada, and Western Europe, team building is designed to forge a collaborative, egalitarian work unit where bosses and employees roll up their sleeves, pitch in, and collectively get the job done. Bosses are commonly greeted on a first-name basis, which contributes to the perception that "we are in this together and little separates us." This is not so in most of the world, nor is it desired. The extreme version of social hierarchy is the caste system in India. But in Middle Eastern, Latino, and Asian culture, egalitarianism is neither valued nor desired. In addition to the culture of place, a person's identity comes from his or her social status and family background, and often part of the social status automatically means less equal. The view of the social order can bring itself to the workplace and have a dramatic impact on team functioning and complicate the dynamics on a group that a manager or consultant is trying to strengthen and unify.

In addition to family and social status, other cultures also place a premium on age and seniority; there is deference to the elder worker and those on the job the longest. This presents another interesting wrinkle in the team-building challenge: Issues of age, gender, and seniority all impact expectations of team members who have been acculturated differently. For example, a manager who recognizes that men from some cultures are not used to working with women, or who learns that most employees are used to having bosses determine the rules, may be hard pressed to get staff members to embrace egalitarian team building. We have worked with a firm where men from Indonesia refused to work for a Latina because reporting to a woman was too degrading. (This example is not an isolated case.) What's needed in situations like this are clear boundaries and expectations. While you want to be sensitive to different upbringings and norms, there are also places where you won't bend because it will create team norms that you can't support and don't want to reinforce.

3. Emphasis on the Group

Validating the importance of the group can create a values overlap that will enable you to speak the figurative language of your diverse team members. In fact, if some people are reluctant to go through a team-building process, one of the best ways to minimize resistance is to position it as a chance to foster good relationships and build trust.

According to our colleague, Dr. Jorge Cherbosque, affiliation is a key norm that relates to the concept of inclusion/exclusion.[3] In some cultures, it is an offensive act to exclude a member. When planning a team-building strategy, a typical U.S.-American response might be to include only those directly involved. However, in other cultures, those excluded might be deeply offended. Think carefully about who belongs in the team-building sessions so that you don't create more problems than you solve, then be able to explain the rationale.

4. Fatalism and External Locus of Control

Team-building sessions designed to solve problems will be impacted by cultural views such as self-determination. It is a common belief system in the United States that our fate is in our control and rests on our own actions. That internal locus of control reinforces individual responsibility for making things happen. The economic slowdown that started in 2008 is currently challenging this view but it is long-held and will die hard; even as we listen to people talk about the wallop the recession is having on them, there is no sense that this basic worldview has been compromised. That take-charge belief lived out each day leads to people identifying and solving a particular problem with the help of a tried-and-true analytical technique or decision matrix: Find the problem and fix it ... that's what you do. In cultures that have an external locus of control, in which predestination or fate is a strong belief, problem-solving may be inhibited. "God's will" may be invoked and can influence a person's willingness or desire to invest in problem-solving. It is assumed that some issues are out of the domain of mortal human beings, no matter how sophisticated the problem-solving systems. What impact does this have on your team building? A manager may determine that a person or a group of people is being difficult, resisting and sabotaging group efforts, when the person or group really is being responsive to cultural upbringing and belief. To understand how culture has influenced your own behavior as a team member, respond to the continuum *Understanding How Cultural Lenses Impact Teamsmanship.*

ACTIVITY 8.2 | Understanding How Cultural Lenses Impact Teamsmanship

---

In order to understand how culture shapes these four values, and the impact of these value differences on the effectiveness of your team, look at the following continua. For each, mark an X at the point that appropriately expresses your values as seen by how you behave. Once you have marked all four, connect the Xs to get a values profile.

1. ....

    Value on harmony   Value on surfacing and resolving differences

---

2. ....

    Status based on family or connections   Status based on merit or achievement

---

3. ....

    Emphasis on the group   Emphasis on the individual

---

4. ....

    External locus of control   Internal locus of control

Suggestions for Using
"Understanding How Cultural Lenses Impact Teamwork"

Objectives:

- Illustrate the impact that culture has on values
- Show, graphically, how culture and values impact team dynamics and behavior on a regular basis
- Gain awareness about cultural similarities and differences between self and team members in four key areas that influence team performance

Intended Audience:

- A diverse work team, HR professional
- Managers or facilitators of diverse teams
- Internal/external consultant or trainer

Processing the Activity:

- Distribute learning activity and a different color of marker or pen for each participant.
- Discuss four cultural values and the opposite ends of the continuum regarding each. Next, ask participants to put an X at the spot that most accurately reflects their values.
- Tell participants to draw a values profile by connecting dots. Put their name on the paper and, with masking tape, put their profile on the wall.
- Ask participants to get up, walk around the room, and see the different profiles. When finished, they come back to their seats. In different locations, have a spokesperson speak at each site.

Questions for Discussion:

- What surprised you, or what did you notice about yourself when marking your own responses?
- When you walked around and saw other team members' profiles, what struck you?
- What areas have the greatest similarity?
- Where are the most differences?
- What can this team do to minimize the conflict from differences?
- How can we make the differences work for us? Make us stronger?

Caveats, Considerations, and Variations:

- If you have some people who seem reticent, process the discussion in small groups first.

All of these differences in values can be worked with. If you are doing this as a manager with your own team, help staff members understand where you're flexible and where you're not. Explain why the values that relate to team cohesion are important to you, while at the same time you extend that same understanding to others. The most important realization for you is that different cultural upbringing will create a different team building reality and perception. Once you interpret behaviors through cross-cultural lenses, you will be less defensive, more understanding, and more open. You can also help all staff members (the old-timers as well as the newcomers) increase their openness. The most effective team building is a hybrid of East and West, old and new, task and relationship.

The Need for Esteem and Belonging: Ways To Build Common Ground

Sondra Thiederman, in her book *Bridging Cultural Barriers for Corporate Success*, mentions Abraham Maslow and the fact that his needs hierarchy crosses cultures.[4] All human beings, regardless of culture, need esteem and belonging. Those two needs are the dominant shapers of functional team behavior. For the manager or the facilitator, the skill comes in realizing that the way esteem and belonging needs are met may vary, depending on the culture. But treating people with dignity and respect never goes out of style and transcends national boundaries.

Lee had this reaffirmed years ago when she visited Professor Joel Kotkin's M.B.A. class at Pepperdine University in Culver City, California. Prof. Kotkin thought Lee might like to talk to his students about their thoughts on what constitutes effective management in a cross-cultural environment. There was not a single student among the eight who was native born. They came from England, Turkey, Japan, Taiwan, and Korea, and all said they plan to return to their respective countries once they have earned their degrees. Some of the questions we wanted answers to were:

- How do you want to be managed? What would your ideal boss be like?
- Describe the team or work environment that gets the best from you.
- How are problems solved, conflicts resolved, or feedback given in your culture? How would you suggest managers conduct these practices effectively in a cross-cultural setting?
- What is the most important piece of advice you would give to a manager trying to manage a diverse workforce today?

The theme that came up repeatedly was the need to be treated with dignity and respect. The students talked about having a strong need for self-confidence and a feeling of competence. They said they believe a boss can help build and reinforce esteem by letting employees know what they're doing well. All the students agreed that they could even handle negative feedback without feeling a loss-of-face if a boss told them what they did well before he or she told them where they needed to improve. This classroom discussion reaffirmed our view that people are much more alike than different. The need for validation and connection provides ample common ground. There are several aspects central to team building that impact esteem and belonging needs. As you read, think about how these issues are, or might be, dealt with on your team. Then turn to Activity 8.3, *Increasing Esteem and Belonging on Your Team* on page 169, as a catalyst for your action plan.

1. Identify and Build on Shared Values

For any group to function well as a team, there must be a commonly shared set of assumptions, expectations, and priorities that arise out of organizational values. Some examples might be (1) We at hospital X offer the highest quality of health care; (2) At store Y, the customer is always right and every effort at customer satisfaction is warranted; (3) In our company, we do whatever it takes to stand behind our product; and (4) In this organization, every human being is entitled to equal dignity and respect, no matter what the job. The values behind these four statements are a commitment to excellence in quality and delivery of services, product accountability, and the intrinsic worth and value of each human being. These values are supported, at least in theory, by most cultures with whom we come in contact. Agreement on their merit is a starting point in building common ground, and operationalizing these values would increase the feelings of worth and belonging of employees. We bet it would also lead to better performance and results in good times and tough ones.

2. Get Commitment to the Group's Goals and Objectives

While values may define a workgroup, the concrete goals and objectives are its life's blood and vitality. Meaningful goals help create a sense of belonging because employees feel connected by participating in a worthwhile venture. Each job needs to be valued for its unique contribution, and those who do the work need to decide how it can best be accomplished. Employees who clean tables and empty trash will know far better what systems glitches might impede cleanliness than a CEO who is far removed from the task. Creating an environment where employees want to offer suggestions is one factor that separates high-performing organizations and teams from those that muddle along. "Throw your two cents in" at meetings is expected in the U.S. business culture. However, there are many cultures where this is not so, particularly if giving input could be construed as diminishing an authority figure who, by virtue of position, is considered to have the answers. Getting information from employees informally or one-on-one is an acceptable way to get feedback, refine goals, and ultimately, develop a more productive team. If you seek this information from your team members in a way that's comfortable for them, you will get not only the feedback you want but commitment, as well. And here is a bonus: The process of getting commitment to team goals builds esteem and belonging in the process.

3. Reward Excellence

It is always smart, humane, and worthwhile to reward excellence, but it only feels like a reward if someone is acknowledged in a way that he or she values. In some cases, calling attention to people through awards, announcements, and pictures on bulletin boards works, but it can also embarrass and intimidate. In some cultures, or for some personalities, this kind of attention would be an embarrassment or an affront. Being singled out can make employees feel validated and appreciated, but it can also make them feel awkward and uncomfortable. It is important to acknowledge excellence as a way to reinforce and strive for continuing high performance. However, a manager that really knows his team can do so in a way that is appropriate both individually and culturally.

Our friend and colleague Dr. Cherbosque relayed two relevant and real examples. To the question "When is a reward not a reward?" Jorge's answer is, "When an employee who thrives on contact with others is rewarded by being given an office of his own that isolates him from his colleagues, no matter how good the intentions, his 'reward' will turn to ashes and the result will be decreased motivation." Cherbosque's second example was interesting because it involved using money as a motivator in an industry that was having financial difficulty. Management's desire to show employees appropriate gratitude resulted in a 20 cents per hour raise for first -line workers. Some employees were insulted by the modest increase, and management was outraged by what they viewed as a lack of appreciation for their effort in this largely symbolic gesture. What to make of this example as it relates to your organization? Just this: One of the most significant team-building rewards is getting people involved in the conversation and process of what constitutes a reward. Management's good intentions were not enough in the last example. Focus on your company and think about some ways you can show your team members appreciation, starting with having a conversation about what seems like a reward, and for certain, what does not.

Maybe a very quiet "thank you," or a simple nod of the head and a smile when looking at a report or a product, would be a valued reward for some employees. Use this private moment to ask the employee if he or she would object to a public acknowledgment. Abraham Maslow undoubtedly would advise you to reward the performance to build esteem and belonging; we suggest rewarding it in a way that validates and enhances the individual.

4. Demonstrate an Appreciation for Each Person and Each Culture's Uniqueness

Paying lip service to valuing differences is easy—the hard part is making it come alive in the workgroup. We saw this with one of our clients last Christmas. Because the United States is a predominantly Christian country, it never dawned on one group we worked with that non-Christians such as Muslims, Buddhists, and Jews wouldn't necessarily want to partake in Christmas festivities at work. Poinsettia plants and Christmas decorations found their way to all cubicles. Through a series of casual conversations, it became clear that not only do all people not celebrate Christmas, but awkwardness or unnecessary discomfort results when the assumption is made that they do. As with so many of our examples, there is almost never an intention to hurt or minimize people, and it seems that knowing people well enough to realize and appreciate the differences goes a long way. That can lead to rich conversations about good ways to acknowledge all people's unique backgrounds. Respect for these differences builds good will and extends cooperation. More important for long-term team effectiveness, acknowledging and making room for differences can, paradoxically, create a deep sense of unity and belonging.

5. Acknowledge Cultural Conflicts

Conflict is normal and natural in any workgroup, but seldom do we stop to realize that, on a diverse team, conflict can often be the result of cultural differences rather than personal ones. One executive team we worked with was primarily white, but there were a few people of color. An African-American woman who had previously worked at a very large organization had a hard time acculturating to a different industry and transplanting herself from the big city to a smaller suburban area. Furthermore, her style of dealing with conflict was very different from her co-workers. As an African-American woman who had faced numerous obstacles in life, she had been reared to stand up for herself so she would not be taken advantage of. Her style of management on this executive team of 12 was abrasive by the others' perceptions. Her own staff loved her, but her colleagues questioned her willingness to be a team player.

There were many dynamics operating, but none of these differences were dealt with openly because everyone denied that race or culture had anything to do with the differences. Unfortunately, we'll never know if this team could have become cohesive if the conflicts been openly dealt with. The sad part, and the end result, is that the woman and five other vice presidents left the organization by choice; no one could stand the stress and underlying conflict. Avoiding a critical conversation that acknowledges the importance that culture has on shaping all of us can lead to conflict that builds neither esteem nor belonging.

6. Learn To Read the Group Accurately by Becoming More Culturally Sensitive

It is human nature to ascribe meaning to actions. The difficulty in doing this in a culturally diverse group, or any workgroup for that matter, is that you may be wrong and reach harmful conclusions. Workgroups can accommodate differences, but not until we know what the differences are and understand them. A manager from abroad may think Americans are loud and aggressive. On the other hand, we may define speaking up as being industrious and a sign of being a real go-getter. The natural inclination is to use one's own culture as the yardstick by which all other actions are judged or esteemed. But the probable inaccuracy of the messages and stereotypes that result is almost always harmful and destructive. Learn the cultural norms of others, and team-build at the same time by pairing people from different backgrounds so they can help one another. Buddy systems can simultaneously build relationships and increase cultural sensitivity and knowledge.

7. Engage in "Activity Team Building"

The essence of activity team building is doing something together and being active in a nonwork environment. By definition, it means that a workgroup, in either a recreational setting or an atypical environment, finds ways to interact that build a sense of belonging. Recreational functions include company picnics, bowling leagues, or sporting and cultural events. Some organizations even form soccer or basketball teams. The emphasis in recreational team building is fostering harmonious relationships through just plain fun. Work may be your initial connection, but in this circumstance it is not the emphasis.

There is another kind of activity team-building where the activity is one part of a process of consciously applying the learning from simulations or experiences to work back at the office. An example of this is the ropes course, famous for building trust, developing leadership skills, and enhancing risk-taking and cohesion amid natural surroundings. The intent is that participants have a good time in a beautiful environment. But the higher priority is that, in a surrounding far from the ritual and familiarity of the office, team members get to know one another in a different light. This course, while very safe, tests people in untraditional ways. Physical strength and skill are on the line, as is psychological mettle. The intent is that depending on one another in the natural wilds should transfer to counting on one another in the organizational wilds. Maria Rubly, vice president at Baxter, told us of her organization's trip for top execs. They went to Alaska to fish together and to get to know one another in a different setting. When we talked, she had just returned from the experience, so it's hard to calculate long-term effects, but it is clear that the experience was meaningful and provocative. It enabled her to build esteem because she overcame some of her own barriers, and it increased belonging because she enhanced her relationships with her co-workers.

There is one more suggestion to consider in activity team-building that combines the structured with the informal. We use it with some of our clients as a finale in team-building sessions. The group is asked by a facilitator or manager to answer a few critical questions, such as, "Who are you as a team? What do you stand for? What are your purposes and goals?" Then their task is to create, with Tinkertoys, Legos, or some building blocks, a structure that best represents their team. It is not only fun for them but also instructive. They get so involved in the process that they pay no attention to their team dynamics, but we function as observers who give them feedback about the roles everyone played in accomplishing the task. Inevitably, this example of activity team building, along with others previously mentioned, invokes group pride and a strong sense of cohesion. It also crosses cultural barriers. Activity team building may mean that there are some learning methods and bonding tools that are more effective and pertinent in some cultures than in others. The idea is to find the most culturally appropriate vehicle. We know that regarding sports worldwide, soccer is king. What else creates energy and engagement? Find out what would be most effective with your employee population.

8. Acknowledge Cultural Differences and Use Them to Your Advantage

A team-building session may be designed to educate employees about cultural differences. The *Cross-Cultural Team-Building Scale*, in Activity 8.4, which measures sameness and difference, can be helpful in this process. Before you use that tool with your team, first talk about and apply the eight suggestions that are part of *Increasing Esteem and Belonging on Your Team*. Working on this tool before the *Cross-Cultural Team-Building Scale* will lead to more openness and honesty so that the team-building scale conversation is richer and more useful.

Beyond cross-cultural knowledge, one important definition of being a good facilitator comes from the feelings of validation, safety, inclusion, and respect people at your team meetings experience. To see how you can enhance esteem and belonging on your team, look at the eight behaviors you just read about, and engage them in a conversation about what you are already doing that works, and where you also need to set some goals to improve.

ACTIVITY 8.3 | Increasing Esteem and Belonging on Your Team

Directions: In the space below, write down your suggestions for increasing esteem and belonging of all team members. You are undoubtedly doing some things already, but think of what you can do better, individually and collectively, to impact the whole.

Behaviors that Show Esteem and Belonging	Suggestions for How To Do It
1. Identify and build on shared values.	
2. Get commitment to the group's goals and objectives.	
3. Reward excellence.	
4. Demonstrate an appreciation for each person and each culture's uniqueness.	
5. Acknowledge cultural conflicts.	
6. Become more culturally sensitive.	
7. Engage in activity team building.	
8. Acknowledge cultural differences.	

Suggestions for Using
"Increasing Esteem and Belonging on Your Team"

Objectives:

- Explore ways to have all team members feel more valued and included
- Gain commitment of all team members toward this goal
- Create realization that all team members are responsible for the climate or atmosphere on a team

Intended Audience:

- Members of a diverse work team
- Manager, facilitators, internal/external consultants, HR professionals, or trainers charged with the task of creating a more cohesive, high-performing team

Processing the Activity:

- The manager, facilitator, or trainer discusses the importance of members' getting esteem and belonging needs met in order to have a highly productive unit.
- Discuss each of the eight items on the worksheet and what they contribute to increased esteem and belonging needs, and their collective impact on performance.
- Next, divide the team into small groups of approximately four to seven participants in each, depending on the number of people.
- Give groups the task of coming up with suggestions for each of the eight areas. How many each group is responsible for depends on the number of groups you have.
- Each group will write their ideas on chart paper so the suggestions can eventually be typed up and distributed.
- After brainstorming, each group will report their suggestions to the whole group, which will provide an opportunity to add suggestions, answer questions, or modify any comments.

Questions for Discussion:

- Where can we pat ourselves on the back for already creating a healthy climate and helping employees meet their esteem and belonging needs?
- Were some of the eight items harder to come up with suggestions for than others? If so, which ones? What made these items more difficult?
- How do we (you) hold one another accountable so these suggestions become our norm?
- Which ones might make the most and best difference in our (your) functioning?
- What is the one thing I (you/each of us) will begin doing tomorrow to make this happen?

Caveats, Considerations, and Variations:

- The questions need to be asked with a *we* pronoun if the manager is working with his or her own team. The *you* pronoun is appropriate for an outsider working with the group.

- Depending on the size of the group, you can have people self-select groups. For example, any group size of 24 or more would enable you to put chart paper and markers at eight stations around the room, each labeled with one of the eight areas. You can tell people to select the area they want to work on, but also tell them the number of people at each station so that each of the eight stations is covered.

- The report from each group at the end and the subsequent discussion is time-consuming, so set clear parameters and give precise directions.

ACTIVITY 8.4 | Cross-Cultural Team-Building Scale

Directions: All human beings have values preferences that significantly impact workgroup cohesion. To see your values profile, mark an X along the continuum for each item and then connect the Xs. The benefit of this exercise to your team is that you will see, graphically, where the similarities and differences are. From there, the next step is to discuss how you make your individual differences a collective advantage.

Value Change . . . . Value Tradition

Direct, specific . . . . Indirect,
communicator   less specific
                                                                                             communicator

Analytical, linear . . . . Intuitive, lateral
problem-solving   problem-solving

Emphasis . . . . , ... Emphasis on group
on individual   performance
performance

Communication . . . . Communication
primarily verbal   primarily nonverbal

Emphasis on task . . . . Emphasis on
and product   relationship and
                                                                                             process

Preference for . . . . Focus is on
openly surfacing   harmony
differences

Preference for . . . . Preference
horizontal   for vertical
organization   organization

Likes informal tone . . . . Likes formal tone

Driven by . . . . Driven by
competition   collaboration

Strict adherence . . . . Flexible adherence
to time   to time

Suggestions for Using the
"Cross-Cultural Team-Building Scale"

Objectives:
- Understand how different values impact workgroup cohesion
- Identify cultural differences that influence team functioning

Intended Audience:
- Members of any functional work team, either on-site or virtual
- Any manager, facilitator, internal/external consultant, HR professional, or trainer charged with the task of creating a cohesive team
- Managers of diverse teams

Processing the Activity:
- Discuss and define each of the items on the continuum.
- Ask team members to mark an X where they see their own values, then connect the dots to see the values profile.
- Divide members into small groups. Ask them to compare their individual profiles.
- You can also reproduce the training tool itself as an 18" x 24" enlargement. Reproduce enough so that there are no more than six people at every station and with different color markers. Have each person plot his or her profile on the enlargement. When all are on the chart, talk about what team gains and losses and what gaps have to be covered. This can be done simultaneously at different locations and lead to very fruitful conversations.
- Come back to the whole group for discussion.

Questions for Discussion:
- What values similarities and differences were most notable among group members?
- What surprises, if any, did you find in the responses of any of your team members?
- When you look more closely at the values differences, what impact do they or might they have on the team?
- How can we make those differences work in the team's favor?

Caveats, Considerations, and Variations:
- Refer back to the worksheet in this chapter called *Understanding How Cultural Lenses Impact Teamsmanship*. The suggestions for processing that activity may be appropriate for the *Cross-Cultural Team-Building Scale* as well.
- After people fill out the scale, compare the various profiles and talk about the implications of the differences. Ask the group for their suggestions on how to use this information productively while honoring the existing ground rules and cultural norms. Depending on the size of the team, you might break people into small groups, getting a good cross-cultural mix in each. But asking the group to come up with some suggestions for how to get maximum input, involvement, harmony, and support while respecting values differences will be helpful and enlightening. The responses will give you pertinent information, while the process will help you create a team where esteem and belonging needs are met.

We are suggesting a number of potentially beneficial tools that can foster good conversation either face-to-face or virtually, but however the discussions are led, the facilitator and participants will have far better results if facilitation skills are consciously developed and polished. To see how effective you stack up as a facilitator, start with the facilitator assessment in Activity 8.5 and then spend some time also perusing Table 8.1, *Impact of Cultural Norms on Meetings with Your Team.* The facilitator assessment and the knowledge presented on the chart about norms at your meetings will give you a lot of help in creating an open climate and also in understanding behavior across a wide array of differences.

Facilitating team meetings or workgroup sessions results in more effective outcomes and the process is easier when you do have an understanding of cross-cultural norms. Table 8.1 has pertinent information for managers, team leaders, and consultants (whether internal or external). It can also help virtual or global team members understand one another better. The usefulness of this chart is that it gives you not only the norms, but also the impact of those norms on meetings and what you can do about them. It is a descriptive and prescriptive chart designed to have practical benefits.

ACTIVITY 8.5 | How Effective a Facilitator Are You?

Directions: Rate yourself from 1 to 5 on the following facilitator skills. The closer you are to a 5, the more skilled you are at facilitation.

Facilitator Behavior	1	2	3	4	5
1. Remains neutral.					
2. Does not judge or contribute ideas.					
3. Keeps the group focused on a common task.					
4. Asks clarifying, helpful questions that suggest alternatives.					
5. Creates a climate free of attack or criticism.					
6. Encourages and structures participation.					
7. Helps the group find win/win solutions.					

Suggestions for Using
"How Effective a Facilitator Are You?"

Objectives:

- Evaluate facilitation skills
- Determine areas for growth

Intended Audience:

- Managers facilitating meetings of diverse teams
- HR professionals, facilitators, consultants, and trainers with diverse groups who lead meetings, problem-solving sessions, or workshops where their neutrality is essential

Processing the Activity:

- Distribute the questionnaire and ask participants to focus on a meeting or seminar they recently led.
- With that session in mind, ask participants to rate themselves on a 1 to 5 scale, 5 being best.
- Have participants then pair up (or use small groups) and discuss their evaluations.
- Ask them to focus on what this questionnaire suggests their facilitation strengths and weaknesses are and what they need to do differently.

Questions for Discussion:

- How did you feel while you were filling this out?
- Would your answers change depending on the group you are facilitating? If so, what does this information suggest?
- What good news did you discover about your facilitation skills?
- What do you think those who attend your workshops and meetings would say about your skills?
- What do the data suggest you need to do differently in order to improve your skills?
- What suggestions can you give one another (in pairs or small groups) that will be helpful to you?

Caveats, Considerations, and Variations:

- Small groups increase feelings of safety and security when people can freely discuss their insights and then get feedback.
- Putting two sets of pairs together for the last discussion questions may increase the number of ideas offered.

TABLE 8.1 | The Impact of Cultural Norms on Meetings with Your Team

Cultural Norms	Impact on Meetings	What To Do
Respect for authority	This norm leads to an unwillingness to challenge ideas from those who are older or in a position of authority; inhibit solutions to problem-solving and can lead to a more formal climate.	State expectations emphasizing the need for participation because it will benefit the company. Loyalty is also a norm that you can use here. Show respect to the group's informal leader because of age, knowledge, title, and overall influence. Solicit this person's help and give leaders the same esteem groups do.
Emphasis on group over individual	This may lead some managers to assume people are unmotivated or lazy because they keep pace with the team rather than seek individual glory or promotion.	The group is your best cultural ally. Use it! Stress teamwork, harmony, and collaboration. Structure group tasks and focus on group accomplishment.
Fear of shame and loss-of-face	Because people are afraid to lose face or make mistakes, there might be less willingness to take risks or share unconventional ideas.	Talk about the importance of taking intelligent risks and reinforce this even when the group makes mistakes. Avoid finger pointing or blaming. Make the group motto be "We're all in this together." Encourage their risk-taking and reward their efforts.
More contextual, less direct communication	It is harder in less direct cultures to figure out what is really on someone's mind. This can result in miscommunication, both in and out of meetings.	Develop a good, trusting relationship over time. It will take time to understand the subtle nuance as well as to get people to open up. You may never get straight talk the way Americans give it. But you can pay attention to the subtle nonverbal cues. With trust and a good relationship, you'll develop understanding over time.
Value placed on harmony and collaboration	This norm can work to your advantage in having people create a positive working environment. The downside may be an unwillingness to discuss painful truths for the sake of harmony, even though it may be necessary.	Use the question-asking skills presented in the chapter on interviewing. In sensitive ways and an unthreatening tone, seek information that may be necessary, and do so through the informal system. Remember to use the group; that provides safety and minimizes the sting.

TABLE 8.1 | The Impact of Cultural Norms on Meetings with Your Team

Cultural Norms	Impact on Meetings	What To Do
Family as the first priority	There are times when people, particularly from Mexico and Central America, may need to leave to take care of family priorities. They may miss meetings, and more important, the assignments that result from them. Deadlines may not be met.	Work with people to find the middle ground. No one wants to be insensitive in times of family emergency. There are always tradeoffs. Explain them. The group may pick up a person's slack for a short time. If a pattern develops that permanently inhibits workflow, some choices will have to be made.
Time consciousness: some cultures hold tighter timelines than the dominant culture, and some cultures hold looser timelines.	The rules need to be the same for everyone or there will be disgruntlement. Be careful not to interpret some flexibility regarding time as indications of laziness or lack of caring.	Make clear what the meeting norms and expectations are. Once you decide how strict or loose you are going to be regarding timelines, reinforce your "rules." Position being on time as showing respect to other members of the group.
Problem-solving that is less linear and analytical	You sometimes may feel like you aren't getting anywhere, because again, U.S.-American directness likes to go straight for the solution. But lateral, intuitive thinking adds its own unique contribution to the process.	Learn to value and use different ways of thinking. This difference is truly one of the biggest gifts from diversity. Don't immediately discount nonlinear methods.
Goal setting and planning influenced by fatalism	The external locus of control mentality mentioned earlier may create the appearance in some cultures that people are less driven or motivated. Again, it's probably cultural. Belief in God's will is a powerful shaper for some.	Help your workgroup experience the direct connection between the responsibility they accept and the results they get. This will be a whole new way of viewing the world for those whose life experience has not shown them that they have much influence over their own world. Patience, respect, and positive reinforcement will help.

Ten Dimensions of Cross-Cultural Team Building

Building a cohesive work unit among people of diverse backgrounds is an exciting challenge and opportunity. We suggest using the following criteria to help in measuring your team's progress. As you read about each of these factors, conduct your own mental audit to see how your group stacks up so far, then check out the accuracy of your perceptions by having the team rate itself as well.

1. A Clearly Articulated Mission

In any effective and profitable company or group, the *raison d'etre* is clear. Why employees show up for work involves more than a paycheck. Especially in a recessionary economy, economic health for the company also means being able to provide jobs so people can live, eat, take care of families and contribute to their communities. Beyond economic well being for individuals and community, the job itself should be meaningful as well. For example, we can imagine that the mission of the Walt Disney Corporation involves bringing entertainment and joy to people's lives, whereas the mission of most hospitals is to save lives while providing quality care and service. Both of those purposes are meaningful, and employees involved in either venture could legitimately feel that they contribute to improving the lives of others in some way. Having a clear mission is just as important for teams as for organizations. It is critical for diverse teams to do so. It is your compass.

2. A Realization That Team Members Are Functionally Interdependent

Team building in any culture is irrelevant if group members are not tied together by the functions they perform. We interviewed a "team" of scientists who are doing research on independent projects. It is clear they are a team in name only: They do not need data, information, or much of anything else from one another in order to get their respective jobs done. However, imagine the astronauts on any shuttle mission trying to go it alone. Their success and effectiveness are contingent on coordination between astronauts and mission control in Houston, Texas, as well as close coordination and cooperation with one another in the space capsule. They could not conduct their experiments or successfully complete their missions if they operated alone. Before you invest any time in team building, regardless of cultural differences, determine whether or not you are functionally interdependent.

3. Well-Defined Roles and Responsibilities

Another critical aspect of creating a hyper-performing work team involves having a clear sense of who does what. This area of team building requires delineating each person's role on the team and what his or her responsibilities are. The following *Goal and Role Clarification* tool, which combines questions on mission statement, functional interdependence, and roles and responsibilities, can help achieve this clarity. Remember though, that when working with new immigrant staff, predefined roles might work best, at least in the beginning, because that seems most comfortable for some staff members.

ACTIVITY 8.6 | Goal and Role Clarification

A team's mission determines its goals and direction. A team's reason for being is an essential step in developing team unity and is effective to the degree that the mission is both clear and agreed on. As a beginning step in goal clarification, define your team's mission as you perceive it.

Goal Clarification

My team's mission is: _____

_____

_____

_____

What goals logically follow from this mission? _____

_____

_____

_____

_____

Role Clarification

To implement these goals, my role/responsibilities are: _____

_____

_____

_____

Other member's roles and responsibilities are: _____

_____

_____

_____

Name Role

To carry out my responsibility, I need to get from and give to you:

Name	Need To Get	Need To Give

Suggestions for Using
"Goal and Role Clarification"

Objectives:

- Articulate and define the team's mission
- Determine what goals follow from this mission
- Clarify roles and responsibilities in order to accomplish these goals

Intended Audience:

- Members of any functional work team or task force
- Any manager, facilitator, internal or external consultant, HR professional, or trainer who is helping the team define its purpose and clarify who does what

Processing the Activity:

- Ask each team member to fill out the mission statement first. This process can be done easily on virtual and global teams. Remind people that the mission is overarching and general, not a specific objective. For example, the mission of a diversity council might be to build a culture of inclusion.
- Record each team member's statement on an easel in front of the group.
- Look for points of agreement and build on those. Reword till all agree with the statement.
- Next, ask each person to list the top three goals that logically follow from that mission statement.
- Go around the group and again, on an easel, list all suggestions. Indicate repeated suggestions with checks in a different color marker from that with which you are writing.
- Discuss all suggestions and decide on the top three.
- Based on that outcome, have each person write down his or her responsibilities and those of other team members as the person sees them.
- Then, in rotating one-on-one rounds that last about 15 minutes each, have people negotiate their roles and expectations with one another.

Questions for Discussion:

- Are there any semantic or language issues that are getting in the way of defining our mission? If so, how can we say things so all people support the statement?
- Of all the goals listed, which will help us get closest to accomplishing our mission?
- Is there any role or responsibility that is still not clear after negotiations?

Caveats, Considerations, and Variations:

- This is a lengthy process. Rarely do groups have the luxury to do it all at once. But you can break it up into parts that break naturally. The mission statement definition may take one or two sessions: Defining goals can take one, and defining roles and responsibilities another. If you do this at a team-building retreat rather than on work time, it can be done in one session.

4. Formal and Informal Mechanisms for Giving and Soliciting Feedback

In mainstream business culture, a formal team-building setting is seen as a great opportunity to get and give feedback. Do you want to know how people view working on this particular team? Are you curious about what is going well and what isn't from each team member's perspective? What obstacles inhibit staff from getting their jobs done in a timely and effective manner? Would you like to know how employees see the ideal work environment? Just ask. The norms in these sessions favor U.S.-American directness. Again, the more acculturated the employees, the more comfortable they will feel in giving and getting feedback directly. Try the following technique, using the *Team-Building Response Sheet*, as a way to build trust and get feedback at the same time. Use small groups to provide safety for team members less comfortable with this directness. When discussing operational issues, if you are offering individual suggestions regarding performance, one-on-ones are best.

ACTIVITY 8.7 | Team-Building Response Sheet: A Tool To Increase Cohesion Through Feedback

This series of open-ended statements is intended to help you discover and clarify your reactions, opinions, and thoughts about your job and organization. It can be used equally well with teams that are virtual or in person. You will have a chance to share and learn from other group members' responses. Directions are as follows: (1) Take turns initiating the discussion; (2) responses can be written out first or done orally with no writing (use whatever works best for your group); and (3) respond to statements in any order you choose. If you are dispersed, you can use Skype, or have people e-mail responses to a person who records comments for a future conversation with the whole group, or to one person for a future one-on-one conversation.

1. Basically, my job is…

2. Usually, I am the kind of person who…

3. When things aren't going well, I…

4. When I'm confused or not sure what to do, I…

5. On the job, I'm best at…

6. One place where I could use some improvement is…

7. The best boss I ever had…

8. The strength of this group lies in…

9. One thing this group could do differently to feel more connected as a team is…

10. A workgroup is positive and constructive for me when…

11. I am most involved and excited about my job when…

12. When I am approaching a deadline, I…

13. As a member of a team, I…

14. I prefer to work with people who…

15. I can help my team by…

Suggestions for Using the
"Team-Building Response Sheet"

Objectives:

- Clarify and discover each team member's reactions, opinions, and thoughts about the team, job, and organization
- Learn more about other team members' reactions, opinions, and thoughts
- Build trust and openness on the team
- On virtual or dispersed teams, build a sense of connection that is hard to achieve in the absence of face-to-face contact

Intended Audience:

- Members of any functional work team
- Any facilitator, manager, consultant, or HR professional leading a team through trust-building or feedback activities

Processing the Activity:

- State purpose of activity. In-person groups do not have to write answers down; they can simply discuss responses orally. That would also work for Skype or video or teleconference, but they also can be e-mailed.
- Structure will change depending upon proximity, but have people discuss responses.
- Discuss some responses in the whole group afterward.

Questions for Discussion:

- What information or responses were the most surprising or interesting to you?
- Which were easiest for you to answer? Which were most difficult?
- What's the biggest insight or learning you got about yourself? Your team members?
- For virtual team members, which information here is not helpful?
- What should we do with this learning?

(continued on next page)

Suggestions for Using the
"Team-Building Response Sheet" (continued)

Caveats, Considerations, and Variations:

- The biggest consideration is face-to-face teams or virtual and or global.
- When working face-to-face, the way you divide people (pairs or larger groups) and whether or not you ask them to group with those they know best or least has to do with trust level and your objective.
- Even with those who think they know each other best, there will be new information and surprises.
- Pairs are best when trying to provide safety and security; bigger groups are better when trying to show breadth of differences and perspectives.
- Giving people time to write their answers is helpful for non-native English speakers and more reflective thinkers.
- Another variation on a theme is to take two or three statements from this list and put them on a chart. Depending on the size of the group, have people discuss the questions in small groups. Then you can either get random responses to all of the questions or go around the group and hear from every person present. Here's a sample of how this works:
  1. The best thing about being a part of this team is…
  2. The diversity on this team strengthens us by…
  3. One thing that might improve our team functioning is…

You could select one of those three statements to hear from everyone or get random responses on all. This can certainly be done on phone or teleconference.

The process we have been describing works well on any team where there is high trust. It can also be used to build trust by encouraging people to open up appropriately, a little at a time. Furthermore, it can help create an understanding of cross-cultural norms on teams that have people from different backgrounds, or even new staff members. Whenever possible, people can converse in their native language if English is still limited. Doing so will give employees security and privacy and you can still get data about the team.

If you want to get or give individual feedback, do so privately as opposed to making it part of the team-building session. Make sure you give the good news first, and then suggest specific behaviors that you are looking for. You can go to the informal group leader for suggestions as to how feedback might be given to a particular person in an appropriate way so that it will be heard.

The key adaptation to make as you look at getting and giving feedback in a diverse environment is that much of it is done informally through the strength of your relationships. We have a colleague who was managing a plant in Puerto Rico. He held management staff meetings every Friday afternoon and could not understand why his normally motivated group turned glum and irritable at these meetings. Staff members did show up, but all of the manager's attempts at getting participation fell flat. Finally, he went out for a beer with one of the fellows after a frustrating session and found out that the staff was irritated because they considered Friday afternoon the beginning of their weekend and meetings were infringing on their time. Once the manager got that piece of feedback, he changed the meetings to Thursday. The group's irritation was gone, and meetings were productive. This manager solicited feedback in the informal system, and he had good enough relationships to get an honest answer. No one would have told him in public, nor would anyone have volunteered the information. Good relationships, and being sensitive to others, are critical to getting and giving feedback in any culture.

5. Mutual Support, Both Psychological and Task-Focused

A colleague of ours, Dr. Natasha Josefowitz, states that we all need three kinds of support. In no particular order, they are, "a shoulder to cry on," "a brain to pick," and "a kick in the pants."[5] Dr. Josefowitz's definition of support is applicable to all persons, regardless of cultural programming. There are times we need comfort when our feelings get bruised. We also need ideas and suggestions from others as we try to effectively make choices and decisions in our jobs or lives. Finally, the kick-in-the-pants aspect of support functions like a full-length mirror, giving an honest, realistic snapshot of us, or our lives at a given moment. All three kinds of support are essential to having an effective team. They can contribute to better problem-solving, higher morale, and genuine commitment; but like any other aspects of team building, while universal in need, support is culture-bound in its manifestation.

Regarding the kick in the pants, U.S.-Americans profess honesty or directness and don't often do it. Recall the memorable fable "The Emperor's New Clothes." No one in this fable wants to be honest with the emperor, who harbors the illusion that he is magnificently dressed when in reality he is stark naked. Finally, one person has the courage to tell the emperor the truth. How often are people in your own organization afraid to speak their version of the truth when they have perceptions that differ from those in power? Employees, even at high levels, are often afraid of retribution when they're honest. If you really want to reinforce kick-in-the-pants honesty on your team, you have to reward those who bring you bad news. Thank them for it. This is hard to do in U.S.-American business culture, and almost impossible to do in some other cultures, but you must do it if you want to build a supportive culture on your team.

Two strategies will help you give support regardless of acculturation or the level of trust. The first is observation. In cultures with more contextual communication, the things people can't or won't say are often the loudest. Pick up the nonverbal cues. Watch faces. Notice relationships. Be a real student of the interpersonal dynamics on your team. The second strategy to pursue is continued relationship building, because over time, as trust builds, honesty will increase. In that way, you will experience more of all three of the kinds of support identified by Dr. Josefowitz.

6. An Ability To Deal with Conflict in a Mutually Satisfying and Positive Manner

Conflict, viewed from a North American perspective, may not be pleasant, but it can be a useful catalyst for change. Of all the criteria on the list of cross-cultural team-building dimensions, how a workgroup resolves its differences is one of the most significant. Unsolved differences remain an obstacle to commitment and productivity.

However, the pragmatic view of conflict held by the U.S.-American business culture is in contrast to some other parts of the world. Elsewhere, conflict is seen as disruptive to balance or harmony. We gave you a method for cross-cultural conflict resolution in Chapter 6. Nevertheless, we want to reemphasize a few points regarding conflict as it relates to team building:

- The use of informal leaders, elders, or intermediaries is a very effective way to help deal with differences.
- As you build a cohesive team, focus on expanding everyone's repertoire of behaviors, helping newcomers learn to acculturate while assisting old timers to be open, sensitive, and nonjudgmental.
- Create a climate where being genuine and maintaining integrity is the norm and where these differences can be discussed in a low-stakes, productive way, an inch at a time.

We recently saw all these factors at work in varying degrees on a team that was mostly Filipino. The group was not meeting some of its objectives, and when the manager, who was African American, convened a meeting to deal with various issues, the staff didn't have the experience of openly surfacing problems. The manager had developed good relationships and built trust with everyone, especially the group's informal leader. She asked each staff member to write down the problems as he or she saw them. At first, there was reluctance, but the leader received help when the first few team members participated, and after a time, they all did it. She collected the data and compiled it on the spot so the group could use it. To everyone's surprise, she got full participation. Team members got more interested and involved than they intended. The manager was encouraged because she could see her staff's individual and collective growth. She realized that none of her staff members were born in the United States, and none had been taught to deal with conflict openly. Nonetheless, they had done so with her. She felt the relationships and the process she used had moved the group noticeably closer as a team. Team members saw that no one was hurt by dealing with the conflicts caused by these problems, and in fact the group was helped.

7. Acknowledgment of the Impact of Cross-Cultural Values and Norms on the Team

Two important factors are critical in dealing with values and norms related to team building. The first is a realization by team members that values lead to different ways of seeing and of being a team member. Whether you were reared in Armenia or Australia; the idyllic 1950s; the rebellious 1960s or the greedy 1980s; the affluent 1990s or the technologically driven new century; or places as different as rural Mississippi and New York City will create a vast difference in how you see the world and the values by which you live. The connections between where you're reared, what you value, and how you behave are strong. Here's a case in point: A young man, who grew up in the United States and played on athletic teams before Title IX, would probably have been around the traditional locker room talk where women were the subject of suggestive comments and innuendos about sexual conquest and where gays were the butt of degrading jokes. In this environment, what message would have been transmitted to this young man about women? About gays or lesbians? About their place in society and the value they add to this world? In his adult professional life, what difference might the messages sent years ago make on the corporate team, where some of his colleagues are women or gays? Values and norms shape us all, but sometimes we aren't aware of their influence.

An effective team needs recognition that different norms and values lead to different behaviors and can cause team conflict. If you want to move your team forward in acknowledging and dealing with these differences, we offer a technique that's important because it honors the values of all cultures. It is direct enough to surface the issues but provides enough indirectness and safety not to hurt anyone's feelings. The directions are given in the *Norms/Values Worksheet*.

ACTIVITY 8.8 | Norms/Values Worksheet

1. Pass a sheet of paper out to each team member.

2. Ask participants to think about values or norms they currently see at work. Once they identify several, have them make two lists as indicated below, with those values they like in one column and those that are difficult to deal with in the other.

3. The manager or facilitator collects the information from each person and then has someone read the data aloud while the manager/facilitator charts the information on a chart paper or white board. If you prefer to have each team member involved in reading the data aloud, shuffle the lists, then redistribute them and have each person read the data aloud from a colleague's list.

4. Once the data are posted, you can ask the group to identify benefits of the values that are hard for people to deal with. Use the expertise of group members who have found a way to deal with different cultural values successfully. End with concrete suggestions for how to handle the ones that may get in the way. If this is facilitated well, it can be enormously helpful. Before facilitating this conversation, refer to Effective Facilitator Behaviors in this chapter.

Norms/Values I Like and Enjoy	Norms/Values That Are Difficult for Me

Suggestions for Using the
"Norms/Values Worksheet"

Objectives:

- Identify values and norms that may be difficult for individual team members to deal with
- Identify ways to more effectively deal with those values and norms that are difficult

Intended Audience:

- Members of any functional work team or task force, can be in person or virtual/global
- Any facilitator, trainer, manager, internal or external consultant, or HR professional who will lead the discussion

Processing the Activity:

- Distribute the worksheet to each team member in person or send the worksheet online ahead of time.
- Ask them to think about values or norms they see on the job.
- In one column, list those they like and enjoy; in the other, list those that are difficult for them.
- Collect the information from everyone and have one member read all answers aloud or distribute the data online. The facilitator charts or collects all the data.
- Get suggestions from group members about how to deal effectively with those that may be hard for some while not so hard for others.

Questions for Discussion:

- Around what values are there differences of opinion?
- What ways have some of you found to deal with these values that no longer make them difficult?

Caveats, Considerations, and Variations:

- Collecting data and having it remain anonymous is important regardless of whether teams are dispersed or face-to-face.
- You can collect and redistribute data so no one has to be accountable for reading his or her own.

8. Effective Problem-Solving and Decision-Making Processes

Remaining or becoming competitive, profitable, and productive means that group problems will need to be solved and decisions will need to be made. There are two cross-cultural norms that could impede your team's problem-solving capability. The first is that less acculturated employees or hourly workers from any part of the globe may see their jobs as more implementation than problem-solving. If you're the boss, in deference to your title, employees may feel awkward and uncomfortable being treated as an equal whose input is valued and sought. It will take some time and patience on your part to create a new norm. It is doable, particularly if you work with informal leaders and position this involvement as loyalty to the boss.

The other cross-cultural norm that could work against effective problem-solving and decision-making is the external locus of control, which has previously been mentioned. This idea that outside factors determine the course of one's life makes team members less participative problem-solvers. The Japanese use consensus a great deal to solve their problems. The complaint, made by some Americans who do business there, it is that takes forever to reach a decision in Japan. While the process may be time-consuming, it also gives you maximum support for decisions because it gets the buy-in of the whole group, and the battles are won and lost in that support.

9. Commitment to a Common Goal

A team's cohesion is significantly enhanced when it has a common goal it deems meaningful. The most dramatic and clear-cut goals are found on athletic teams—the 1980 U.S. Olympic hockey team winning its gold medal, for example. In business, "winning" may be harder to quantify. Is it increased market share? Greater profitability? Getting that new product to market in a timely manner? Being first out with the latest technological advancement? Whatever the multiple answers are, your team will be more cohesive and effective if members strive for a goal that is clear, achievable, and meaningful.

10. Diagnostic Processes for Assessing the Health of the Team

Part of what keeps any excellent team effective over the long haul is its ability to look at its own operation and make changes as necessary. The very process of analyzing a team's content (what it's doing) and its process (how it's doing whatever it does) is a predictable part of U.S. business culture.

We have included three diagnostic tools here. In different ways, they all advance teamwork. The first, *Window on the Team*, gives individuals a chance to look at the team and its functioning. It also provides an opportunity to look at individual comfort and skill development. This will be a good tool to use when there is some level of trust and acculturation. To use this tool and lessen the discomfort, have team members fill it out by themselves and then process it in small groups where there is a high level of trust. Have a recorder put everyone's data, unattributed, on a large sheet of paper that duplicates the four quadrants. Then the data can be processed more anonymously and safely for employees who do not want to offend the boss. While this tool is a natural for in-person meetings, it can also be used very effectively with virtual teams.

ACTIVITY 8.9 | Window on the Team

What's going well on this team?

_____
_____
_____
_____
_____
_____
_____
_____
_____
_____
_____
_____
_____
_____
_____

What are the areas of concern?

_____
_____
_____
_____
_____
_____
_____
_____
_____
_____
_____
_____
_____
_____
_____

What skills, if you developed them, would help you be a better team member?

_____
_____
_____
_____
_____
_____
_____
_____
_____
_____
_____
_____
_____
_____
_____
_____

What kind of support do you need from others to become a better or more productive team member?

_____
_____
_____
_____
_____
_____
_____
_____
_____
_____
_____
_____
_____
_____
_____

Suggestions for Using
"Window on the Team"

Objectives:

- Stimulate individual thought and discussion that will lead to usable information to develop the team
- Gain perspective and information about the team

Intended Audience:

- All members of any functional work team, whether in one location or many
- Managers, facilitators, consultants, or HR professionals who can facilitate the activity

Processing the Activity:

- Distribute the worksheet at the session and ask participants to fill out information in all four quadrants. Distribute ahead of time when meeting electronically.
- Pair up to discuss, in person. Set pairs up electronically so conversations predate the meeting.
- Have facilitator get information in top two quadrants from everyone and chart it on an easel and flip chart. Have a conversation about bottom quadrants as well, with people being very vocal about what helps them do better.

Questions for Discussion:

- What does this tell you about this team?
- What kinds of support would help you be a better team member?
- What do the data suggest you (we) need to do to be stronger?

Caveats, Considerations, and Variations:

- In a small group (six or seven people), you can share data from everyone.
- You can change the questions or areas of focus to suit any need you have at a given time.

The second diagnostic tool, the *Team-Development Survey*, helps a team identify its weak link. This sample tool gives the team a place to start its assessment. These are standard team-building questions we designed for our clients, but you can change them and substitute other questions more pertinent to your issues. We combined numbers and words in the analysis to provide comfort for all team members because some members put faith in objective data, some in subjective. In the sense that the responses come from individual perception, they are all subjective, but using both numbers and words should allow all participants to feel comfort somewhere in the diagnostic process. The variety gives you a better chance to hit each person's comfort level.

Finally, we offer the *Group-Experience Rating Form*. This makes a good pre- and post-team-building tool. You can have individuals evaluate the team on all 20 items for starters; then, once the data indicate areas of strength and weakness, the team can focus on specific areas for improvement. Identify the skill areas team members need in order to add more value to the group.

These last three tools, and in fact all the tools in this chapter and throughout the book, can be used globally. Table 8.2 helps you figure out how technology can be an asset as you work across borders and time zones.

ACTIVITY 8.10 | Team-Development Survey

Respond to items 1 through 6 by circling the appropriate answer. There is no right answer, only your answer, honestly given, based on your perception. Data will be reported collectively so the anonymity of each person is assured.

	Rarely		Sometimes		Almost Always
1. I am clear about our team's goals and priorities.	1	2	3	4	5
2. I feel as though I have a voice in setting priorities and making decisions.	1	2	3	4	5
3. As a team, we are effective in dealing with our differences.	1	2	3	4	5
4. On this team, it is safe to honestly express my values and ideas.	1	2	3	4	5
5. We have clear roles and responsibilities.	1	2	3	4	5
6. The goals of this team and this organization are meaningful to me.	1	2	3	4	5

Please respond to the following questions by writing down your candid responses on the lines below.

1. The strengths of this team are: _____

_____

_____

_____

_____

_____

2. In order for this team to be more effective, it needs to: _____

_____

_____

_____

_____

_____

Suggestions for Using the
"Team-Development Survey"

Objectives:

- Give the team feedback about itself in a number of different areas
- Gain information objectively and subjectively through numerical responses and open-ended statements

Intended Audience:

- Members of any diverse work team
- Facilitators, managers, consultants, or HR professionals leading a team through trust-building or feedback activities

Processing the Activity:

- Ask team members to fill in their responses and collect the worksheets or distribute electronically.
- The facilitator compiles data and feeds the compiled data back to the group.

Questions for Discussion:

- What does this information tell you (us) about what the team is doing well and what it is not?
- How do you account for the range in numbers (from a low score of 2 to a high score of 5, for example)?
- How do the objective data fit with your open-ended responses?
- Based on this information, what issues does the team need to address?

Caveats, Considerations, and Variations:

- You can collect this information ahead of the session and use it to plan the agenda of a team-building meeting. It legitimizes the direction you take with a group because the content comes straight out of their information. You can also use this right at the session and tabulate the data on the spot to generate discussion on various dimensions of team effectiveness. This on-the-spot tabulation can be done virtually and face-to-face.

ACTIVITY 8.11 | Group-Experience Rating Form

Instructions: Rate the problem-solving performance of your group by responding to the questions below. Indicate for each question the rating (1-5) that describes your observation of the group experience. Simply circle the appropriate number. The scale is as follows:

		Rarely		Sometimes		Almost always
1.	Take time to find out what the problem really is.	1	2	3	4	5
2.	Listen and try to understand multiple viewpoints.	1	2	3	4	5
3.	Understand the feelings I may be experiencing.	1	2	3	4	5
4.	Help me to clarify my thinking by asking insightful, pertinent questions.	1	2	3	4	5
5.	Share their feelings about the team's strengths and weaknesses.	1	2	3	4	5
6.	Offer loyalty, support, and encouragement as a team norm.	1	2	3	4	5
7.	Encourage my contributions.	1	2	3	4	5
8.	Help me explore alternatives without pushing their own solutions.	1	2	3	4	5
9.	Set out to find the facts.	1	2	3	4	5
10.	Take time to set goals and objectives.	1	2	3	4	5
11.	Take time to evaluate how we are doing individually and collectively.	1	2	3	4	5
12.	Put talk and decisions into action.	1	2	3	4	5
13.	Seek and accept help from others.	1	2	3	4	5
14.	Provide different functions to the team at different times (e.g., leader, clarifier, summarizer, etc.).	1	2	3	4	5
15.	Say clearly and tactfully what they need or expect from me and others team members.	1	2	3	4	5
16.	Acknowledge disagreements and seek to understand them.	1	2	3	4	5
17.	Seem to care about me and other team members and whether or not we accomplish our goals.	1	2	3	4	5
18.	Give honest, nonjudgmental feedback.	1	2	3	4	5

Suggestions for Using the
"Group-Experience Rating Form"

Objectives:

- Assess the function and behaviors of the team
- See which behaviors add to team effectiveness and which detract
- Get a sense of the various perspectives team members hold

Intended Audience:

- Members of any functional work team. This can be used easily on virtual teams with the help of technology, and data can remain anonymous if desired.
- Any facilitator, manager, consultant, or HR professional leading a team through trust-building or feedback activities

Processing the Activity:

- Ask each team member to rate the team by responding to the 18 items.
- Discuss responses in pairs or small groups first, then in large groups if you are on-site together. If done by teleconference, have the facilitator lead whole-group discussion.
- Based on responses, determine an area to work on.

Questions for Discussion:

- What are the areas of greatest strength? Greatest weakness?
- What does this rating form suggest this team needs to do differently?
- Focusing on what item will help this team the most?

Caveats, Considerations, and Variations:

- If 18 items feel like too many, divide items in half or quarters. Start smaller and eventually work through all 18 items.
- Feel free to use the items as they are, or adapt them to your own group. Remember that being analytical and linear ("The team has a problem ... let's fix it") is very Western, as is the directness of the tools. But using small groups to process the tools can increase safety and security for members from different backgrounds as all team members try to acculturate to the collective norms of the organization and their own team.

TABLE 8.2 | Enhancing Task and Relationship Functions Through the Use of Technology[6]

TECHNOLOGY	TASK	RELATIONSHIP
Electronic meeting systems	Allows group to work together on any number of tasks. The strength is that participants have free flow of input and data, and, if desired, comments can be anonymous. Suggestions or ideas can be added at will.	In some nations and economies, technology has been used in face-to-face settings for a while. It is now being used in disbursed teams to enable collaboration with people in different locations.
Teleconference	This can be helpful in bringing people together to exchange viewpoints, give or get feedback, share ideas and think through different approaches.	When relationships have already had face-to-face contact and some trust exists where people say what they really think and feel, enabling a group to reach agreement.
Video conference	This is a commonly used tool but the effectiveness of it depends a lot on the quality of the video transmissions. Often, time zone differences and uneven quality of the technology limit usefulness.	It is a good tool for discussing opinions and, because it is video, participants can see one another, and get nonverbal information in real time.
E-mail	This is certainly the most used computer-mediated technology for people working together over distances. It is readily available, easy to use, and can be both relational and task-focused. It is quick and efficient, but still allows people time to reflect and get back to one another. You can send attachments and it is an easy, cost-effective way to communicate.	Ground rules on the "what and how" of e-mail are helpful for a team. Communication styles differ, and from written communication one can even infer, in addition to national styles, generational styles. People reared on technology are more staccato in style while those 50ish and older who wrote letters have more solutions and formal closures. If there is enough privacy in e-mail, team members can be real and truthful with their ideas, thereby resolving differences. See suggestions for Netiquette below.
Company's Intranet	If a company has its own Intranet, a new division/section /area could be added specifically for teams working on a specific project. There could even be separate areas for each team. Communication is enhanced with worldwide accessibility, posting of questions/answers and questionnaires. Similar to e-mail but can be shared (not required) by all.	As in use of e-mail, ground rules are important as is the role of the webmaster in being responsive to the needs of the various teams.
Internet Newsgroups	When a company does not have an Intranet in operation, the members of teams can form a newsgroup where all can share the contributions of team members. This method is not as flexible, especially in the use of questionnaires, nor as private as an Intranet location, nevertheless it can be a useful tool. Most newsgroups are shared with others from all over the world. As such, it can be a plus for those reaching out and looking for similar experiences and possible outcomes.	Same as e-mail and company's Intranet. See below for suggested Netiquette.

Five Ways To Foster Appreciation of Difference

Not all differences and not all sources of team conflict will be a result of racial, gender, ethnic, cultural, or lifestyle differences, but some may be. It doesn't matter what the source of the differences is. The first step in creating a cohesive team is to start with the premise that individuals are unique. Any workgroup will naturally reflect the differences. Step two is to realize that in spite of the predictable differences, we're all human. There will also be areas of sameness that can provide a fragmented group with bridge-building opportunity.

1. Value It

You can talk all you want about valuing differences, but what you *do* will tell the real story. If someone on your team is known to be a lesbian, how is this person treated? What kind of discrimination or judgment does she face? Can your team accommodate other differences? It is hard to have a cohesive team without valuing and using them. One way to walk the talk of valuing around generational differences is to have a mentoring process where younger employees coach seniors and vice versa.

2. Acknowledge It

There are those who live in denial about the differences between us. They try to be color-blind in an attempt not to be prejudiced. This denial, however well intentioned, is not helpful. We can make more strides in our racial behaviors and attitudes if we acknowledged and deal with race or other differences that we try to deny. There is a saying in Gestalt therapy that is appropriate here: "The only way out is through." You can't get beyond the differences until you first acknowledge they exist and then deal with them. Either course of action, acknowledging or denying, will affect team performance and morale.

3. Model It

Talk has always been the cheapest commodity around. Modeling an appreciation of difference means taking action. If you manage a team, you may have to listen to, consider, and implement suggestions that are different from your own. Sometimes it may be hard for you to walk that proverbial mile in another person's moccasins, but a person who models an appreciation of differences will be less likely to have knee-jerk rejection of others' ideas when they're suggested. These ideas must at least be given serious consideration. Allowing your staff to implement solutions they believe in, even when these ideas aren't your preference, is an excellent way to make good on the example of modeling behavior that shows appreciation for different perspectives.

4. Reward It

When staff members demonstrate, through their discussions and decisions, that they see and appreciate each person's uniqueness, your group is on the way to becoming a team. You need to reward their behavior. The opportunity here comes in understanding individual team members, about and beyond culture, to tailor rewards so that what is given actually feels like a gift. For some, a private thank you means everything and public acknowledgement is humiliating. Others live for the chance to get public recognition. Some people are thrilled to get a new learning opportunity, while some might want an expansion of job duties that stretch skills and talents.

5. Learn from It

Using what you learn from staff whose value base and experiences are dissimilar from your own will send a powerful message that you find worth in differences. In fact, it is one of the best strategies for creating a climate where others also want to learn from you and feel they can do so without losing their own culture. We've seen this operate dramatically in the area of language acquisition. Managers who have learned Spanish, for example, tell us it motivates their Spanish-speaking staff members to try to use English more frequently because they have less fear of sounding foolish. What develops when you are willing to learn from others is more acculturation by all parties, greater rapport, and mutual respect.

Trust: The Indispensable Element on Any Potent Team

The ability to guide any team, but especially one that is comprised of staff from diverse backgrounds, rests heavily on the trust and credibility of the leadership. Jack Gibb, in his book, *Trust: A New View of Personal and Organizational Development*, says, "Trust begets trust, while fear escalates fear."[7] One of the most important organizational insights Gibb makes is that "When trust is high relative to fear, people and people systems function well." Relationship building is a critical aspect of developing trust on any team and even more important on a diverse team.

How much of a relationship nurturer are you? In Activity 8.12, put a check by any of the behaviors you engage in on a regular basis if you are on-site, and think about how contact can be extended on virtual teams. The same needs and behavior apply across locations.

ACTIVITY 8.12 | How Much of a Relationship Nurturer Are You?

☐ I spend time or connect with every staff member each week, in person or virtually.

☐ I make it a point to circulate through the areas of my department every day.

☐ Employees often come to see me, or use technology to make contact.

☐ I often eat lunch or take breaks with my employees.

☐ I know a little about the personal lives of each of my staff people.

☐ I can usually tell when someone needs to talk.

☐ Employees seem relaxed and comfortable around me.

☐ I sometimes talk about nonwork-related topics with my staff members.

☐ I let my staff know I appreciate them.

☐ I greet each employee every day.

☐ I help staff through the rough times.

The more of these you engage in, the more trust you'll reap. Any effort on your behalf to nurture relationships will build trust and increase cohesion and commitment to the team and the task.

Suggestions for Using
"How Much of a Relationship Nurturer Are You?"

Objectives:

- Gain a sense of how much time you spend with people on your team
- Look at the different ways you make contact and engage
- Consider how these necessary behaviors can be carried out or adapted for dispersed teams

Intended Audience:

- Managers or team leaders who want to build more cohesive teams
- Trainers, facilitators, consultants, coaches, or HR professionals who want to help groom managers to be more connected to their teams

Processing the Activity:

- Have participants fill out the *How Much of a Relationship Nurturer Are You?* checklist.
- In pairs or small groups, have participants share, focusing on what they are already doing and what they could do more of.
- After paired or small-group discussions, bring the group back together and have one large conversation.

Questions for Discussion:

- Which of these behaviors do you engage in regularly?
- Which seem to be very natural and comfortable for you?
- Which ones do you seldom engage in?
- Have you intentionally thought about which of those behaviors you engage in and or those you don't? If so, explain, at least to yourself, what the reasons are in either case.
- What have you learned?
- What are the consequences, pros and cons, for doing these behaviors, or avoiding them?

Caveats, Considerations, and Variations:

- Identify one or two behaviors that you are willing to do more frequently as a way to nurture others.
- Keep a journal, recording the evolving nature of your relationship as you try these strategies.

Building High-Performance Work Teams in a Diverse Environment: Six Key Ingredients

As you've read in this chapter, the factors involved in building a powerful work team are numerous and complex. There are a few simple principles worth remembering that will help you get started on the right foot as you team-build in a complex, global environment.

1. Acknowledge Differences

Today's workforce in not homogeneous by race, age, religion, ethnicity, gender, physical ability, world view, sexual preference, values, or much of anything else. Start your attempt at team building with that reality. It is helpful to acknowledge these real differences and the opportunities they present because then you can move on to find the strength in your sameness as well.

2. Find the Common Ground

Even members of nuclear families who love one another have their interpersonal rubs with each other. Your team won't escape the rough spots, either. But just as the differences are a reality, so is the common ground. In spite of all the differences just mentioned, if you work for the same boss on the same team in the same organization, you already share significant commonalities. Undoubtedly, there are others. Make those your glue and build on them. We frequently hear about team members scattered over all sorts of miles and geographies. We were inspired and amazed recently when one such group told us they had a virtual baby shower for one of their team members via teleconference. Gifts were collected and shipped from a variety of places to a team member few had met in person. Limits of time and space do not have to be limits of their common ground, interpersonally or in task accomplishment.

3. Identify Individual Interests, Strengths, and Preferences

Identifying individual interests, strengths, and preferences will help you identify individual talent to be used for the good of the group. Focusing on individual strengths doesn't have to conflict with cultures reflecting strong group emphasis. Any group is only as talented as the individuals who comprise it. This is your chance to ensure that people are in the right jobs based on their interests, talents, and strengths. In so doing, you gain commitment to the team as well as topnotch performance.

4. Clarify Expectations

There is a legitimate tightrope to walk between having clear standards of performance and being flexible enough to accommodate differences. As a team leader, you're the one who can best determine where to bend and when you break. Decide what issues are worth going to the mat for as you mold your team. Everything can't be a do-or-die issue, but some things must be. Once you are clear about what your expectations are, tell the troops and reinforce the standards.

5. Collectively Shape Group Culture

As leader or manager of a team, you are a very critical piece of it, but you aren't the whole of it. The effective group reflects the experiences and values of all its members. Make room for the richness of the totality. Humans are not static; don't expect groups to be. Even in a group of first-line staff that prefers everything spelled out, you can help team members grow and increase their input.

6. Create a Feedback Loop

When all is said and done, a team is measured by how it performs. Is the job getting done? Where are the levels of excellence? What areas are ripe for improvement? Use the suggestions we have made in other chapters about getting and giving feedback; they will enable individual team members and the group itself to learn and grow on the job. Ultimately, feedback on job performance is the organizational insurance policy for achieving peak performance.

In truth, each individual is a minority of one. The challenge and the joy of team building lies in taking diverse individuals and forging their uniqueness into a whole that is greater than the sum of its parts. Doing so is critical. The good news is that by using the techniques offered here, it is also doable.

CHAPTER 9.
Performance Evaluation in a Diverse Organization

• •

This chapter will give you:

- An understanding of culture- and diversity-related variables that impact the performance evaluation process

- Information about the sources of resistance to performance evaluation and how to overcome them

- Ways to overcome cultural blind spots in performance evaluation

- Examples of effective and ineffective performance evaluation

- A step-by-step guide for planning performance evaluation sessions

- Techniques for getting employee buy-in and commitment in the process

- Self-assessment tools to help you analyze and improve your effectiveness as an evaluator

- Tips for avoiding common performance evaluation pitfalls

It is a rare person who doesn't find the performance evaluation process difficult and tense. On both sides of the desk, apprehensions and nervousness are apt to be felt. The evaluator worries about being accurate and fair, avoiding hurt feelings, and not producing conflict. The person being evaluated, on the other end of the process, anticipates potential criticism, judgments, and embarrassment. Yet for all its difficulties, evaluating employee performance is the main way organizations have found to maintain accountability and to reward employees equitably. Like it or not, this system is generally accepted as standard procedure in U.S. business life. At its best, the process gives employees a chance to find out how they are doing so they can improve their performance. It also gives them an opportunity to highlight their accomplishments and reap the rewards of their hard work.

Why Diverse Employees May Resist Performance Evaluation

Employees who are not part of the dominant culture of the organization may have even more apprehensions about the performance evaluation process. Knowing the source of their tension can help you overcome some of their resistance. Think for a moment about how you might feel if you were:

- An older female employee being evaluated by a younger male boss
- A young Filipina nurse with a temporary work permit, awaiting your green card, being evaluated by an American nurse manager
- A long-term Latino factory worker being evaluated by your African-American female supervisor
- A paraplegic male engineer being evaluated by your able-bodied male manager
- A male Vietnamese immigrant bookkeeper being evaluated by your boss, a Euro-American female accountant

What assumptions might you make? What expectations might you have as you approached your evaluation session? Some of the following factors might contribute to the resistance you might be feeling.

1. Fear of Repercussions

Most of us would feel less safe in any organization or culture where we are not the dominant group. Diverse employees, knowing they are not the power wielders, may experience fear when being evaluated by those who are in power. They may perceive they have no recourse to any judgment. They may also fear losing their jobs or their work permits. They may see the evaluation itself as a formalized reprimand, a wrist slapping for past mistakes, and hence they may be reluctant to participate.

Suggestion for Managers:
- Explain the purpose of the evaluation, emphasizing that it is not a disciplinary meeting and that the employee is not going to lose his or her job.

2. "Not One of Us" Syndrome

The U.S. judicial system mandates that every person on trial be judged by a jury of his or her peers. It is felt that only those in similar circumstances can make a fair judgment. In diverse organizations, the evaluator is not necessarily of the same group as the person being evaluated. The employee may feel that it is not possible to be fairly evaluated by someone who may have little understanding or empathy for the problems of the employee. When individuals do not perceive they will get a fair shake, they are apt to resist.

Suggestion for Managers:
- Sit next to the person being evaluated at a table or in chairs rather than across a desk. Show empathy; for example, you could state, "People sometimes feel a little nervous at performance evaluation time. I feel that way, too, when I get evaluated."

3. Lack of Understanding of the Process

Employees of all stripes often see performance evaluation as a reprimand or dressing-down session. Because they do not fully understand the reasons behind the evaluation, nor the actual form and process, they may balk. In addition, the forms used may be confusing and intimidating for someone not used to such administrative paperwork.

Suggestion for Managers:
- Explain the performance evaluation process to the whole staff, telling them the reasons for it, how it can benefit them, and how they can help. Explain this again briefly at the beginning of each evaluation session.

4. It Is a Foreign Experience

For employees who are from other cultures, the whole process may be strange and confusing. In many countries, rewards such as promotions and raises are a result of seniority or family connections rather than performance. They may never have experienced this kind of formalized feedback process. The employee may have little experience with the notions of individual responsibility, goal setting, and monitoring of performance that underlie the evaluation process in U.S. firms.

Suggestion for Managers:
- Use the evaluation as a teaching opportunity, explaining how individual performance and accomplishing goals leads to rewards.

5. All Task and No Relationship

In the more structured setting of an evaluation session, the employee may be taken aback when the task takes precedence over the relationship—suddenly the evaluation form with its boxes and categories seems more important than the person. If the employee has had a comfortable relationship with the boss, he or she may feel betrayed, as though the boss who was so friendly this morning is now cold and all business.

Suggestion for Managers:
- Try to maintain the same tone in the evaluation session that you generally have in relating to the employee. Talk about each section in normal everyday language, making sure to avoid using "legalese."

Why Existing Performance Evaluations Don't Work with Diverse Employees

Performance evaluation generally has three major functions. First, it serves as a tool to help improve performance by giving employees clear feedback about what they are doing well and where they need to improve. Second, it gives the organization a measuring system to help in doling out rewards equitably. Finally, it helps employees in their own career growth, giving them feedback and assistance in professional goal planning.

Performance evaluation fails in accomplishing these objectives when employees do not understand the constructive purpose for it. Furthermore, when they see the feedback as hurtful rather than helpful, they do not use it to grow. Finally, when they are faced with a different system of standards for reward than they are used to, confusion, frustration, and irritation build on both sides. Both bosses and employees find themselves required to go through the motions of a process that seems to be missing its mark; a waste of time at best, and a morale and productivity sapper at worst. For performance evaluation to serve its purpose with diverse employees, it needs to be clearly explained and perceived as constructive.

Helping Diverse Employees Understand the Evaluation Process

Imagine that you have suddenly been transported to India and find yourself in the middle of a cricket field. You are dressed in the regulation white outfit and have an odd-shaped bat in your hands. All the players speak English, though with a different accent. The game is about to begin, and you are told to play. How would you feel? Bewildered? Embarrassed? Anxious? What would you do? Start asking other players? Walk off the field? Observe and try to figure things out?

Some of your reactions might be similar to those of diverse employees attempting to "play the game" in your company, and making sense of the performance evaluation process is one more perplexing part of that game. It may be just as foreign an experience. Just as you would have been helped by a pregame briefing, the employee also needs the rules of the game to be explained to him or her. Since most of us are more receptive when we understand the reasons, the first place to start in the performance review process is to explain its purpose.

Emphasize the benefits that both the organization and the employee can derive from the evaluation. Using an analogy can help. If the person is interested in sports, for example, you might use a basketball analogy: "How would you learn how to make more baskets, if you had to play in the dark? You'd never know when you made a basket and when you didn't, so you wouldn't know how to improve your shots. Performance evaluation is a way of telling you how close you're getting to the basket, which balls are making it, and which aren't. Without the feedback you get in performance reviews, you'd always be in the dark."

You might want to talk about something that you learned in a performance review that helped you improve your own productivity. It is also important to explain that everyone in the organization goes through this experience, and that you and your bosses get evaluated, too.

How Diversity Impacts Performance Appraisal Systems

Managers and employees bring their diverse backgrounds and cultures to work, and these variations touch every part of the organization's systems. Performance appraisal is no different: Both cultural and experiential variables of diverse employees have a significant effect on the process of evaluating employee performance.

Table 9.1 outlines the effects of diversity-related variables on performance evaluation. Once you have reviewed it, you can analyze one of your own performance appraisal experiences by using *Pinpointing Diversity-Related Influences That Impact Performance Evaluation*. Recall a recent review session, and then check any of the factors that you felt influenced the process. Next, jot down the employee behavior that indicated this factor was operating. In the far right column, write any actions you could take to improve communication and get buy-in from the employee.

TABLE 9.1 | The Impact of Diversity-Related Variables on Performance Appraisal

Cultural Factors	Impact on Appraisal	Behavior
Avoidance of loss-of-face	Anxiety on the part of the employee and unwillingness to discuss any criticism	Smiling and laughter may be signs of embarrassment; missing conferences or absenteeism on performance evaluation day may be signs of avoidance
Emphasis on harmony	Agreement to items not clearly understood	Saying "yes" even when not understanding or when disagreeing
Respect for authority	Unwillingness to question the review or disagree with any points made by the evaluator	Lack of eye contact and not entering into a dialogue with the boss
External locus of control	Difficulty in seeing the consequences of behavior; not connecting the review with his or her own behavior	Comments may show that the employee does not make the connection between his or her performance and the evaluation ratings
Emphasis on relationship rather than task	Task accomplishment not seen as the critical variable in job success; relationship with boss, seniority, and group status takes precedence	Attempts to please the boss as well as bewilderment shown by a blank facial expression
Difficulty in separating self from performance	Taking the review personally and finding comments hurtful; "But I thought you liked me" attitude; seeing criticism as an affront rather than as helpful feedback	Showing feelings of hurt, betrayal, or embarrassment
Emphasis on group over individual	Difficulty in distinguishing own performance from team's as evaluating individual performance may be a different paradigm for employee used to group results being the focus of evaluation Calling attention to individual contributions is perceived negatively Employee may also find calling attention to him or herself awkward and disloyal to co-workers	Signs of discomfort, confusion, or embarrassment such as smiling, withdrawal, or clamming up
Other Diversity Factors		
Lack of common base of experience	Employee may feel misunderstood and unfairly judged if evaluator has not had to deal with similar obstacles or outside of work problems (e.g., older worker, single parent, or employee with elder-care responsibilities)	Sulking silence or defensiveness
Previous discrimination	Employees who have experienced discrimination in the past are apt to be distrustful and skeptical of the value and results of formal appraisal systems	Lack of participation, sarcasm

ACTIVITY 9.1 | Pinpointing Diversity-Related Influences That Impact Performance Evaluation

Check any of these factors that you felt influenced a recent performance evaluation process. Jot down the employee behavior and any actions you might take to improve communication.

Cultural/Diversity-Related Factors	Employee's Behavior	Manager's Action
☐ Avoidance of loss-of-face		
☐ Emphasis on harmony		
☐ Respect for authority		
☐ External locus of control		
☐ Emphasis on relationship rather than task		
☐ Difficulty in separating self from performance		
☐ Emphasis on group over individual		
☐ Lack of common base of experience		
☐ Previous discrimination		

Suggestions for Using
"Pinpointing Diversity-Related Influences That Impact Performance Evaluation"

Objectives:

- Identify diversity-related variables affecting performance evaluation
- Gain information that will help determine actions to take to overcome diversity-related obstacles to performance evaluation effectiveness

Intended Audience:

- Managers wanting to increase effectiveness of performance evaluation with diverse employees
- Trainees in a managing diversity seminar

Processing the Activity:

- Facilitator gives brief explanation of the diversity-related influences that impact performance evaluation.
- Using the worksheet, individuals analyze a recent performance evaluation experience with an employee from a different background. They check any of the variables they perceived as influencing the process, then jot down the employee behaviors that indicated this factor was operating. In the final column, they write any actions the manager could take to improve communication and get buy-in from the employee.
- Small groups can discuss those variables checked and behaviors observed, and then brainstorm additional actions the manager could take.
- The whole group discusses brainstormed suggestions for managers.

Questions for Discussion:

- Which variables had the most impact?
- What was the effect these variables had on the performance evaluation?
- What could the manager do to deal with these variables and overcome any potential obstacle?
- What insights have you gained?

Caveats and Considerations:

- This worksheet can be used as a coaching tool in helping managers develop more effective performance evaluation skills.
- This worksheet can be used by managers as a planning tool when setting up future performance evaluation sessions.

There Is No "Culture-Free" Performance Appraisal System

Try a little experiment with yourself. Close your eyes and imagine the ideal employee in your department. Picture the individual at work in your organization's setting. Notice everything about the way this person goes about working and interacting with others. Now, answer some questions about this ideal worker. Was the person male or female? What racial, ethnic, or cultural group did the person belong to? Did the individual have any physical limitations? How old was the employee? How close are you to this ideal image? What does this experiment tell you about your own performance expectations and their relationship to diversity? If you are like most people, that ideal worker bears a resemblance to you. This experiment illustrates how difficult it is to have a culture-free performance evaluation.

Four types of performance evaluations most frequently used in organizations appear to be those that use:

1. Rating scales
2. Forced distribution
3. Critical incidents
4. Performance-based criteria

All four of these share characteristics of the U.S.-American culture. Because that culture reveres logic and linear thinking as well as fairness and task accomplishment, there is an emphasis on the objective, rational, and impersonal nature of appraisal. These systems are attempts at quantifying and objectifying a very subjective process. Yet, no matter how one analyzes the ratings or manipulates the statistical comparisons, the difference between an "excellent" and a "very good," between a "3" and a "4," or between employees ranked 5 and 6, is a subjective judgment. In addition, these evaluation systems presuppose an acceptance of the American cultural notion that performance is separate from the person. This view is contrary to that held in most other cultures such as those of the Middle East, Mexico, the Philippines, and much of Asia, which make little distinction between the person and his or her behavior. U.S. Americans tend to believe you are worthwhile because you do; others believe you are worthwhile because you exist. Finally, appraisals rest on a solid foundation of cause-and-effect, find-the-problem-and-fix-it thinking, which relies on an internal locus of control, the belief that achievements are the result of one's effort and ability. While this paradigm is prevalent in most Western countries, it is not a universal one. In many areas of the world, outcomes are seen as the result of fate, luck, or other factors out of the control of humans. These cultural foundations often present "blind spots" for those from other backgrounds who are not acculturated to U.S.-American norms.

Overcoming Diversity Blind Spots in Each Type of Performance Appraisal

Overcoming diversity blind spots means teaching employees a different way of thinking and looking at the world. One way of doing that is to help employees understand the overlap areas between their thinking and that of the dominant culture. You can emphasize common ground, for example, by showing the employee how the performance evaluation is subjective at its base, too, and that feelings about people do enter into the judgments.

It might also help to ask the employee to evaluate the performance of some hypothetical employee who is a nice person but an unproductive worker. Discussing these differences might highlight the separation between performance and the person. Showing employees the results of their work and giving them tangible and immediate rewards helps them mentally connect their performance with consequences. Another way to empower employees and help them develop a more internal locus of control is to ask them what they can do or would suggest about a particular problem, which works to develop the employee's inner sense of capability and responsibility. It also builds rapport and relationship.

Specific performance review systems, however, pose special problems. The forced distribution method, similar to placing employees on a bell curve by ranking employees against one another, is a case in point. It would be like asking which fruit is the best—an apple, cantaloupe, strawberry, or mango. Not only does the answer depend on the rater's preference, but it has meaning only to the evaluator. In addition, comparisons generally put those who are different from the norm at a disadvantage. If this method is used, there need to be specific behavioral performance standards on which the comparisons are based. Even in using the rating-scale method, which allows the evaluator to independently rate employees using a number scale, there is an implicit comparison between workers: Are Mohammed, Erik, and Rosario all 4's even though they work differently? If I rate Tranh a 5, does that mean everyone else is a 4 because Tranh is always finished first?

The critical-incidents method may be more difficult to use in jobs where the product depends on group effort and individual contributions are not as clearly distinguishable. This may be especially true among employees who value group loyalty and harmony over individual achievement; the workers themselves may make it impossible to determine which individual is responsible for which product, step, or part. Another difficulty with this method arises because those who are not in the mainstream may stand out and be noticed more than other employees. Examples of both superior and inferior performance can be exaggerated and demeaning: for example, "Wow, that was a dynamic presentation, and I thought Asians were not good at this sort of thing." In addition, incidents that reinforce the evaluator's expectations are apt to be noticed, while those that do not may be ignored: for example, "I knew he'd have trouble with this because of his crutches."

No evaluation method is ever completely unbiased as long as human beings do the evaluating. However, using performance-based criteria leaves the least room for bias against diverse employees. Performance objectives are results-oriented: for example, "Customer complaints were reduced 25 percent," rather than "Communicates well with customers." Care must be taken to make sure criteria relate to the specific job responsibilities. This method requires careful explanation to the employee of the standards expected as well as the levels of competency. Once the employee understands these, he or she can choose how hard, and at what level of excellence, to work. Practice in writing performance-based criteria is provided in Activity 9.2 on the list that follows. In addition, the examples of an ineffective and an effective performance evaluation are given in Tables 9.2 and 9.3.

TABLE 9.2 | Ineffective Sample Performance Evaluation

I. General Information

Name_____   Review Period _____

Reviewer_____   Date of Review_____

II. Performance

Objectives	Rating
1. Learn foreign side of business	Exceeds expectations
2. Participate in in-house training	Meets expectations
3. Respond to company reports	Meets expectations
4. Reduce operating costs	Exceeds expectations

TABLE 9.3 | Effective Sample Performance Evaluation

I. General Information

Name _____   Review Period _____

Reviewer_____   Date of Review_____

II. Performance

Objectives	Results Achieved	Rating
1. Contact foreign clients and negotiate one international contract	Negotiated two successful international contracts	Exceeds expectations
2. Complete in-house managing diversity seminar and put information to use in own department	Completed course and made three changes in department due to learning in seminar	Exceeds expectations
3. Respond via memos to monthly regional reports	Writes and distributes accurate, informative memos within three days of receiving reports	Exceeds expectations
4. Reduce departmental operating costs by 5 percent each year	Reduced operating costs by 7 percent by consolidating forms and streamlining reporting procedures	Exceeds expectations

ACTIVITY 9.2 | Performance-Based Criteria

Trait/Characteristic	Performance Behavior
a. Careful and conscientious	*e.g., Continuously monitors quality of work, stopping to correct errors immediately*
b. Neat and well-groomed	*e.g., Wears uniform that is clean and pressed everyday*
c. Cooperative and congenial	*e.g., Volunteers to help others when own tasks are completed*
d. Responsible	*e.g., Calls in to advise boss when using sick leave*
e. Productive	*e.g., Suggests improvements that increase productivity*

Employee Evaluation Tools That Can Enhance Performance in Any Culture

1. You

As a manager, you are the most important tool in evaluating employees. Your ability to build relationships with staff, show them respect and appreciation, and value them as human beings is not something you do only at performance review time; relationship building with staff is an everyday process. This doesn't mean you need to socialize with staff outside of work or become best friends. Doing so may, in fact, cause problems and decrease productivity in workgroups where employees come from traditional cultures that respect a hierarchy and show deference to authority figures. What it does mean is that you show employees dignity by such behaviors as the following:

- Greeting them every morning and saying "good-bye" at the end of the day.
- Noticing them as human beings and speaking to them about the details of their lives.
- Helping them solve problems.
- Listening to their complaints and suggestions and taking action to respond to them.
- Asking for and using their input appropriately.
- Teaching them new skills and showing confidence in their ability to learn and grow.
- Trusting them with responsibility.
- Noticing and rewarding their accomplishments in culturally valued ways.
- Suggesting new opportunities for growth and learning.
- Recommending them for special projects, programs, and awards.

When employees feel accepted and valued, they are more open to learning and adapting. When they do not feel accepted and valued, their energies will be directed at resisting organizational procedures and processes, whether actively or passively. When this happens, performance review becomes a useless task that produces negative results for the organization and the employee.

As a manager, it is important that you get honest with yourself about your own feelings, assumptions, and biases about your employees. In one organization, for example, the manager of the legal department was honest enough to admit that he had difficulty accepting the fact that one of the lawyers working for him was gay. Because the boss was able to face his own biases and admit his own stereotypes, he was in a better position to keep them from directing his behavior and influencing his decisions. This meant he could actively work on being a better, fairer, and more effective boss to this employee. To help yourself in this process, make it a point to look for examples of behavior that break the stereotypes you hold about particular groups. Watch for performance that exceeds your expectations. Try to prove your prejudices and biases wrong, not right.

2. The Employee

The second most important tool is the employee. Only the employee has the ability to use the performance evaluation information to improve performance. Evaluations that do not include the employee in self-evaluation, goal setting, and action planning miss the mark. Without real employee involvement, you've gone through the motions and filled out the forms, but you have not achieved the results you intended.

Getting this kind of involvement may be difficult if the employee is from a culture that does not support this kind of participation. In more traditional settings, where hierarchies are more rigid and authority is not questioned, there is no expectation of employee input; helping individuals become active participants in their own growth and development is a teaching/coaching process done a step at a time. Use every opportunity, from staff meetings and one-on-one conferences to informal lunches and breaks, to talk about the employee's plans, goals, dreams, and accomplishments. It is important to remember that you may need to be the initiator.

3. Talk First, Paper Second

Overemphasis on the evaluation forms can be off-putting to employees from cultures that emphasize relationships over tasks. Spend time at the beginning of the evaluation session in icebreaking small talk, and then proceed to talking about the employee's performance in general. Invite the employee to loosen up and participate by using open-ended questions such as the following:

- How have things been going for you here?
- What have you been learning?
- How do you feel about your progress?

Also give your own views using "I" statements such as the following:

- I've noticed an improvement in …
- I've been pleased with your progress in …
- I've appreciated the way you …

Once you have each given a general overview, then you can get into the specific performance criteria on the evaluation form.

4. Performance-Based Criteria

Ratings based on traits and characteristics evaluate the individual and tend to produce a defensive response from the individual being evaluated. This type of evaluation also allows for more subjectivity on the part of the evaluator, making room for charges of discrimination and accusations of prejudice. This system may also trigger resistance in managers who balk at "playing God" in making these judgments. Ratings based on performance and behavior are less personally focused and tend to produce less defensiveness. In addition, behavior can be observed, quantified, and measured in more objective and equitable ways. Try your hand at changing these trait/characteristic criteria into performance behavior statements. Then compare your responses to the suggestions at the end of the chapter (see Table 9.4 on page 228).

5. Patience

While we may, in theory, subscribe to the axiom that patience is a virtue, few of us in the U.S. culture practice it. However, it is a virtue that can bring you surprising payoffs in a diverse environment. Having patience in listening in the evaluation session makes the employee feel attended to. When you get impatient with a circuitous explanation that sounds to you like "beating around the bush," the employee will feel rushed and put off. Make sure you set aside enough time for the evaluation so you do not have to keep looking at your watch because you have the next appointment in 20 minutes. Also, in evaluating performance, be patient with the rate of growth you notice in the employee and yourself; none of us changes or learns overnight. Watch for incremental steps that show progress rather than huge transformations. When you look back over time and trace the growth, you may see some significant change.

Guidelines for Conducting the Performance Review in Any Culture

Seat-of-the-pants performance review is a road to frustration and failure. Having a plan gives you confidence and a clear process. It also gives the employee security in a setting that produces anxiety. There are three areas in which to focus your planning. First is the preplanning arena, which sets you up for success. The second part involves the steps in conducting the review itself. The final step is the aftercare portion, which ensures that outcomes of the review bear fruit.

Preplanning for Productive Performance Reviews

1. *Set performance standards.* Analyze the job, writing the desired standards in relationship to performance behaviors and conditions, not personal qualities.

2. *Explain and clarify the standards to the employee.* It is critical that employees understand what the job requires and on what criteria they will be evaluated. Get employee input and involvement in that process.

3. *Help employees understand the review process.* Explain the reasons for reviewing performance and the part they play in the process. Show employees the forms with samples of criteria.

4. *Observe employee performance periodically.* Make notes about examples and instances. There is a tendency for evaluations to reflect the few weeks just before the evaluation session rather than the total six-month or one-year period covered by the evaluation. By making notes all year, you will have ample information to write a complete, representative review.

5. *Give the employee the forms for self-evaluation.* Clarify the criteria and evaluation rating system to be used. Discuss any questions or areas of confusion. Remember, most employees won't ask when confused, so give an explanation without requiring them to ask for it. "Lots of employees ask about this part of the review," or "This part may seem confusing. Let me show you how it works," might be ways to open up the subject.

6. *Set the time and place for the review session.* Give both yourself and the employee enough time to prepare the review forms. Set aside enough time in the review appointment for discussion, and reserve a private location in which to meet.

Conducting the Performance Review Session

1. *Explain the purpose of the review session.* Emphasize that it is not a disciplinary meeting. Give the employee a brief idea of the agenda of the session so he or she knows what to expect.

2. *Set the tone.* Start with a general discussion about how things are going from both your perspectives. Take enough time to make a personal connection and get used to the sound of each others' voices. Coffee, tea, juice, or soda might also help create more warmth and feeling of hospitality. In addition to the inherent inequality in boss/subordinate relationships, be sensitive to diversity-related reactions that may affect the climate of the meeting. A man being evaluated by a woman boss, for example, may feel discomfort. It may be the first time he has been evaluated by a woman since his mother or teacher did so years ago. A person of color may carry memories of past experiences of prejudice into the session.

3. *Have the employee present his or her self-evaluation.* Listen carefully to the employee's assessment. Do not interrupt or refute the employee's analysis at this point. Be careful even in asking clarification questions such as "What do you mean ... ?" because they are apt to sound like disagreements and can produce defensiveness.

4. *Present your evaluation.* Make sure to give specific examples of behaviors and conditions. Give a balanced view, beginning with the good news. Emphasize both positive, productive performance as well as areas of needed improvement. Identify points of agreement between the two evaluations. Use the techniques learned in the feedback section of the communication chapter, such as using the passive voice and giving positive directions.

5. *Jointly identify problems and obstacles to improved performance.* Put your heads together and discuss improvement needs:
    *   What seem to be the most difficult areas?
    *   What task seems to be the most difficult?
    *   Where does performance slip?
    *   What is getting in the way?

6. *Jointly make a plan for improving performance.* Continue discussing, at this point focusing on problem-solving:
    *   How can the obstacle be overcome?
    *   What does the employee need to do differently?
    *   How can you help him or her in that process?
    *   What are the employee's goals for growth?
    *   How can these be worked on?

7. *Agree to the evaluation and commit to a plan of action.* Both employee and manager need to work together until there is agreement and commitment to it.

8. *End on a positive note.* Complete the session with a summary of the evaluation and next steps and a final positive comment. Show appreciation, give a compliment, and show you value the employee. Thank the employee for participating, and end with a handshake or a formal closure.

Aftercare

1. *Assess yourself as a performance evaluator.* Use each review as a dress rehearsal for the next so you can continue to improve your own performance as an appraiser. *The Evaluating Yourself as a Performance Evaluator* checklist that follows can help you assess yourself.

2. *Set checkup times with the employee.* Put notes in your file to check back with employees periodically about how they are doing on their plans in both new goal achievement and performance improvement. Have a mini evaluation session at these checkups. You will need to initiate these sessions, as it is rare for employees of any culture to do so.

3. *Help the employee work through any difficulties.* Perhaps the goal needs to be reassessed, or maybe a different solution is in order. Whatever the case, help the employee figure out what to do.

ACTIVITY 9.3 | Evaluating Yourself as a Performance Evaluator

		Yes	Sometimes	No
1.	I explain the performance expectations of the job to employees.	_____	_____	_____
2.	I check employees' understanding of the role and performance expectations.	_____	_____	_____
3.	I explain the reasons for performance review to employees, emphasizing benefits to the organization and the individual.	_____	_____	_____
4.	I explain the steps in the evaluation process from the setting of standards and the use of forms to the actual evaluation session.	_____	_____	_____
5.	I give employees the time and the opportunity to do self-evaluation before the joint session.	_____	_____	_____
6.	I listen openly to employees' perceptions of their performance.	_____	_____	_____
7.	I remain objective and nondefensive in the session.	_____	_____	_____
8.	I observe the employee in action throughout the year and make notes on my observations.	_____	_____	_____
9.	I use performance criteria based on observable behaviors and measurable results.	_____	_____	_____
10.	I give myself time to prepare the evaluation document with thought and care.	_____	_____	_____
11.	I plan the evaluation session, setting it for the most productive time and place.	_____	_____	_____
12.	I create a comfortable, inviting climate at the evaluation session.	_____	_____	_____
13.	I spend a few minutes initially in the session talking with the employee to break the ice and open communication.	_____	_____	_____
14.	I am willing to modify my evaluation, incorporating ideas and comments from the employee's self-evaluation.	_____	_____	_____
15.	I require the employee to set his or her own goals and make an action plan for achieving them.	_____	_____	_____

Suggestions for Using
"Evaluating Yourself as a Performance Evaluator"

Objectives:

- Assess strengths and weaknesses as a performance evaluator
- Identify behaviors that could enhance effectiveness as a performance evaluator
- Trigger thinking about self-development regarding this management responsibility

Intended Audience:

- Managers seeking to increase their effectiveness as performance evaluators
- Trainees in a managing diversity seminar

Processing the Activity:

- Individuals rate themselves by placing checks in the appropriate column on the worksheet.
- Individuals share, in pairs or small groups, their ratings, identifying strengths and weaknesses and discussing potential areas for development, responding to the following questions:
  - » What did I do well? What do I need to work on to do better next time?
  - » What is one specific way in which I can make the next evaluation more effective?
- Group discusses reactions, insights, and learning.
- Individuals make a contract for self-development by targeting one or two behaviors to work on that would increase their effectiveness as performance evaluators.

Questions for Discussion:

- Which behaviors are easiest/hardest for you to do?
- What is the consequence of not doing those that are hardest?
- What would be the consequence of incorporating these?
- Which behaviors are you willing to do more often to make your performance evaluations more effective?

Caveats and Considerations:

- This worksheet can be used in one-on-one coaching sessions with managers as well as in supervisory/management training sessions focusing on performance evaluation.
- It can be used as a self-evaluation tool after each session and as a guide in planning future evaluation conferences.

Avoiding the Five Most Common Performance Review Pitfalls

1. Catching Their "Disease"

Anxiety and nervousness are contagious, and so is defensiveness. As a manager, it is easy to pick up on your employees' emotional state and respond in kind. It is not uncommon for managers to catch the tension or defensiveness their employees bring to the performance review process. First, deal with your own nervousness. It is normal to feel some anxiety; admitting it to yourself reduces some of its power. Also, look at the positive side of your feelings. Your nervousness may come from a concern for fairness and your desire to do a good job. Next, don't take it personally. Defensiveness on the part of the employee is not an attack on you or your assessment. It is an attempt to restore lost self-esteem. You can avoid this trap by not judging, accusing, or threatening the employee. You can also keep out of quicksand by not responding with your own defensiveness, but rather by showing empathy and listening to what the employee is saying.

2. Fearing Being Seen as Unfair or Prejudiced

All human beings have a need for approval. We have yet to meet the person who wants to be ignored, rejected, or talked about. Yet when your need to be perceived as a nice person takes precedence over your responsibility to give clear, direct, and honest feedback, you sabotage the process of performance evaluation. Not giving employees accurate feedback does a disservice to all. The employee does not know how to improve and may be confused by your mixed messages: "You tell me I'm doing great, yet you seem irritated with me." And you build resentment because the employee is not intuiting your desire for improvement. Remind yourself that you are not helping employees when you allow them to get by with less than they are capable of or less than is required. Take the acid test: Ask yourself, "Would I make this assessment if the person were of a different group?"

3. Assuming Employees Understand the Performance Review Process

Employees of all groups often see the evaluation as a test they are nervous about passing. They worry about failing, getting reprimanded, and losing face. In a diverse staff, many employees may have little or no experience with such a process, so it is even more important to make sure employees understand the purpose for the review. Help them see how it serves both the organization and themselves, and how it is tied to rewards and promotions. Finally, employees need a clear understanding of how the process will be handled. Showing samples of past reviews, having them meet with employees who have experienced the process, and discussing performance review at staff meetings are examples of ways you can do this. You may even do a mock review session using a role-play at a staff meeting to give employees a taste of what it is like. Having employees share the best thing they got out of their last review and brainstorming benefits they can derive from the review process are two other ways you can help further employees' understanding of performance evaluation.

4. Missing the Coaching/Teaching Opportunity

One of the richest and most overlooked benefits of the performance review process in a diverse staff is the chance to teach employees and help them acculturate to the norms of the organization. The joint problem-solving and goal-setting process helps employees develop a more internal locus of control. Setting standards and self-evaluation helps employees develop skill in participating in shared decision-making and giving input. Recognizing that these may be new and uncomfortable experiences for the employee can help you use them as teaching opportunities, or perfect chances to show employees the ropes and develop rapport at the same time.

5. Going It Alone

No matter how difficult it may be to get employee participation in performance evaluation, involvement is essential. If it is your responsibility and your review, there will be little investment from the employee to use it for improvement. Make the review a joint project from the setting of the performance standards to the targeting of goals for the future. Work on getting this across to the employee in as many different ways as you can. You can say, "While I'm responsible for evaluating you as your boss, you're the real expert on your performance. I need your help and input in this process," or "I can help you in achieving your goals if I know what they are."

Building Managing Diversity into Managers' Performance Reviews

If diversity is to be made an organizational asset, then management's ability to capitalize on a diverse workforce must be developed. One way organizations can actualize their commitment to diversity and inclusion is to evaluate managers on this aspect of their role. In organizations that have made progress in creating a more inclusive environment, managers are evaluated on and rewarded for their effectiveness in managing diversity. Performance standards reflect such behaviors as those in the *Diversity-Related Performance Standards for Managers* checklist.

ACTIVITY 9.4 | Diversity-Related Performance Standards for Managers

☐ Hiring, retaining, and promoting individuals from diverse backgrounds.

☐ Coaching and grooming diverse individuals for advancement.

☐ Building cohesive, productive work teams from diverse staffs.

☐ Resolving diversity-related conflicts between staff members.

☐ Maintaining a low rate of discrimination and harassment complaints.

☐ Developing staff through delegation.

☐ Planning and leading effective meetings with a diverse staff.

☐ Learning about the cultural norms and values of employees.

☐ Helping new employees acculturate to the organization's norms.

☐ Providing cultural-sensitivity training for staff.

☐ Attending cultural-awareness training and applying learning with own staff.

Which of these are part of your performance standards? On which is your boss evaluated? How would you rate yourself and your organization against these standards? Which do you need to work on to be a more effective manager of your diverse staff? When performance in these areas is made part of the manager's job duties and responsibilities, and evaluated periodically, its importance is validated. It is one way in which organizations show real commitment, not lip service, to diversity.

Performance evaluation is an important management tool that, when used effectively, can enhance employee performance, increase commitment, and strengthen the relationship between manager and employee. However, if not understood and dealt with, cultural differences and other diversity-related variables can sabotage the effectiveness of the process. Using the information, techniques, and approaches given in this chapter can help you maximize the output of your performance evaluations with all staff.

Suggestions for Using
"Diversity-Related Performance Standards for Managers"

Objectives:
- Identify appropriate performance standards for managers regarding dealing with diversity
- Assess existing and/or desired practices regarding the management of diversity
- Assess effectiveness in managing a diverse staff

Intended Audience:
- Managers wanting to increase their effectiveness in leading diverse staffs
- Executives and HR staff seeking to increase their organization's effectiveness in managing diversity
- Trainees in a managing diversity seminar
- Task forces charged with designing performance standards for managers

Processing the Activity:
- Individuals can use this checklist in a number of ways: they can check those criteria that are presently part of their performance standards; and they can star those they think need to be added. Executives can do the same with regard to subordinates' standards. Task forces can be asked to rank these to identify top-priority criteria. In still another variation, individuals can use these standards to measure their own performance, checking those they do or rating themselves on a scale of 1 to 5 (low to high) on each criterion.
- Groups can discuss their responses, ratings and/or priorities. If they are groups such as task forces making proposals about performance standards by executives deciding on those to be included, they can work toward consensus on a decision.
- Individuals can also identify those performance standards they would like to add to their own review and make plans for their own development in those areas.

Questions for Discussion:
- Which of these are/are not part of your performance standards and the performance standards in your organization?
- Which do you think should be included in your evaluation? Other managers' evaluations?
- What other performance criteria related to managing a diverse staff would you add?
- Which do you need to work on to be more effective with your team department or work unit?

Caveats and Considerations:
- This tool can be used as an assessment for individual managers as well as an activity to clarify the thinking of those designing standards to support the management of diversity.

TABLE 9.4 | Examples of Performance-Based Criteria

The following are suggested performance behavior statements:

a. Dresses in a manner that inspires customer/client confidence in his or her ability.

b. Helps others with work without being asked.
    Responds positively to delegated tasks.
    Volunteers for task forces and special projects.

c. Completes projects on schedule.
    Takes initiative to correct errors, fix equipment, and/or solve problems.

d. Fulfills job responsibilities completely.
    Accomplishes assigned tasks within given time frames.

SECTION 2

Integrating Diversity Into Your Organizations:

Modifying Systems To Capitalize on the Benefits of a Pluralisitic Workforce

Creating an Inclusive Culture That Leverages the Strength and Power of Diversity

• •

This chapter will provide you with:

- An explanation of how to create an inclusive culture

- An identification of the losses that influence a person's possible resistance to change and inclusion

- Tools for assessing the openness of your organizational climate and the barriers to inclusion

- Ways to use inclusion as a retention tool

No culture can live if it attempts to be exclusive.

—MAHATMA GANDHI

Language that advocates creating an inclusive mind-set is everywhere—it is heard when people talk of creating a new world order, living in a flat world, getting more adaptive in a global world, and making diversity and inclusion the prevailing norm in their organizations. Inclusion will be realized when employees are fully engaged and their talents and energy are thoroughly used. Finding a way to make inclusion really happen in a time of rapid change and bad economics is a serious challenge. James Baldwin astutely said—years before the demographic revolution, the information revolution, the technological revolution, the women's revolution, worldwide political revolutions, and most of the other major revolutions we have recently witnessed—that "any real change implies the breakup of the world as one has always known it, the loss of all that gave one identity." He was a wise man: He understood the subtle but complex issues involved in trying to harness both planned and haphazard, but definitely inexorable, change. Among demographic change, probably the biggest shift in your organization's culture has to do with generational and technological differences. In a Twitter world when BlackBerry devices are ubiquitous and MySpace is almost old news, you know life changes daily and constantly. It is tough, in this environment, to create and build an inclusive psychological climate that is open, feels safe, and values differences. Achieving true inclusion is a tall but necessary order.

Inclusion: A Mind-set That Pays Dividends

Inclusion is a term used often where people have a diverse work environment. It implies a comprehensive openness—an environment that welcomes any person who can do the job, regardless of race, age, gender, sexual orientation, religion, ethnicity, physical ability or any diversity dimension one sees every day on the job. How does this attitude show itself in real organizational life? For starters, it means that if I'm 55 and applying for a job, it is not automatically assumed that I'm unemployable because I'm too old. If I'm a 25-year-old, it is not assumed that I am always texting, multi-tasking, unable to focus, and only interested in tweeting. The 55-year-old can be valued for work and life experience, and he or she may also be literate in technology and change-oriented. The 25-year-old can be welcomed for knowledge, skills, talent, energy, and a viewpoint that any surviving organization sorely needs. It also means that when promotions are made or opinions are sought, it won't be assumed that women are too soft and too nurturing to handle the bottom-line tasks, that Asians will be too silent or too meek to make good managers, or that African Americans will be too aggressive to be team players. In an inclusive environment, what counts is a person's ability to do the job, and no one is disadvantaged because of background. The exercise *Symptoms of Inclusivity* can be a good barometer to see how your organization or team rates in the inclusion category.

ACTIVITY 10.1 | Symptoms of Inclusivity

Directions: Put a check next to any items that currently exist in your company.

_____ Employees are welcome and accepted regardless of lifestyle variations.

_____ All segments of your population are represented in the executive suite.

_____ Air time at meetings is not dominated by any one group and ideas are welcome and wanted from every level.

_____ Ethnic, racial, and sexual slurs or jokes are not welcome.

_____ Cliquishness between groups is absent.

_____ Variety in dress and grooming is the norm.

_____ Warm, collegial relationships exist between people of diverse backgrounds.

_____ There is sensitivity and awareness to different religious and ethnic holidays and customs.

_____ Selection of food and refreshments at organizationally sponsored functions or food facilities takes into account religious and personal preferences.

_____ Flexibility exists to accommodate personal responsibilities outside of the job.

Suggestions for Using
"Symptoms of Inclusivity"

Objectives:

- Assess the inclusiveness of your workgroup or organization
- Identify a starting point for creating more openness in climate and utilization of ideas and talent

Intended Audience:

- A CEO or vice president of human resources who wants to stimulate a discussion among executive staff about opening up the organization
- Trainers teaching managers to create a more open climate

Processing the Activity:

- Explain the directions as stated in the inventory. Ask each participant to check off those items that indicate inclusivity. This can also be done virtually by having people do it themselves then bring collective data to the discussion on a teleconference.
- Put people in pairs or small groups and ask them to discuss the symptoms they see. Suggest illustrating their perceptions with concrete examples.
- Tell participants to use all perceptions, no matter how similar or different, as data for group discussion.
- Bring all the small groups back to the big group to discuss as a whole.

Questions for Discussion:

- Where are your perceptions about symptoms of inclusivity the same as others'? Where are they different? How do you account for the differences?
- Think about the places where your workgroup or organization lacks openness. What does it cost you in individual and team performance?
- Think about times when you have felt excluded. What has been the impact on your performance? Where are others being left out and what does your team or organization lose by not hearing them?
- If you were to begin creating more openness by focusing on one of these symptoms, what one would you choose?
- What can you do to start the process?

Caveats, Considerations, and Variations:

- Remind participants that culture change is slow. Small starts, reinforced over time, can add up to bigger change, but it won't happen overnight.
- Openness and flexibility need to be modeled. Employees learn behavioral norms more from what you and other leaders do than from what you say.

Focus on the inclusivity symptoms you'd like to see but you don't. Which ones can you identify? What does their absence cost your company or workgroup? Select one symptom you'd like to work on as a starting point toward creating a more inclusive environment. What might you gain in productivity and commitment if, for example, it was no longer acceptable to tell jokes at some group's expense? What would be the result of acknowledging the different holidays or celebrations of your employees in a company newsletter or in the cafeteria? These things are not hard to do, but they do have to be valued to be realized. What's in it for you to recognize and embrace those differences?

An Inclusive Environment Captures Commitment

An inclusive environment has, as part of its bone marrow, the acceptance of people as they are. That doesn't mean that feedback is not given, but it does mean that, theoretically, each person is accepted for who he or she is and room is made to use the valuable talent he or she brings to the task at hand. Employees rarely produce their best work when they have to fit into someone else's mold. An atmosphere that has, as its credo, acceptance of a person's genuine self will get top performance from its staff. It will also minimize resistance and maximize commitment.

Identifying Organizational Barriers to Diversity and Inclusion

If creating a diverse and inclusive workplace is beneficial, how come there is so much resistance to doing so? For starters, there are numerous concerns that erect strong barriers to moving forward with diversity and inclusion, some conscious and predictable while others are unconscious. In either case, it is important to identify and acknowledge barriers so the case can be made for the benefits diversity and inclusion bring.

Cost of Implementation

Milton Friedman's quip "There are no free lunches" applies to organizations as well as individuals. If a company is serious about creating a culture that embraces diversity and inclusion, does this necessitate a full-time minority recruiter? How much will outreach to colleges and universities cost in order to create and cultivate the connections that give you first crack at top talent? And what about training? There will be a need for management training to help managers handle the predictable difficulties that arise as diversity grows. There will also be a need for awareness training to sensitize employees of all backgrounds to one another, and training to help new employees find common ground in the organization. If all of this training takes place—and it is necessary if the diversity effort is going to be successful—who will be cranking out the work while staff is being trained and how will the organization pay for it in a time of job cuts and tight resources? The time to plan for a long and successful future is now, even amidst difficult financial challenges. Some knowledge and training can be found online, but other conversations about changes and appreciating and using different points of view can only happen when people talk to one another. There is no substitute for convening people and discussing options. We can make a strong case for saying that the short-term cost may be high but the long-term benefits are worth it. Since the dominant U.S.-American business culture is notoriously short-term in both thinking and the desire for gratification, a commitment of time and money can be a major obstacle. However, organizations that talk a good game but fail to make a real commitment risk losing the trust of their employees and the markets they serve. Those companies that focus on future opportunities even in these tough economic times will be well served. Cost effectiveness matters—and so does planning for the future.

Fear of Hiring Underskilled, Undereducated Employees

Another barrier to greater inclusion in hiring is the fear of hiring people with inadequate skills and effectiveness. Sometimes, there is erroneous belief that hiring women, people of color, and other segments of the population that fall under the diversity banner will mean sacrificing competence and quality. Common stereotypes hold that members of some groups are undereducated and therefore inadequate in a work environment. It is no secret that high school dropout rates in this country are disgracefully high, and they are even worse in communities where there is poverty or little support for education from parents. We hear in the news repeatedly about how difficult it is to find qualified people in this country to do basic jobs. Since people are being laid off, that may be less of an issue in the economic downturn but a tough economy won't last forever. Business leaders are concerned about the investment they will have to make in bringing potential employees up-to-speed. An even bigger concern is, "If the investment is made, will employees be able to do the work?"

Strong Belief in a System That Favors Merit

There is a bias toward equal treatment in this country that in itself is commendable. What makes this otherwise admirable attitude a barrier toward diversity and inclusion can be seen in the subtle aphorism that advocates "the best man for the job." In the United States, not only has the best, or only, person for a job traditionally been a man, but it has been a white man. Not infrequently, organizations have been dragged kicking and screaming toward affirmative action as a way to level the playing field, but the perception still exists that any affirmative action candidate is someone chosen to fill a slot and not because he or she may happen to be the best candidate for the job. Our socialization is so strong and our biases so subtle that rarely is a women or person of color actually considered the best person for the job. What this myth of meritocracy also overlooks are the traditional practices that ignore merit by giving advantage to some candidates because of their connection-based factors such as legacy admissions to universities or executive's children getting sought-after internship positions.

Annoyance at Perceived Reverse Discrimination

Reverse discrimination raises the hackles of those fair-play advocates who say that it doesn't help to end discrimination of one group at the expense of another. As long as one person's gain is perceived to be someone else's loss, fears of reverse discrimination will provide very strong resistance to diversity and inclusion. In interviewing people about their recruitment practices, organizations that were effectively dealing with diversity were looking for employees from varied backgrounds. Sometimes, based on numerous factors, the applicant pool did not allow them to be as diverse as they liked. They did not sacrifice quality, but what they did do, when they found a number of excellent candidates from different groups, was take into consideration the ethnic makeup of their employee base and the customers they serve. Having customers see themselves in an organization whose products or services they might buy is a powerful motivator to reframe reverse discrimination so that there is less annoyance at the belief that one person or group gains at the expense of another.

Perception That There Has Been a Lot of Progress

In the eyes of some, any progress that exists is proof that the system is opening up. If it opens at a snail's pace, so what? The perception of increased openness will exist more strongly now that we have a bi-racial president with a very eclectic cabinet, and the progress that has been made is undeniable. Thankfully, we are seeing gains in selecting people more for talents, skills, and experience, regardless of their backgrounds or visible differences. But we also cannot fool ourselves that we have arrived in a utopia of diversity and inclusion. One client told us recently that he hired the first African American in his organization and was treated as the "anti-Christ" because of that hiring decision. That example is less isolated than we would like to believe. We are balancing the conflicting truths here—progress has definitely been made and we also have a long way to go.

Diversity and Inclusion Are Not Seen as a Top-Priority Issue

In a long list of organizational priorities, especially amidst the current economic downturn, diversity may not be seen as crucial. An organization would need forward-thinking leadership to make diversity a top priority when people are losing jobs right and left. In some sense, the world and demographics have changed so much that pluralism is simply our reality. But real vision and leadership are shown in difficult economic times when surviving and keeping the doors open is the highest priority and diversity stays on the radar.

The Need To Dismantle the Existing Systems To Accommodate Diversity and Make Inclusion a Higher Priority

The sheer weight of rethinking or changing existing systems is frightening to many people. Some fear the changes because of what they perceive they'll lose. "If, for example, the selection process, reward structure, or performance review system is changed to create a more inclusive environment, what will that mean to me?" worries the employee who sees limited resources. If you are charged with the task of modifying the existing system, a lot of work will be involved in getting buy-in. If you are charged with implementing the new system, it means learning and teaching new methods of operation to others and then setting up a feedback loop. And if you are an employee impacted by these changes in an uncertain time, you don't know for sure what it will mean, and that might be the scariest position of all.

The Size, Rituals, and History

Large organizations are like the 2,000-pound elephant: They can't turn on a dime, nor can they change direction quickly like the hummingbird. Actually, smaller organizations we have worked with don't change all that easily either. Organizations have history, systems, norms, and a whole lot of mythology and folklore, but change eventually alters them all in some way, either by design or happenstance. Your organization is analogous to a human system whose primary function is to sustain and perpetuate itself. Any outside intervention is viewed as threatening, so the system closes to protect itself from intrusion. The result is that sheer inertia will keep the system moving on its own steady course; hence, organizational and personal responses to change almost guarantee that reversing or changing direction will not happen easily, and there has to be strong motivation and payoff to making inclusion the way you do business. Consider how all of these factors play out currently in your organization. Which obstacles seem to be the most intractable? Is there an appetite to harness change, or a stronger desire to just let it happen? Is there currently support for dealing with any of these barriers? If so, where is the most hopeful place to begin? If you are truly determined to create a more open and responsive organization, these issues will have to be acknowledged, dealt with, and overcome. Try the exercise *Identifying Organizational Barriers to Diversity and Inclusion* in order to pinpoint the biggest obstacles in your organization.

ACTIVITY 10.2 | Identifying Organizational Barriers to Diversity and Inclusion

Directions: Rank the following list of obstacles as they occur in your organization. The most significant obstacle rates a 1 and the least important an 8. You must use all 8 numbers.

_____ Cost of implementation

_____ Fear of hiring underskilled, undereducated employees

_____ Strong belief in a system that favors merit

_____ Annoyance at reverse discrimination

_____ Perception that there has been a lot of progress and this is not needed

_____ Diversity and inclusion not seen as a top-priority issue

_____ The need to dismantle existing systems to create greater diversity and inclusion

_____ The size, rituals, and history

Assessing Your Culture's Openness to Change

Identifying the barriers to diversity and inclusion is important, but it is really part of a larger issue that involves your organization's openness to change. George Bernard Shaw said, "Progress is impossible without change and those who cannot change their minds cannot change anything." Shaw's quote is as relevant today as when he said it. The measure of any successful organization in today's world ultimately rests on how adaptive a company or team is to the changing times. If you want to find a clear example of how adaptation means survival, you need look no further than Apple.

Apple is an organization that values excellence and innovation, and that emphasis does not change. What do change are their offerings. Think about the journey from iMac to iPods to iPhones and iTunes. They have changed and stayed relevant even as they keep looking for new ways to do business, new products to offer, and new ways to matter to their customers in a time of huge competition. In the midst of this troubling recession, as of April 2009, they are one company whose stock prices still go up.

Take a look at your own organization and see where it stands on the change issue. The following 15-item questionnaire will help you focus on where you are doing well with regard to change, and where you have work to do.

Suggestions for Using
"Identifying Organizational Barriers to Diversity and Inclusion"

Objectives:

- Identify obstacles that participants think prevent the organization from dealing with the issue of diversity and inclusion
- Compare perceptions of various participants
- Determine consensus on barriers and future courses of action

Intended Audience:

- An executive staff willing to work on removing obstacles that inhibit becoming a more open organization
- Top management of a division willing to do the same
- A change agent who works with top management to identify barriers to diversity and inclusion
- Any team willing to wrestle with the barriers it sees

Processing the Activity:

- Ask all participants to rank the obstacles from 1 to 8. Number 1 is the biggest obstacle; number 8 is least important. Again, as with other tools, this can be done virtually by mailing ahead of time, collecting data, and then having a teleconference meeting about what the data suggests.
- Have participants discuss their responses in small groups. Have the group reach consensus on what the biggest obstacles are and determine a starting point for change.

Questions for Discussion:

- Are there any barriers you would like to add that were not on the list?
- What is the impact to the organization of not dealing with each of these barriers?
- Based on answers to the last question, which three obstacles are most significant or costly?
- What do you see happening to morale and productivity if you (we) do nothing?
- What needs to happen in order to tear down some of these barriers?
- Where is a good place to begin?

Caveats, Considerations, and Variations:

- Make certain that all participants have their say. Everyone needs to contribute to the discussion.
- Keep asking questions that help participants see the high cost of exclusion.
- This can also be used as an exercise to teach consensus. Each person ranks his/her responses from 1 to 8 and then the group or the team in groups of seven to nine people are charged with achieving consensus on the ranking. It can teach a decision making strategy while also providing great discussion content. The same questions for discussion are viable, and all that needs to be added are comments about how the group handled the process of reaching consensus.

ACTIVITY 10.3 | How Open and Flexible Is Your Organizational Culture?

Focus on your organization as you read questions 1 through 15. Then place a check in the appropriate column.

Questions	Almost Always	Often	Sometimes	Almost Never
1. In my organization, change is viewed as a challenge and an opportunity.				
2. Policies are reviewed annually to assess effectiveness.				
3. Rewards are doled out to suit the preference of the rewardee.				
4. Our personnel department is creative in finding new ways to attract top talent among diverse groups.				
5. There is an openness to suggestions from people at all levels of the organization.				
6. Our strategic plan is evaluated once a year and revised as needed.				
7. "We've always done it that way" is a philosophy that describes my company's response to new ideas.				
8. When problems emerge, there is a willingness to fix them.				
9. Our products and services reflect the awareness of a more diverse consumer base.				
10. My boss values new ideas from people at different levels and implements them quickly.				
11. Performance evaluations in this organization measure an employee's adaptation to change.				
12. Top executives in this company solicit innovative ideas and listen to people throughout the organization.				
13. We can and do make midcourse corrections easily.				
14. There is little variation in style of dress among employees.				
15. People at all levels of the organization are continuously trying improve products, processes, and services.				

(continued on next page)

ACTIVITY 10.3 | How Open and Flexible Is Your Organizational Culture? (continued)

Directions for Scoring "How Open and Flexible Is Your Organizational Culture?"

Numbers 1-6, 8-13, and 15

Almost always . . . . . 4 points
Often . . . . 3 points
Sometimes . . . . 2 points
Almost never . . . . . . 1 point

Numbers 7 and 14

Almost always . . . . . 1 point
Often . . . . 2 points
Sometimes . . . . 3 points
Almost never . . . . . . 4 points

1._____   6._____   11._____

2._____   7._____   12._____

3._____   8._____   13._____

4._____   9._____   14._____

5._____   10._____   15._____

Total:_____

Answer Key

50 to 60: The culture of your organization is open to change. You are able to react and adapt quickly and are open to new ideas. This openness should translate to greater inclusion of new people and ideas, and greater innovation from using varied points of view.

40 to 49: Your organization understands that change is a reality. In some ways you are open to it, but you haven't fully embraced it, nor are you harnessing change to make it work for you.

30 to 39: Your organization understands the value of change, but you need to be more open to its reality and quicker in the implementation process.

15 to 29: If you don't get better at adapting, you won't be around long.

Suggestions for Using
"How Open and Flexible Is Your Organizational Culture?"

Objectives:

- Help a workgroup or part of an organization assess how open its culture is to change, thereby impacting its ability to be inclusive
- Identify places where an organization or group is not open or flexible
- Determine what, if anything, needs to be done to make the culture more open, flexible, and inclusive
- Create an environment where talent from different backgrounds and places feels safe, welcomed, and valued

Intended Audience:

- Executive staff conducting its own assessment of the climate
- An internal or external change agent working with the CEO and executive staff or management staff of any division
- An internal or external change agent using this assessment at various levels of the organization to gather feedback that can be fed upward to top management and compared against their collective perceptions

Processing the Activity:

- Distribute questionnaire to each participant and clearly identify the group being evaluated. Is it the whole organization? One division? A smaller workgroup? It would be very interesting to do small business units then the whole. That picture would reveal a great deal.
- Ask participants to check the most appropriate answer for all 15 questions.
- Explain directions for scoring, and ask each participant to come up with a total.
- On a flip chart, record all the scores so the group can get an idea of how varied the perceptions are. There is no need to match names to scores.
- Then, depending on the size of the group, have small-group discussions. Anything from pairs to foursomes is good. Have participants review their one- and two-point answers.

Questions for Discussion:

- Look at your one- and two-point answers. What do they indicate about the openness and inclusiveness of your culture?
- What areas are ripe for change as you review your responses?
- What are you willing to do to begin the process of becoming more open and inclusive?

Caveats, Considerations, and Variations:

- The higher the level of management willing to act on data from this questionnaire, the greater the opportunity to impact change in the culture.
- This tool has the possibility of providing valuable feedback from all levels of the organization. How it's presented to top management will influence receptivity. Get their buy-in before you use it.

The numerical score is a beginning assessment of how fluid and potentially inclusive your organization is. An even more instructive way to use this questionnaire is to do an item analysis. Circle all your one- and two-point answers, then reread the questions and think about the issues embedded in them. For example, if your score on item number 12 was either one or two points, is it because top executives are too insulated? Maybe their creativity never filters down to the lower levels. More important, maybe employee creativity never floats upward. If executives operate as phantoms who are figuratively and literally out of touch with the troops, that might account for the score. Being unapproachable precludes an open and inclusive environment because executives will have limited access to full information.

As you contemplate some of your answers, think about why your organization or workgroup scored low in certain areas. People resist change for many reasons, but underlying them all is the fear of loss. If you want to create a more change-oriented culture, you will need to come face-to-face with the losses people fear.

Acknowledging these losses is a critical first step. Later in this chapter, we present an activity that will help you or your workgroup deal with them. It is tempting to look for a way to short-circuit the pain of these losses, but that is not possible. The fact that there will be hurt and discomfort in this process is unavoidable. Before you can create an organization that truly embraces diversity and practices inclusion, both losses and gains need to be dealt with and acknowledged. To help yourself sort through the issue and achieve some clarity, fill out the four quadrants in *Sample of Anticipated Losses and Gains on the Path to a More Inclusive Climate*. The questions to answer are, "What do I stand to gain and to lose in a more diverse and inclusive organization? What does the company stand to gain and lose?" A sample answer is listed in each square in order to help you fill out your own answers. You can use this exercise with your own workgroup if you detect their resistance to becoming more open, or as a coaching tool with any individual who is having a particularly difficult time.

ACTIVITY 10.4 | Sample of Anticipated Losses and Gains on the Path to a More Inclusive Climate

	Anticipated Losses	Anticipated Gains
Me	Career opportunity	Marketable experience in managing and functioning in an open, multicultural work environment
Organization	Confusion and disorganization in the culture change process	Creates opportunity to respond to employee needs; can also lead to increased job satisfaction through a more attentive environment

Suggestions for Using
"Anticipated Losses and Gains on the Path to a More Inclusive Climate"

Objectives:

- Foster the idea that the path towards a more inclusive culture presents both advantages and disadvantages
- Help people, who are impacted by this change, acquire a broader perspective and thereby lessen the stress and resistance
- Explore, with co-workers, different views of possible culture change and the gains/losses that accompany it

Intended Audience:

- Managers helping individuals or workgroups move towards greater inclusion
- Any training professional who leads an inclusion process
- Internal or external consultants who have to help resistant workgroups or organizations deal with change and move toward greater inclusion

Processing the Activity:

- In each of the four quadrants, have participants list anticipated losses and gains for themselves and the organization.
- In pairs, have participants discuss these possible losses and gains in each area.
- On a flip chart and easel, list the losses and gains from the random responses of group members.
- Conduct a discussion with the whole group about the data that surfaces, and what it all means. Focus specifically on the group's ability to manage and guide the process for best possible outcomes.

Questions for Discussion:

- What gains and losses have you personally experienced or which ones do you expect to? Which do you anticipate in the organization?
- What strikes you about these gains and losses?
- What can you take from this experience to the next change?

Caveats, Considerations, and Variations:

- There may be some participants who refuse to anticipate any positive outcomes in some of their changes. Acknowledge their anger and accept their feelings or reactions.
- Use one-on-one with participants who are stuck when the possibility of or need for change emerges.

Losses: The Seeds of Resistance to a More Inclusive Culture or any Other Kind of Change

Let's pretend that you're at a meeting and an enlightened manager is trying to enlist your support in helping her create an environment that embraces diversity and inclusion. Among her arguments for this openness are the following:

1. You can be seen and valued for who you really are with no hiding or censoring yourself.
2. The psychological safety and freedom you feel will enable you to be more creative and productive.
3. The organization will be more permeable, and because it is, your ideas may exert more influence.

Once your manager puts these benefits forward, would you sign on to bring about change? The answer ought to be a knee-jerk "yes," but it isn't always. Change frightens people and saps them of conviction. Why this resistance? William Bridges, Ph.D., provides a list of losses in his book, *Surviving Corporate Transition*.[1] See which of the perceived losses ring true for you.

Perceived Losses During Change

1. Loss of Attachments. If you already like, value, respect, and enjoy working with the group you are part of, why would you want to open it up more and risk messing with the dynamics? Sometimes people tell us they already have open climates with the people who are there and they are not interested in being more inclusive, no matter how good the talent might be. They like what they have, and the idea of moving people around and losing their connections isn't attractive.

Attachments to home, loved ones, and the familiar run deep. Years ago, in one organization that was downsizing, we conducted seminars that helped their middle managers deal with the significant changes attached to either relocation or job loss. While some longtime employees were being laid off, others could keep their jobs if they were willing to move halfway across the country. The only certainty was that when the dust settled, everything would look different. One story of loss moved us because the attachment was both deeply personal and very unusual. One of the participants mentioned that he was a gardener by avocation, growing rare apple trees. He was grafting a number of different kinds of apples that were so unique you would never find them in your supermarket. It had been a five-year process, and he was just starting to see the literal and figurative fruits of his labor. He was proud and invested in this orchard. He said, "I can't go to my boss and say, 'I don't want to move to Texas because I don't want to leave my apple trees.' But I can tell you that I don't want to move to Texas because I don't want to leave my apple trees." Attachments come in all sizes, shapes, and colors. All of us, native borns and immigrants, have them. Any change that forces us to leave these attachments is threatening.

2. Loss of Turf. Gang wars are literally fought over turf. In organizations, turf wars may not be fatal, but they can be devastating. Being more inclusive asks people to open the boundaries of who counts, and to let in people who are not part of "your group." One of the most volatile turf issues often centers on which languages are used in the workplace.

Beyond the obvious loss individuals might feel when they literally can't communicate, the greater loss, conscious or unconscious, might be in the areas of power, dominance, and organizational influence. If we are more inclusive, does that dilute our influence? We think not: Actually it broadens it but fear of turf loss can make people put up emotional fences.

3. Loss of Structure. The loss of structure gets to the heart of some key organizational systems such as promotional, accountability, and reward systems. Answers to questions like "What do you have to do to be promoted in this organization?" or "What behaviors get rewarded in this company?" will change if the organization is more open and inclusive. If you are a talented, competent white male who has been working hard to move up the ladder, and the new structure rewards an able, competent woman with the position you have coveted, will you feel cheated and angry that these systems no longer automatically favor you? Loss and frustration will be among the paramount feelings as you adjust to this change, and inclusion as an idea might seem better than inclusion as a reality.

4. Loss of Future. The demographic shifts portend a different racial/ethnic cultural configuration, hence a different power structure. Being white and male is probably no longer a guarantee of preeminence. On the other hand, if you are a woman or a person of color, your professional future might hold more opportunities as sheer numbers shift the balance of power.

5. Loss of Meaning. All human beings have a set of operating principles by which they live their lives. These assumptions act as a bedrock and function smoothly in times of stability, but they are severely challenged in a time of change. These principles lend fundamental meaning to people's lives by assigning significance and order to the world. For example, it is not uncommon for those reared in the United States to hold to the belief of fairness, equity, and treating people well. As a nation of immigrants, part of our history is that we are truly open to others who differ from us in any number of ways. A less obvious but still bedrock U.S.-American belief is about the nature of capitalism. We know that capitalism is an unforgiving economic system that offers potentially high rewards but it is also high-risk. The basic belief is that if you get the benefits of the reward on the upside, then you must be willing to take your lumps on the downside. It feels like that belief is being violated when big banks get bailouts and people lose jobs. There is anger and frustration: On one level, it is about perceived injustice but at a deeper level, one of our core principles that give our life meaning and structure is amiss.

In regards to inclusion, the issue of meaning spills over into other losses already mentioned such as those of structure and future. Meaning is the most subtle of the losses, and it is very powerful. Changing your assumptions and expectations about the culture, its openness, and entitlement is important to opening the organization up to change. It also is intimately connected to the sixth fear, loss of control.

6. Loss of Control. The overriding loss during change is the loss of control that encompasses all the other losses. When people feel out of control, it is harder for human beings to be open and inviting to others. Our need for predictability is threatened and any outsider, even an organizational insider just transferred from one department to another, is less welcome. When working in organizations where significant numbers of people around us don't speak our language, we may feel like strangers in our own house. Not knowing how to give directions to a blind employee might make you feel out of control or inadequate.

When we don't know how to manipulate our world anymore, we feel threatened and powerless. What follows are anger and exclusion, not openness and inclusion. If organizations are populated with people who feel they can't control globalization, a recession, demographic changes, or the ability to create a more inclusive environment, there may be enough anger and resentment about diversity to resist it rather than accommodate it. The issue of loss of control is most definitely not limited to white males. One African American called us after reading a magazine article we had written on today's multicultural workforce. She was a deeply angry woman because, in her view, the implied promise made to blacks about securing a bigger piece of the pie has never been fulfilled, and now she has to share limited resources with so many other immigrant groups. She feels her own opportunities are diluted. Again, change comes—she can't control it. Her anger makes it hard for her to be open to creating a climate that welcomes and invites others.

In an organization that is focused on becoming more inclusive and changing its hiring and promotional patterns, some in the organization will feel their informal contract was broken. We have met countless women who bought into the assumption that they would be judged, evaluated, and promoted by the job they did. They strove to deliver continuously excellent performances, but when promotion time came around, the prize was not there. Again, this represents to the individual a "contract" broken, an assumption violated, a world out of control. Doing superb work is not enough … now what? Spend a few minutes thinking about your own workgroup and the actual or anticipated changes you are going through, or expect to. What will its impact be on you, or the group as a whole? What are the consequences of these losses on your ability to have a more inclusive climate?

Losses and gains are an inevitable part of facing the diversity-and-inclusion issue. They are also a central in dealing with change and the resistance to it.

ACTIVITY 10.5 | Losses From Change:
Possible Impediments to an Inclusive Climate[2]

Directions: Think about the diversity you and your workgroup are dealing with. In the boxes below, make notes about how each loss impacts a desire to be more or less inclusive for both you and your group.

Loss	Impact on You	Impact on Your Workgroup
1. Attachment (e.g., losing two colleagues to job cuts)	*I am going to miss Robert and Jorge. Losing them makes me sad and unfocused.*	*All of us will have more work so we'll miss not only their energy and enthusiasm but also feel more burden from having to do their share of the workload.*
2. Turf		
3. Structure		
4. Future		
5. Meaning		
6. Control		

Suggestions for Using
"Losses From Change: Possible Impediments to an Inclusive Climate"

Objectives:

- Help individuals and workgroups identify the losses they are experiencing or expect to experience from any change, and the impact those changes may have on developing an inclusive climate

Intended Audience:

- Leaders in an organization who want to shape climate
- Trainers and managers who can help individual employees and workgroups deal with the frustration, stress, and anger sometimes associated with change
- Teams or groups of people dealing with change

Processing the Activity:

- Ask participants to write down both real and perceived losses (as an individual and as a member of a group), then talk about what this does to your creating an inclusive, welcoming environment.
- In pairs or small groups, have people discuss their comments.
- Discuss perceptions among the whole group, looking both for common viewpoints of loss as well as different reactions.

Questions for Discussion:

- Where do you feel the greatest loss personally? In the workgroup?
- Were there some areas where you felt no loss? Even without anticipating losses, could you envision any possible gains?
- What was your reaction to writing this down and seeing your thoughts on paper?
- What were the most interesting reactions that surfaced in your group? Any surprises?
- Based on comments you heard from others, are there any of your losses you are willing to rethink? If so, which ones?
- How can you help yourself stay open, welcoming, and truly inclusive when you are going through tough times? How can you use this mental process next time you feel a loss?
- People have strong feelings about these losses. Provide enough time for venting and good discussion. Be certain that, in addition to processing the losses from change, people also talk about what a climate of loss does to inclusion. Also, make certain that you ask people to think about potential gains. What upsides can be envisioned?

- Create a trusting climate, but suggest people group themselves with those they don't know too well in the discussion segment. It might offer a varied perspective.

  A few things should become obvious from analyzing your losses from change.

  1. Stimulate discussion of both gains and losses so that employees can see hope and possibility as well.

  2. Perception is critical. Often the only difference between a gain and a loss is how someone sees it.

  3. Whether the changes result in a loss or a gain depends on how they are handled. A manager can do some problem-solving around areas where there are perceived losses, such as fear of shrinking resources and fewer career opportunities. Those feelings can create an opportunity for some team building that will be to everyone's advantage.

From a Monocultural to an Inclusive Workplace: Designing Incentives That Work

Commitment to becoming an organization that embraces diversity necessitates becoming inclusive by using the differences that exist. The road to hell, as the saying goes, is paved with good intentions. In many organizations, that road is littered with diversity efforts stopped midstream. Some companies and personnel just have no idea of what they were getting into and what kind of resources would be required to make a real effort work. Good intentions and noble objectives are not enough. Before you embark on the long journey to real inclusion, take a reality check. Every organizational journey of 1,000 miles begins with a single step. The following list presents your first dozen. Use these 12 steps to guide your own change effort toward greater openness and engagement.

Twelve Steps on the Road to Inclusion

1. **A Long-Term Change Effort Is Required To Realize Significant Culture Change.** In our 30-second-sound-bite culture, sustained long-term effort requires more tenacity than we are normally willing to invest. The kind of change we are advocating impacts the bone marrow of the organization. It can be successful, but it will not be quick, it will not be easy, and it will need eternal vigilance. It is not an effort for the faint of heart. Set clear expectations with employees from the very beginning so they understand you are embarking on a several-year, systemic change as opposed to eight hours of diversity training.

2. **Time, Energy, Money, and Emotional Commitment Are Essential.** If so many resources are involved, and if commitment is usually only lukewarm, why do it? In a word: survival. To paraphrase the L'Oreal commercial, it may be expensive, but you're worth it! Smart, competitive organizations will not look at this as only a diversity effort; they will frame it as it should be framed—a change effort designed to produce a quicker, leaner, more open, and more competitive organization. Becoming more inclusive is just one piece in the global powerhouse puzzle.

3. **Support from the Top Is Critical to Success.** No one can dispute that support from the top is critical to success. What's also critical is to determine what that support looks like. Is the CEO willing to continue financial support for this change effort in tough economic times? How accessible will he or she be to consultants, internal or external, who facilitate the change? When you get to the training sessions, does he or she need to kick them off? If the answer is "yes," does that mean all of them? Does he or she need to do so in person? Is video an acceptable medium to indicate that this is a top organizational priority? These are tough questions. Lip-service support is easily detectable and it won't work. In a culture change effort of this magnitude, that failure can be deadly. The stakes are too high, the cost too great, and the consequences too important not to define the terms very clearly ahead of time. Support and communication are essential.

4. **Don't Raise Expectations That May Eventually Be Dashed.** We meet a lot of cynical people as we travel around in our work. Most have been hurt over the course

of their professional lives by organizations that raised their hopes but didn't come through. The end result is lowered expectations and cynicism. If you don't plan to go where the path leads, you are better off never starting the effort of revamping the organization and making it more responsive to all your employees. Tokenism will be detected. Contrary to what P.T. Barnum said, suckers are not born every minute, or if they are, don't count on the fact that they live in your organization. If you start this effort, you need to be open enough to go where the data take you, have ego strength enough to not be defensive, and have courage enough to implement changes. There are no sacred cows once you start the process.

5. **Expect Discomfort: Change Is Unsettling.** Organizational transitions lead the troops, at least for a time, to a no-man's-land, which is not a comfortable place to be. It's that undefined area between what your culture is and what it is striving to become. As said earlier, when looking at losses that unsettle us in change, the human species likes predictability and homeostasis. Change disrupts them both. Your effort should be centered on creating an organization that's nimble. If you can create a psychological climate open to the rich diversity that exists, you will also end up with an organization that is more open to new and different ideas.

6. **Be Clear About the Depth and Breadth of the Effort.** Whether the people guiding the change effort are internal or external, they need to coach, facilitate, and guide the organizational leadership. It is not hard to imagine a CEO that signs up for a top-quality workplace with the promise of establishing a highly talented workforce from diverse backgrounds and who also conducts business productively and profitably with staff. Who wouldn't want that? What he might not ask, however, is, "At what price?" Even with the most elaborate plans, all outcomes cannot be anticipated, but you will do yourself a favor if you define your commitment level before you ever start.

7. **Work To Modify the Systems You Already Have in Place.** Don't throw out the baby with the bathwater. If you need a new promotional system to encourage broader representation among diverse groups, look at your existing system. What parts are working? What adaptations have to be made as your objectives change? If you have performance reviews conducted in ways that are offensive to people from various cultures, see what communication norms are incompatible or offensive. Determine what kind of changes need to be made in giving feedback so that employees will be open to suggestions that are useful. Revising systems you already have is much smarter and less threatening than starting from scratch.

8. **Help Employees Understand the Big Picture and Get Beyond Themselves.** Helping employees understand the big picture is not so easy to do in mainstream U.S.-American culture because we focus so extensively on individual need fulfillment. It will be a much easier task in most immigrant cultures where personal satisfaction usually takes a backseat to the collective good.

9. **Set Measurable Criteria**. As you engage in the process of becoming more multicultural and, in some cases, truly global, what are your criteria for success? What results need to occur in order for staff to determine that the efforts are warranted? Your chances of success are greater if you determine the criteria before you get

started, not after the fact. If you are trying to create a more inclusive culture, there needs to be something in it for everyone. Get data from the troops. Find out what needs revamping. Does the flexible benefits package need to offer domestic partner benefits? In terms of career development, are there mentors or coaches available? What particular classes or educational opportunities could make the performance review system more tailored to the variety of people and culture norms present in your company? Set measures ahead of time that tell you how well you have achieved these goals.

10. **To Get Support for the Changes, Employees Must Be Shown Something Better Will Result Than What Currently Exists.** Years ago, the city of San Diego, California, was involved in a major change effort to value and embrace a diverse workforce. As so often happens in these efforts, the perception initially existed that what the organization's real end game was "slotting minorities" into management positions. When two consultants from the organizational effectiveness program went around to various groups to explain the program, they talked about many things, among them the flexible benefits package that gave every employee in the city an extra $600. This was initially intended to help with child care, but each employee could use the money as he or she saw fit, even taking it in cash. Additionally, a child care coordinator was hired by the city to investigate different child care centers and contracted with several of them to give city employees discounts of between 10 and 25 percent. At the end of one of their briefings, a white female told one of the consultants how glad she was they had come to talk to her group because before they explained the program, she thought this was just designed to help certain people. Now she can see this effort is for everybody. If you want yours to work, then it, too, has to have benefits for everybody. Don't be bashful—tell people loudly and clearly what those benefits are.

11. **Training Is Necessary but Not Sufficient.** Training is undeniably an important part of any long-term change, particularly as it relates to systems changes that revise organizational culture. Your training content should fall into three areas: (1) awareness, (2) knowledge, and (3) skills. Employees need awareness about their own reactions to different cultural norms specifically and to change generally. They also need knowledge about what culture is, about how it impacts everyone, and about change as a universal human phenomenon. Lastly, managers need skills in areas such as managing intercultural conflict, structuring an effective work team or task force, and leading meetings in a diverse group. The umbrella for all of this training is creating an inclusive culture where people feel safe, connected, committed, and counted. Inclusion is the main mantra because it will establish the expectation that everyone counts and is valued.

12. **There Is No "There" There**. After all your effort, you will see some wonderful, satisfying results. You'll also undoubtedly have experienced some frustrations. But the most sobering reality will be the awareness that as you have created openness and solved certain problems associated with closed systems, inclusion presents its own set of challenges. New problems will be spawned, new answers will be needed, and new products will be developed to meet competition in the marketplace. There

is no laurel on which to rest: At best, you get a temporary stopping place for a moment, where you can feel the warmth of the sun and the satisfaction of accomplishment. But organizations are rapidly changing and are always in evolution, so your best bet is to look at this a little bit like Tom Sawyer's fence: You've got some willing and committed painters, but by the time they get to the end, they may need to go back and touch up a few spots.

Inclusion as a Retention Strategy

There are many good things that an inclusive environment brings to an organization. We believe that one of its best gifts is retention because people want to work for, and will stay at, organizations where they feel valued, have their skills utilized, and feel connected. As we write this book, the unemployment rates are exceedingly high so this moment in time could be an aberration in terms of retention, but there is a big difference between staying at an organization because there are so few jobs in the larger market, and staying because you love your organization and want to give it your all. Organizations that are seen as inclusive much more frequently get full commitment.

If organizations are truly interested in the kinds of policies and procedures that will compel people to stay, it is helpful to get feedback. The retention questions in Activity 10.6 are useful in both one-on-one interviews and in focus groups. Compiling the data into themes enables executives or managers of business units to take ideas and make them actionable. These questions are a good first step in getting your arms around the retention-and-inclusion issue especially if you seek information from a diverse representation of your workforce.

Another way to get feedback is to have managers distribute the *Managing Retention and Inclusion* questionnaire (Activity 10.7) to people who report to them. A diversity council could also use this 15-item questionnaire and give the data to the manager or appropriate person in the larger organization. As you can see from looking at the Managing Retention Model (Figure 10.1) and the questionnaire, a manager, diversity council, workgroup, executive, or whoever uses this data needs to focus on three areas: (1) Individual attitudes and beliefs; (2) managerial skills and practices; and (3) organizational values and policies.

The individual attitudes and behaviors look at how people treat each other in one-on-one situations and what kind of peer consequences there are when people violate norms of respect and inclusion. A welcoming, safe, respectful environment is the expectation. The second part of the model, managerial skills and practices, looks not only at how managers define retention and inclusion as part of their role, but also how they behave as managers and integrate these practices into the workplace operations and meetings.

Finally, the organizational values and policies look at what the organization must do in its systems to hold people accountable. How is more access and opportunity given to employees? Are there policies which may unintentionally exclude people, and if they do, what needs to happen to change them? What consequences exist for managers who don't stop bullying or racial epithets immediately when they see them take place at work?

ACTIVITY 10.6 | Retention

1. What do you like best about working here?

2. What gets in the way of productivity, morale, and satisfaction for you?

3. How well are your skills, talents, and ideas used? What could this organization do to tap more of your potential?

4. What are the biggest frustrations you face on the job?

5. What keeps you working here?

6. What would tempt you to leave?

7. What could another employer or position offer that would entice you to leave?

8. What is the most important thing this organization can do to keep you?

There is no shortcut to developing behaviors, policies and procedures that foster, promote, and reinforce retention. The behaviors advocated in this 15-item questionnaire are among those most employees desire in a workplace. They are inclusive and, in the end, environments like this will do a lot to retain people even in times where perks like bonuses, money for more education or promotions are not readily available. Those benefits are "nice to have," but they won't keep people. On the other hand, an inclusive climate will go a long way toward doing so, or at the very least, give people a number of things to consider before they ever leave.

FIGURE 10.1 | Managing Retention and Inclusion

An Example of Inclusion in Action

In April 2009, the *Los Angeles Times* had an article about a small business (66 workers) in three locations: Rancho Cucamonga, California, Chicago, Illinois, and New Jersey. The article was about Primary Freight Services, a company which had the predictable financial trouble most companies are experiencing in the recession of 2009. Sales since the beginning of the year fell 21 percent, but rather than lay people off at this point, John Brown, the owner, cut hours and pay of all employees by 20 percent.[3] He has done the following, as well:

1. He, as owner, and his sister, Kathy Hagar, as CEO, have stopped taking personal pay checks to try to avoid layoffs.
2. He has provided video conferences, two hours each week for six weeks, to help people deal with anger, stress, and job burnout.
3. He has shared the sales numbers in company meetings, left benefits unchanged, and answered all questions from employees. This is real transparency.
4. He sent personal letters to the home of each employee to acknowledge his awareness that cutting back hours would impact not just the employee but their families as well.

ACTIVITY 10.7 | Managing Retention and Inclusion

Think of your organization as it relates to managing a diverse staff, then read the following 15 questions and respond to each by putting a check in the column that is most true and appropriate for your organization.

		Usually	Sometimes	Rarely
1.	Employees of all groups feel valued, respected, and included.			
2.	Managers engage staff in discussions about job satisfaction and career development.			
3.	Changes in systems and processes are initiated to create more equity and accessibility.			
4.	Employees spend time (e.g., lunch, breaks) with people who are different from them in a variety of ways.			
5.	Managers are coached on how to deal with diversity-related problems that lead to turnover.			
6.	Policies are reviewed annually to assure they are inclusive.			
7.	From a policy and relationship standpoint, it is clear that ethnic, gender, racial, religious, etc., jokes are off limits.			
8.	Retention issues and obstacles are discussed at regular management or work team meetings.			
9.	Managers are held accountable for fair treatment and respectful behavior.			
10.	People speak up when necessary to let others know that derogatory comments and exclusionary behaviors are out of bounds.			
11.	Managers have effective resolution strategies for use when there are conflicts in the workplace.			
12.	The strategic advantages for retention and inclusion are made clear to all.			
13.	Staff members make an effort to include newcomers.			
14.	Managers see retention and inclusion as part of their responsibility.			
15.	Leadership speaks publicly and supportively about the organization's retention-and-inclusion initiatives.			

Scoring:

Usually: 2 points; Sometimes: 1 point; Rarely: 0 points

Individual attitudes and behaviors; items 1, 4, 7, 10, 13 _____

Managerial skills and practices; items 2, 5, 8, 11, 14 _____

Organizational values and policies; items 3, 6, 9, 12, 15 _____

Total _____

From a quick scan of the data, where is your group doing well? What opportunities exist for moving forward? What aspects (individual, managerial or organizational) need the most attention?

John Brown is a smart and decent man. He is decent because of how he is treating people—no special treatment; everyone is in it together; employees are kept in the know. He is smart because he knows that within five years a predicted labor shortage looms as baby boomers leave the workforce. Companies want to hang on to capable, talented, committed employees. Investing in his employees is a good use of resources that will give him a competitive edge over the long haul.

March figures indicated an 18 percent increase in sales figures, some perhaps because John Brown made more trips to clients abroad, but also because after the training, his employees were more confident in asking potential customers questions about additional business. It is too soon to write the final chapter on Primary Freight Services. There is hope, but not certainty, that the company will survive. By mid-May, they will decide whether to restore full pay and hours or make the painful decision of more deduction of hours and layoffs.

Being inclusive in how you work with people does not mean everything always ends well, although we hope this will. What it does mean is that people are considered and they are an integral part of the process. When Brown was asked why he went to such efforts, he talked about the importance of minimizing disruption and he kept his eye on the larger prize: "My business would have suffered because it would have given the impression that it's all about the numbers and not the people. We were just trying to stay true to our culture as well as get through these tough times."

This is a man who understands what it is like to include people during the good times and the bad. He believes they matter as individuals and he knows they really are his best resource. His behavior in a tough time illustrates the message of this chapter.

Diversity and Inclusion as an Organization Development Intervention: Culture Change That Works

• •

This chapter will provide you with:

- A look at saboteurs which derail diversity-and-inclusion initiatives

- A seven-step process for achieving long-term culture change that develops a culture of inclusion

- Examples of methods and practices used at each stage

- Tools for engaging appropriate groups in planning and implementation

When one looks at the results of diversity initiatives started over the last 25 years, the outcomes appear to be decidedly mixed. There are success stories to be sure, and these have a few things in common: They are part of change efforts that are based on strategic drivers that connect to the organization's goals, they are long-term processes, and they focus on achieving meaningful systemic change. These are organizations that have stuck with the effort through all manner of obstacles. We have seen so many aborted and disappointing efforts to accomplishment of culture change, too, so we start this chapter with a list of the top saboteurs, factors that make long-term diversity-and-inclusion culture change at the very least an uphill battle, and, at worst, ineffective. The following list of saboteurs will reveal potential obstacles so they can be dealt with.

Identifying Major Diversity Roadblocks

Perceived Lack of Relevance

While all the obstacles listed are pertinent, relevance is a key factor because unless employees believe that the accomplishments from a diversity initiative matter, they don't. However, relevance is also relative. Why should someone whose "plate is too full" care about a diversity initiative? "What's in it for me" is the answer to the question of relevance. How diversity initiatives impact competitive advantage, productivity, financial results, product development, team dynamics, or job security and opportunity are important and have to be emphasized. Relevance has to be demonstrated up close and personal in very clear ways to get the attention of busy people who are often overworked and stressed. Some important questions to ask yourself and others regarding relevance are:

- How are diversity and inclusion central to the daily functioning of individuals, teams, and the organization?
- How are people treated and where might that sense of respect or dignity need to be improved?
- How might our economic or interpersonal indicators change if we attend to this issue?
- What happens if we do nothing?
- What's currently going on that makes diversity important to both consumers who buy our products/services and employees who work here?

If your answers to these questions indicate that life goes on exactly the same with or without a diversity-and-inclusion initiative, think twice about trying to move forward.

Not Using Data To Drive the Initiative

What would make an initiative relevant is having data which says, for example, that turnover is high and good people are leaving; or the organization loses out when it tries to recruit good people because it is not perceived as diversity friendly in the job market; or there are discrimination suits and employees feel disconnected and totally uncommitted to getting the job done; or we have a changing customer base that we are serving. Data can come from a number of places: employee surveys, focus groups, interviews, or customer feedback, for example. Observational data can be useful as well. Things such as who sits together in the cafeteria or how frequently employees call in sick, or how quickly they exit work at the end of a day, all offer information that is helpful in diagnosing. Relevant questions regarding data are:

- What data have the most credibility with your audience?
- What traditionally happens to data in your organization once it's collected?
- What current data do you have that can be used rather than starting from scratch and seeking whole new information?
- How many ways can that existing data be cut? (e.g., department, exempt, nonexempt, gender, age, etc.)
- Once you look at the data you have, what's still missing? What's the most cost-effective and information-rich method of getting what you need?

The biggest benefit from data is that it can delineate where exclusions are hindering or where greater inclusion could help, and it can provide the information that legitimizes paying attention to diversity.

An "Us vs. Them" Mentality

Frequently, resistance to diversity initiatives is due to the sense of polarization employees feel or anticipate. This happens if white males are singled out as the all-powerful, while other employees are seen as powerless victims. Resistance and polarization also happens when any group (e.g., ethnic, racial, gender, departmental, or union) is perceived as the beneficiary of diversity change initiatives and the winner of the resources battle at the expense of other employees. Setting up any program in this "some benefit at the expense of others" mind-set creates more problems than it can ever solve. Showing the benefits for everyone minimizes polarization.

Questions to be asked:

- How can this, or any, initiative benefit all parts of the organization?
- What groups feel disenfranchised or excluded?
- What departments, age groups, ethnic groups, for example, seem underrepresented when opportunities for growth exist?
- When are there entrenched differences where can you build common ground?
- Who perceives potential losses from this initiative?
- Who are the leaders from various constituencies who could serve as bridge builders?

Lack of Understanding at the Top Regarding the Nature and Implications of Commitment

It tends to be much easier to get verbal commitment from executives to engage in diversity initiatives than to get real, sustained change. In theory, the potential benefits of diversity done well sound good, but the realization of what that commitment requires on a daily basis tends to chip away at energy and effort. Perhaps the evolution of priorities in a rapidly changing world means that what made sense yesterday no longer works today. The point of changing priorities can be seen by applying Abraham Maslow's needs hierarchy to organizations. At the top of the pyramid is self-actualization. Organizations want to grow, develop, and be all that they can be. Diversity is fashioned as a tool to help achieve this growth. But until a connection is made that diversity is also linked to Maslow's lower-level needs for survival, or the esteem and belonging needs of people in workgroups, diversity initiatives will continue to be seen as a luxury, free to be abandoned at the first sign of a crunch. A legacy of fair-weather commitment has left a residue of broken trust, the "flavor of the month" syndrome, and little faith that anything lasting can happen. Questions to be asked include:

- What is the organizational demonstration of commitment? How do people know when something really matters in this organization?
- In coaching the CEO and executive staff to demonstrate commitment, what specific behaviors do you want or need from them?
- What are the consequences of appearing to have commitment, starting down the road and seeing it evaporate?
- How can you clearly articulate these consequences to the executive staff in a way that motivates them to respond thoughtfully?

Failure To Set Context

Diversity initiatives that are appropriately implemented are designed to add strength to a company's strategic position. That means the whole landscape of an industry, domestically and globally, has to be looked at. Who are the other players in the industry? From where do we draw our employees? What customers do we serve and how broad is our reach? What skills and knowledge do we need now and in the future? What skills and knowledge are we missing? As you ask these and other questions, and as you survey the scene within your industry, what do the answers imply? Perhaps you are like a large multinational who said to us recently, "We thought 20 percent of our workforce needed to be cross-culturally fluent, but we are doing business worldwide, and everywhere we turn we need greater understanding in moving our business objectives forward." Your diversity initiative doesn't happen in a vacuum and you need to pay attention to the economy and social climates in which you are conducting business. Consider the following questions:

- What information do you need about the industry, employee population, and consumers to understand why diversity matters?
- What big-picture factors in the macro climate might influence the definition and scope of your initiative?
- How does the current economic situation impact the organization with regard to diversity and inclusion?

Not Doing the Upfront Work

A dear friend of ours says that the secret to good gardening is putting a 10¢ plant in a $10 hole. If you do all the prep work on the soil, any plant can thrive. This metaphor about gardening has relevance to setting up a successful diversity initiative: Part of the soil preparation is doing your homework in terms of collecting data, and once you have a sense of why diversity matters in your organization and what needs to be addressed, there needs to be time spent building coalitions, internal advocates, and relationships at all levels of the organization. We have never seen an initiative be successful where internal support wasn't carefully cultivated.

Another part of the upfront work is determining how executives are going to demonstrate their support. Does support mean making a video? Does it involve talking about the importance of diversity every time they get a chance? What about holding their direct reports accountable for inclusion? Furthermore, how are you communicating the purpose of this initiative? What format (e-mail, Internet, memos, meetings, etc.) are you using to inform your end users? Other questions to be asked include:

- What is the history of long-term change initiatives in your organization?
- What are the factors that have been relevant to both success and failure?
- What must you do ahead of time to set this program up for success?
- Who in the organization can give you honest feedback about your communication and implementation strategy?
- Who are the key opinion-makers and informal leaders that you need to include and involve to boost support?

Absence of Clear Goals and Objectives

Our first question to any client who calls for help is, "What's going on that makes you think you need work around diversity and inclusion and what do you want differently at the end of your efforts?" These two questions must be answered at the very beginning because they get to the heart of what an organization's rationale might be. Whether you're doing this to create a more engaging organizational culture, minimize law suits, or understand and respond to diverse consumers more effectively, your goals must be clear. Having a clear rationale for pursuing diversity, identifying changes you're after, and determining how those changes will be measured and evaluated are bedrock questions. Don't even think of beginning an initiative until serious discussion around goals, objectives and measures has taken place. Questions to be asked include:

- What tangible changes do you want from the diversity initiative?
- How will you know if you have achieved them?
- How much flexibility is built into the initiative for changing the goals as organizational realities change?

Lack of Tailoring in Training

One of the most common mistakes is making the training involved in the diversity initiative the only visible change. Training has a valid role to play in any change effort, but it has to be customized and conducted in the service of achieving something tangible and specific. If, for example, you work at a health care facility whose community is changing and becoming multilingual and multicultural, it may be helpful to have cultural-competence workshops that explain the wide range of cultural norms in communication, values, and health care beliefs and practices. To maximize the learning and application, people in housekeeping may need only four hours of training, whereas nurses, for example, may need eight because their patient and family contact is more extensive.

If you are looking at diversity as more of an internal issue, maybe all employees need a basic session so that they are talking the same language and have a clear understanding of how your organization is defining diversity and why it matters. In addition, managers who are responsible for hiring, promoting, coaching, conducting performance reviews, and team-building may clearly need some skill development to help them enhance their repertoire of management techniques for leading a more complicated workforce. If time does not permit you to teach all the necessary skills, which ones are more critical and do those vary by department? It is this kind of tailoring that can make diversity training relevant and helpful.

Questions to be asked include:

- What are your training objectives and how do they relate to organizational goals and individual performance?
- How are you evaluating the success of the training?
- How do the objectives, content, materials, and delivery change depending on position or educational level?
- What adaptations are made for non-English-speaking participants and those with limited literacy?

Human Nature and Reluctance to Change

Finally, when one looks at potential saboteurs of long-term change, one needs to look no further than human nature itself. As a species, we tenaciously hang onto the status quo whether or not it works to our advantage. Weak egos, a desire to control our environments, shaky esteem, and vested interests are among a few of the reasons human beings resist change. Finally, perhaps the biggest reason of all is comfort with the known and fear of the unknown.

Questions to be asked include:

- Who stands to lose and what do they lose if the desired changes are accomplished? (The previous chapter provided tools to assess this.)
- What kind of strategies need to be implemented for everyone to gain something?
- What strategies are available for mitigating people's fears?

These roadblocks, singularly or collectively, can influence the success or failure of your initiative. They are intended to make you think, and to help you do your homework before you ever roll out an initiative. To see which ones can pose problems for your organization, do the assessment in Activity 11.1.

ACTIVITY 11.1 | Identifying Major Diversity-and-Inclusion Roadblocks

Directions: Identify potential obstacles to diversity and inclusion that are operating in your organization. Write down some suggestions for your preplanning to avoid these potentially negative outcomes.

Potential Saboteur	How this is shown	How we can address it
Perceived lack of relevance		
Not using data to drive the initiative		
An "Us vs. Them" mentality		
Lack of understanding at the top regarding the nature and implications of commitment		
Failure to set context		
Not doing the upfront work		
Absence of clear goals and objectives		
Lack of tailoring in training		
Human nature		

Suggestions for Using
"Identifying Major Diversity-and-Inclusion Roadblocks"

Objectives:

- Identify factors that have the potential to sabotage the effectiveness of your diversity efforts
- Determine strategies for overcoming the saboteurs

Intended Audience:

- Diversity Council or task force
- An executive staff looking at the strategic benefits of diversity
- An internal Organization Development department responsible for long-term change

Materials:

- Copies of the worksheet *Identifying Major Diversity-and-Inclusion Roadblocks*

Processing the Activity:

- Ask participants to think about the organization's diversity-and-inclusion change efforts, then identify on the checklist those saboteurs that get in the way and note the ways they are shown in the organization.
- Then ask them to think about strategies for overcoming the obstacles and make notes in the *How we can address it* column.
- In either pairs or small groups, participants discuss the saboteurs, how they show themselves in the workplace, and how they can be addressed.
- Have a recorder chart suggestions in small groups.
- Lead a total group discussion of suggestions and knowledge obtained.

Questions for Discussion:

- Which saboteurs stand out? For what reasons?
- Which ones most seem to undermine the implementation of the diversity strategy?
- If you could try to turn around just one of these barriers, which one would it be and why?
- Which ones seem possible to fix or influence? Which seem intractable?
- How are these saboteurs demonstrated?
- What suggestions do you have for minimizing their negative impact?
- Whose support do you need to make any change(s) happen?

Caveats, Considerations, and Variations:

- Tackling too many of the saboteurs at once may make the change seem overwhelming and dampen enthusiasm.
- Take care not to misread the depth and complexity of the saboteurs; they are easy to understand at a conceptual level but much harder to flesh out a pragmatic level. Allow enough time in the session to have these points discussed fully.
- At the start, you can ask participants to brainstorm factors they imagine might sabotage efforts and chart these. Add these to the list.

Seven Steps to Diversity-and-Inclusion Culture Change

Being aware of the saboteurs can help you avoid the pitfalls. Even so, there's no magic about what, when, or how to generate results. However, the following seven steps used sequentially, and/or simultaneously, are critical to an organization's chances of achieving success.

1. Gain Commitment From the Top

It is common knowledge that for the long-term success of any change process, commitment from the top, including support from the CEO or president, the entire executive staff, and the board of directors, is critical. Committing resources, holding people accountable, and sustaining the long-term effort required to change existing systems necessitates both symbolic and real commitment at the top of the organization from all the formal leadership positions.

A key factor in getting commitment is making a strategic business case that focuses on the bottom line. While many articles have appeared touting the business case, Michael Wheeler when working at the Conference Board, conducted research which identified how U.S. companies were making the case for diversity and how it was integrated into business operations and objectives.[1] Ninety-five percent of those companies that responded said that any initiative, diversity or otherwise, must prove to be an essential part of business operations. His results were interesting but not surprising; they validate what we hear from most organizations. Though it is sometimes challenging to link diversity to economic profitability, there are measures which can show bottom-line results. In spite of the fact that proof positive is hard to come by, the business rationale is being made with the following five items. Ranked in order of importance, they are:

1. Customers and markets
2. Global diversity
3. Productivity
4. National workforce demographic trends
5. Internal workforce demographics.

Customers and Markets

Linking marketing, service, and the sale of products to the broad needs and tastes of diverse consumers served is a case that most top executives can understand. Customers who don't see themselves reflected or represented in services will go somewhere else, which is significant because the profile of the consumer is changing: Eighty-five percent of the consumer dollar is spent by women; older Americans control more than 50 percent of all discretionary income (more than $800 billion annually);[2] and the purchasing power of African Americans, Hispanics, and Asian Americans (in 2003) had increased over 500 percent to $1.684 trillion annually.[3]

Global Diversity

Global diversity ranked second among organizations that responded. Though many are headquartered in the United States, they have operations all around the world. Firms are increasingly treating the world as the appropriate business arena, source of brain power, market, and functional team.

The intense competition for products and services, the increasingly swift, fluid communication channels, the porosity of national borders, and the demand for world-class products has changed the entire scope of the marketplace. Even "domestic" businesses, such as a local bank or hospital, become global when they recruit from around the world and deal with a multilingual, multinational customer base as is the case in many areas around the United States.

IBM has identified domestic and global diversity issues in a "Worldwide Diversity Issues" chart, which incorporates feedback from HR teams in the United States, Canada, Europe, Middle East, Africa, Asia/Pacific, and Latin America.

TABLE 11.1 | Worldwide Diversity Issues-IBM*

Canada	United States
• IBM Representation Women Minorities Disabled Aboriginal People • Bilingualism • Dependent Care • Work/Life Flexibility • Domestic Partners • Credentialism • Old Boys' Network	• Civil Rights Act • Glass Ceiling/Walls • A.D.A. • MacBride Principles • Immigration • Multilingualism • Redistricting • Family Leave • Dependent Care • Work Flexibility • Domestic Partners
Latin America	**Europe**
• Women • Population Growth • Work Flexibility	• Women • Disability • Catholics (Northern Ireland) • Economic Immigration • Social Exclusion • National Origin • Work Flexibility • Race • Aging Population
Asia/Pacific	
• Women • Disability • Aging • Work/Life Balance	

*Source: Wheeler, Michael, *Diversity: Business Rationale and Strategies. A Research Report.* New York: The Conference Board, 1995, pp. 11, 14.

Productivity

Most business leaders instinctively feel that having an inclusive climate—one where everyone belongs and feels utilized based on the unique combination of talents and skills—increases productivity. While connecting diversity and inclusion efforts to productivity increases is difficult to prove, there is a sense that a diversity-friendly climate builds pride in the company and a desire to be more tenacious in completing tasks and solving problems. There is some data indicating that diverse teams trained to leverage their diversity can create better solutions, utilize different perspectives effectively, and minimize conflict. Here are some examples that demonstrate the diversity-productivity connection.

In banking, research shows that having a diverse workforce has beneficial results in performance and service.

- "Diversity in top management teams was associated with greater innovation within bank branches."[4]

- "Racial diversity was positively associated with growth in branches' business portfolios."[5]
- "Gender diversity within regions was positively related to goal achievement as well as speed of response to customers."[6]
- "Ethnically diverse teams performed better when they were embedded in ethnically diverse organizational units."[7]
- "Racial diversity was associated with higher overall performance in [bank] branches that enacted an integration-and-learning perspective on diversity."[8]
- "Branches in which a higher proportion of employees participated in at least one diversity-education program outperformed [in sales productivity] branches with lower participation in these programs."[9]
- "Racial diversity had a positive effect on overall performance in branches that used that diversity as a resource for innovation and learning and a negative effect otherwise ..."[10]
- "... for teams led by managers of color, [there was] a positive relationship between team ethnic diversity and team performance."[11]

The impact of gender diversity is shown by the following:
- Average returns of investment clubs showed that all male clubs had an average of 8.7 percent, all female clubs 9.4 percent, while mixed male-female clubs had a 10.4 percent return.[12]
- Conference Board of Canada researchers found a link between gender diversity and good corporate governance. "94% of boards with three or more women insist on conflict-of-interest guidelines compared with only 58% of all male boards and 72% of boards with two or more women conduct performance evaluations, compared with only 49% of all male boards."[13]

Finally, the overall impact of diversity is shown in the following:
- *Fortune* 500 companies with good results in recruiting and retaining women and people of color had 10 percent higher stock prices than those that did not have good results.[14]
- Firms that had exemplary diversity management practices " ... performed better as measured by their stock prices."[15]

More data connecting inclusion and productivity is clearly needed to demonstrate competitive advantage from diversity.

Workforce Demographics
If a lack of concrete productivity results can fan the flames of doubt, looking at demographics can erase them. According to the Department of Labor's report, *Opportunity 2000*, there are some significant diversity trends that impact diversity initiatives.[16] One of the most significant trends to pay attention to is the graying of the workforce. Not only are numbers of middle age and elder workers rising, but retirement for many is delayed, especially in tough economic times. While the aging of the workforce may be the most significant trend, others also matter: The increase of women, an increasing percentage

of minorities, and a large immigrant population also have high impact. One of the most interesting demographics involves immigrants because while numbers are increasing significantly, they are not so equally in all places. For example, while there are more Hispanics in California and the Southwest than elsewhere, they are also the fastest growing minority in many other areas both urban and rural, in the United States.[17]

Internal Workforce Demographics

Most people in the workplace see the changing population. Looking at the demographics of your area and considering their impact on your current and future workforce will help you decide how to attract and retain highly-qualified people, how you can minimize turnover, how you can build a reputation as a diversity-friendly company, and how diversity can help adaptation and flexibility become the norm in the organization.

What difference does it make if more workers are aging? Or are women? Or are from Mexico? One concrete example involves looking at flexible benefits. Cafeteria plans are more important than ever. For an aging population, medical coverage may emphasize a plan for glasses and eye exams, whereas parents of young children may desire day care more than anything else. The one-size-fits-all plan is irrelevant in a diverse climate. Mostly what does matter is not assuming that broad-brush national demographics will fit your region, industry, or community.

These five factors—customers and markets, global diversity, productivity, and external and internal workforce demographics—require some initiative in tailoring the case to help you deal with your competition, consumer, industry or region.

We have found that the most relevant and compelling business cases are built around a simple framework suggested by the work of Amy Kahn and Steve Gomez that involves four dimensions.[18] (see Figure 11.1) First, diversity is both an internal workforce issue, focusing on those within the organization, and an external marketplace issue related to customers, clients, and the public. Second, managing diversity is called for because there are both opportunities to access and liabilities to avoid. When these dimensions are considered, four categories of reasons for managing diversity can be articulated, tapping potential opportunities in the workforce and in the marketplace while reducing the potential for liabilities in those same arenas. With this framework as a foundation, organizations can begin building a customized business case by collecting data, giving examples, demonstrating needs, and showcasing potential gains in each of these arenas. The charts that follow provide a tool and process to construct this case, with the input and involvement of key players.

FIGURE 11.1 | Making the Strategic Business Case for Diversity*

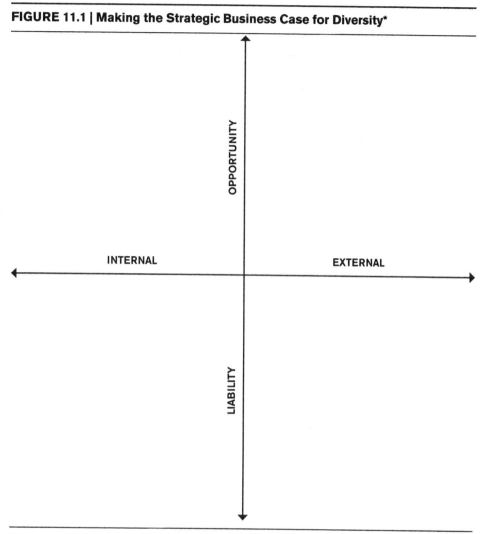

*Adapted from the work of Amy E. Kahn and Steve Gomez; see Amy E. Kahn, *Challenging Diversity: Taking the Next Step*. Phoenix: Budshel Press, 1998.

TABLE 11.2 | Building the Strategic Business Case for Diversity

• What do employee surveys tell you about satisfaction and commitment?	• What are the demographics of your existing and projected customer base?
• Are there disparities between groups regarding perceived treatment?	• How do the demographics of your workforce compare to those of your customer, client, or patient base?
• What is the demographic make-up of your workforce by level? How does that compare to the surrounding labor force?	• In how many countries do you do business?
• Who are you not having access to in recruiting and promoting?	• How many cultures and languages are represented in your marketplace?
• What are your projected recruitment needs in terms of skills and positions?	• How many of those are represented in your workforce?
• What are the statistics in the labor market relative to your needs?	• What do customer satisfaction surveys tell you about missed opportunities and needed improvements?
• Where are there untapped resources of talent within the organization such as overqualified, underutilized, or undeveloped employees?	• What market segments are you seeking to penetrate?
• What obstacles are recruiters facing?	• What employee groups could help you understand those markets?
• What are your organization's critical needs for creativity and innovation?	• How do you tap the experience and knowledge of different employee groups to help in marketing and customer service?
	• What is the demographic makeup of decision-makers in your client organizations?
• What are the statistics in your organization regarding grievances, complaints, and lawsuits?	• What customer complaints have you received?
• How much has your organization spent on legal fees and settlements for discrimination and/or wrongful termination lawsuits?	• What discrimination lawsuits have been brought against your organization by customers?
• Which divisions, departments, or groups are experiencing low morale, diminished performance, or conflict?	• What is the rate of repeat business or customer loss? How does that rate compare to others in your industry?
• What are the statistics regarding absenteeism?	• Are there any instances of negative publicity for your organization such as bad press, boycotts, or protests?
• What is the rate of turnover and what is the cost to the organization of replacing those who leave?	• Where are there negative perceptions about your organization?
• What do exit interviews tell you about why people leave?	• What business have you lost because of a lack of diverse staff?
	• What business have you lost because of poor customer service and lack of understanding of diverse customers?

Suggestions for Using
"Making the Strategic Business Case for Diversity"

Objectives:

- Identify the business drivers regarding diversity
- Build a case that identifies how diversity can be leveraged for organizational success
- Illustrate the negative costs of diversity issues that have been ignored or poorly managed

Intended Audience:

- Executives whose support and buy-in is needed
- Diversity Councils charged with building the strategic business case for diversity
- Managers who need to use diversity as a vehicle to improve teamwork and morale
- Employees at all levels who are needed to support and implement diversity culture change

Materials:

- Copies of the figure, *Making the Strategic Business Case for Diversity* and the table, *Building the Strategic Business Case for Diversity*
- Chart paper and markers
- Tape for putting large replicas of the four areas of the worksheet on the walls

Processing the Activity:

- Facilitator raises the question, "Why pay attention to diversity?" Expect some random responses from the group that mention change, demographics, and increased creativity. After fielding a few responses, the facilitator begins a lecture on the model entitled *The Strategic Business Case for Diversity*.
- The facilitator explains that the business imperative is both internal (people inside an organization have to see how it matters to ongoing work relationships and conflict resolution) and external (consumers know when they are understood and valued through ads and sales pitches). The facilitator also talks about leveraging diversity for gain (opportunity) and reducing liability.
- The facilitator then asks participants to fill out the participant worksheet to define opportunities and liabilities internally and externally as they see them from their perspective.
- Once they have done so, divide the large group into small groups at various stations. Have between four and six people in each group. Enlarged charts and markers will be at each station and each group will put all its data on their chart.
- Halfway through the small group brainstorming of data, distribute Table 11.2, *Building the Strategic Business Case for Diversity* to stimulate additional thoughts.
- After 15 minutes, reconvene the whole group for a large-group discussion.

(continued on next page)

Suggestions for Using
"Making the Strategic Business Case for Diversity" (continued)

Questions for Discussion:

- Which business case opportunities are easiest to make?
- How have you altered the WIFM's (what's in it for me) to suit people at each level of the organization?
- What data do you need to support these drivers?
- Where is it difficult to make the case at all?
- What are the strongest arguments for the external environment, both as opportunity and liability?
- Which benefits talk most strongly to the employees?
- How can you convert any of this to the data that talks to each audience; some is dollars and cents and some in improved climate and culture?

If you can't get the executive buy-in you want, you can try to make a difference on a smaller scale. Focusing on building diverse teams can change the tone and dynamics of team interaction. What you can't change by working on diversity in a small piecemeal fashion are the systems that underlie and support a whole organization. If your only option is to start small at the grassroots level or not to start at all, take the grassroots approach. It takes longer and moves more slowly but change is still possible. But you have to be honest with people and explain that the scope of the impact will be a particular team, unit or task force, not the whole organization. That may disappoint some people, but, to a starving person, half a loaf is better than none.

2. Assessment and Diagnosis

Once initial executive commitment is gained, a plan for the initiative needs to be developed. Assessing the organization by gathering data and analyzing it is the next step in this process. This assessment provides information about diversity conditions and serves as a kind of "state of the organization" report that pinpoints issues, obstacles, and potential areas for growth and development. According to diversity author and consultant Marilyn Loden, data-driven change is one of the 10 critical factors in successful diversity implementation.[19] Much data can be found in reports, statistics, and documents already existing in the organization. It can also be collected through surveys, focus groups, interviews, and observation. Chapter 12 provides detailed information and guidelines about conducting audits, as well as samples of questionnaires and survey tools to use in the process.

3. Diversity Council or Task Force

An organization that is serious about the prospect of long-term change regarding diversity and inclusion needs a group to shepherd the effort and be held accountable for making change happen. A diversity task force, council or action team broadens the base of support and is needed to oversee the process, give and get feedback, acknowledge the milestones, and lead the charge. This group should be a cross-functional, multi-level, diverse team committed to change. It should represent employees from all parts and levels of the organization.

Before it begins its own work, the task force needs to be educated on diversity-related issues, and it needs to go through its own team-building process. Once it has increased its knowledge about diversity and has a sense of common purpose and cohesion, the task force can start the process of articulating its mission, goals, and objectives. While those should be loosely known before the group convenes, the specifics will have to be defined by the group itself once it looks at data, understands its responsibility, learns about its boundaries, and knows for what it will be held accountable.

Frequently Asked Questions Regarding Use of a Diversity Council/Task Force

Does an organization need one?

If you are serious about changing the culture of an organization, you need some group to lead the charge. You don't always have to form a new group; many times an existing process improvement team or other group can take on this role. That can make good sense if all constituencies in the organization are represented in the group.

What would its mission be?

That depends on what's going on in your organization. The broad mission at the abstract, macro level, would be creating an open and inclusive culture; however, the specifics are particular to each organization. Your council's mission should suit the particular values, *raison d'être*, and context of your organization.

What are the usual parameters or responsibilities of a council?

These vary: Some councils are recommending bodies that investigate strategies before suggesting specifics to the executive staff, while others create the strategy and oversee implementation.

How would membership be determined?

The council needs to represent the diversity of your organization and model the inclusion you are creating. The most effective councils are made up of a diagonal cross section of the workforce so that all levels, locations, departments, and groups are represented. You may decide to recruit, or get volunteers, or both. Any group that feels left out will likely sabotage your efforts.

Who does a council usually report to?

The short answer is someone with clout and resources. It could be a CEO, and is often a vice president of Human Resources. Avoid the perception that the effort is just another "HR initiative." If you can get a champion who is the VP of a line function, especially one with clout in the organization, so much the better.

For what would this council be held accountable?

The council's deliverables depend on its charter from leadership. It may be charged with assessing the organization about inclusion, developing the business case, designing the diversity strategy or giving the executive team input on these.

What might someone gain by serving on it, particularly when people are overloaded?

People tell us they are energized by their work on the council. They gain personal insight and awareness, as well as meaningful shifts in how they see and define their world. They also develop relationships with new associates, gain visibility with senior leaders, and gain a sense of accomplishment that comes from being involved in some potentially meaningful change. Finally, people tell us they learn so much about diversity and become more culturally competent

Who would facilitate this council?

It's probably best not to have it be a team member. If you have internal staff such as in the OD (organization development) department, an internal facilitator could do it. If the council is an extension of a process improvement team, the answer is built into that structure. You can also hire external consultants or facilitators to help you.

Once the group is mature, what should it focus on?

The accomplishment of its goals is what the group is after. Go back to your question about a mission. Once the mission is clear and assessment has been done, goals and objectives that give you focus will follow.

Are there some important people who need to be on the council?

People who can make things happen in the organization add value. In one organization, where we were running four task forces simultaneously to deal with four different issues, each council had an executive member as part of the group. They provided leadership and insight. They also added credibility and helped team members gain a more strategic perspective. The perception of diversity as something important will correlate to the clout of people on the task force.

How do you institutionalize the council?

We're not sure you should. It should have an impermanent shelf life … long enough to do a complete and successful job, but not so long as to add to bureaucracy or workload once diversity and inclusion are woven into the organization. The clearest indicators of success are seen when the council works itself out of a job and the initiative is owned by everyone.

How do you empower the group?

Clarity and commitment up front empower the group and are critical in setting the group up for success. Ask questions such as, what are the responsibilities and expectations? From whom? For what will the council be held accountable? By what date? Beyond fundamental questions such as these, commitment, in the form of resources to do the job, are central to feeling empowered. Money for training, and time away from other work without being penalized, is essential.

How do you create a positive attitude toward the council, both serving on it, and throughout the organization?

Part of the answer to this question can be found in your organization's history. Have other councils been and felt productive? Communication is critical. Use newsletters, the organization's web site and Intranet, e-mail, postings in the cafeteria—and highlight results. It will keep people informed, and if the council is doing something relevant to employees, it will be well regarded.

How and when do you communicate with the rest of the organization?

Communication needs to be strategic. Information will change as the work goes along, but letting people know the objectives and scope of the work is critical at the beginning. Checking in at strategic points, and getting and giving feedback, is also essential. Communication is especially critical when an outcome influences daily reality. If, for example, you are rolling out a whole training program that will affect people's schedules, coverage in the unit, and financial resources, don't pull any surprises. Give people plenty of notice, as much flexibility as possible, and a clear and compelling rationale for what you are doing.

Set your council up for success by identifying the factors that can sabotage its effectiveness. Use the following checklist as a tool to get council members to recognize obstacles that could (or already) hinder them. Then come up with strategies to overcome them.

ACTIVITY 11.2 | Diversity-Council-Saboteurs Checklist

- ☐ Lack of team-building
- ☐ Unclear mandate and charter
- ☐ Absence of demonstrable executive and managerial support
- ☐ Discrepancy between broad definition of diversity and narrow affirmative action measures
- ☐ Management resistance to release time for council members
- ☐ Single-issue advocacy from individual members
- ☐ Infrequent meetings and contact
- ☐ No ground rules for operating
- ☐ Fear of resistance and unwillingness to take risk
- ☐ Inadequate measurement and evaluation
- ☐ Little emphasis on strategic and operational application
- ☐ Using training as the major change vehicle
- ☐ Little accountability for task accomplishment
- ☐ Lack of urgency
- ☐ Not gathering and using data to determine direction
- ☐ Lack of diversity education
- ☐ _____

Suggestions for Using
"Diversity-Council-Saboteurs Checklist"

Objectives:

- Identify factors hindering diversity council effectiveness
- Stimulate analysis and discussion of council functioning
- Provide information useful in designing plans for strengthening council operation

Intended Audience:

- Diversity council members
- Diversity coordinators and facilitators
- Executives and managers organizing and chartering a diversity council

Materials:

- Copies of *Diversity-Council-Saboteurs Checklist*
- Pens, pencils
- Easel/flipchart and markers (optional)

Processing the Activity:

- Explain that the most effective diversity councils are those that strategically plan their operation, analyze their functioning, and continue to strengthen themselves. This activity will give them a chance to make progress on this process.
- If the audience is an already functioning council, ask members to respond to the list, checking any of the saboteurs they are experiencing.
- If the audience is a beginning council or comprised of managers organizing a council, ask them to check off those saboteurs they expect to encounter.
- Have participants form into small groups and discuss those items checked, then select the three most critical saboteurs.
- Ask each group to report their three top saboteurs, charting responses.
- Lead a total-group discussion of themes and reactions to saboteurs.
- Assign one or two saboteurs to each small group and have groups brainstorm methods to overcome or deal with them, then select the top two strategies/suggestions for each.
- Have each group report their suggested strategies.
- Get commitment to follow through on suggestions by assigning names and dates to each accepted suggestion.
- Ask each participant to respond to one or both of these open-ended statements:
  - » "The most important thing our council needs to do now is ..."
  - » "The most important thing I can do to help our council move ahead is ..."

(continued on next page)

Suggestions for Using
"Diversity-Council-Saboteurs Checklist" (continued)

Questions for Discussion:

- Which saboteurs create the most serious barriers for your council?

- Which saboteurs are surprising to you?

- What resources are available to help deal with these obstacles?

- What steps can be taken to prevent these from blocking the council's accomplishment?

- What is the most important thing the council needs to do next?

- What can you do to help the council?

- What needs to be included in the council's future development to increase its effectiveness?

Diversity Council Building Blocks

Councils are most effective when they are built on a solid foundation, have a productive team infrastructure, and finally focus on operationalizing the diversity initiative to create real culture change. Figure 11.2 demonstrates these building blocks and their component parts. You can use Activity 11.3, *Rx for Your Diversity Council*, to help your group analyze itself and develop ways to continue to increase its effectiveness.

FIGURE 11.2 | Diversity Council Building Blocks

Operationalizing the Diversity-and-Inclusion Initiative
- Clear measures and evaluation process
- Clear accountability for task accomplishment
- Strategic and operational application
- Training in support of systems change
- Gathering and utilizing data
- Urgency in deadlines
- Management support of release time
- Clear goals and objectives

Team Infrastructure
- Team-building
- Diversity education
- Diversity definition that goes beyond race and gender
- Multi-issue focus
- Ground rules
- Commitment
- Consistent meetings and face time
- Courage

Foundation
- Clear charter and accountabilities
- Demonstrated support
- Council membership

ACTIVITY 11.3 | *Rx* for Your Diversity Council

BUILDING BLOCK	IN PLACE	NEEDS TO BE DONE
Foundation		
Team Infrastructure		
Operationalizing the Initiative		

Suggestions for Using
"Rx for Your Diversity Council"

Objectives:

- Assess strengths and areas of needed development on the council
- Engage all members in increasing the council's effectiveness
- Set goals for the council's ongoing development

Intended Audience:

- Diversity council members
- Diversity directors, coordinators, and council leaders and facilitators

Materials:

- Copies of the *Diversity Council Building Blocks* chart and *Rx for Your Diversity Council* worksheet
- Easel and flipchart

Processing the Activity:

- Ask the group what they think are essential factors for council effectiveness and then chart the responses.
- Explain the *Diversity Council Building Blocks*.
- Have participants fill out the worksheet, making notes about what aspects of the building blocks are in place and what still needs to be done.
- Have participants discuss their responses in small groups and come up with two or three priorities that need to be done.
- Chart priorities from each group.
- Lead a discussion of insights and next steps.

Questions for Discussion:

- What are the aspects of development that have already accomplished?
- In which building block does the most work need to be done?
- What priorities exist for future development?
- How can these be accomplished?
- What are the next steps?

Caveats, Considerations, and Variations:

- This activity can follow the *Diversity-Council-Saboteurs Checklist.*

4. Training

Training can serve some very useful purposes in a diversity initiative. It is always necessary at some stage in the process. Training can help all employees and managers broaden their repertoire of knowledge and skills for dealing with other employees and customers, and minimize misunderstandings. It can effectively enlighten staff about personal attitudes, beliefs, and assumptions, and it can expand cultural knowledge. Training can be focused on skills such as how to alter the performance review process for cultures where shame and loss-of-face is a big issue. Equally relevant might be methods for dealing with anger and conflict, or how to run meetings and build teams when you have people from various ethnic groups and locations around the world.

Training can also go beyond individual growth and have a team-building function. However, there are two caveats with training. The first is to be clear about the limits of what training can accomplish. It will not bring about organizational change, although it can be a catalyst that sparks it. The other caveat is to make certain that the training serves the organization's objectives, is relevant to participants' needs, and is conducted by people who have a track record of effectiveness. If training is done by external consultants, you have to do your homework. Observe the consultant in action, on tape, or get references of others who have used their services. If you use your internal resources, make sure they are well prepared and that you are involved in seeing the agenda and the presenters ahead of time. Pilot programs are one form of insurance. Refinements made after a pilot program increase chances of effectiveness of the training.

Data previously mentioned as critical to culture change is also essential in designing training. Identify skill deficits by looking at customer feedback, or by viewing survey data that indicates where people feel inadequate or are underperforming. Look at organizational goals that aren't being met and see how training can provide some help. If, for example, minority hiring is talked about but not really happening, then perhaps training that focuses on interviewing assumptions, coaching, mentoring biases, and hiring profiles can help managers identify and get beyond unconscious assumptions and barriers.

Once you determine the objectives and relevant training content, then it is important to look at how you group participants. Do you keep managers and supervisors together? Is there ever a time when it is helpful to have managers and supervisors with their own workgroups? The answer to how you group, how long the sessions are, and what kind, if any, follow-up you should have is "it depends." Here are some guidelines:

- It is helpful and important to train managers together when you are teaching managerial skills.

- It is helpful to have managers and supervisors with their own groups when you are teaching broad awareness because you can build understanding by helping them each see the others' perspectives. However, if there is little or no trust, this would not be helpful because frontline staff would feel intimidated and be afraid to speak. The paradox of putting them together is that, while doing so could build trust, if trust doesn't exist, it will be very difficult to gain in the session.

- Regarding length of time or numbers of sessions, it depends on your objectives and your organizational realities. Half days with follow-ups can work very well in having people integrate ideas and skills over time. The downside is that attendance usually declines because other responsibilities get in the way of attendance at follow-up sessions. Full-day modules work well but sometimes the content is so intense people prefer shorter sessions. Shorter modules can work if they are not seen as the complete exposure to the issue. In one 24-hour operation we conducted sessions over 10 weeks from 10 p.m. to Midnight because that was the only way to include all shifts. If short modules are all you can schedule, find ways to get participants there consistently.

- Follow-up needs to be built into skill development. If there are multiple sessions, staff can try the skills, then come back and talk about what worked and what didn't.

A good place to start is deciding if you even need training at all. To do so, look at the *Symptoms That Indicate a Need for Diversity Training*. Check any you see in your organization and add others that are relevant.

ACTIVITY 11.4 | Symptoms That Indicate a Need for Diversity Training

Check any of these symptoms you see in your organization.

_____ 1. Insensitive comments or jokes in the work unit regarding age, gender, ethnicity, sexual orientation, or physical ability

_____ 2. Inability to retain members of diverse groups.

_____ 3. Open conflict between employees from different groups.

_____ 4. Lack of teamwork and cooperation between groups.

_____ 5. Cultural faux pas committed out of ignorance, not malice.

_____ 6. Complaints about language-related barriers in communication.

_____ 7. Misinterpreting or not understanding directions which lead to mistakes, repeating tasks, and low productivity.

_____ 8. EEOC suits and grievances.

_____ 9. People feeling isolated and unconnected to the workgroup.

_____ 10. Perception that one's strengths and background are not valued for the unique contribution that can be made.

_____ 11. Complaints about behaviors of customers or co-workers.

_____ 12. Lack of diversity at different levels in the organization.

Suggestions for Using
"Symptoms That Indicate a Need for Diversity Training"

Objectives:

- Gather input about needs in order to tailor the training.
- Pinpoint specific issues that indicate diversity challenges.

Intended Audience:

- Diversity council members
- Managers and employees in an organization contemplating diversity training
- Training and HR staff members

Materials:

- Copies of the *Symptoms That Indicate a Need for Diversity Training* worksheet
- Easel and flipchart

Processing the Activity:

- Distribute copies of the worksheet and have participants check any symptoms that are evident in the organization. Participants may also add other symptoms they see.
- Poll the group and tally responses on a flipchart to see which symptoms are most evident.
- Lead a discussion of the symptoms and their impact.
- Have the group prioritize the symptoms most in need of being addressed.

Questions for Discussion:

- Which symptoms have the biggest negative impact on teamwork, productivity, or service?
- How might training help address these issues?
- What awareness, knowledge and/or skills would you want training to provide?

Caveats, Considerations, and Variations:

- Data collected using this tool is most useful if it comes from a cross section of employees so you get an accurate representation.

Training That Focuses on Individual Awareness, Attitudes, and Behaviors

We often begin awareness training with a slide that proclaims, "Diversity is an inside job." This is the essence of awareness training. It should help individuals explore their own roots, cultural identify, biases (preferences for or against something), assumptions (preconceived expectations about others), and stereotypes (the fixed mental images accrued over time about groups). Specifically, three areas of training should be part of any organization's awareness segment:

1. Diversity: What and Why

Focusing on the organization's paradigm of diversity is an essential first step. How broadly or narrowly is diversity being defined? Does it encompass a narrow version that focuses on visible diversities such as race, ethnicity, and gender or does it encompass a broader reach, taking into account aspects such as religion, geography, education, and work experience? That clarity and those boundaries must be presented up front, as should a discussion of the business case, the organization's reason for attending to diversity.

2. Culture

Culture as a key shaper of behavior is also part of an effective awareness program. Participants need to understand that culture is the software that programs all human beings and gives them their operating rules. A range of cultural norms should be discussed. Chapters 5 and 6 provide more information about this.

3. Stereotypes and Prejudice

A third segment that should be part of an awareness program involves learning about stereotypes and prejudice. Participants need to learn that stereotyping is a human phenomenon; and no one escapes being either a victim or a perpetrator. That leveling reality creates safety in a training session and frees participants to examine and admit their own blind spots and biases. Doing so is helpful because they learn how their assumptions pigeonhole co-workers and customers and then work to manage these preconceived notions. Chapter 7 provides more information on this topic.

Training That Focuses on Managerial Skills

While awareness training is focused on understanding values, attitudes, and behavior, managerial training needs to focus on skill-building, with direct and immediate application. If done well, a manager or supervisor should be able to take the skills learned and use them on the job the next day. While many specific skills are appropriate, the following list offers a few. These skills are covered in detail in other parts of this book.

1. Performance Review

Evaluating performance always has the potential to be a sensitive subject and it becomes more so when people communicate across cultures. The amount of directness vs. indirectness and active vs. passive voice is important; so is loss-of-face and avoiding shame.

2. Conflict Resolution

Managing conflict becomes more complex in a cross-cultural setting. U.S. directness favors an assertive approach to conflict resolution. But that directness is often seen as upsetting and intimidating to those who place a high value on harmony. For this reason, a wide repertoire of conflict resolution skills is critical. Cultural interpreters, intermediaries, and more indirect approaches work better in some cultures. The key in all these skills is not to replace one technique with another, but rather to add to the existing body of skills.

3. Problem-solving

Problem-solving goes hand in hand with conflict resolution. Managers need to learn to solve problems one-on-one or in a group. The key is to help all parties understand the assumptions and issues from each participant's vantage point. When the parties find common ground they can generate alternatives that work for all involved.

4. Giving and Getting Feedback

As with the other skills, feedback competence is critical for managers. For example, telling employees what you do want, not what you don't, or sticking to behaviors, not labels and judgments, is helpful. "You're so rude" is a judgment but a discussion about interrupting someone while talking involves a behavior. When taking cross-cultural norms into consideration, indirect feedback is of great value as is attending to nonverbal cues.

There are other skills that can be taught, such as team-building and running effective meetings. Training content should be determined by data that indicates needs, gaps, issues, or deficits and it should be tailored to both the realities of the organization and needs of participants.

However, training about diversity doesn't have to be limited to sessions with that label. An effective way to continue helping managers and staff increase their effectiveness in this area is by integrating it into all training. Customer service, leadership development, supervisory skills, safety, and job-skills training can all have diversity woven in. The following checklist suggests specific ways to do that in both the content and process.

5. Systems Changes

Diversity pioneer R. Roosevelt Thomas, Jr., has said that the "… biggest challenge to managing diversity is not the 'isms,' but poor or nonexistent management."[20] His comment points to the critical role of leaders and organizational management systems in setting in motion the mechanisms of change. Individual awareness and skill-building is necessary but clearly not sufficient to make the kind of cultural change required for an organization to move toward real inclusion of all staff and capitalizing on its diversity. To achieve what diversity theorist Taylor Cox calls "equal-opportunity motivation to contribute"[21] requires making changes in the system, the places where the organization touches its employees.

ACTIVITY 11.5 | Integrating Diversity into All Training

Check those steps you have taken to integrate diversity into all training.

CONTENT

☐ 1. A wide range of approaches and methods are taught.

☐ 2. Advantages and disadvantages of each method are discussed.

☐ 3. Diversity is depicted through examples and cases.

☐ 4. Situations and examples do not reinforce stereotypes.

☐ 5. The influence of culture and background is included in explanations and the analyses of behaviors and situations.

☐ 6. Assumptions and preconceived notions are challenged.

☐ 7. Visual materials depict a diverse array of individuals.

☐ 8. Language used is nonsexist and nonracist.

☐ 9. Trainers and curriculum designers have a solid understanding of diversity concepts such as cultural differences, stereotypes, and prejudice.

☐ 10. Training content reinforces understanding and responding to differences in others.

PROCESS

☐ 11. A variety of learning and teaching methods are used.

☐ 12. Participants are clustered in various kinds of groupings.

☐ 13. Trainers represent diversity in dimensions such as age, gender, ethnicity, race, level, and education.

☐ 14. Both written and visual materials are used.

☐ 15. Written materials are provided at an appropriate level of literacy and in other languages if needed.

☐ 16. Training is designed and reviewed by a diverse group of staff members.

☐ 17. The cultural and individual needs and preferences of participants are assessed and taken into account.

☐ 18. Ethnic, gender (or other) slurs, jokes, and comments are not tolerated in training sessions.

☐ 19. Participants are not singled out for embarrassment or ridicule.

☐ 20. Learning activities are comfortable and engaging for participants.

Suggestions for Using
"Integrating Diversity into All Training"

Objectives:

- Assess the degree to which diversity is being integrated into all training content and process
- Suggest ways to integrate diversity into other training

Intended Audience:

- Diversity coordinators, managers, and leaders of diversity processes
- Diversity council members
- Training and development professionals

Materials:

- Copies of the worksheet *Integrating Diversity into All Training*
- Pens/pencils

Processing the Activity:

- Facilitator introduces the topic by asking participants to brainstorm all the training and development offerings provided in their organization.
- Facilitator explains that one of the ways to make diversity a relevant part of everyday operations is to integrate it into training of all kinds.
- Facilitator may review the four aspects of the training/learning environment: content, process, climate, and results (*The Diversity Tool Kit*, Section I) or explain that all training consists of both content and process.
- Facilitator asks participants to respond to the checklist.
- Participants discuss their responses in pairs or small groups, focusing on strengths and potential areas for improvement.
- Facilitator leads a total-group discussion of learning, application, and next steps.

Questions for Discussion:

- In what ways have we already integrated diversity into existing training programs?
- What items have not been checked?
- What diversity awareness, knowledge, and skills are relevant to the content of training programs we offer?
- What training processes take into account participant diversity?
- What changes, modifications, and adaptations could be made to increase effectiveness with diverse groups?
- What actions or steps do we need to take?
- Who else needs to be involved in this process?

Caveats, Considerations, and Variations:

- Trainers may be resistant to considering integrating diversity as they may assume it changes their courses. Explain that it is intended to enhance training programs and increase the engagement of participants of all groups.

The Organizational Universe Model: A Blueprint for Systems Change

A framework for organizational change is helpful when implementing a culture transformation as all-encompassing as that required by diversity and inclusion. The Organizational Universe Model, by John E. Jones, offers a construct that shows the directly controllable elements of the organization's systems as well as the aspects that can only be influenced indirectly (see Figure 11.3)

FIGURE 11.3 | The Organizational Universe Model*

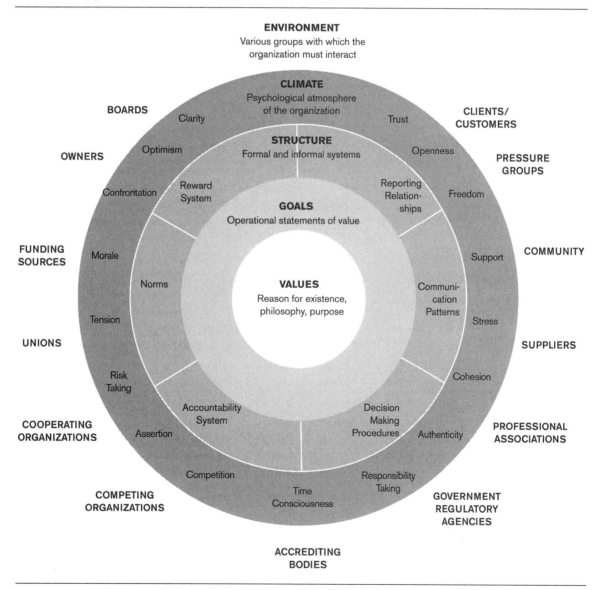

*Adapted from John E. Jones, "The Organizational Universe," in William Pfeiffer and John E. Jones, eds., *The 1981 Annual Handbook for Group Facilitators* (San Diego: University Associates, 1981).

An organization's culture is built around its core values, those basic tenets that form its foundation. Values such as return on shareholder's investment, providing compassionate care, creating innovative solutions, or doing groundbreaking research might be examples of these. Goals represent the way to make those values operational, the ways in which the organization seeks to act on its values. In the third circle, we come to the structure of the organization, the ways in which it marshals the talent and energy of employees to achieve the goals. It is this layer that is critical to the implementation of diversity-and-inclusion culture change, because it is in the six parts of the structure that the organization and its culture can be touched, manipulated, and moved. It is only through these six that direct action can be taken. The fourth layer, the psychological climate, is where much of what is desired through culture change (such as tolerance, inclusion, trust, and respect) resides. However, these can't be accomplished directly but rather through action taken in the six areas of the structure or from pressure from the external environment. Understanding the six aspects of the structure can help focus energy in diversity implementation by pointing out six concrete areas where diversity initiatives transform the system and influence the climate. Working through these six areas uses the existing structure and builds on it—so as to integrate diversity into all aspects of the organization.

1. Accountability

This aspect of the structure delineates clearly who is responsible for what and where the buck stops. When diversity-and-inclusion programs falter and fail, a common complaint is that there was no accountability. Everyone's responsibility becomes no one's. Projects lose steam, tasks fall through the cracks, and credibility is lost when there is no clear accountability. This is particularly true when dealing with a process as long-term and amorphous as diversity. Specific tasks, behaviors, and results need to be assigned, then measured, which requires that someone be held accountable. In one organization, where diversity and empowerment were intertwined, one senior manager continued to drag his feet, making nasty comments about the process. When his boss got word of his uncooperative stance toward shared decision-making and team-based management, he swiftly removed him from his position, sidelining him to a staff role where he would not have the line responsibility nor power to sabotage the culture change efforts. This action sent shock waves through the organization. It also sent a clear message that leaders would be held accountable for implementing this process.

In many organizations, accountability for systems changes, whether in recruitment, work/life balance, promotion, or benefits, is insured through incorporating diversity performance objectives into existing performance measurement and evaluation. Managers and employees at all levels can be held responsible for achieving relevant diversity objectives. Increasing employee engagement scores, developing skills to serve diverse customers, gaining additional language proficiency, building diverse teams, mentoring staff of different groups, and recruiting diverse employees are examples of objectives that hold staff accountable for developing individual competence and helping the organization capitalize on diversity. Another global organization uses an innovative approach to hold leaders accountable for leveraging the creative potential of diversity. Each business unit is required to "sell" and "buy" one best practice to and from another unit in the organization. This reinforces collaboration across the organization and increases business success.

2. Reward

According to behaviorists, human beings continue behavior that is reinforced while behavior that is not reinforced is extinguished. Not all reinforcements come from the organization, but many do in the form of rewards. Whether in real or psychic dollars, a pay check or pat on the back, public acclaim, or self satisfaction, reward motivates behavior. Positive diversity changes are reinforced when company awards are given to teams, departments, or divisions which have made exemplary progress. Pay differentials for language acquisition or proficiency, promotional points for those who mentor, or increased visibility for those who serve on diversity task forces are additional ways organizations reward inclusion work. One forward-thinking organization built in rewards for its diversity trainers; they got bonuses for the extra duty work they did in facilitating training sessions.

Rewards are also embedded in the compensation and benefits package. Greater flexibility in these offerings is a trend seen across the country. Twenty-three percent of organizations with 5,000 or more employees now provide health care benefits for unmarried domestic partners.[23] Services such as on-site day care, gyms, ATMs, and takeout meals are perks that have been added at many worksites. These aids for harried workers reduce stress and are used as extra recruitment inducements.

3. Reporting Relationships

The organization chart, chain of command, or who reports to who, is another aspect of the structure that can be used to increase inclusion. Changing systems for promotion opportunities, hiring, career development, and mentoring would be involved in this aspect. Making internal promotions more equitable through open job posting, more active recruiting for diverse candidates, both internally and externally, and mentoring are methods often used to get a broader mix into higher levels in the organization. Another strategy used is the creation of a dedicated diversity position. While titles differ from coordinator, director or manager to vice president, this position entails responsibility for the diversity initiative and generally reports to a top executive. Debates continue about whether this position should be a part of Human Resources or not, and whether it should encompass affirmative action and EEO or be separate. Each organization needs to build its own rationale for its decision.

4. Communication

Both formal and informal channels of communication are needed to carry the message about diversity and get input from staff. Memos and newsletters, as well as the grapevine, are needed. Effective diversity communication informs, teaches, and generates commitment. Since employees are generally jaded by "organization-speak," the more real, unusual, and personal, the better. Heart-to-heart talks by the CEO and employees telling their stories, as well as statistics about marketplace opportunities or workforce demographics, all have their place. Diversity web sites and diversity columns in regular organizational newsletters are often used, as are topical forums and brown-bag sessions.

Table 11.3 gives you some ideas about leveraging various vehicles and communicators, as well as potential content and audiences in your communication plan. Don't stop with this list—work with your diversity council to create additional avenues.

TABLE 11.3 | Developing a Diversity Communication Plan*

Vehicles	Content
_____ In-house television broadcasts	_____ Why (business case)
_____ Newsletter	_____ What (obstacles and issues)
_____ Videos	_____ How (plan/strategy)
_____ Town Hall sessions	_____ When and where of events
_____ Brochures	_____ Information about stereotypes, culture, and dimensions of diversity
_____ Web site	
_____ Employee handbook	_____ "Did you know?" tidbits
_____ Internal memos	_____ Case studies/dilemmas with different perspectives
_____ New employee orientation	
_____ Meetings	_____ Personal stories/experiences
_____ Training sessions	_____ Innovative practices
_____ One-on-one contact	_____ Customer trends and feedback
_____ Local, regional newspapers	
_____ Posters	
_____ Calendars	
_____ E-mail, Internet	

Communicators	Audiences
_____ CEO	_____ Board
_____ Executives	_____ Executives
_____ PR Department	_____ Managers/Supervisors
_____ HR Department	_____ All staff
_____ Informal leaders	_____ Community/Public
_____ Trainers	_____ Shareholders
_____ Managers	_____ Industry
_____ Supervisors	_____ Regulatory agencies
_____ Board members	_____ Professional associations
_____ Focus groups	_____ Investors
_____ Consultants	_____ Job seekers
_____ Diversity council	_____ Recruits
_____ Employee Associations/ Affinity Groups	

(* Developed in conjunction with Patti Digh, diversity consultant and author.)

5. Decision-Making

Who makes decisions and how they are made is another key element of the organization's structure. Involving a wider range of employees, and therefore a broader spectrum of views, generates far greater creativity in ideas and solutions. It also increases the chances that faux pas will be avoided and that decisions made will be supported and will achieve their objectives. Using diverse hiring and promotion panels is an example of this. Those who work directly with an issue or problem have critical knowledge that is needed when making decisions about it. This was made evident in one organization where a well-meaning and committed CEO attempted to address a diversity concern without the involvement of those most affected by the problem. An organizational audit had identified that a major obstacle for employees with small children was the long hours, especially the frequent weekends at the office, that were required to get the job done. Responding to the problem, this well-intentioned leader offered to provide child care professionals on-site on Saturdays when employees needed to come in. However, this suggested solution missed the point: The working parents' issue wasn't child care, but rather the long hours that kept them away from their children. Involving those with the problem might have generated a more effective solution.

Some businesses regularly tap their employee diversity networks or affinity groups to get ideas for marketing to particular segments of their customer base. They also call on them for suggestions and help in recruiting employees from those groups. Internally, these employee networks can be called on to give insight into problems and suggest appropriate responses. In one organization, when graffiti with slurs about a particular group appeared on walls, the CEO immediately consulted the employee support group that represented the group that was the target of the slurs. They advised him not to create a major issue and possible repercussions by instituting an organization-wide campaign with sensitivity training for all employees. Instead, they suggested he write a very clear response in his regular column in the corporate newsletter stating his view and clarifying the company's policy prohibiting such acts and delineating the punishment. It worked; no further graffiti appeared.

Finally, the most common method of widening the involvement in decision-making regarding diversity is creating a diversity council or task force. Whether its function is input-giving, solution-generating, or strategic planning, this group can help keep diversity initiatives on target and generate wider support within the organization.

6. Norms

One of the most difficult aspects of the organization's structure to work with are the norms, the informal, yet powerful rules of behavior. Rarely written in any employee handbook and seldom even explicitly explained, they are strong shapers of workplace culture. When ethnic jokes, teasing, and hazing are part of peer group camaraderie, when horseplay verges on harassment, or when employees separate into ethnic, racial, or gender enclaves, norms can be problematic.

Many organizations have found that diversity celebrations in which groups share food, music, and customs is one way to break down barriers. Recreational activities such as picnics, sports events, and outings can bring employees of a variety of backgrounds together in relaxed social settings where new relationships can be formed. Cross-training, mixed groups in meetings and training sessions, and buddy systems for new employees are also ways of creating a greater understanding between people of different groups.

Changing norms can also be modeled by leaders. John Scully, former CEO at Apple, sent a clear message about the organization's stance regarding sexual orientation by marching in a national gay rights parade. When asked why he did it, since he wasn't gay himself, he responded that he saw it as a human rights issue. A leader at mid-management level modeled inclusion in another way. As a HR manager in a large medical center, her regular hours were 8 a.m. to 5 p.m. Yet many of the staff, who were her internal customers, worked evenings and nights. So as not to ignore them or their needs, or require them to come in to see her during nonwork hours, she works one day each week on the night shift, 11 p.m. to 7 a.m. Her behavior emphasizes a norm that says employees on all shifts matter.

Managers can also model negative norms that sabotage diversity efforts. When prejudicial comments are overlooked, or when slurs and jokes are allowed in the workplace, the manager's refusal to confront is seen as tacit approval that allows such unproductive norms to continue or even escalate. Managers also can have an even more active role in stonewalling diversity. When bosses make comments such as "You don't have a chance because you're not the right color," diversity is positioned as the opposite of quality and the misconception that any woman or person of color is there only because of gender, race, or ethnicity rather than skill or ability is promoted. No one benefits from such inaccurate conceptions; women and people of color feel diminished, while white men feel deprived of opportunity. A less supportive, more adversarial environment is created for all employees. Managers who want to create positive norms around diversity need to reframe the issue.

Table 11.4 provides examples of some ways organizations are working within the six areas of the structure to make systemic change and create more inclusive, productive cultures. You can use these six aspects of the structure to analyze your organization to identify diversity obstacles as well as generate strategies to overcome them. Activity 11.6 can help you in that analysis.

Suggestions for systems changes can also be generated from benchmarking (learning from other organizations). Checking their web sites and interviewing diversity directors can be ways to gather best practice ideas from others. Most of the specific programs and changes instituted as part of diversity-and-inclusion culture change center around those listed on the following chart. From expanded benefits, flexible schedules, and on-site child care to mentoring and recruitment, best practices span a wide array of interventions touching various aspects of the structure. Using Activity 11.7 can help you assess what your organization is currently doing regarding each of these best practice areas and pinpoint areas where you can improve existing programs or institute new interventions.

TABLE 11.4 | Integrating Diversity and Inclusion into the Existing Structure*

ASPECTS OF STRUCTURE	EXAMPLES OF DIVERSITY-AND-INCLUSION INITIATIVES/CHANGES/ACTIONS
ACCOUNTABILITY	• Diversity objectives made part of manager's regular performance review • Mentoring diverse employees made an objective for all managers • Diversity demographics objectives set for each department • Diversity training made an objective for all employees • Diversity action plan made an objective for all managers • Requirement that managers interview diverse group of applicants before making hiring decision
REWARD	• Pay differentials for additional language proficiency • Tuition reimbursement for wider range of courses (e.g., technical) • Diversity management objectives tied to compensation • Increased flexibility in benefits package to meet diverse needs of employees • Awards for exemplary diversity and inclusion accomplishments of unit/department/division • Pay equity reviews • Management compensation incentives for diversity-and-inclusion gains from for recruiting underrepresented groups • Rewards for recruitment referrals
REPORTING RELATION-SHIPS	• Establish dedicated diversity position (e.g., director or coordinator) • Job posting expanded • Mentoring programs • Succession planning • Cross training • Internships • Review of internal candidates precede external search • Increased recruitment efforts (e.g., wider net)
COMMUNICATION	• Video by CEO • Diversity logo, buttons, mugs, and posters • Diversity web site • Column in regular newsletter or organization's Intranet • Column by CEO and other executives in newsletter • Training sessions introduced by executive staff members • Panels of diverse employees talk to senior managers • Communication pieces, signage, and materials provided in other languages • Diversity-and-inclusion awareness and skills training for all staff • Diversity-and-inclusion training for communication staff • Diversity-and-inclusion training included in new employee orientation • Diversity-and-inclusion best practice sharing • Diversity-and-inclusion survey • E-mail messages • Diversity-and-inclusion presence in organization's web site or Intranet • Diversity-and-inclusion calendar

(continued on next page)

TABLE 11.4 | Integrating Diversity and Inclusion into the Existing Structure (continued)

ASPECTS OF STRUCTURE	EXAMPLES OF DIVERSITY-AND-INCLUSION INITIATIVES/CHANGES/ACTIONS
DECISION-MAKING	• Employee networks tapped for creative approaches to new markets and recruiting • Diversity-and-Inclusion Council/Team/Steering Committee made up of diagonal cross section of workforce designs diversity plan • Diversity-and-inclusion action teams responsible for creating strategies to overcome diversity-related obstacles • Diversity-and-inclusion connected with empowerment or safety programs • Employee focus groups • Process-improvement teams tackle diversity-and-inclusion issues • Task forces and teams have diverse make-up • Diverse hiring and promotion panels
NORMS	• Flexible schedules and telecommuting • Work/life balance programs • Executives leverage work/life and leave programs • Diversity-and-inclusion celebrations and events • Diversity-and-inclusion brown-bag forums • Diversity-and-inclusion training conducted with mixed-level groups • On-site child care • Community internship program (employees work in community agencies) • Employee diversity-and-inclusion networks/affinity groups/support groups • Organization-sponsored recreation (basketball, soccer, baseball, etc.) • One employee cafeteria for all levels

*Adapted from John E. Jones, "The Organizational Universe," in William Pfeiffer and John E. Jones, eds., *The 1981 Annual Handbook for Group Facilitators* (San Diego: University Associates, 1981).

ACTIVITY 11.6 | Implementing Diversity: Making Structural Change*

Aspect of Structure*	Diversity Obstacles	Suggested Strategies
Accountability		
Reward		
Reporting Relationship		
Communications		
Decision-Making		
Norms		

*Adapted from John E. Jones, "The Organizational Universe," in William Pfeiffer and John E. Jones, eds., *The 1981 Annual Handbook for Group Facilitators* (San Diego: University Associates, 1981).

Suggestions for Using
"Implementing Diversity: Making Structural Change"

Objectives:

- Assess current diversity culture change strategies
- Identify areas for additional strategies
- Stimulate discussion and creation of strategies to use the structure of the organization to enhance inclusion

Intended Audience:

- Executive staff
- Diversity council
- HR and OD staff

Materials:

- Copies of worksheet *Implementing Diversity: Making Structural Change* and Table 11.4 *Integrating Diversity into the Executive Suite*
- Markers and chart paper

Processing the Activity:

- Explain the Organizational Universe Model, emphasizing the six areas of the structure and giving diversity change examples for each.
- Ask participants to jot down changes already in place and those needed in each of the six areas.
- Post large chart for each of the six areas of the structure around the room. Each chart has two columns, one labeled "Diversity Obstacles" and the other "Suggested Strategies."
- Count off participants into six groups, each at one of the posted charts.
- Participants take five minutes to write and discuss their responses on both columns on the chart.
- Groups rotate for five more rounds, repeating the process at each chart—writing additional suggestions to those already written.
- Each group returns to its original chart, reviews what has been written, and prioritizes selecting the two suggested strategies that would have the most positive impact in creating inclusion.
- Each group shares their top two suggestions.
- Lead a total-group discussion of suggestions and next steps.

Questions for Discussion:

- Which areas of the structure are we already using well for inclusion?
- In which areas do we need to do the most work?
- What obstacles do we face?
- Which suggestions would have the most positive effect on increasing inclusion?

ACTIVITY 11.7 | Benchmarks in Diversity and Inclusion

SYSTEMIC ISSUES	WHAT YOUR ORGANIZATION IS DOING
Flexible Benefits	
Child Care	
Training	
Career/Professional Development	
Recruitment/Hiring	
Accountability	
Work/Life Balance	
Performance Review	
Reward	
Communication	
Promotion	
Continuous Learning	

Suggestions for Using
"Benchmarks in Diversity and Inclusion"

Objectives:

- Generate discussion about systems changes in diversity and inclusion implementation
- Stimulate creativity in responding to diversity-and-inclusion needs
- Compare diversity-and-inclusion strategy with best practices in other organizations

Intended Audience:

- Diversity council or task force
- Executive, senior management team
- HR staff

Materials:

- Copies of the worksheet *Benchmarks in Diversity and Inclusion*

Processing the Activity:

- Individuals fill out the chart, listing what the organization is doing in each area.
- Groups discuss programs and activities in place.
- Groups determine priorities for needed action.

Caveats, Considerations and Variations:

- This list can be overwhelming as each category contains so many aspects that could be explored. It may be helpful to limit the discussion to a few areas at a time.
- This analysis may spur participants on to investigate programs and interventions in other organizations, then report back to the group.

Tips for Making Systems Change

The following can serve as a checklist of suggestions as you proceed with your systems change process.

Avoid short-term focus. Thinking of diversity-and-inclusion culture change as a quick fix is a recipe for disaster. The process is a long and continuous one. Expectations for quick, tangible results are unrealistic and sabotage commitment when immediate improvement is not seen. Implementation requires tenacity, perseverance, and patience. Experts generally estimate that real changes won't be seen for at least five years. Preparing the organization, diversity team, and individual employees for the reality of this long-term process is critical so that more realistic and achievable objectives can be set and so adequate resources are allocated.

Involve the "right" people. Making systemic changes requires both the objective and subjective "right" answer. Objectively, this means that those with the clout to make things happen, as well as those with the necessary knowledge and information, need to be involved. On a subjective level, it requires that those who own the problem and who will be needed to implement the solution be involved in order to generate commitment and avoid resistance that can derail the most carefully crafted plan.

Utilize existing systems. Diversity changes work best when they build on existing mechanisms in the organization. Rather than starting from scratch, focus on enhancing current programs, integrating diversity elements, and working through already organized systems. Career development programs are often enhanced to achieve diversity goals. HR professionals can analyze ways that compensation and benefits can be expanded. Performance management and incentive programs can be augmented.

Communicate effectively. Any change is apt to create some resistance, and good, clear communication is required to overcome the misconceptions that emerge from the rumor mill. Explaining the business reasons for changes and highlighting the benefits to each employee is critical. Without a clear understanding of the "why" behind the change and the "what" it means to each employee, it is apt to be seen as something for others.

Consider the repercussions of the changes. Disgruntlement and new inequities result when the outcomes of changes are not thought through clearly. In one organization, changes in health benefits to include same-sex domestic partners brought a wave of complaints from those with opposite-sex domestic partners who wanted equal treatment. In another company, a minority mentoring program was restructured to be open to all employees when nonminority staff members complained of unfairness.

Don't be derailed by resistance or complaints. Commitment is seen as paper thin when changes are abandoned at the first sign of resistance. One organization stopped all training when the CEO received two letters from angry employees. On the other hand, when a different organization received negative feedback about an announcement about the formation of a gay and lesbian support network that appeared in the company newsletter, it saw a prime opportunity to educate employees. It responded with an explanation of its position on an inclusive work environment and a clarification of the requirements for any group that wished to start a network.

Avoid shooting from the hip. Making changes in the organization without adequate analysis and data generally leads to ineffective or even counter-productive actions. Careful planning is needed. Investigating to find out what the real obstacles are to the full utilization of all staff is critical. Once these are clearly understood, setting clear objectives and considering a wide range of options to overcome the obstacles is the next step. Examining innovative and effective practices in other organizations can help at this point, then gaining the support and commitment of those who will be needed to drive the change is required. Finally, allocating the necessary resources to implement, monitor, and improve the process is needed. An approach with a variety of diversity quick-hits won't generate or sustain real change. A diversity web page, celebration, posters, or slogans might be effective aspects of an overall plan; however, they are wasteful and misdirected if they are done in a hit-or-miss fashion. Equally ineffective is a poorly thought out response to a crisis situation.

7. Evaluation and Measurement

This critical aspect of the diversity process is often the one most talked about and, at the same time, the least well implemented. Measurement tells the organization what is working and how well. It gives evidence of impact that generates support. Finally, it provides information that stimulates continued change. Yet the benefits of measurement can only be reaped if it is done effectively. Chapter 15 gives information about strategies and methods of evaluation as well as sources of measurement data that can be gathered and analyzed. Effective evaluation depends on setting clear criteria before any implementation is begun and on having a strategic strategy for tracking that is carried out throughout the process. Measuring after the fact, without having collected initial baseline data, generally limits the usefulness of the process. In addition, both the process (how well did we do what we set out to do, and what did and did not work) and the results (what difference did it make, did it achieve the objectives set out and what is the return on investment for the organization) need to be evaluated.

8. Integrating Diversity Into the Fabric of the Organization

The last stage of the diversity process is that of continuing to weave diversity into the fabric of the organization. From new employee orientation to the annual report, from the board of directors to the sales staff, on agendas at executive staff meetings and team sessions, as well as on organizational brochures and in the parking lot, diversity is seen as a regular part of the way business is conducted. Integration is the result of effective implementation of the first six steps of the strategy; however, momentum needs to be maintained. When staff in the communications department routinely check all brochures to make sure a wide variety of employees are depicted, or when managers request help in soliciting more diverse applicants, the diversity process is part of the culture. Organizations continue to reinforce this through calendars, events, performance objectives, newsletters, and rewards. They also remain vigilant, continuing to look for new diversity obstacles and additional ways to make the culture more inclusive to get the best from every employee.

Some strategies to ensure integration that are used in organizations are:
- Rotation of membership of the diversity-and-inclusion council
- Review of curricula with diversity segments added to augment training programs (e.g., communication, interviewing, and conflict resolution)
- Diversity-and-inclusion items included on employee and customer surveys

- Diversity-and-inclusion performance objectives for all staff
- Utilizing diverse teams for task forces and projects
- Employee input and feedback mechanisms
- 360° feedback processes
- Cross-training and job rotation
- Regular reviews of benefits, compensation, and leave policies
- Regular reviews of marketing and advertising materials
- Diversity-and-inclusion film series with facilitated discussion
- Brown-bag sessions and webinars on current diversity-and-inclusion issues (e.g., generational differences, sensitive online communication)

Activity 11.8 can help your diversity-and-inclusion council or leadership team analyze your diversity-and-inclusion process in the seven steps, identifying what's been accomplished and what still needs to be done.

Another way to gain insight into the diversity-and-inclusion implementation process is to get a close look at organizations that have experienced this change; doing your own benchmarking research can give you important information and deeper understanding of what lies ahead. It is even more effective when this research responsibility is shared by a group such as the diversity-and-inclusion council, with each member investigating two organizations, one in the same industry or field and one in a different one, then all pooling their findings and discussing learning. The following questions in Table 11.5 can help guide your investigations.

No one thinks diversity-and-inclusion implementation is easy or painless. It is an arduous process that requires tenacity, courage, and imagination. It also requires being savvy about your organization and knowledgeable about the larger world. Our goal in this chapter was to give you information and guidelines that can validate where your organization is already effective; tools for engaging others in the process of culture change; suggestions for identifying vulnerable spots; and methods for implementing successful actions.

ACTIVITY 11.8 | Steps in Managing Diversity

STEP	WHAT'S IN PLACE	WHAT NEEDS TO BE DONE
I. Executive Level Commitment		
II. Assessment and Diagnosis		
III. Diversity Task Force		
IV. Training		
V. Systems Changes		
VI. Measurement and Evaluation		
VII. Integration		

Suggestions for Using
"Steps in Managing Diversity"

Objectives:

* Generate discussion about the organization's progress in managing diversity and inclusion
* Identify areas of needed work and development in the implementation of diversity and inclusion

Intended Audience:

* Diversity-and-inclusion council or task force
* Executive, senior management, or leadership team

Materials:

* Copies of the worksheet *Steps in Managing Diversity*

Processing the Activity:

* Facilitator briefly explains the seven steps in managing diversity and giving examples.
* Participants working individually fill in the chart.
* In small groups, participants share information, charting combined responses.
* Groups report collected responses.
* Total-group discusses areas of needed development, setting priorities, and planning action.

Questions for Discussion:

* What is already in place and how is it working?
* What areas are most in need of work?
* What are the top priorities that need to be attended to?
* What could interfere with/block making progress in these areas?

Caveats, Considerations, and Variations:

* The group that works through this analysis needs enough information to be able to respond. They also need to have some power in stimulating action.

TABLE 11.5 | Benchmarking Questions

1. What are the objectives of your diversity-and-inclusion initiative?

2. What are your criteria for success?
   - Culture and climate measures
   - Business/productivity measures

3. How does your executive management demonstrate support for diversity and inclusion?

4. How did you get buy-in from staff?
   What kind of resistance did you encounter? At what levels of the organization?
   How did you overcome or deal with it?

5. Describe the structure and process of your initiative? (e.g. Do you have a council? Are you collecting data? If so, how so?)

6. What are the priorities and objectives of your initiative?

7. What are your most effective strategies and processes?

8. What are or have been your most important discoveries to date regarding both successes and failures?
   - What mistakes have been made?
   - What would you do differently next time?

9. Did you benchmark in your own planning? If so, what did you adapt from other organizations' best practices?

10. What is the most important piece of wisdom you would share with another organization embarking on a diversity-and-inclusion initiative?

CHAPTER 12.

Conducting a Diversity Audit: Taking an Organizational Snapshot

• •

This chapter will provide you with:

- A clear understanding of the advantages and disadvantages of three types of assessment methods

- A series of diversity assessment tools, questionnaires, checklists, and surveys

- Guidelines for conducting focus groups and interviews

- Sample questions to use in focus groups and interviews

- Tools for pinpointing diversity-related problems and training needs of managerial and nonmanagerial staff

"Know thyself" is as important a dictum for organizations as it is for individuals wanting to increase effectiveness. Before your organization or workgroup can figure out how to manage diversity, it needs to examine and assess existing conditions, practices, attitudes, and skills. Without accurate baseline information, plans and changes are built on unstable foundations.

The Role of Assessment: What It Can Do

Assessment is a tool for diagnosing organizational conditions. It is analogous to a physical examination where a patient's temperature and blood pressure are taken and lab tests and X rays are done to check the body's functioning. Many different methods of checking are used to give the doctor critical information needed in making a diagnosis. Likewise, the many tools of organizational assessment provide information that serves your organization in five ways.

Provide feedback. Assessment data reported back to the organization function much like biofeedback for an individual. By seeing information in black and white, with words, charts, graphs, or other visual depictions, managers and other staff get an accurate picture of the diversity-related aspects in the organization. This information serves as a springboard for making decisions and taking action. Seeing these effects and conditions is a first step in doing something about them. Often, having this information made public within your team, management group, or whole company is enough to get change started.

Determine baseline data. Assessment also provides information that serves as a "state of the union" report. This baseline information is essential for strategic planning and as a reference for future comparison. How far your organization has come can't be assessed unless you know where you started.

Make latent issues public. Assessment also uncovers problems, concerns, and obstacles that might not have been openly discussed before. Like underground reefs, unseen on the smooth surface of the sea, they can be treacherous if not discovered. Assessment brings them out into the open where they can no longer be ignored.

Identify staff development needs. Data from assessment also uncover areas of needed development of staff, both managerial and nonmanagerial. Attitudes, skill levels, and knowledge can be assessed and determinations made about needs for training and growth experiences.

Generate commitment through input. Because data come from people in the organization, staff are more apt to "own" the information and feel committed to any plans or actions built on it. Getting input in this initial stage sets the tone for participation throughout any change process.

In understanding the positive outcomes of assessment, it is important to heed a caveat. As one colleague of ours used to sagely caution, "Don't open up a can of worms unless you have the recipe for worm soufflé." In other words, assessment can open up volatile issues. If an organization is not prepared to deal with the information, the result may be expectations initially raised, then dashed. Unless an organization is ready to make use of assessment data and has a clear purpose for doing so, it is better not to embark on the process of data gathering in the first place.

Before you begin the process, the following questions can help you plan and structure the most effective audit for your purpose.

What do you want to find out? For example, do you want to assess staff attitudes about the many cultures in the workplace, perceptions of employees from nonmainstream groups, or skills of managers in working with diverse staff?

What part does this data collection play in your larger organizational plan? Assessment needs to be in the service of a larger goal. Is it part of a plan to increase demographic diversity at all levels in your company process? Is your aim to pinpoint areas of exclusion that are hindering effectiveness? Or perhaps the development of more cohesive work teams is part of your process-improvement program.

Who needs to be involved? Your purposes and your budget will help you decide the answer to this. Do you need an organization-wide survey, focus groups from certain segments of the workforce, or a questionnaire for managers, for example?

How will data generated be used and communicated to others? Will information be used by a diversity task force or executive management? Will the data be fed back only to those who participated or communicated to all staff? How will that process be managed?

What methods will be used to collect data? The answers to the questions above will help you decide the most appropriate assessment options.

Who will be most appropriate and effective in collecting data? What staff personnel or outside resources are best suited to conduct the process or aspects of the process?

What cultural factors may influence the audit process? The language and reading level of any instruments, the values at the base of the process, and the methods used will all be influenced by the cultural backgrounds, the designers, and data collectors, and need to take into account those of the involved participants. This chapter will help you formulate your own answers to these questions.

Three Types of Assessment: Survey Isn't the Only Way

Assessment generally calls up images of paper-and-pencil or electronic instruments such as your last employee opinion questionnaire or your customer satisfaction survey. While such written assessment tools represent one way to collect data, there are two others. A method borrowed from marketing research, and one that is being used more frequently in internal assessment, is that of focus groups. These discussions serve as a kind of group interview. Questions are posed for participants that enable them to share their opinions, perceptions, and feelings on the topic being investigated. Finally, a third avenue of assessment is through individual interviews with appropriate staff members. Table 12.1 takes a look at the advantages and disadvantages of each.

There is no need for exclusivity when choosing an assessment method. A combination of two or all three methods may be used in one assessment project. For example, interviews with top executive staff members and a random sampling of managers may help determine the areas to be investigated and questions to be asked on a written questionnaire. Even further, this information may be used to set up focus groups. Then a two-pronged approach using focus group data collection and an organization-wide questionnaire survey can be used. Combining the two provides breadth and depth.

TABLE 12.1 | Assessment Methods Compared

Method	Advantage	Disadvantages
Questionnaire	Data can be obtained from everyone in the organization in a cost-effective way. Data are collected anonymously so employees feel free to be more honest. Provides data in comparative form from all respondents that can be quantified and statistically analyzed. Takes relatively little time from employees and can be done simultaneously in many locations. Simple to administer, either electronically or paper and pencil.	Requires literacy and possibly translation into other languages. Oneway communication offers no way to get clarification or explanation about responses. Responses tend to be limited by information requested in questionnaire. May get lip service and perfunctory answers rather than thoughtful responses. Impersonality and lack of human touch may put off employees, especially those from highly relational, high-context cultures that prefer face-to-face communication and storytelling.
Interviews	Interviewees may feel freer to speak openly without others present. Problems and issues surfaced can be explored in depth. Permits collection of examples, anecdotes, and stories that illustrate the issues and put them in human terms. More personal touch allows for person-to-person communication.	Least time efficient and most labor intensive and costly method. Requires skilled interviewer to guide sessions. Data collected from a limited number of people may provide a narrow slice of information if only staff at certain levels are interviewed. Affects the least number of staff so may generate only limited commitment.
Focus Groups	Serve as a teaching tool, building respondee awareness about diversity. Produce richer data through in-depth discussions about topics and issues. Two-way communication permits clarification and explanation of information given. More personal and human. Subtle information from nonverbal clues and body language can be picked up. More time efficient to get information from groups rather than individuals one at a time. Interaction generates more data. Comments spark other ideas so new information may emerge. Participants' hearing of each others' views may expand their understanding of the issues.	Require skilled facilitation in sessions. Generally only provide a sample of views, not everyone's. Peer pressure may influence participants' comments. Takes time to coordinate sessions and schedule the pulling of employees from jobs. People may be uncomfortable in a new setting and an unfamiliar experience. Participants may be reluctant to open up and speak freely for fear of repercussions or because of cultural norms that discourage negative or critical comments.

An important consideration is whether to use internal or external data-gatherers. Using in-house resources, such as staff in human resources or EEO/affirmative action departments, may seem more cost-effective. Insiders have a greater knowledge of the organizational culture and so may have a sense of which issues to pursue. Their informal networks and information pipelines can help in getting beyond the level of superficial observations. However, their association with existing programs, such as affirmative action, may cause employees to question the purpose and objectivity of the assessment process. On the other hand, an assessor from the outside has greater objectivity and clarity in looking at the organization. This outsider usually has no vested interest, no relationships with other staff, and no history with the organization to color his or her thinking. Assessment may get more honest, candid responses from employees who have greater trust in the objectivity of an outsider. Having an external data-gatherer may also cause employees to see the assessment in a larger organizational context, not just another project from a particular department. Deciding who should conduct the various aspects of your assessment does not have to be an either-or. The assessment can be a collaborative effort of insiders and outsiders, getting the best of both worlds.

Once you have decided on the who and how of your organizational audit, there is a need to focus on the what—the tools and techniques that will help you get the information you want and the answers you need.

Assessing How Effective Your Organization Is at Managing and Capitalizing on Diversity

In examining an organization's overall management of diversity, three areas need to be investigated. First, because organizations' effectiveness and productivity depend on the human beings who work in them, there is a need to look at individual attitudes and behaviors. Issues such as how open employees are to people who are different, how comfortable staff is with change, and how people deal with one another across lines of difference are important areas of assessment. Beyond the individual level, it is essential to look at organizational values and norms. How does the organizational culture encourage or discourage diversity? Is diversity tied to the vision and strategic goals of the company? Finally, it is critical to look at the place where the organization and the employees interface, the management practices, and policies. How do managers use such organizational systems as accountability, reward, and decision-making to capitalize on diversity? How adept are managers at getting maximum commitment from all segments of the workforce? When all three of these levels of organizational functioning work in concert, diversity is effectively managed as a corporate asset. The *Managing Diversity Questionnaire* in Activity 12.1 can be useful to you in assessing an organization at these three levels.

ACTIVITY 12.1 | Managing Diversity Questionnaire

In this organization...	Very True	Somewhat True	Not True
1. I am at ease with people of diverse backgrounds.			
2. There are no double standards. The rules are the same for everyone.			
3. Managers have a track record of hiring and promoting diverse employees.			
4. In general, I find change stimulating, exciting, and challenging.			
5. Gender jokes are tolerated in the informal environment.			
6. Managers hold all people equally accountable.			
7. I know about the cultural norms of different groups.			
8. The formation of specific support groups is encouraged.			
9. I'm comfortable going to my manager with a diversity problem.			
10. I am afraid to disagree with members of other groups for fear of being called prejudiced.			
11. There is a mentoring program that identifies and prepares talented people for promotion.			
12. Managers are comfortable dealing with differences such as age, race, gender, and sexual orientation.			
13. I feel there is more than one right way to do things.			
14. Racial and ethnic jokes are tolerated in the informal environment.			
15. One criteria of a manager's performance review is developing the diversity of his or her staff.			
16. I think that diverse viewpoints make for creativity.			
17. There is high turnover among specific groups.			
18. My manager asks for my opinion and uses my input.			

(continued on next page)

ACTIVITY 12.1 | Managing Diversity Questionnaire (continued)

	Very True	Somewhat True	Not True
In this organization...			
19. I am aware of my own assumptions and stereotypes about others.			
20. Policies are flexible enough to accommodate everyone.			
21. Managers get active participation from all employees in meetings.			
22. I'm uncomfortable with people speaking other languages on the job.			
23. If I don't get help from my manager, I know where else I can go when I have a diversity issue.			
24. Multicultural work teams work together harmoniously.			
25. Staff members spend their lunch hour and breaks in mixed groups.			
26. Recruiting a diverse array of talented people is a priority.			
27. Managers know how to deal with language differences or other culture clashes.			
28. I feel that working in a diverse staff enriches me.			
29. Promotional systems are transparent and fair.			
30. Managers have effective strategies to use when one group refuses to work with another			

SCORING:

_____ Items 5, 10, 17 and 22   Very true = 0 points, Somewhat = 1 point, Not true = 2 points.

_____ All other items   Very true = 2 points, Somewhat = 1 point, Not true = 0 points.

_____ INDIVIDUAL ATTITUDES AND BEHAVIORS   Items 1,4,7,10,13,16,19,22,25,28

_____ ORGANIZATIONAL VALUES AND NORMS   Items 2,5,8,11,14,17,20, 23,26,29

_____ MANAGEMENT PRACTICES AND POLICIES   Items 3,6,9,12,15,18,21,24,27,30

_____ TOTAL SCORE

Suggestions for Using the
"Managing Diversity Questionnaire"

Objectives:

- Assess three levels of an organization's effectiveness in managing a diverse workforce: individual attitudes and behaviors, organizational values and norms, and management practices and policies
- Increase awareness and knowledge about aspects of managing diversity
- Target areas of needed development

Intended Audience:

- Staff at all levels in an organization who are working to increase effectiveness in managing diversity and who desire to understand perceptions of employees about the issues
- Executive and/or middle management involved in planning diversity development strategies
- Executive staff and diversity council members charged with organizational strategy regarding diversity
- Trainees in a managing diversity seminar

Processing the Activity:

- Individuals are asked to respond to the questionnaire based on their perceptions of the organization and how it functions. They are told that responses are anonymous and are asked to be candid. They are also told how the data generated will be used, who will see them, and what will be done with them.
- Questionnaires are collected and scored.
- Data are compiled and analyzed by item, by the three levels of functioning, and by demographic groupings of staff.
- Data are reported to appropriate executive and or management staff, and a summary of findings is communicated to all participants along with an indication of next steps.

Questions for Discussion:

- What are our organization's strengths and weaknesses?
- How similar or disparate are perceptions of different groups, divisions, or levels within the organization?
- What issues need further investigation or clarification?
- What issues need attention?
- Who or what (positions, levels) needs to be involved in dealing with these particular issues?

Caveats and Considerations:

- Do not embark on a process of this type until you have a clear plan about how the data will be used and a commitment that they will be considered in planning.

- This questionnaire can be used as an awareness builder for managers who want to increase their own effectiveness and/or for those involved in diversity task forces. It can also be used as a jumping-off point for discussions about managing diversity in execution and/or management staff meetings.

- Questionnaires can be coded by level, department, length of time with the company, type of work, and so on to give more specific categories for analysis.

The overall score has a range of 0-60. The higher the number of points, the more effectively the organization is managing and capitalizing on diversity. However, analyzing scores by item and by the three levels—individual, organizational, and managerial—provides additional information. Item analysis can help you pinpoint diversity weak spots, your organization's figurative Achilles' heels. For example, if the lowest-scoring item is number 15, then perhaps including managerial performance standards about developing diversity might need to be addressed. If number 7 is a collective low-point, your company might want to consider providing cultural awareness training to staff so they can learn about the cultural backgrounds of groups with whom they work. The information gained from this survey can be fed back to executive staff or the diversity council so they can make use of it in their strategic planning. It can also be fed back to managerial staff so they can problem solve around the weaknesses surfaced; for example, coming up with ways to offer more appropriate rewards to a diverse staff.

Analyzing scores at the three levels of organizational functioning can give you additional information. If, for example, the individual attitudes and behaviors score is lowest, then training might be called for to help staff understand and accept differences. If the organizational values and norms score is lowest, then perhaps a feedback session with executive staff is called for, giving leadership the questionnaire data so they can use them in their strategizing. Finally, if the management practices and policies score is low, then perhaps management development training regarding diversity and problem-solving sessions are called for. In one organization that used this audit, scores showed a large disparity between executive and first-line staff regarding perceptions about management policies and practices. Sharing these respective realities might be a place to begin dealing with diversity in this organization. In all cases, executive management needs to see the data and be involved in setting a course of action.

The most critical aspect of any organizational assessment is using the data. To conduct this type of a process and then to merely report the findings misses the point. Something needs to be done with the information gathered. Analysis needs to be done, and "so what" questions need to be asked.

- So what does this tell us about our organization?
- So where do we need to improve?
- So what do we need to do to improve our effectiveness?

Having staff at appropriate levels grapple with these questions is a critical step in milking assessment tools such as this for their full usefulness.

If an organization is in the initial stages of addressing diversity as an issue, there may be a simpler and more basic question to answer: "How do we know if we need to address this issue at all?" One straightforward way to get a collective answer is to use an uncomplicated checklist that requires respondees to indicate any of the problems they are experiencing (see Activity 12.2).

ACTIVITY 12.2 | Symptoms of Diversity-Related Problems: Internal Checklist

Check any of the following situations you notice and/or are experiencing in your organization:

_____ Lack of a diverse staff at all levels in the organization

_____ Complaints about staff or customers speaking other languages on the job

_____ Resistance to working with or making negative comments about another group (ethnic, racial, cultural, gender, religion, sexual orientation, or physical ability)

_____ Difficulty in communicating due to limited or heavily-accented English

_____ Ethnic, racial, or gender slurs or jokes

_____ EEOC suits or complaints about discrimination in promotions, pay, and performance reviews

_____ Lack of social interaction between members of diverse groups

_____ Increase in grievances by members of specific groups

_____ Difficulty in recruiting and retaining members of different groups

_____ Open conflict between groups or between individuals from different groups

_____ Mistakes and productivity problems due to employees not understanding directions

_____ Perceptions that individuals are not valued for their unique contributions

_____ Ostracism of individuals who are different from the norm

_____ Barriers in promotion for diverse employees

_____ Frustrations and irritations resulting from cultural differences

_____ Other diversity-related problem—Explain:_____

_____

_____

_____

_____

_____

_____

_____

_____

_____

_____

_____

_____

_____

Suggestions for Using
"Symptoms of Diversity-Related Problems: Internal Checklist"

Objectives:

- Identify diversity-related problems within the organization
- Raise awareness and spark discussion about such issues
- Provide a jumping-off point for taking action to deal with diversity-related problems

Intended Audience:

- Managers, supervisors, and first-line staff in a diverse organization
- Trainees at a managing diversity seminar
- Executive staff attempting to identify obstacles to productivity and morale
- HR staff attempting to reduce turnover and grievances

Processing the Activity:

- Individuals are asked to check any of the problems they have experienced within the organization. They may also add others that are not listed.
- Groups can discuss problems checked to get an idea about which issues seem to be most prevalent. They may also assign priorities regarding dealing with the problems, discuss how widespread the problems are, and/or determine which parts of the organization seem to be most affected by particular issues.
- Follow-up will depend on the group involved. Data can be used by managers in solving the problems in their own departments/divisions; by executives in developing or modifying plans or policies; and by HR staff in making recommendations to executive management and in modifying their own procedures. Finally, data can be used in planning management development activities.

Questions for Discussion:

- What seem to be the most frequent problems surfaced?
- How widespread are they? Which sections of the organization seem most affected?
- What is the cost to the organization of these problems? What will happen if these go unaddressed?
- What additional information do we need in order to address these? From whom?
- Where/how do these issues need to be dealt with?
- What do we need to do to address these problems?
- What support, skills, and training do managers need to deal with these issues?
- What organization systems or policies need to be examined and possibly modified?

Caveats, Considerations, and Variations:

- Be careful not to make any premature commitments regarding actions to address these problems. Undoubtedly, further clarification about the problems is needed before solutions can be planned.
- This activity can be modified for use by a manager to get feedback from his or her workgroup.

The beauty of this tool is that it is quick, easy to administer, and can be used to pinpoint the organization's problem areas related to diversity. Pay particular attention to the frequency with which problems are identified. When the same data surface repeatedly, employees are sending a message. This checklist can be used in deciding whether diversity does present problems to the organization and, if so, what those obstacles are. If problems are uncovered, more investigation and assessment would be needed to answer such questions as the following:

- How widespread is this problem?
- Which groups are most affected?
- How is the problem getting in the way of productivity, morale, and service?
- Is the problem a result of individual attitudes and behaviors, organizational norms and values, or managerial policies and practices?
- How can these issues best be addressed?

Answering these questions may require the use of a survey questionnaire and/or focus group data collection. They may also be addressed at management staff meetings.

Stages of Diversity Survey: An Organizational Progress Report

Dealing with the phenomenon of diversity is an evolutionary process, not a revolutionary one. No organization has a homogeneous workforce or exclusive culture one week and a diverse staff or inclusive culture the next. In fact, the evolution is a gradual process of change that involves a shift in not only the demographics but attitudes and practices in the organization as well. An organization can have a very diverse staff yet continue to function as a monocultural system, as though its staff were all of similar backgrounds. Bailey Jackson and Evangelina Holvino hypothesize that organizations experience three stages in this evolution: monocultural, nondiscriminatory, and multicultural.[1]

In the monocultural stage, the organization acts as though all employees were the same. While staff may be somewhat diverse, there is an expectation to conform to a standard that is, in most cases, the white-male model, which puts heterosexual white men at an advantage. Success is achieved by following the expectations and norms of this model. Women, people of color, immigrants, and others who are different are expected to assimilate, to adopt the dominant style of the organization. The motto might be "When in Rome, do as the Romans do." Differences are underplayed, and there is an attempt to be "color and gender blind."

As the organization evolves, it reaches the second stage: the nondiscriminatory stage. Usually because of governmental regulations and the threat of employee grievances, organizations begin to pay attention to affirmative action requirements and EEO regulations. In this phase, there is much attention paid to meeting quotas in hiring and promotion and in removing roadblocks that inhibit diverse groups from moving in and up. The goal is to eliminate the unfair advantage of the majority group. Generally, the two groups that have been most affected at this stage are women and African Americans. Training in gender equity and reducing stereotypes and prejudice is often done during this period. For diverse employees, there is a push/pull between the need to assimilate and a desire for the organization to accommodate to their needs. Compromises are usually the method of resolving these conflicts, with each side giving in a little in order to gain some as well.

Sooner or later, because of workforce changes in ethnicity, lifestyle, and values, the organization comes to the third stage: the multicultural stage. In this stage, there is not only a recognition that there are clear differences of culture, background, preferences, and values, but a valuing of those differences and the benefits they bring. Assimilation is no longer the model for success. Rather, new norms are created that allow more leeway for employees to do things their own way. Organizational policies and procedures are flexible enough to work for everyone, and no one is put at an exploitive advantage. This nirvana-like state is a worthwhile goal, but we have yet to see an organization so evolved that it fits entirely in this stage. Use Activity 12.3 to assess where your organization is in its evolutionary process.

The *a* responses describe an organization in the monocultural stage, the *b* responses describe an organization in the nondiscriminatory stage, and the *c* responses depict an organization in the multicultural stage. The category in which you have the highest number of checks indicates the probable stage of the organization. However, scores in the other two categories are important as well. Because organizations function at many levels simultaneously and evolve unevenly, most will have some points in all the stages. The most instructive part of this questionnaire may emerge not from the score but from an examination of the specific responses checked or not checked. Which of the *c* responses were not checked? What goals or strategies might that suggest?

ACTIVITY 12.3 | Stages of Diversity Survey: An Organizational Progress Report

Directions: Check each response that is true of your organization. You may check more than one response for each item number.

1. In this organization:

   _____ a. There is a standard way to dress and look.

   _____ b. While there is no dress code, most employees dress within a conventional range.

   _____ c. There is much variety in employees' style of dress.

2. In this organization:

   _____ a. Newcomers are expected to adapt to existing norms.

   _____ b. There is some flexibility to accommodate the needs of diverse employees.

   _____ c. Norms are flexible enough to include everyone.

3. In this organization:

   _____ a. Diversity is an issue that stirs irritation and resentment.

   _____ b. Attention is paid to meeting EEO requirements and affirmative action quotas.

   _____ c. Working toward a diverse staff at all levels is seen as a strategic advantage.

4. In this organization, dealing with diversity is:

   _____ a. Not a top priority.

   _____ b. The responsibility of the HR department.

   _____ c. Considered a part of every manager's job.

5. People in this organization:

   _____ a. Downplay or ignore differences among employees.

   _____ b. Tolerate differences and the needs they imply.

   _____ c. Value differences and see diversity as an advantage to be cultivated.

6. Demographics of this organization show that:

   _____ a. There is diversity among staff at lower levels.

   _____ b. There is diverse staff at lower and middle levels.

   _____ c. There is diversity at all levels of the organization.

7. Money is spent on training programs to help employees:

   _____ a. Adapt to the organization's culture and learn "the way we do things here."

   _____ b. Develop diverse staff's ability to move up the organization ladder.

   _____ c. Communicate and work effectively with diverse staff and customers.

(continued on next page)

ACTIVITY 12.3 | Stages of Diversity Survey:
An Organizational Progress Report (continued)

8. Managers are held accountable for:

    _____ a. Motivating staff and increasing productivity.

    _____ b. Avoiding EEO and discrimination grievances and suits.

    _____ c. Working effectively with a diverse staff.

9. Managers are held accountable for:

    _____ a. Maintaining a stable staff and perpetuating existing norms.

    _____ b. Meeting affirmative action goals and identifying promotable talent.

    _____ c. Building productive work teams with diverse staff.

10. Managers are rewarded for:

    _____ a. Following existing procedures.

    _____ b. Solving problems in the system.

    _____ c. Initiating creative programs and trying new methods.

11. This organization:

    _____ a. Resists change and seeks to maintain the status quo.

    _____ b. Deals with changes as they occur.

    _____ c. Is continually working on improvement.

12. In this organization, it is an advantage to:

    _____ a. Be a white male.

    _____ b. Learn to be like the "old guard."

    _____ c. Be unique and find new ways of doing things.

Directions for Scoring:
Count the total number of checks next to each letter (a, b, c) and fill in the totals below:

_____ a. Monocultural

_____ b. Nondiscriminatory

_____ c. Multicultural

Suggestions for Using the
"Stages of Diversity Survey: An Organizational Progress Report"

Objectives:

- Determine an organization's stage of development in dealing with diversity
- Give feedback to executive management about the organization's status regarding dealing with diversity
- Provide data for strategizing regarding organization development

Intended Audience:

- Middle- to lower-level staff in a diverse organization
- Management and supervisory staff
- Members of diversity task forces or planning teams
- Executive staff involved in strategic planning

Processing the Activity:

- Individuals are asked to check each response that they perceive as a true statement about the organization. They may check more than one response for each item.
- Questionnaires are collected and scored. If used by a task force or planning team, they may be scored in the group.
- Scores are analyzed, and data are interpreted and then presented to the planning group.

Questions for Discussion:

- Where is our organization in its development regarding diversity?
- What surprises or new information is there?
- What issues need to be addressed?
- What kind of planning or development is indicated for growth?

Caveats, Considerations, and Variations:

- While this instrument leads to a score that places the organization in a particular stage of development, its purpose is not to label the organization but rather to serve as a tool for exploration and growth. Help those with the information use it for that purpose.
- Individuals may disagree with some of the statements. They may also find some indicators of particular stages not desirable. In these cases, use disagreement to provoke discussion of desired organization goals and indicators of their achievements.

Diversity Readiness: Analyzing Individual Awareness

Awareness precedes choice, as our friend and mentor, organization development theorist, author, and consultant John E. Jones use to say. A beginning point in dealing with diversity is awareness about differences, about individuals' attitudes and prejudices, and about the impact of diversity in the workplace. Activity 12.4 can give you a quick assessment of the awareness level of a group or staff. Armed with this information, you can proceed to design a diversity training program that meets people where they are.

This tool can serve as a jumping-off point in beginning discussions about diversity. It can also show you the degree of acceptance or resistance that exists regarding diversity. Armed with this information, you can tailor your intervention to suit the group: a more aware group may be able to jump into experiential training activities right away; a more resistant group, conversely, may need a more cognitive approach initially. Beginning with statistics and demographic data supporting the strategic business case for dealing with diversity would be a less threatening first step and would probably give you the best chance for acceptance with a less aware, more resistant group.

Measuring Employee Perceptions: How Much Is Diversity Valued?

Perceptions and attitudes are difficult to measure with self-report assessment tools because most people are "test wise" and smart enough to pick up on which is the "right" answer. In addition, most of us are uncomfortable with our own prejudices, so we often deny them, even to ourselves. However, there is value in having people respond to questionnaires such as the *Diversity Opinionnaire* in Activity 12.5 to get some information on professed attitudes as well as to open people's minds to some of the issues involved in dealing with diversity.

ACTIVITY 12.4 | Diversity Awareness Continuum

Directions: Put an X that represents where you fit along the dotted line for each continuum below.

I am not knowledgeable about the cultural norms of different groups in the organization.	. . . .	I am knowledgeable about the cultural norms of different groups in the organization.
I do not hold stereotypes about other groups.	. . . .	I admit my stereotypes about other groups.
I feel partial to, and more comfortable with, some groups than others.	. . . .	I feel equally comfortable with all groups.
I gravitate toward others who are like me.	. . . .	I gravitate toward others who are different.
I find it more satisfying to manage a homogeneous team.	. . . .	I find it more satisfying to manage a multicultural team.
I feel that everyone is the same, with similar values and preferences.	. . . .	I feel that everyone is unique, with differing values and preferences.
I am perplexed by the culturally different behaviors I see among staff.	. . . .	I understand the cultural influences that are at the root of some of the behaviors I see.
I react with irritation when confronted with someone who does not speak English.	. . . .	I show patience and understanding with limited-English speakers.
I am task-focused and don't like to waste time chatting.	. . . .	I find that more gets done when I spend time on relationships first.
I feel that newcomers to this organization should adapt to our rules.	. . . .	I feel that both newcomers and the organizations in which they work need to change to fit together.

Draw your profile by connecting your Xs. The closer your line is to the right-hand column, the greater your awareness regarding diversity; the closer to the left-hand column, the less aware you may be about diversity-related issues.

Suggestions for Using the
"Diversity Awareness Continuum"

Objectives:

- Assess individual awareness and attitudes about diversity
- Give management information about staff attitudes and potential sources of resistance to diversity
- Give individuals information about potential areas of personal/professional development

Intended Audience:

- Members of diverse and/or changing work teams
- Managers dealing with diverse staffs
- Trainees in diversity awareness and managing diversity seminars

Processing the Activity:

- Individuals place an X representing where they fit along each continuum on the sheet. They then connect their Xs.
- In groups or in a team, they discuss their responses, focusing on the farthest-left and farthest-right marks. Discussion continues about reactions and feelings about diversity, and the consequences of those reactions.
- Individuals target one or two areas for personal development.

Questions for Discussion:

- Where are you most/least aware and knowledgeable about diversity?
- What do you need to learn?
- What is the impact of these?
- Where are your greatest strengths and weaknesses?
- What are the team's/group's greatest strengths or weaknesses regarding diversity?
- What do you need to do as a team to grow? As an individual?

Caveats, Considerations, and Variations:

- In addition to its value as a tool for growth for the individual and team, this activity can provide data to training and development professionals developing diversity training programs.
- It also serves as a subtle teaching tool, suggesting areas of development regarding diversity.

ACTIVITY 12.5 | Diversity Opinionnaire

Please respond with a rating that represents your feelings about each opinion below.
5 = strongly agree, 4 = agree, 3 = uncertain, 2 = disagree, 1 = strongly disagree.

_____   1.   Everyone who works in this organization should be required to speak English.

_____   2.   Diversity brings creativity and energy to a workgroup.

_____   3.   Immigrants should be expected to forsake their own cultures and adapt to American ways.

_____   4.   Multicultural teams can be stimulating, productive, and fun.

_____   5.   People should leave their differences at home and conform to organizational standards at work.

_____   6.   Showing flexibility and accommodation to people's individual needs and preferences increases commitment and motivation.

_____   7.   Diversity brings unnecessary conflict and problems to a workgroup.

_____   8.   Women and people of color are underrepresented at higher levels in this organization.

_____   9.   Increasing workforce diversity has led to a decline in quality.

_____   10.   People are more motivated and productive when they feel they are accepted for who they are.

_____   11.   Women and people of color are oversensitive to prejudice and discrimination.

_____   12.   Stereotypes exist about all groups.

_____   13.   Racial and ethnic groups tend to stick together.

_____   14.   Differences often make people uncomfortable.

_____   15.   Some groups are more suited for or talented at certain jobs.

_____   16.   There should be no double standards. The rules should be the same for everyone, regardless of gender, race, age, ethnicity, and so on.

_____   17.   America would be a better place if people would assimilate into one culture.

_____   18.   America would be a better place if people were allowed to preserve their individual cultures.

_____   19.   People are reluctant to disagree with employees of certain groups for fear of being called prejudiced.

_____   20.   Training is needed to help employees understand each other and overcome communication barriers.

Scoring:

_____   Total score for odd-numbered items

_____   Total score for even-numbered items

Suggestions for Using the
"Diversity Opinionnaire"

Objectives:
- Assess attitudes about openness toward diversity
- Identify potential sources of resistance to diversity
- Uncover personal prejudices and feelings about diversity

Intended Audience:
- Staff at all levels in a diverse organization
- Managers dealing with a diverse staff
- Trainees in a diversity awareness or managing diversity seminar
- Individuals wanting to increase their own awareness and sensitivity regarding dealing with differences
- Members of a diversity task force or planning group needing to "get their own house in order" before working with the organization about this issue

Processing the Activity:
- Individuals respond by assigning a number, from 1 to 5, to each of the statements.
- If used as an organization assessment, questionnaires are collected, scores are tabulated and analyzed, and then data are reported to the appropriate planning group.
- If used by individuals or groups for their own information and growth, individuals score their own and then discuss results and their significance.
- Individuals can target areas for personal growth, while teams or groups can pinpoint areas for group development.

Questions for Discussion:
- What is the workplace impact of these attitudes?
- How can these opinions affect relationships with diverse groups?
- How do they affect manager/subordinate relationships?
- Which attitudes represent obstacles to making diversity an asset to the organization or team?
- What needs to be done to deal with these perceptions? How?

Caveats, Considerations, and Variations:
- Discussion is apt to be heated, and there may be a tendency for individuals to want to defend their opinion, attack another's, and/or argue for their own point of view. It is important to remind people that attitudes and perceptions are neither right nor wrong; however, they are realities for those holding them. Keep the discussion centered on the effect of the attitudes and the consequences of the behaviors they provoke. Focus on the impact on the organization, team, and individual.
- As a variation in process, signs with the numbers 1-5 can be posted around the room. As questions are read, people can go to the number of their response. The facilitator can stop and lead a discussion when there are interesting patterns in responses.

The odd-numbered items are opinions that represent a more monocultural view and a resistance to diversity. The higher the total for these items, the stronger this view is held. The even-numbered items are opinions that represent a more multicultural view and a valuing of diversity. The higher the total for these items, the stronger this view is held. An overall score for comparison purposes can be obtained by subtracting the odd score from the even score. The result may be a positive or negative number. The higher the number is on a positive scale, the greater the acceptance and receptivity to diversity. Again, as with all the other tools offered, this data can be a catalyst for (and can legitimize) action.

Staff Diversity Needs Analysis: Awareness, Knowledge, and Skills

In order for individuals of many backgrounds to work productively together, they need information and abilities on three levels: awareness, knowledge, and skills. First they need awareness. It is critical that they recognize differences and are aware of their own assumptions about those differences: "What are my unconscious expectations of African Americans? Latinos? Gays and Lesbians?" "Am I surprised when all secretaries and nurses are not women or when I meet doctors or pilots who are?" Beyond awareness of their own subtle expectations or assumptions, there is a need for knowledge about different cultural norms, needs, and preferences of individuals from different groups.

Second, they need knowledge. Information is needed to answer such questions as the following: "Why do people nod and say 'yes' when they don't understand?" "Why do gay men and lesbians feel the need to come out of the closet?" "What are the myths and realities about aging?" "Why do some employees speak their native languages at work even when they know English?" "Why do others react negatively when I speak my native language on the job?"

Third, they need skills. Employees need to have the ability to deal with one another in sensitive ways: "How can I resolve a conflict with someone who won't admit anything is wrong?" "How can I communicate with a co-worker whose English is limited?" "What can I do when I encounter racist remarks or ethnic slurs?" Activity 12.6 can give you an idea of the training and development needs of your employees at these three levels.

ACTIVITY 12.6 | Staff Diversity Needs Analysis

Please respond to the questions below by answering true or false.

_____ 1. I am comfortable working with individuals who are different from me in race and cultural background.

_____ 2. I am sometimes confused by the behavior of employees from different backgrounds.

_____ 3. It is difficult for me to understand people who speak with thick accents.

_____ 4. I'm reluctant to disagree with employees of different groups for fear of being considered prejudiced.

_____ 5. I know about my own cultural background and how it influences my behavior.

_____ 6. I am able to resolve conflicts with employees who are different from me in cultural background, gender, race, and sexual orientation.

_____ 7. My behavior is influenced by gender differences.

_____ 8. Prejudice exists in every individual.

_____ 9. I feel comfortable talking about differences in race, culture, and sexual orientation.

_____ 10. Racial and cultural differences influence my behavior.

_____ 11. Stereotypes are held about every group.

_____ 12. I'm not sure what labels to use in referring to different groups.

_____ 13. My behavior is influenced by differences in sexual orientation.

_____ 14. I understand the different cultural influences of my co-workers.

_____ 15. I get frustrated when communicating with limited-English-speaking individuals.

_____ 16. I am most comfortable spending time with people who are similar to me in background.

_____ 17. I find the behaviors of some members of other groups irritating.

_____ 18. I'm fearful of offending individuals of other groups by saying the wrong thing.

_____ 19. People of some groups are treated differently because they act differently.

_____ 20. I find myself thinking, "Why don't they act like us?"

_____ 21. I'm able to resolve problems easily with co-workers who are different from me.

_____ 22. I recognize my own biases and prejudices.

_____ 23. Certain behaviors of groups bother me.

_____ 24. I am able to work with people so I feel I fit in, no matter how different we are.

_____ 25. I wish we were all more similar.

_____ 26. I understand some of the reasons why there is cultural clash and conflicts between groups.

_____ 27. When dealing with differences, I am able to "walk in someone else's shoes."

_____ 28. I find differences among us interesting and stimulating.

_____ 29. I understand the reasons for my own reactions to others' differeces.

_____ 30. I find many similarities between me and my co-workers of different backgrounds.

Scoring—Give each answer a point value as follows:

Items 1, 5, 6, 8, 9, 11, 14, 21, 22, 24, 26, 27, 28, 29, 30:   True = 1 point, False = 0 points.

Items 2, 3, 4, 7, 10, 12, 13, 15, 16, 17, 18, 19, 20, 23, 25: True = 0 points, False = 1 point.

_____ Awareness = Total score for items 1, 4, 7, 10, 13, 16, 19, 22, 25, 28

_____ Knowledge = Total score for items 2, 5, 8, 11, 14, 17, 20, 23, 26, 29

_____ Skills = Total score for items 3, 6, 9, 12, 15, 18, 21, 24, 27, 30

_____ **Total**

Suggestions for Using the
"Staff Diversity Needs Analysis"

Objectives:

- Identify training and development needs of staff regarding diversity
- Pinpoint specific areas for development
- Give information to individuals regarding personal training and/or development needs

Intended Audience:

- Staff at nonmanagerial levels in a diverse organization
- Trainees in a diversity training seminar
- Individuals wanting to increase their own ability to deal with diversity

Processing the Activity:

- Individuals respond to the statements by marking them true or false.
- Questionnaires can be collected and scored for use as a training needs assessment.
- Questionnaires can be scored by the individuals and then discussed in groups. Discussion can focus on strengths and weaknesses and areas of needed growth.
- Individuals can prioritize needs and target specific areas for growth.
- Training and development professionals can analyze scores to determine appropriate training content and design.

Questions for Discussion:

- What strengths and weaknesses emerge?
- Where are the greatest needs for growth: awareness, knowledge, and/or skills?
- How do weaknesses in these areas affect productivity? Morale? Service?
- What does this tell us about training needed by staff in specific departments?
- What do we need to find out more about?

Caveats, Considerations, and Variations:

- This questionnaire can serve as a catalyst for discussion within a team dealing with diversity. The group can identify collective weaknesses and target areas for growth and development.

There is a possible total of 10 points for each of the three areas: The higher the score in each, the greater the mastery of that area; the lower the score, the greater the need for training and development in that area. Overall totals may be compared, by group, staff, age, ethnicity, gender, and position to see if there are significant differences. For example, it may become apparent that employees in the customer service department need help in dealing with limitedEnglish-speaking clients/customers or that recruitment staff need to become more aware of their own attitudes and prejudices. The data can help you in tailoring training sessions and in structuring problem-solving at staff meetings to help employees develop the awareness, knowledge, and skills they need.

Management Development Diversity Needs Analysis: Awareness, Knowledge, and Skills

Managers have many of the same awareness, knowledge, and skill needs as other employees when it comes to dealing with diversity. However, they have additional skill needs in the area of management responsibilities, such as giving feedback, reviewing performance, and building productive work teams. They need answers to such skill-related questions as the following: "How can I give directions to someone who won't tell me when he or she doesn't understand?" "How can I give a performance review that does not cause a decline in motivation because of hurt feelings?" "How do I keep my staff from segregating into separate ethnic, racial, or gender groupings?" The *Management Development Diversity Needs Analysis* in Activity 12.7 can give you an idea of the training and development needs of managers regarding their awareness, knowledge, and skills in managing diversity.

There is a possible total of 10 points for each of the three areas: The higher the score in each, the greater the mastery of that area; the lower the score, the greater the need for training and development in that area. Overall totals may also be compared by age, ethnicity, gender, education level, and position to see if there are significant differences. It may be that supervisory-level staff have different skill needs than middle management, or that younger managers have different attitudes toward diversity than older managers, for example.

In addition to using this questionnaire, the *Management Development Diversity Needs Assessment Checklist* in Activity 12.8 can be filled out by managers as part of your training-and-development needs assessment process. This gives managers a chance to give direct input about their training needs and to participate in their own development.

The data produced by this checklist can help the HR department target and focus management development activities. Using the checklist in this fashion not only gives you information about training needs, but also serves as a diversity awareness-builder for managers and can lead to insightful discussions as managers begin to grapple with these challenges.

ACTIVITY 12.7 | Management Development Diversity Needs Analysis

Please respond to the questions below by answering true or false.

_____ 1. I am comfortable managing individuals who are different from me in race and cultural background.

_____ 2. I am sometimes confused by the behavior of employees from different backgrounds.

_____ 3. I'm able to resolve problems easily with employees on my staff who are different from me.

_____ 4. I'm reluctant to disagree with employees of different groups for fear of being considered prejudiced.

_____ 5. I know about my own cultural background and how it influences my behavior and my expectations of employees.

_____ 6. I know how to give feedback so employees of different cultures don't "lose face."

_____ 7. My behavior toward employees is influenced by gender differences.

_____ 8. Prejudice exists in every individual.

_____ 9. I feel comfortable talking with my staff about differences in race, culture, and sexual orientation.

_____ 10. My behavior toward my staff is influenced by racial and cultural differences.

_____ 11. Stereotypes are held about every group.

_____ 12. I am able to give constructive performance reviews with employees of different groups.

_____ 13. My behavior toward my staff is influenced by differences in sexual orientation.

_____ 14. I understand the different cultural influences of the people I manage or supervise.

_____ 15. I get frustrated when my staff segregates into subgroups along cultural or racial lines.

_____ 16. I am most comfortable managing people who are similar to me in background.

_____ 17. I find the behaviors of members of some groups on my staff irritating.

_____ 18. I'm fearful of offending employees of diverse groups by saying the wrong thing.

_____ 19. People of certain groups are treated differently because they act differently.

_____ 20. I find myself thinking, "Why don't they act like us?"

_____ 21. It is difficult for me to manage people who speak with thick accents.

_____ 22. I recognize my own biases and prejudices.

_____ 23. Certain behaviors of some groups on my staff bother me.

_____ 24. I am able to resolve conflicts among employees of different cultural backgrounds, genders, races, and sexual orientation.

_____ 25. I wish my staff were all more similar.

_____ 26. I understand some of the reasons why there is culture clash and conflicts between individual employees and groups of employees.

_____ 27. I'm not sure what labels to use in referring to different groups.

_____ 28. I find differences among us interesting and stimulating.

_____ 29. I understand the reasons for my own reactions to others' differentness.

_____ 30. I am able to build a cohesive work team from my diverse staff.

Scoring—Give each answer a point value as follows:
Items 1, 5, 6, 8, 9, 11, 14, 21, 22, 24, 26, 27, 28, 29, 30:   True = 1 point, False = 0 points.
Items 2, 3, 4, 7, 10, 12, 13, 15, 16, 17, 18, 19, 20, 23, 25: True = 0 points, False = 1 point.

_____ Awareness = Total score for items 1, 4, 7, 10, 13, 16, 19, 22, 25, 28

_____ Knowledge = Total score for items 2, 5, 8, 11, 14, 17, 20, 23, 26, 29

_____ Skills = Total score for items 3, 6, 9, 12, 15, 18, 21, 24, 27, 30

_____ **Total**

Suggestions for Using the
"Management Development Diversity Needs Analysis"

Objectives:
- Identify management development needs regarding diversity
- Pinpoint specific areas for training
- Give information to individual managers regarding personal development needs

Intended Audience:
- Managers dealing with a diverse workforce
- Trainees in a management development series or a managing diversity seminar
- Management teams wanting to increase their effectiveness in dealing with diversity

Processing the Activity:
- Individuals respond to the statements by marking them true or false.
- Questionnaires can be collected and scored for use as a management development needs assessment by the training department.
- Questionnaires can be scored by individuals and then discussed in groups. Discussion can focus on strengths, weaknesses, and areas of needed growth.
- Groups and individuals within them can prioritize needs and target specific areas for growth. They can even brainstorm ways to accomplish that growth.
- Training-and-development professionals can analyze scores to determine appropriate training content and design.

Questions for Discussion:
- What strengths and weaknesses emerge?
- How do the weaknesses impact management effectiveness? Productivity? Morale?
- Where are the greatest needs for growth in general areas (awareness, knowledge, skills) and/ or specific issues (e.g., communication with limited-English-speaking staff)?
- Where do we need to focus our own development?

Caveats, Considerations, and Variations:
- Dealing with the issues in this questionnaire may provoke heated discussion if there has been no previous groundwork laid regarding managing diversity. This is best used after a general session discussing changes in workforce demographics and a broad definition of diversity, where venting can be done and where executive management explains organizational goals and strategy regarding diversity.

ACTIVITY 12.8 | Management Development Diversity Needs Assessment Checklist

Check any of the following you would like to learn more about.

☐ Understanding differences regarding race, culture, gender, sexual orientation.

☐ Dealing with prejudice and stereotyping.

☐ Understanding norms, practices, and values of different cultures.

☐ Understanding communication differences among groups.

☐ Learning to reward appropriately amid diversity.

☐ Using nondiscriminatory language and labels.

☐ Communicating with limited-English-speaking individuals.

☐ Motivating effectively in a diverse environment.

☐ Resolving cross-cultural conflicts.

☐ Dealing with prejudice on my staff.

☐ Building multicultural work teams.

☐ Giving feedback in culturally sensitive ways.

☐ Enhancing trust in a diverse staff.

☐ Communicating more effectively with diverse employees.

☐ Coaching, grooming, and mentoring diverse employees.

☐ Conducting productive performance reviews with diverse staff.

☐ Recognizing the special needs of different groups.

☐ Creating an environment where all employees feel included.

☐ Understanding and dealing with generational differences.

☐ Other: _____

. . . .

Suggestions for Using the
"Management Development Diversity Needs Assessment Checklist"

Objectives:

- Identify management development needs regarding diversity
- Give information to training-and-development professionals regarding perceived needs
- Increase awareness about skills and knowledge essential in managing a diverse staff

Intended Audience:

- Managers and supervisors leading diverse staffs
- Potential trainees in a managing diversity seminar
- Executive staff wanting to increase the effectiveness of managers and supervisors in dealing with diverse staffs

Processing the Activity:

- Managers check those aspects of managing diversity in which they need development.
- Groups can discuss items checked and assign priorities to them.
- Training-and-development staff can then use this information in planning training for managers.
- Executive staff can discuss data and assign priorities for management training.

Questions for Discussion:

- Which items were checked?
- What themes or issues do these items relate to?
- What is the effect of these deficiencies on the job?
- What are the consequences if these go unaddressed?
- Which are most/least widespread? Critical?

Caveats, Considerations, and Variations:

- This tool gives only preliminary data; more information is needed before action is taken.
- If managers responding to this checklist are new to dealing with diversity, they may not recognize needs they have.
- This checklist can also be used as a self-assessment by managers by changing the directions and having them rate themselves, either with a plus/minus or on a scale of 1 (not very good) to 5 (very good) on each of the items.

. . . .

Incorporating Diversity Assessment into Existing Survey Instruments

In addition to the substantial financial cost of conducting organizational assessments, they can also be taxing in the time and energy they require. It's common for organizations to tell us that they do not want another questionnaire to collect data because their people are "surveyed out." Often, the resistance to surveys has its roots in a history of poorly used and communicated results from past assessments. "Why should we do another one? They never do anything with the information anyway," is a common employee response regarding surveys. Whatever the cause or reason, conducting a full-scale diversity survey may not be the best approach for an organization. Yet, because information is still needed, diversity-related data can be obtained from existing survey instruments, both by reviewing data that has already been obtained and by augmenting collection and analysis methods in future surveys.

Many organizations conduct some type of employee survey aimed at measuring a variety of employee perceptions—from satisfaction and attitudes to needs and concerns. The input from these feedback instruments often contains pertinent diversity information. Demographic cuts of the data comparing employees within different diversity dimensions can point out obstacles. Results are usually tabulated by department so managers can share and discuss findings with workgroups and divisions. This same analysis can be made by comparing employees along other dimensions such as age, seniority, level, gender, education, or marital status. Startling diversity information may emerge from such analyses. For example, in one manufacturing firm, survey results showed that white-male hourly employees were the least satisfied employees. These data prompted leaders to conduct focus groups to identify the specific concerns and issues underlying the dissatisfaction. Without understanding and addressing the concerns of this large group of employees, it is doubtful that any other diversity work could make headway.

Seeing differences in ratings between staff with children and those without, between those with college degrees and those with less formal education, or male and female managers can signal possible roadblocks to diversity. It is essential to figure out the reasons behind the differential ratings. Specific problems or barriers can only be addressed after they are pinpointed.

Another way of obtaining diversity data through an existing survey process is to augment the instrument by adding items and soliciting additional demographic information. If managing diversity has been positioned as a strategic business competence, and if your present survey is categorized by topics, a diversity segment could be added. On the other hand, diversity items can be integrated into the questionnaire in a more subtle way by interspersing them throughout. When adding items, the same guidelines used for a dedicated diversity questionnaire apply. Be clear about what you want to find out. Are you assessing attitudes, competencies, training needs, and/or organizational obstacles? Different questions are needed for each type of information sought. Then, make sure questions give you specific and useful data. "My boss treats me fairly" solicits less specific information than "My boss accurately and clearly evaluates my performance" or "My boss solicits my opinions and ideas." "Promotional opportunities are equitable" gives less clear data than "I know how to find out about career opportunities within the organization," "Developmental opportunities are available to me to advance my career," or "I can get the coaching and help I need to groom me for promotion."

The data you obtain from surveys will undoubtedly point up issues and obstacles that need further exploration. Why aren't existing mentoring programs being used by a wide range of employees? What keeps people from taking advantage of tuition reimbursement benefits? Why aren't top performers applying for management positions? What is your organization's image among potential recruits in various communities? Why is there a higher rate of turnover among a particular segment of the workforce? What might entice people to stay? This kind of specific information generally requires a deeper investigation, which can be achieved with focus groups.

How To Use Focus Groups To Get Information About Diversity

Focus groups can be a rich source of information about diversity. In a small group setting, where there is comfort and safety, employees are often willing to be more candid and open about diversity problems and concerns. In addition, issues can be explored in greater depth through discussion than through a questionnaire. In order to get the most from your focus group needs assessment, a number of factors need to be considered. Attention needs to be paid to selection of participants, group composition and size, time and location of sessions, facilitation of discussions, and topics and questions to use in stimulating and guiding discussions.

Selection of Participants

Since focus group participants represent a larger constituency, they need to cover as wide a spectrum of views as possible. In a large organization where a number of focus group sessions will be held, selecting participants by random sampling techniques (every 20th employee from an alphabetical list, for example) might be appropriate. In smaller organizations, or where only a few groups will be conducted, selecting members from different opinion "camps" and diverse groups would help ensure a wider spread of views and inclusion of employees from all groups. Accepting only volunteers skews your sample. While those who would volunteer probably have a greater interest in the issues surrounding diversity, they may also have some of their own axes to grind or their group's vested interests to promote. They may not be representative of the larger group of employees. While you may include some volunteers, you may need to recruit more reticent employees to get divergent views.

Group Composition and Size

Different groupings will serve different purposes in your needs assessment. If you want the specific views of particular groups—Latino, African American, Korean, or Filipino employees; middle managers; immigrant employees; assembly-line staff; or differently-abled workers, for example—then forming like groups would be indicated. In these groupings, individuals are more apt to be open and candid about their true views and feelings about prejudice, discrimination, and other touchy topics because they generally feel safer and more accepted while not having to worry about offending someone from another group. On the other hand, like groupings may reinforce stereotypes and not give participants a chance to hear the perspectives of other groups. Having mixed groups allows participants to hear how different co-workers experience diversity at work. For example, it might be eye opening for Euro-American heterosexual males to hear the frustrations of Latino, African American, gay or lesbian or female employees, and vice versa. In one organization where diversity was being discussed in a culturally-mixed group of peers, the Euro-American males were shocked to hear one of their colleagues, an Asian American, talk about his experiences with prejudice and discrimination in what they thought was an open, accepting, and equal environment for all. It can also be insightful for different groups to realize they are not alone in some of their concerns and frustrations. Finally, it may be surprising for groups to learn that they are both the victims and the perpetrators of prejudice. It is important to choose the type of grouping that best suits your purposes.

Group size is another factor that will affect results of focus group data collection. The smaller the group, the greater the comfort and participation. However, if the group is too small, there may not be enough energy and divergence to spark a lively discussion. Generally, groups of 8 to 12 make for optimum discussion.

Time and Location

Since the purpose of focus groups is to elicit feelings, attitudes, and perceptions about a topic that is apt to generate strong emotional responses, enough time needs to be allotted for the discussion. It is frustrating for both participants and data collectors to have to cut off a lively and informative discussion midstream. Therefore, schedule at least 1 1/2 hours per focus group session with a 30-minute cushion between sessions in case the discussion goes over the scheduled time frame. If it seems that there is more discussion needed, you always have the option of scheduling a follow-up session with the group. The 30-minute cushion also gives the data collector time to jot down observations and reactions.

Another important logistical element is location. Focus group discussions will tend to be more open and honest if held away from the work environment, far from the possibility of eavesdroppers, curious passersby, and work distractions such as BlackBerry devices, phone messages, or other interruptions. It is also helpful to have a meeting or conference room that allows for chairs to be arranged around a conference table or in a circle so that participants can face one another.

Capturing Data

Information from discussions can be captured for later use in a number of different ways. With the permission of participants, the discussion can be taped and comments transcribed later. Comments can be charted or notes taken; however, this usually necessitates two facilitators—one to lead the discussion and the other to take notes or chart information. Another method sometimes used is for the facilitator to make notes immediately after the discussion. However, this may result in some data being lost.

Facilitation

Sessions need to be led by experienced and skilled facilitators, either in-house staff in the HR department or external consultants. The role of the facilitator is to create a safe and comfortable environment, keep discussion focused on the topics being investigated, encourage active participation of all individuals present, and set and enforce the ground rules of the discussion. In addition, the skilled facilitator is adept at questioning to probe for additional information and feelings about points made. The advantages and disadvantages of both internal and external facilitators have been discussed earlier in this chapter. Whichever is chosen, sessions need to have a structured agenda so that participants feel a sense of security and so that the objectives of the discussion are achieved. Notice the facilitator's role in the *Sample Focus Group Agenda* in Table 12.2.

Topics and Questions for Discussion

In formulating focus group questions, remember that open-ended questions stimulate the most discussion, while topics related to issues of real concern for participants will elicit the most participation. Questions that will give you data about the issues you are investigating should then be formulated. Because they will produce much response, it is probably a good rule of thumb to limit the number of questions to six to 10. Depending on your objectives, the *Sample Focus Group Questions* can give you examples of questions to stimulate discussion (see Table 12.3).

TABLE 12.2 | Sample Focus Group Agenda

1. Introduction of facilitator and explanation of the general purpose of the focus group sessions, as well as who will see the data.

2. Self introduction of participants by name.

3. Objectives of the group discussion:
   - Gain employees' perceptions about how the organization is dealing with a diversity.
   - Learn about diversity-related barriers to teamwork, productivity, and motivation (or service, care, etc.).
   - Hear employees' concerns, ideas, and suggestions about dealing with diversity more effectively.

4. Ground rules of the session:
   - Confidentiality of sources, with input reported anonymously.
   - Each person speaks for self.
   - Every perception is valid; no arguing with perceptions.
   - One person speaks at a time.
   - Get permission to tape (if tape recording responses).
   - Only the facilitator or assessment team sees the notes or hears the tapes.

5. Present questions for discussion, giving participants time to jot down ideas and points. (Questions may be on slide, flip chart, and/or handout.)

6. Facilitate discussion:
   - Keep participants focused on the questions asked.
   - Chart comments and responses as stated or take notes.
   - Clarify points and ask for specific examples when vague comments or generalizations are made.
   - Maintain objectivity and do not enter into the discussion.
   - Reinforce ground rules and intervene if there is inappropriate behavior.

7. Wrap up the discussion, summarizing themes or making a concluding statement that refers back to objectives.

8. Thank participants and tell them what will happen with data.

TABLE 12.3 | Sample Focus Group Questions

These questions are examples of the kind of discussion "pump primers" you can use to get people talking and to focus their comments on the areas you are investigating.

- What are signs that this organization values a diverse workforce?

- What obstacles prevent you from doing your best?

- What organizational practices, policies, or norms keep people from succeeding and/or moving up?

- What keeps you here in this organization? What would tempt you to leave?

- What kinds of prejudicial or discriminatory have you faced or seen, if any?

- What do you wish members of other groups knew about you or your group?

- What do you wish your manager understood about you and your needs?

- What do you wish management understood about your group?

- What contributions and behaviors are most valued and rewarded in this organization?

- What do you need to do and/or know to get ahead in this organization?

- What would you like to know and/or learn that could help you succeed here?

- How comfortable, accepted, and valued do you feel in this organization? Why?

- What groups are easiest/hardest for you to work cooperatively with?

- What behaviors of other groups are most difficult for you to deal with or most irritating?

- What do you think the organization could do to get the best from everyone?

Diversity Quotient: Analyzing Organizational Demographics

One source of fruitful information in the overall assessment plan is in the area of organizational demographics. Statistics about your workforce can give you an unvarnished look at diversity within the company. Some of this information may be on file in your HR department; however, some may not have been collected. Before embarking on the data collection, be aware that you may get some resistance to this kind of assessment. In one organization, for example, many managers refused to respond to the surveys about the ethnic and racial composition of their staffs because they felt it was both irrelevant and an invasion of individuals' privacy. Ethnic labeling brought images of totalitarianism and government identity cards. It is important to tell staff why you are collecting this information and how it will be used so you can allay fears and reduce resistance. "We need to find out about the composition of our staff so we can meet the needs of everyone. That's why we are gathering information about all employees. The data will remain anonymous and will not be connected with anyone's name."

As a first step, you will need to determine which demographic statistics you require and where you can obtain this information; see the *Analyzing Organizational Demographics* Activity 12.9.

ACTIVITY 12.9 | Analyzing Organizational Demographics

	Executives Number/Percent	Managers Number/Percent	Supervisors Number/ Percent	Staff Number/Percent
Staff Composition				
Gender:				
Male	____ / ____	____ / ____	____ / ____	____ / ____
Female	____ / ____	____ / ____	____ / ____	____ / ____
Total	____ / ____	____ / ____	____ / ____	____ / ____
Ethnicity				
Euro-American	____ / ____	____ / ____	____ / ____	____ / ____
African American	____ / ____	____ / ____	____ / ____	____ / ____
Latino	____ / ____	____ / ____	____ / ____	____ / ____
Middle Eastern	____ / ____	____ / ____	____ / ____	____ / ____
Asian	____ / ____	____ / ____	____ / ____	____ / ____
Pacific Islander	____ / ____	____ / ____	____ / ____	____ / ____
Native American	____ / ____	____ / ____	____ / ____	____ / ____
Other	____ / ____	____ / ____	____ / ____	____ / ____
Total	____ / ____	____ / ____	____ / ____	____ / ____

Languages Spoken	Number	Percent
Native English speakers	_____	_____
Fluent, accented-English speakers (strong accent)	_____	_____
Limited-English speakers (strong accent)	_____	_____
Non-English speakers	_____	_____
Bilingual		
Spanish/English	_____	_____
Tagalog/English	_____	_____
Japanese/English	_____	_____
Vietnamese/English	_____	_____
Chinese (Mandarin)/English	_____	_____
Chinese (Cantonese)/English	_____	_____
Arabic/English	_____	_____
Korean/English	_____	_____
Armenian/English	_____	_____
Hebrew/English	_____	_____
Russian/English	_____	_____
English	_____	_____

Personal Data	Men Number/Percent	Women Number/Percent
Married	____ / ____	____ / ____
Single	____ / ____	____ / ____
Dual parent	____ / ____	____ / ____
Single parent	____ / ____	____ / ____

Suggestions for Using
"Analyzing Organizational Demographics"

Objectives:

- Examine organization demographics related to diversity
- Provide data for analysis and decision-making regarding diversity

Intended Audience:

- HR professionals collecting data for diversity planning
- Diversity development task forces gathering baseline data

Processing the Activity:

- Data collectors gather statistics about each category, compiling information and computing percentages. Data can be gathered through self-report questionnaires, personnel records, and/or management observation.
- Data can be analyzed, summarized, and reported to appropriate planning group.

Questions for Discussion:

- What does your survey of demographic data tell you about diversity within your organization?
    - » What do our demographics say about the diversity of our staff at each level?
    - » How closely do our percentages mirror the local population and workforce? Our client/customer base?
    - » Are there groups that are underrepresented? At what levels?
    - » What surprises are there in the figures?
    - » What challenges does this information present?
- Are there changes called for in light of demographic trends in the larger society? In our client/customer base? How do organizational statistics compare with those of the workforce in the area? Population in the area?
- What surprises or questions are there?
- What do these statistics indicate for the organization in terms of needs, potential opportunities, and possible problems?

Caveats, Considerations, and Variations:

- Some individuals may regard information requested as too personal and may balk at the categorization.
- Some individuals will see the categorization as divisive rather than as a first step in remedying deficiencies that may exist.
- Careful explanation of the purposes of this survey and its use in identifying organization needs is required.

Analyzing Turnover Statistics for Clues to Diversity Management

Another method of getting information about an organization's diversity management is to analyze existing statistical data regarding turnover. In analyzing this data, you may be able to zero in on specific causes—whether diversity-related or not—which can only be addressed once they are uncovered. In one organization, for example, an African-American female professional was recruited away by another organization. Even though this "raiding" of employees is a common practice, management spent time investigating her reasons for leaving. Though the new position was exciting and challenging, it involved a move to another city. Management wanted to know what factors influenced her to accept the offered position. They found that she had continuously felt she was bumping up against a brick wall in the organization and was frustrated by the constant inability to get people to hear what she was saying. When asked why she had never complained, she said it was obvious to her that this "deaf ear" to the concerns of women and minority group members was sanctioned organizational practice. While it was too late to keep this employee, management got some critical feedback that led them to question their communication and promotion practices and begin working on making conditions more inclusive. These kinds of subtle underlying issues and problems can be the undoing of even the best diversity efforts. This kind of information often emerges only through in-depth exit interviewing.

Organizational feedback can also be obtained from turnover statistics by searching for answers to such questions as:

- What are the rates of turnover in each department, section, division, or unit? How do these compare to other units? To industry or profession standards?
- What is the gender, ethnic, and racial breakdown of the turnover percentages?
- Are they at parity with overall turnover percentages within the organization?
- Are there departments, groups, or areas that stand out because of their higher or lower percentages?
- What factors within these groups might lead to these higher or lower turnover rates?
- What information is uncovered in exit interviews? What reasons do employees give for leaving? (Is there in-depth exit interviewing to get beyond superficial responses?)
- To what do managers attribute the high or low turnover rates of diverse employees?

Information obtained from this analysis may be able to give you clues about how to retain diverse employees and why they leave. This information can be helpful feedback for individual managers and valuable input in designing management development programs.

Observation Checklist for Assessing Morale and Workgroup Cohesiveness

As a manager, you may not be in a position to institute organization-wide programs in diversity training or the development of diversity at all levels of the company. However, you can and do manage the workgroup environment of your staff. In that role you may need a tool to help you assess the morale and cohesiveness of your staff. Many of the tools you have already learned about can be used or adapted for use with your staff. You may also be able to assess these factors without questionnaires or focus groups by using your own observation skills. The *Morale-and-Workgroup-Cohesiveness-Observation Checklist* in Activity 12.10 can help you in that process. It can also be used as a workgroup checklist by simply asking staff members to react based on their own observations.

ACTIVITY 12.10 | Morale-and-Workgroup-Cohesiveness-Observation Checklist

Check those statements that describe your staff most of the time.

_____ Employees of different groups help one another without being asked.

_____ Staff members eat lunch and spend breaks in mixed groups.

_____ Employees talk freely and openly with one another.

_____ There are no cliques or in-group/out-group divisions among staff.

_____ Employees take initiative in solving problems and making suggestions about improvements.

_____ Employees do not blame one another for problems.

_____ Employees freely voice their views to their manager.

_____ Employees are proud to work in this department/unit/division.

_____ There is low absenteeism.

_____ There is low turnover.

_____ There is laughter and good-natured humor in the workgroup.

_____ No employees are left out of workgroup camaraderie.

_____ Employees of different backgrounds work together cooperatively.

_____ There is little friction between staff from different cultures or groups.

_____ There is seldom petty gossiping or backstabbing.

_____ Employees are willing to help each other out during stressful or demanding times.

_____ The workload is shared equitably by all.

_____ Employees celebrate together.

_____ Employees make an effort to help newcomers become part of the team.

_____ Employees go out of their way to understand employees whose English is limited or accented.

Suggestions for Using the
"Morale-and-Workgroup-Cohesiveness-Observation Checklist"

Objectives:

- Assess workgroup morale and cohesiveness
- Pinpoint obstacles to teamwork
- Identify employees' irritations, concerns, and problems that may be blocking productivity

Intended Audience:

- Managers and supervisors seeking to increase the cohesiveness and morale of their teams
- Trainees in a management/supervisory development class or managing diversity seminar
- Members of a diverse workgroup seeking to strengthen the team

Processing the Activity:

- Individuals check those conditions and factors they observe in their work team.
- Groups discuss those items checked and not checked, focusing on strengths and weaknesses of the team.
- Items not checked are discussed with regard to their impact on the team.
- Weaknesses are listed and prioritized, and areas for development are targeted.
- Individual managers can target specific areas to begin working on to strengthen their own team.

Questions for Discussion:

- What strengths and weaknesses are indicated?
- What is at the root of the weaknesses?
- Which issues have highest priority for attention?
- How can these areas be strengthened?
- What can you/we do to begin working on the problems surfaced?

Caveats, Considerations, and Variations:

- Managers making observations of their own staffs will tend to lack objectivity. It is helpful to suggest having a few other people (in the group or the whole team) respond to get a more rounded view.
- Weaknesses indicated need to be investigated further to find out underlying reasons, conditions, and organization systems that may be at the heart of the problem.

The more items checked, the greater the workgroup morale and cohesion. Those descriptions not checked may indicate problems in motivation or relationships. Checking into these areas may turn up the underlying differences in cultural programming that are causing individuals to misinterpret each other's behavior, act on inaccurate assumptions, or make prejudicial judgments. These kinds of problems can signal a need for cultural-sensitivity training and diversity-related team building. They may also be a sign that the manager needs to restructure roles and responsibilities so that people of different groups learn about each other by working together. Assigning tasks or projects across race, gender, cultural, physical ability, and sexual orientation, for example, is one way to structure this workgroup desegregation.

Using Interviews as a Method of Collecting Data

A third method of gathering assessment data is through one-on-one interviews. While time-consuming and expensive, interviews can be a rich source of in-depth information about attitudes, conditions, and problems. Interviews need to be conducted by individuals skilled in this process and by those who have objectivity regarding the issues and personalities involved. The following tips can guide you in getting the most from this method. In addition, the material on interviewing found in Chapter 13 can be helpful.

Know what you are after. Determining what information you are seeking helps you select the most appropriate individuals to talk with and the most relevant questions to ask. If you want to find out about problems between supervisors and their staffs, interviewing executive managers won't help, while asking supervisors about organizational diversity strategy will also miss the mark.

Establish rapport and build trust. Begin the interview with a few minutes of person-to-person contact, explaining the purpose of the interview, why the interviewee has been selected, how the data will help their organization, and how the information will be used. Assure the individual of confidentiality and anonymity in the reporting of data.

Use carefully constructed questions. Ask questions that get to the information you are after; however, be careful not to be so direct that you are perceived as intrusive. In addition, you may miss important data if your questions do not come at the issue from different directions.

Use your questions as a guide, but be flexible. Your objective is to get information, not to finish all your questions. Be careful not to have the interview become nothing more than an oral questionnaire. Listen to the interviewee's response and use that to prompt your next question. Ask for clarification, examples, and specifics as well: "Can you tell me more about that problem?" "Give me a specific example of that issue." "In what ways is that attitude a problem?"

Don't be afraid of silence. Jumping in with the next question to fill the void may cause you to miss important information. Interviewees generally give the safest and most superficial information first and get more candid as they talk. Wait and listen.

Listen for the unstated message. Pay attention to nonverbal cues. One of the advantages of this method is that it gives you the opportunity to pick up the more than 50 percent of the communication that is not in the words. Pay attention to tone and speed of speech.

Also watch body language and facial expressions. You can pick up much about the feelings and attitudes—such as uneasiness, tension, irritation, or disbelief—from rolled eyes, crossed arms, and furrowed brows, for example.

Capture the data. Use the most comfortable and effective method for keeping the data from the interview. Either taping, with the permission of the interviewee, or taking notes during the interview is generally used. Waiting until after the interview risks losing much information.

While you will need to construct questions that suit your purposes, the three sets of sample interview questions (for leaders and policymakers, underrepresented employees, and nonminority employees) in Tables 12.4, 12.5, and 12.6 can trigger your thinking.

TABLE 12.4 | Sample Interview Questions for Leaders and Policymakers

1. What have been the biggest benefits of having a diverse workforce? What are the biggest problems and frustrations?

2. How are diversity and inclusion strategic business issues for the organization?

3. With an increasingly diverse workforce, what changes do you see?

4. What challenges does this present to your organization?

5. What is your organization doing to help your managers meet these challenges?

6. What do they need to learn to do differently?

7. How do you measure and reward your managers in this area?

8. What is your organization doing to enhance the upward mobility of underrepresented group members? What obstacles prevent this mobility?

9. What processes do you have to identify and develop a diverse pool of talented employees?

10. What does your organization do that shows you value cultural diversity?

11. What is your organization doing to accommodate differences in values, norms, and practices?

12. Why have you decided to invest your organization's resources (time, energy, money) in making diversity and inclusion a priority? What results do you expect to see?

13. What organizational systems, practices, and policies present obstacles to fully developing and using your diverse workforce?

14. If your organization does nothing to address diversity and inclusion, what do you predict will happen?

TABLE 12.5 | Sample Interview Questions for Underrepresented Employees

1. What do you like about the culture of this organization?

2. What do you find difficult about it?

3. What did you expect to find when you came to work here? What was your biggest surprise? Biggest joy? Biggest disappointment?

4. What kinds of experiences made you feel welcome in this organization? Unwelcome? What did you do to help the situation?

5. What is your professional goal? What do you hope to achieve here?

6. How has this organization helped you toward your goal? How could it help more?

7. Have you ever felt it was a mistake to come to work here? If so, what made you feel this way?

8. How have you been treated by bosses and co-workers (both good and bad news)?

9. How do you get along with people of other groups in the workplace?

10. On a scale of 1 to 10, how much do you feel a part of the organization? What needs to happen to make you feel more a part of it?

11. What is the most important thing the organization can do to help you do your best here? What can you do?

TABLE 12.6 | Sample Interview Questions for Nonminority Employees

1. What have been the biggest changes in this organization the past few years?

2. What have been the biggest benefits of being part of a diverse workforce? What are the biggest problems and frustrations?

3. How does diversity in the workforce impact you? Your workgroup? This organization?

4. What has been the biggest "culture shock" for you in working with diverse groups?

5. What kinds of experiences make you feel comfortable with employees from different groups? Uncomfortable? What did you do to help the situation?

6. How have you been treated by employees of diverse groups?

7. What is the most important thing your organization can do to help diverse group members adapt to this organization?

8. What is the most important thing these employees can do to help themselves adapt?

Bringing Your Organizational Snapshot into Focus

While this chapter has given you a variety of assessment techniques, all the tools in the world won't help if you don't ask the right questions in planning your audit and in analyzing the data once they are collected. The following can be helpful guides in designing your audit:

1. What do we want to find out?
2. What are the most useful tools we can use?
3. Where can we find the information we need? (Which organizational statistics? Which individuals? Which groups?)
4. Who should coordinate and conduct this audit for optimum results?
5. What kind of a budget do we have to work with?
6. What do the collected data tell us?
7. What next steps are indicated? Where do we go from here?
8. What kind of commitment are we willing to make? What are we willing to do about what we have found out?

An organizational audit will give you the clearest, most revealing picture of your organization if you choose the most appropriate tools, focus on the richest sources of information, and seek the most relevant data to answer your questions. The process involves careful planning, thorough implementation, and thoughtful analysis of the collected data, and finally, the application of findings to strengthen the organization.

CHAPTER 13.

Recruiting and Hiring a Diverse Workforce

• •

This chapter will provide you with:

- Tools to use for creating a less culturally biased interview process

- Strategies to enhance your recruitment and hiring of diverse individuals

- Suggestions for ways to expand your cross-cultural network

- Skills in asking interview questions in culturally sensitive ways

- Information about how values, assumptions, and biases impact hiring and recruitment

There is a saying by Ralph Waldo Emerson pertinent to assessing an organization's commitment to recruiting and hiring a diverse workforce: "I can't hear what you're saying because who you are rings so loudly in my ears." In today's fast-paced world, we say, "Actions speak louder than words" or, shorter still, "Walk the talk." What do any of these admonitions about practicing what we preach have to do with hiring or recruiting a pluralistic workforce? Simply this: It is easier to talk about valuing a diverse employee base than it is to intentionally find, hire, and recruit one. In Chapter 10 we address not only what it takes to create a welcoming and inclusive environment that makes people sign on, but also what it takes to retain them once they do.

Make no mistake, words are important in sending a message about the value of achieving diversity and inclusion in your environment, but beyond the rhetoric, a key question remains: What is your organization doing to secure and develop a diverse workforce? We aren't talking about quotas where you find a person of a particular color, ethnic background, age, or sexual orientation to fill a slot; we are talking an organization's willingness to truly open up the applicant pool and provide hiring and promotional opportunities to talented, experienced people regardless of gender, skin color, age, physical abilities, sexual orientation, religious beliefs and practices, and so on.

We can already hear the chorus of people saying, "We want to hire a diverse staff but we just can't find the people." Well, this chapter is about helping you uncover creative ways to find the talent which is clearly out there. That's the easy part. The hard part lies in creating an organization where the environment is inclusive and accepting enough that a person who is different from the dominant group feels comfortable, wants to join you, and, more important, wants to stay. This is why Chapter 10 and this chapter are companion chapters; they help you see the intersection between an inclusive environment, reaching out to get great talent, and the ability to hold on to them. As we said earlier, talk is cheap, but actions speak volumes. Your company's commitment to this issue is demonstrated in tangible clues. To find out if your company has this commitment, do a little investigative work. Put on your sleuth hat and respond to the following questions:

1. What is the ethnic, racial, and gender composition of your workplace?
2. What is the age span of the workers?
3. What percentage of top management are people of color, women, or those who are challenged physically in some way? How do the percentages change when applied to middle management? First-line staff?
4. Is the ethnic and cultural distribution the same from top to bottom in the organization, or are all white males in the executive suite and all Hispanics in environmental engineering?

Responses to these questions give you a partial answer to the level of your organization's commitment or level of readiness regarding implementation on this issue. But while some companies have demonstrated their commitment for years through their recruitment and hiring practices, others aren't yet sold on the idea of diversity being factored into the hiring equation. For them, the case still needs to be made.

Should Diversity Be a Part of the Hiring and Promotion Equation?

The short answer to the above question is "yes," but only if you want your organization to survive and thrive. We say that, not because it is a moral or ethical imperative (although we believe it is), but because the demographics and interconnectedness of the world demand it. As we write this book, the world is in a global recession—jobs are being shed, visas being cancelled, and protectionist impulses are on the rise. But even though all of that is happening and we understand why it is, the complexity of globalization and a world truly knitted together cannot be undone. Reflecting the reality of the world seems to make more long-term sense than trying to shut it out. Even if we could shut the door, let's look at some of the business imperatives that indicate attention to this issue is both warranted and critical as we strive to remain open.

Planning Requires Short- and Long-Range Goals

Remaining competitive in a global economy necessitates forecasting on any number of issues; among them are capital outlay, research and development, and the skill level and availability of the labor pool. It is this last issue that ties directly to the question of diversity as part of the equation. Whether we're talking about short- or long-range goals, considerations regarding the labor pool lead to the same conclusion. This is not an issue that can be ducked in most companies. If you doubt the validity of that statement, consider this: A worldwide affirmative action manager for Hewlett-Packard made the observation that, 40 years ago, most engineering graduates were white males. Those numbers are dramatically different today. If Hewlett-Packard and other companies as well want to remain industry leaders, there is no viable alternative to attracting, hiring, and developing the current diverse workforce into effective managers—and a good part of that search probably will direct some focus toward India and China.[1]

The Composition of the Workforce Changes Before Our Eyes

The case cannot be made strongly enough for taking the issue of workforce composition changes seriously. Check out the following facts:

1. While the number of white males in the workforce is declining, in the next decade, 64 percent of the growth in the labor force will be from women.

2. Gender is only one aspect of diversity. Age is another, and the reality of the aging workforce, like age itself, is creeping up on us. In fact, generational differences are becoming the most prominent diversity issue. In addition to intergenerational conflict, there is also the enormity of baby boomers who were poised and ready to take their expertise and ride off into the sunset. The financial crisis might stem some of the workforce and experience loss temporarily but then you have newcomers and old-timers competing for fewer jobs. According to the Social Security Administration, the number of people age 65 or older is expected to more than double, from 30 million to 68 million, by the year 2040.[2] The age issue, however, is more complex than even the aging of the workforce and implications for Social Security. It is also about people working longer if they can due to the recession, and about the need for intergenerational communication and understanding as we witness a span of four or five generations in some workplaces.

The Diverse Employee Base Is Paralleled by a Diverse Consumer Base

The percentage growth of Hispanics and Asians is dramatic. Hispanics made up only 7 percent of the labor force in 1986 but currently constitute 15.1 percent, according to the U.S. Census Bureau, and there are indications that in cities like Los Angeles, the growth in the Latino population has been underreported. Nationally, it has grown from 8 million to almost 19 million, and this group runs more than 400,000 businesses in the United States. It remains to be seen what the fallout will be on immigrant population due to the recession. There will be fewer immigrants, both documented and undocumented, because there are fewer jobs, but complex demographics are still in place and the recession won't last forever. What constitutes making an issue a bottom-line consideration? Those kind of numbers and dollars, for starters. Smart companies will be ahead of the wave in reaching out to address the needs of the diverse communities that are part of their consumer base. How best to do that? By understanding the group you are trying to serve. This understanding comes most easily when you hire employees who are part of that community.

The "Grapevine" Never Rests—Your Reputation Will Precede You

Attracting the best talent occurs when the word gets out that yours is a comfortable, welcoming company in which to work, a company where talent and individual differences are respected and rewarded. Apple and Google, for example, do not have to cheerlead or shout about what inviting companies they are, or about how much opportunity they provide for people of any background who are willing and able to do the job. Their hiring and promotion decisions speak for them, as well as the climate they have created.

Neutralizing the Application Process

An organization that is truly committed to recruiting and hiring a diverse workforce will pay attention to just how "applicant friendly" the company is, both in perception and reality. It is of little comfort to open the doors to applicants if they struggle with the application process. "Applicant friendliness" involves cultivating and welcoming talent among groups of individuals from different backgrounds whose norms, values, and customs may not be identical to those of your existing workforce. Do employees in your company have to be stamped out of a cookie cutter to get ahead? Try to imagine yourself a different age, ethnicity, gender, or race. Would you feel comfortable working in your organization? Imagine walking the proverbial mile in another person's moccasins. Doing so will shed light on your organization's openness to pluralism. The answers your imagination gives you can offer insight that could lead to equalizing the process for everyone, so answer the questions in Activity 13.1. If others also use this checklist, it can be a catalyst for identifying obstacles in your organization.

ACTIVITY 13.1 | Neutralizing-the-Application-Process Checklist

Answer each of the questions below by putting a check in the column that most accurately reflects your organization.

Questions	Rarely	Sometimes	Often
1. All applicants are given the same information and get their questions answered.			
2. When language problems exist, our organization finds a way around them through the use of pictures, interpreters, etc.			
3. Every interviewee for a particular job is asked the same questions. While interview style may change due to personal and cultural differences, the interview process is standard.			
4. Interviewers avoid prejudging applicants based on appearance.			
5. Interviewers don't jump to conclusions about someone's ability to do the job based on race, gender, age, ethnicity, or physical ability.			
6. Interviewers and managers recognize and compensate for their own hiring preferences.			
7. Applicants are interviewed by a diverse team.			
8. There is a male/female mix on the interview team.			
9. Interviewers are aware of cultural "hot spots" and try to avoid issues that may offend applicants.			
10. Written application questions have been tested for cultural bias and ease of understanding.			

How To Score the "Neutralizing-the-Application-Process Checklist"

For each *Rarely* answer, score 1 point. For each *Sometimes* answer, score 2 points. For each *Often* answer, score 3 points.

1._____   3._____   5._____   7 _____   9 _____

2._____   4._____   6._____   8._____   10._____

Total: _____

Interpretation

Warm   27-30 points   Your organization has an applicant-friendly environment, warm and open to differences. You are successfully creating a neutral application process.

Temperate   21-26 points   Your organization is making progress in neutralizing the application process but you've got a way to go. Don't rest on your beginning accomplishments.

Cool   10-20 points   Yours is a cool organization, not applicant-friendly. Diverse talent will pass you by. If you want to remain competitive in this labor pool, start making your application process more friendly

Use this information as a starting point. Your one-point answers will give you some clear indications of where your organizational Achilles' heels are in the interview domain. That can be the beginning of some helpful and necessary changes. For example, most people try to avoid judging others by appearance but it is difficult to do. Question #4 also could be the start of not only good conversation but some important actions that might bring change to the process.

· ·

Suggestions for Using the
"Neutralizing-the-Application-Process Checklist"

Objectives:

- Gain a sense of the openness and neutrality of your organization's application process for new hires
- Get feedback from those in positions to hire or recent new hires
- Educate those in a position to bring new people on board

Intended Audience:

- HR professional in charge of recruiting and hiring or in charge of educating managers about hiring
- Managers who do their own hiring
- Work teams who interview and pick new hires
- Vice president in charge of HR who wants to raise the issue at top levels of the organization

Processing the Activity:

- Distribute the questionnaire to those charged with the task of interviewing and hiring new employees. This can be given in a workshop setting or to individuals.
- Ask them to respond by putting a check in the appropriate column. Next, score the checklist.
- Whether in a workshop setting or discussed one-on-one, ask respondents to look at one- and two-point answers.

Questions for Discussion:

- What do the data from this questionnaire indicate about your application process?
- Where can you or your interview team pat yourselves on the back for creating an open and neutral application process?
- What do you still need to do to make it even more so?

Caveats, Considerations, and Variations:

- This checklist can be given to the whole interview team to look over and discuss before the next interview.
- This would be a good tool to use as a catalyst for feedback from new hires and then make the feedback useful to the appropriate sources.

· ·

How To Find, Recruit, and Hire a Diverse Workforce

Before you can do a first-class job of recruiting and hiring the kind of candidates you want, you need to have a sense of what could sabotage your effectiveness. Look at the list of potential obstacles to recruiting and see how many of them are (or can be) roadblocks. The more checks you have, the more dense the obstacles are, but the good news about identifying them is that you have information about what is holding you back and where you need to do your work.

ACTIVITY 13.2 | Potential Obstacles To Recruiting in Your Organization

Directions: Check any that sabotage recruiting efforts. If you have questions about these, there is a brief explanation of each following the "External" and "Internal" lists.

External

1. _____ Image of the community
2. _____ Lack of a critical mass
3 _____ Perception that "there's no one like me"

Internal

4. _____ Diversity vs. quality paradigm rather than diversity and quality
5. _____ Absence of pipelines to the community
6. _____ Perception that "there aren't any out there"
7. _____ Lack of knowledge about what candidates want
8. _____ Emphasis on "quotas"
9. _____ Assimilation model
10. _____ Projecting bias onto customers
11. _____ "Like me" bias
12. _____ Time commitment
13. _____ Inflexible policies
14. _____ Strategic relevance not understood

Explanations of Potential Obstacles to Recruitment

External

1. How is the community seen where you are trying to recruit? What stereotypes exist about it?
2. There is not a sizeable group of people who are similar to each other but different from the majority population, nevertheless, they still have legitimate and unique needs and norms.
3. The sense of being an "only" can get very old and tiring after a while

Internal

4. This paradigm is based on the false belief that a diverse hire sacrifices quality; as someone once said, "It's the B team."
5. No pipeline or connection to the community exists, therefore there are no advocates for you or your organization and no entry to a broader community.
6. This inaccurate belief can exist if people don't build the connections and pipelines in diverse communities they need to really see and grasp the richness of talent that exists everywhere.
7. You have to talk to people and find out what sells. No company appeals to everyone. Know who you are and find out what the candidates you value are seeking.
8. Emphasis on quotas as the rationale or driver is totally passé. It is a nonstarter.
9. The idea of hiring diverse candidates is to expand your company's experiences and possibilities. Don't lure them for that and then remake them in your image.
10. This belief is scary, but we still see it. For example, it is too common to hear or observe that an individual won't buy a product or service from someone of a particular background or go to a doctor who speaks with an accent.
11. We all feel a comfort with those like us. It is pretty human to do so.
12. "It takes too much time," is a common refrain. Time invested in building the initial pipeline is a great investment.
13. There are companies that won't change. It will do them in eventually.
14. If people don't understand that this is a strategic long-term investment and commitment, they won't do it. It's about the future.

The most common complaint we hear from companies that say they truly want to expand the diversity of their population is that they don't know where to find the personnel. For those of you who fit into this category, help is now on the way. Your search becomes much simpler when you realize that there are only two main scouting locations: outside the organization and inside. Both have benefits and costs attached.

Recruiting Outside

The biggest cost to recruiting outside the organization is not the recruiting cost itself, although that is not cheap. It is the demoralization of those who are on the inside. The unselected employee's question will be, "Why not me? I know the organization, I'm committed to it, and I have a good track record. With a little training, I'd be perfect." There is no culture where feeling rejected is painless or comfortable. But in some cultures, the consequences are larger than in others. Those who are overlooked may feel they have lost face and been embarrassed. Some may even quit. This situation could lead to disaffection among colleagues and supporters of the employee who was not promoted. That doesn't mean, however, that the cost of employee discontent should deter you from not looking outside when it is appropriate. Just be aware that there could be a cost to pay for doing so.

With so many potential negatives to outside recruiting, why might an organization choose to do it anyway? For starters, there may not be an existing pool of candidates from whom to draw. If you are actively seeking a broader employee base among many dimensions of diversity, you may have to look outside. In addition, organizations balance the inside/outside question when new blood is needed to get the organizational adrenaline pumping again or for purposes of gaining a different perspective. Maybe you are seeking skills or experience that no one currently employed seems to have. One thing is for certain: the need for ego validation transcends culture and language differences, so any promotion or recruitment needs to be handled with great sensitivity to all involved. With these considerations in mind, let us give you a number of places to scout the local talent. Among companies using creative recruiting strategies, a grocery store chain in Southern California wages the battle for effective recruitment and retention on several fronts (see Table 13.1). But there are other good strategies as well, and we begin with a list of nooks and crannies.

Explore Community Nooks and Crannies. Good, reliable, and effective recruiting practices have been around for a long time; they just aren't followed enough. Look at the tried and true practices of Estella Romero, president of Estella Romero Enterprises, a consulting firm that specializes in marketing strategies and community outreach to the Latino consumer in Southern California. She gets tremendous results by cultivating her local community. Some of the sources she mentions can be tapped in any community. Among them are the following:[3]

- *Adult education classes:* Many new immigrants congregate here for the purpose of learning English. Besides language skills, they also learn other skills in order to find gainful employment. There is a ripe and ready workforce here, eager for training and opportunity.

- *Parent advisory groups and the PTA:* Some parents associated with local schools have skills, need, and drive but lack the confidence and know-how to convert these skills to paying jobs. Giving them an opportunity and some on-the-job training will result in loyal employees.

- *Local churches, synagogues, mosques, or other religious centers:* These are wonderful places to network because they are among the most active in helping immigrants and disadvantaged groups get into the economic and social mainstream. Those in these religious centers are already being helped through the acculturation process, so their learning and adaptation curves accelerate.

- *Ethnic student associations on local college and university campuses:* This avenue provides targeted outreach to a specific population. It can be a good source of networking for both present and future jobs.

- *Government job training programs:* These programs provide skill and training, job preparation, and placement services.

- *Refugee resettlement agencies:* Such social service agencies help immigrants adjust to life in the United States. This might involve learning the language, finding a job, or taking care of others' resettlement needs. These agencies are nonprofit organizations that generally target one nationality or ethnic group.

- *Employee referrals:* Who you know can open doors at every levels of organizational life. In one utility company, a personal relationship got somebody a job in the housekeeping department. This is the first time the newly-hired immigrant has ever had health benefits and a steady job without waiting on street corners every day looking for work. He was asked by a number of employees how he got the job because their brothers and cousins are on the waiting list. He acted innocent, but in truth, a professional colleague who worked with the division head plead his case and he was hired. In your continuing efforts to attract top talent, one satisfied employee can be your best recruiter. In communities that have not always felt embraced by mainstream America, an endorsement by a fellow employee can mean a lot.

- *Elementary school outreach:* The personnel officer we met at Olive View Medical Center in the San Fernando Valley starts his recruiting efforts in elementary school. He targets fourth and fifth graders at career fairs. Armed with balloons, pencils, and information, he plants the seeds early about good job opportunities in health care that are realistic and reachable.

Instead of going to a career fair, a sheriff in Los Angeles County did some unintended recruiting when he went to address the questions and concerns of a class of local elementary school kids. The indirect recruiting happened like this:

The students are given a weekly assignment of writing a letter to someone in the news about an issue of importance to them. One particular week, after a young man had been shot and killed by the sheriff's department in a local housing development, this class of primarily Latino students wrote the sheriff about this incident in search of answers to questions that troubled them. Rather than answer 35 separate letters, the sheriff called the teacher and asked for permission to come to class and talk to the kids. He spent two hours answering their questions and making a pitch for a life of education rather than drugs and gangs as the best way to avoid this young man's tragic fate. When one little girl in a wheelchair asked if she could become a sheriff, he told her that if she got her education she could probably become anything she wanted to. At the end of the two hours with the class, when asked how many students might someday be interested in a career with the sheriff's department, every hand in the class went up, including the teacher's. To her, he sent an application. To the students, he planted seeds about the value of education. In one way or another, law enforcement will hopefully reap the rewards. Recruitment is not a short-term strategy; good recruiting is a combination of strategic thinking and the willingness to make a long-term investment.

TABLE 13.1 | Recruitment and Retention Strategies: One Example from a Southern California Supermarket Chain

Group	Recruitment Strategies	
Minorities	Early school links Explain opportunities Identify career paths	Image enhancement Role models Cultural awareness
Homemakers	Increased flexibility Child-care considerations School-term-only jobs	Image enhancement Wage/benefit information
Retirees	Increased flexibility Image enhancement Role models	Recruitment targets Wage/benefit information Part-time shifts
Students	Increased flexibility School-term-only jobs Image enhancement	Wage/benefit information OJT programs Identified career paths
Mentally/physically challenged	Agency contacts Explain opportunities Role models	OJT programs Job-content flexibility

All of these nooks and crannies offer good places to start the search.

Be Creative in How You Sell Your Company by the Pluses You Offer. Flexible benefit packages, as well as flexible work hours, can make your company very attractive. For example, looking at benefit packages that contain provisions for child care, or offering flextime that allows two new mothers to share one full-time position will not only help you hire an able workforce but will enable you to retain them as well. To recruit female employees, offering provisions for elder care can also be an inducement.

Tap the Talent of Underutilized Groups. Two such groups come to mind immediately: One is retirees and the other is people with physical disabilities. Employment statistics on our aging workforce make seniors a particularly interesting group to tap. With the over-55 market ballooning, this is an experienced, responsible group with much to offer. In a country that for years has extolled and worshipped the virtues of youth, an emphasis on age and experience rather than youth and potential may take some getting used to. Nevertheless, this group can contribute to an organization's bottom line in a full-time, part-time, on-call, or project basis. Seniors have the reputation of being devoted and dependable employees who still have a strong, reliable work ethic. Think of it this way: Your company gains a dedicated worker, the retiree gains a sense of being useful and making a difference, and all of society gains because we aren't discarding our human resources. We have seen this work magically in the field of education where retired "lifers" come back to tutor kids and work with teachers in a variety of ways. A little ingenuity can bolster both people and organizations.

Build Ties That Bind. It's time to take a page from the book of organized athletics. For years, college coaches have been masters of building ties to local high school coaches, and the pros have done the same with the colleges and universities. Everyone who follows sports can recall some story about a heavy recruiting battle for top talent. While an athlete's high school coach can't make the decision about where his star athlete should play college ball, he very likely will have some influence. In fact, he can start the process by contacting a college coach.

What works in sports will work in business, law enforcement, or any other place you want to recruit. We remember well the example of a police officer we talked with in the Asian immigrant community. Recruitment there has been a difficult task for several reasons. First of all, for most Asian refugees, police were part of the larger social and political problem in their former countries, so this is an occupation where there is no trust. Furthermore, particularly in the Chinese and Japanese communities, police work is not viewed by parents as a desirable profession for their sons and daughters. The officer we interviewed stated that recruiting in the Asian community is "analogous to recruiting star athletes. You sit down with the family and convince everyone involved that this is a worthy endeavor." The law enforcement agency uses Asian recruiters and gets help from Asian community groups. Nevertheless, his work is cut out for him. What brings him success is building the ties like coaches have done for years. You gain reputation, credibility, and, ultimately, traction and history for the organization and its relationship to the community. This is an invaluable and trustworthy ritual that will pay dividends at universities, local community colleges, trade schools, community organizations, or wherever else you set up a talent pipeline.

Use Professional Associations and Organizations such as National Society of Hispanic MBAs (NSHMBA), which holds an annual career conference where 8,000 or more highly educated and qualified Hispanic professionals can be found.

Integrate Your Commitment to Diversity Recruitment With Overall Search for Full Representation of a Global World. No one you hire will like being thought of as a statistic or someone who just fills a slot. In the case of a woman of color, she won't be any happier to think she fills two slots. In a recent presentation made by Steve Pemberton, Chief Diversity Officer at Monster.com, one of the most interesting things he stated is that diverse candidates don't want to be singled out or selected for their diversity; they want to be known and selected for their talent. They want to lead with, be recognized, and sought after for the gifts they have and the experience they bring, not the slots they fill. However, they do care about the fact that diversity matters in the organization. In fact, in September 2003, John Forsythe revealed the following:[4]

- 91 percent said that diversity programs make organizations better places to work.
- 97 percent of all minority candidates would rather work in a diverse workplace.
- A company's image is critical to attracting minority candidates.
- 65 percent of minority candidates look at an organization's reputation, and supporting diversity is a factor in where they apply for jobs.

Among the interesting pieces of information in Forsythe's article is the data that said after supporting work/life balance, for minority candidates, the next most important factor that influences application for a job is the "reputation for hiring and cultivating diverse employees." It was notable that both hiring managers and job seekers think that diversity is very important. It brings people in, and when employees think that doing so matters to the organization, it also keeps them. Open up your mind-set as you view the huge range of talent out there and go for that. Then you will get the diversity you seek.

Monster.com shared interesting information about places that employers look for candidates and where candidates themselves look for jobs. These are mostly managerial positions and the information is important for what it reveals, and equally noteworthy for what has changed over the years. As you can see in Table 13.2 the big differences is between where employers put their resources in looking for candidates and where candidates themselves are putting their efforts. Career fairs are No. 1 on the list for employers while that is the tenth priority for those seeking jobs. The only place employers and seekers are in sync is in company Intranets.

TABLE 13.2 | Resources: Where Employers Look for Candidates, and Where Prospective Candidates Look for Jobs*

	Employer Resources	Seeker Resources
1	Career Fairs	10
2	Company Intranet	2
3	College Web Sites	13
4	On-campus Recruiting	19
5	Face-to-Face Networking	6
6	Large Online Job Sites	1
7	Referral Programs	18
8	College Career Office	16
9	Newspapers (print)	3
10	Employment Agency	9

(*Monster.com, 2009.)

The biggest differences are seen in the fact that minority job seekers use online job web sites more than white job seekers do, and face-to-face/word-of-mouth is more used by white job seekers. The latter is not as much of a surprise because contacts and who you know always matters, and, traditionally, whites have had more access to jobs that use recruiting services. The surprise to us is the big difference between minorities and whites using online web sites. This is significant information if you are trying to recruit.

TABLE 13.3 | Methods Used To Look for Jobs in the Past 12 Months*

Method	Minority Job Seekers	White Job Seekers
Large online job web sites	41%	35%
Company's Intranet web site	39%	37%
Newspapers (print)	34%	36%
Newspapers (online)	29%	29%
Local job web sites	23%	24%
Face-to-face networking/word-of-mouth	22%	29%

(*Monster.com, 2009.)

As you look at the following list, notice the differences just a few years makes. The up arrows indicate biggest movers and the down arrows indicate biggest drops. The message is to stay current and don't necessarily let history be your guide or you could end up missing the good candidates you seek.

TABLE 13.4 | Biggest Drops/Biggest Movers in How Diverse Candidates Find Employers (Between 2005 and 2008)*

2005-How Diverse Candidates Find Employers		2008-How Diverse Candidates Find Employers		
1	Local Job Web Sites	1	Large Online Web Sites	↑
2	Newspapers	2	Company Intranet	↑
3	Newspapers (online)	3	Newspapers (print)	
4	National Job Boards	4	Newspapers (online)	
5	Career Fairs	5	Local Job Web Sites	↓
6	Government-sponsored Sites	6	Face-to-Face Networking	↑
7	College Web Sites	7	Contacted co-direct	
8	Trade/industry	8	Help Wanted	
9	Headhunters	9	Employment Agency	
10	Diversity-specific	10	Career Fairs	↓

(*Monster.com 2009.)

Recruiting Inside

Looking inside the organization is the other invaluable way to find diverse talent. The main benefit of staying inside the company is that you build loyalty within the existing workforce. It's also cheaper. The learning curve is shorter since your internal candidates are already acculturated to company norms. Rewarding those on board sends a message to other employees that hard work, good performance, and dedication will pay off. The downside of promoting from within is that you can miss some top talent by looking only inside. You can also become too inbred. Sometimes, that outsider can blow a much needed breath of fresh air through a musty environment. Deciding whether to recruit from inside or hire from outside requires balancing the organization's objectives against the skills and experience of the existing labor pool. In the economy of 2009, organizations have the chance to get superb talent with more ease at better prices than in times that are more affluent or stable. Regardless of where you look, there are five important values in mainstream American business culture (on the following pages) that are different from those in many other cultures. It will be helpful for you to think about these considerations and views so that cultural bias doesn't affect your recruitment or hiring decisions, no matter where you find prospective employees.

TABLE 13.5 | Recognizing Values Differences in Your Hiring and Promotion Process

Mainstream U.S. American	Most Other Cultures	Impact
1. Work and obligation to the job are a high priority for many.	Primary obligation is to family and friends.	This values difference often causes U.S.-American managers to question the loyalty and commitment that diverse employees have toward the company, as well as their motivation to do the job.
2. An organization has the right to terminate an employee. An employee has the right to leave a company for a variety of reasons.	Employment is for one's lifetime.	If an employee from another culture is terminated for not meeting performance standards, it may disgrace the employee. In addition to loss-of-face for the individual, there is the possibility that members of the same group will interpret termination as an affront. It could demoralize and affect group commitment and loyalty. The expectation of lifetime employment may make some managers gun-shy when they consider hiring someone from a diverse background.
3. There is a strong drive for personal achievement.	Personal ambition is frowned upon; what matters is the collective good.	People who frown on personal ambition and who place group loyalty before personal reward may be perceived as lazy or unmotivated. Individuals from cultures where "tooting your own horn" is discouraged may not feel it is appropriate to seek promotion or even mention an interest in doing so. Managers will need to keep a special lookout for these "diamonds in the rough" and encourage them to take advantage of developmental activities, or sign up for promotional exams.
4. Competition is a valued way of stimulating performance.	Competition upsets balance and harmony.	People from immigrant cultures may not indicate interest in promoting or setting themselves apart from the crowd because loyalty to the group and a harmonious environment are more important. The danger here for the U.S. manager is the false assumption that the person isn't motivated to do an excellent job and that he isn't aggressive or assertive enough to get the job done.
5. Loyalty is to the organization.	Loyalty is to individuals, such as bosses or informal group leaders.	Employees from cultures that emphasize personal loyalty may see promotion as an act of disloyalty and lack of gratitude toward one's boss. Organizations need to understand the strong pull of boss and peer-group loyalty when offering promotions and understand why this opportunity might not be received enthusiastically.

Not recognizing these subtle but powerful aspects of culture may cause you to sell some applicants short and mistake a lack of self-promotion for a lack of interest, or an emphasis on collaboration rather than competition as a lack of drive. Recognizing these cultural influences should help you have more discerning judgment as you go through the recruiting and hiring process.

There is no one-size-fits-all recruiting strategy. The business you are in, the level and skills of the employee you need, your purposes for wanting to fill a job, and the resources you have, both to seek candidates and to pay salaries, all impact the kind of strategies you will use. The list of a dozen strategies for increasing your diversity recruiting is not science, and in some cases it is decidedly old school, but we have seen all of these work for any level. They all have pieces of useful truth so read them and see which ones provide opportunities for you to bring in people you need.

Activity 13.3 would be an interesting tool to share with your recruiting committee. Have some conversations about what you are using, what works, what might be obsolete, and where the missed opportunities are. Beyond the conversation itself, a very valuable outcome would be commitment to action on one or two strategies.

ACTIVITY 13.3 | Strategies for Increasing Your Diversity Recruiting

Directions: Put a checkmark by each strategy you currently use. If there are strategies you would consider using but aren't currently doing so, put a star next to them.

Currently Use	Strategy	Examples of How To Do It
_____	Partner-Up	Have executives go with recruiters to conferences and job fairs.
_____	Tap Insiders	Get help from employee associations in outreach and recruitment.
_____	Connect to the Community	Have leaders and managers participate in community organizations.
_____	Involve Managers	Give managers techniques and hold them accountable for participating in recruiting.
_____	Incentivize Employees	Reward employees for finding candidates.
_____	Pay for Expertise	Offer compensation for needed skills and knowledge.
_____	Showcase the Community	Play up the advantages the area offers.
_____	Dispel the Myths	Give information that corrects misconceptions about the community.
_____	Review Language	Modify language in job ads, titles, and requirements that may be exclusionary or off-putting to potential recruits.
_____	Expand Communication Channels	Go beyond traditional established media.
_____	Talent Scout Approach	Visit homes of target recruits to engage families.
_____	Diverse Hiring Panels	Use diverse perspectives in interviewing candidates.

Creative Cultural Networking: Your Ace Recruiting Tool

We once wrote an article entitled "Who You Know Does Count!" for a newspaper in Los Angeles. It was directed to job seekers and touted the value of building relationships. Our article stated that in today's volatile job market, your only job security may be in the contacts you develop and nurture. As an employer, the proverbial shoe is on a different foot; nevertheless, some of the main points are still relevant. Your ability to attract top talent will be impacted in part by the extent of your contacts. Building a "rainbow rolodex" requires some creative cultural networking.

Cultural networking is your ability to develop individual relationships with people from diverse backgrounds, and in so doing, build a large bank of resources that you can call on when needed. Some of your best leads can come from your own employees but you also want to be sensitive to becoming too inbred. We know one hospital that hired its first Filipino in the accounting department, and every hiree after that was a Filipino recommended by that first person. Not only does this not create a diverse workforce, but it is a questionable practice because it can lead to a monocultural department.

Joining professional associations may help you get personnel leads when you need them. Maybe someone will take the initiative and call you about the one person you absolutely must interview. Perhaps some contact can tell you where you can go to comfortably ask questions regarding diversity-related issues or find out about cultural norms as you try to educate yourself and minimize faux pas. This cultural network may lead you to developing good friends from various backgrounds, but whether or not that is either achieved or desired, what it should enable you to do is get access to the invaluable talent pool that exists in every environment. Activity 13.4 can be helpful by showing you what you are already doing to build your network and what actions you may still need to take.

This self-assessment tool is primarily designed for those whose responsibility it is to expand the mix of employees at all levels of the organization through recruiting and promotion efforts. A single individual can take this assessment, see the results, and use it as a blueprint for greater outreach. If there is a company-wide or division-wide effort to expand the employee mix, this could be useful in a workshop setting to determine an organization-wide strategy.

ACTIVITY 13.4 | Creative-Cultural-Networking Checklist

Put a check by any statements that reflect what you are currently doing to expand your cross-cultural network.

_____ 1.   I belong to a professional or social group where the membership is very diverse.

_____ 2.   I consciously attend group functions where I am an outsider, where I don't know many people, and where some of them are of a different group (e.g., gender, ethnicity, race, or religion).

_____ 3.   I create collegial relationships, friendships, or arrangements at work with people who are different from me.

_____ 4.   At meetings, functions, or professional conferences, I make it my business to expand my contacts with people from diverse groups.

_____ 5.   I attend various cultural support groups such as the Black Employees' Association at work, even though (by background) I am not a member of those networking groups.

_____ 6.   I attend community functions, lectures, art exhibits, or holidays that celebrate diverse cultures.

_____ 7.   I join civic groups apart from work where I have a chance to broaden my contacts.

_____ 8.   I have hosted a networking party where I invited people from diverse backgrounds and asked them all to invite a friend or colleague.

_____ 9.   I keep nurturing the relationships I have already developed so that my base of contacts grows.

_____ 10. I have joined an organization or currently subscribe to a publication whose top priority is cultural diversity.

Directions for scoring: Count your checks. The more you have, the more effectively you are currently creating your cultural network. Our suggestion is that you target one or two of these specific items as a beginning point toward expanding your cultural network.

1. One thing I will do to more creatively develop my diversity network is _____ and I will do so by (date)_____.

2. One thing I'm already doing well but could improve on a little is _____.
   I plan to capitalize on this networking technique by doing the following: _____

Suggestions for Using the
"Creative-Cultural-Networking Checklist"

Objectives:

- Offer suggestions about various places to expand contacts and gain greater access to a pluralistic workforce
- Assess current outreach efforts

Intended Audience:

- HR professional or manager in charge of hiring and promoting
- Affirmative action officers in charge of hiring and promoting
- External consultants specializing in diversity management who want to expand their network
- Managers whose responsibility it is to recruit

Processing the Activity:

- Have participants check the responses they are currently engaged in. See what activities are not being covered by the group; then determine what efforts need to be made.
- The facilitator can take each item, one at a time, and see who is doing what. Areas ripe for exploration will emerge in the discussion.

Questions for Discussion:

- How many of you are involved in item number ___ (pick any number)?
- What have been your results?
- What makes this work well?
- Are there things that might make this strategy more effective?
- Where should we put our energy as a group?
- Let's define commitment more specifically. Where are you willing to put your energy?

Caveats, Considerations, and Variations:

- This can be very effective as a tool for individuals. Vice presidents of HR may want to share it with appropriate people on an as-needed basis.

To give you a little extra help, the following section presents some networking tips. If followed, they will pay big dividends when you need help in the find, hire, or promotion stages.

Creative Networking Tips

Focus on Building Excellent Relationships with Good People of All Backgrounds

Invest your time in cultivating people. You have limited time and energy, so you need to be discerning, but the effort can have a very high payoff. U.S.-American culture can disadvantage us on the world stage because while we know relationships grease the wheels of business, we're too short-term and time conscious in our thinking to invest the necessary time in building strong bonds. Many other cultures pay more attention to building relationships and nurturing people. They realize that the ability to transact business rests on trust, which builds slowly. If you are genuine and treat people as though they are worth getting to know, you will end up with memorable interactions, worthwhile colleagues or associates, and the results you want when you need them. It is sometimes difficult to remember in our fast-paced and easily disposable society that genuine relationships pay dividends over the long haul. But the truth is they do. Creative cultural networking, unlike Federal Express, does not deliver the goods overnight.

Let People You Meet Know What Kind of Jobs Your Company Has Available

Networking can be a very cost-effective way of advertising or recruiting. If you are actively seeking candidates or contacts, don't keep it a secret. We frequently see this in our business. People call to find out whether we teach accent reduction or are bilingual and can work with different groups on a variety of organizational issues. When the work that is requested is not our area of expertise, we always refer the caller to other consultants. Sometimes the people to whom we refer the caller are not exactly right, but they usually know someone else who will be. It works for everyone. There is a method to this madness that has unwittingly been set to poetry. Part of a line from Robert Frost's "The Road Not Taken" is applicable here: "way leads on to way." In other words, one person will lead you to another (and perhaps another) and you'll continue to grow and experience new opportunities.

Develop Patience and Realize Some Goals Are Accomplished Indirectly

The punctuality and goal orientation of mainstream U.S. culture can come into direct conflict with the slower, more deliberate pace and emphasis on relationship-building in Mexico, Central America, Asia, and the Middle East. It is difficult for a culture that espouses the aphorism "Time is money" to realize that the direct route is not always the fastest or best. We have an acquaintance who managed a project in Kuwait. He invested a full 30 percent of his time in building relationships. His bosses back in the United States were totally frustrated at the pace of the project, but he told them it had to be done his way or he'd leave. He understood the culture he was living in and was willing to live by Kuwaitis' values. By building trust and nurturing relationships, he brought the project in on time. Sometimes the shortest distance between two points is not a straight line.

Give as Well as Take

Symbolic tokens of appreciation are significant in most cultures. Sometimes that means giving gifts. We remember a consultant who did a lot of work in Japan, and she spent a considerable amount of time investigating protocol to find an appropriate gift for her host. When President Obama went to London for the meeting of the G20 in April of 2009, there was a lot of press and TV time paid to the question of what gifts he would take to Queen Elizabeth. The fact that he took an iPod loaded with pictures of the Queen's trip to the United States in 2007, and music from some of her favorite American musicals, was an attempt by the President to give a gift that showed personal attention to his host. Gifts matter as a huge part of international protocol; however, it is more about thoughtfulness then the gift itself. The generosity of time you spend helping people in little ways will be very meaningful, indeed. The saying, "What goes around comes around" is trite, but it is also true. Said a little differently, if you give the gift of time or information to others when they need it, particularly to those who may be reluctant to ask for it, they will be in your debt. They will also return the favor. Giving and getting help should be a win/win practice for all involved.

Acknowledge and Show Respect for the Special Events of Different Cultures

All cultural groups have their own unique celebrations. By remembering to acknowledge those celebrations through sending cards, attending events, or simply wishing someone a happy holiday, you go a long way toward helping people feel validated. This kind of consideration builds goodwill and understanding. It is part of what cultural networking, and in fact all networking, is really about. Lee sees this all the time with her friends and colleagues who are not Jewish. During Passover or Yom Kippur, she receives good wishes and holiday cards. Her non-Jewish friends of many years feel at home at the seders. Every January 7, Lee shares Serbian Orthodox Christmas with Anita's family. We all feel richer for these exchanges.

Become a Master of Follow-Up

When you meet someone who may be helpful in expanding your network, follow up the initial contact with a note, an appointment for lunch, or an after-work drink. Take the initiative, show interest, and always let people know that you appreciate their help. We have been in business close to 30 years. In that time, we have been shocked by a lack of common courtesy on so many occasions that we have decided the very term is an oxymoron. We have also been delighted by uncommon gestures. Some colleagues of ours who are classy and smart businesswomen always send a small box of chocolates when they get a referral. It's a nice gesture that distinguishes them from the crowd, but even a "thank you" note will make you stand out. Anything you do to build and strengthen ties is a plus, and a gracious acknowledgment to someone crosses language and cultural barriers.

Put Yourself in the Appropriate Places To Increase Your Contacts

When we worked with the UCLA Business Operations Division in its diversity development effort, one of the many things that impressed us about this group was the diligence with which they made an effort to recruit diverse candidates. Managers in this unit systematically socialized, joined organizations, and attended events or workshops with an eye toward meeting and networking with people who could lead them to the workforce they were seeking. You never know where a contact may come from or where it may lead.

Set Goals for Expanding Your Network of People Whose Backgrounds or Experiences Differ From Yours

It is human nature to feel most comfortable and secure with people who are like you. But skin color, physical abilities, or age are only some of ways in which people are the same or different. Explore values, special interests, hopes, and dreams with people who are different from you; you may be surprised at how similar you are. We know that all people are different, even those who look, or are, a lot like us. Your own family can be a fertile learning ground for appreciating differences. Let the differences you discover be a source of stimulation and fun. Not only will you expand your network, but more importantly, you may expand your vision.

Cultural Etiquette

When you are honest enough to realize and acknowledge that you might be guilty of excluding applicants based on cultural differences, then you're on the right track. Determine if some of the rubs are etiquette issues. If you have read Chapter 6, then you already understand the influence, consciously and unconsciously, that etiquette can have. It is sometimes subtle, sometimes not. But it can have a dramatic effect on social interaction, relationships, and, ultimately, hiring and promotion.

There are certain examples of this etiquette that will come to light the first moment you see someone in an interview. Do you shake hands? If so, how much firmness is appropriate? How do you address prospective employees? If you are a woman interviewing a Middle-Eastern man, are you prepared for the confusion or discomfort when he does not shake your hand? Culture has programmed you and the prospective employee with a different set of rules.

Tips for Not Being Sabotaged by Your Own Cultural Programming

Understand How Truly Powerful Culture Is and Have a Generosity of Spirit About the Differences

Culture is powerful and pervasive. All humans come with a set of operating rules, but those rules differ depending on where we are reared. Simply hiring or promoting someone in your organization who came with a different "instruction manual" won't result in instant acculturation. You won't be able to negate that person's previous years of training or behavior anymore than you could negate your own. Just imagine yourself moving to a foreign land or even to a different part of the United States. We transport our patterns and habits with the move. The only difference between personal habits and the furniture we move is that you and others can immediately see the furniture—it is tangible, while our patterns are more illusory and take longer to discover. But they are just as real. Moving to a different country sometimes involves major culture shock. The adaptation process gets even tougher in stressful times. Remembering the effort involved in that acculturation can increase your sensitivity toward others.

Expect That People You Hire Will Be Reshaped by the Organizational Culture, and in Turn, the Company Will Also Become Different

The people you are hiring are trying to become successful in an existing company with an already powerful culture of its own. To do so, they will need to fold into this organization. But the adaptation isn't strictly one-sided; both the company and the individual will become a little bit different through the interaction. Both want to thrive, not just survive. The goal of thriving necessitates identifying a common set of operating rules that function like glue, keeping the place together. Making those rules elastic and inclusive enough so that all the people you hire or promote feel comfortable and stick around is essential to your company's financial health.

Be Tolerant and Respectful of Different Cultural Values

Dealing with differences is difficult, but it also can be infinitely rewarding. As we wrestle with the impact of these differences, it is important to remember that all values in every culture cut two ways.

As a case in point, look at the ways different societies view women. In Saudi Arabia, women don't drive, nor do they generally work outside the home unless there is some special circumstance involved. There are prescribed standards of dress and, in general, much less freedom than women in the industrialized world have come to expect. While the lack of freedom can be problematic for a Westerner, it isn't for Saudi women, who esteem their role for its importance in transmitting the values of the culture. Having women manage the family helps the society maintain a tightly knit structure, and some of the West's greatest ills, such as drugs and crime, are almost nonexistent in Saudi society. The lack of freedom brings a control and order to their society that works for them. We can appreciate that it works for the Saudis and admire some of the effects of these dictates without wanting that cultural norm in the United States. And we can expect that if we went to Saudi Arabia, we would need to honor their customs. Likewise, people coming to this country find different core values than they are used to. But tolerance goes two ways. A man coming to the United States from a different culture may not be used to reporting to female managers or even to seeing women in a professional context. However, if that man wants to live and work in this country, he will need to make the adjustment.

Read About, Learn About, and Become Familiar With the Cultural Norms of Your Employee Population

Learning about different customs and the reasons behind them will make the "rules" less foreign and sometimes less irritating. You may find some different customs interesting and become more accepting. There may be others that are difficult for you to understand. We interviewed a number of American women who had worked and lived in Japan and, when they returned to the United States, had continued to work for Japanese companies. They talked about their adjustments. One that gave them pause and got a good chuckle was the one where they were not able to leave the company before their Japanese bosses at the end of the day. That took some getting used to because the Japanese have notoriously long days. Conversely, one woman described the shock her new Japanese boss got when he came to do his rotation in California. At 5 p.m. on his first day of work, he witnessed a mass exodus. Very perplexed and confused, he inquired where everyone was going. When he found out that everyone was leaving because it was the end of the workday, he could not fathom this. Adjustments are required all around.

Come to Terms With Your Humanness

Part of being human is having limits and being imperfect. Acknowledge that some behaviors may be more difficult for you to deal with than others. However, acknowledging the difficulty doesn't give you license to be intolerant. Understanding why certain behaviors are hard for you can be the beginning of dealing with them. For example, Lee is involved in a professional group with people who view their once-a-month meetings as a great opportunity for socialization. A strict time frame is not a big issue for them, but it is an issue for Lee. She tried to facilitate faster conclusions to these sessions. There was much teasing between the group members and Lee. Humor was a help—so was the group's commitment to end all meetings within two hours. But the fact is that Lee will always be impatient even with two-hour meetings and downright irritable when they go longer.

Be Willing To Ask Questions

Within your organization, you have resources—people who can explain customs, educate you, and assign meaning to certain cultural behaviors unfamiliar to you. Use these resources so you can minimize your feeling of frustration or irritation at certain behaviors that don't seem very credible for someone job hunting. Finding out why it is not unusual for an Asian applicant to smile all through the interview or why an African American listens with no nonverbal affirmations (nods and "uh-huhs") would help you avoid misinterpreting the behavior.

Be Honest With Yourself

In many cases, a candidate's name gives you information about his racial, cultural, or ethnic background. The issue is not the applicant's background, but rather the interviewer's reaction to it. Do you immediately have expectations, both positive and negative, about what that person can do? Do you assume that any person with an Asian name will be a technological whiz? Do you just as quickly assume that any African American seeking a promotion to management probably got into engineering school as an affirmative action candidate and therefore might not be fully qualified? Both high and low expectations based on anything but performance do all people an injustice. One of the easiest things in the world is pigeonholing people, but it is also one of the most costly. You can't afford to be anything but honest about your prejudices—that way there is less chance they will limit or control you.

Assess Your Cultural Awareness and Sensitivity

To see just how much awareness you have of the impact of culture on your evaluation of potential employees, respond to the *Cultural-Awareness Questionnaire* in Activity 13.5.

This tool can be used for groups being educated about cultural differences. It can also be given to managers of other individuals who need cultural awareness because they interview, hire, or promote.

ACTIVITY 13.5 | Cultural-Awareness Questionnaire

Directions: Please respond to each of the questions below with a check in the appropriate column.

	Yes	No
1. I know that different cultural values and behaviors may influence my perceptions of a person's competence, confidence, and social graces.		
2. I have ways of being less direct in asking questions of someone from Mexico or the Middle East in order to get information and help the interviewee feel at ease.		
3. In cultures where the group is more important than the individual, I have ways to gain information about a person's performance by focusing on group goals and the individual's part in them.		
4. Regarding introductions, I appropriately use first names and surnames.		
5. I understand that not making eye contact is often a way of showing respect, not a lack of assertiveness.		
6. I realize the inclination to use either a sturdy or a soft handshake, depending on the culture.		
7. I understand that vagueness or indirectness in answering a question is often culturally correct.		
8. I conduct the interview formally because the informality of American culture can be intimidating for an interviewee whose comfort comes partially from a hierarchical structure.		
9. I am conscious of the fact that standing very close to someone is appropriate in Middle Eastern culture.		
10. I realize that the loudness or softness with which people talk is often cultural.		

The more yes answers you have, the more culturally aware you are. If any of the cultural behaviors embedded in these 10 questions surprised you, start paying attention to them as you see them in the work arena. Look at your no answers. Have you ever come across these behaviors? If so, can you remember your responses or reactions? In order not to have any of these behaviors impede your selection of new personnel, look at how some of them might be your own cultural barriers. Then respond to the questions on *Overcoming Cultural Barriers in Interviewing*.

Overcoming Cultural Barriers in Interviewing

1. Which of these behaviors are most troublesome for you?

_____

_____

2. How do you interpret these behaviors? What is the reason they are problematic?

_____

_____

3. What are you willing to do, or how are you willing to see things differently, in order to make sure this behavior does not negatively impact the interviewing you do?

_____

_____

Suggestions for Using the
"Cultural-Awareness Questionnaire"

Objectives:

- Educate interviewers about cultural norms that may impact how they treat and view a potential employee
- Provide an assessment tool that increases cultural and self-awareness

Intended Audience:

- HR professionals or affirmative action officers in charge of interviewing and hiring or in charge of educating managers about interviewing and hiring
- Managers who do their own interviewing
- Work team or hiring panel members who interview and pick new hires
- Vice president in charge of HR who wants to educate and sensitize the executive staff

Processing the Activity:

- If used with a group, pass it out to participants and have them discuss in pairs or small groups.
- Discuss questions in whole-group. Be sure that the last three questions, on overcoming culture barriers, are discussed as well.

Questions for Discussion:

- What cultural behaviors or values surprised you?
- Which of these behaviors are most troublesome for you?
- How do you interpret these behaviors? What makes them problematic?
- What changes are you willing to make in your own interviewing?

Caveats, Considerations, and Variations:

- HR professionals or affirmative action officers can give this to managers of people who need it and discuss it one-on-one. It can be a useful coaching/teaching tool.
- You can make this tool more culturally specific if you are trying to educate your staff to deal more effectively with a particular consumer or employee base.

Five Ways To Ask Questions That Set Up Any Candidate for Success

Awareness of the norms and customs of other cultures that impact the communication process is critical. These communication patterns are particularly significant when you look at the interview process and see how people from different cultures solicit information from one another. U.S. Americans, quite accurately, have a reputation for being direct. The mainstream culture would say we are "efficiently so." Other cultures might say we are "aggressively or rudely so." Clearly, your style in asking questions, whether you are seen as efficient or rude, has a lot to do with culture and your effectiveness in communicating and soliciting information.

The process of asking questions is by nature a prying, intrusive one, so we can't stress strongly enough the importance of investing time up front to put people at ease. There are many people born and reared in the United States who are sometimes intimidated by the directness with which questions are asked. This process is even more difficult for someone from a culture that is more private and less open. As an interviewer, you have a responsibility to get the information you need in order to make a good hiring decision. But how you ask these questions, or elicit the information you want, is critical to your success. Using the five techniques described below and summarized in the table that follows should help you get the information you need.

Open-Ended Questions

The open-ended question is designed to help a person explore options or design possibilities. By nature, it is an expansive technique and best used when you want to assess a person's judgment or critical-thinking skills. The question allows the interviewee to give a lot of information beyond the parameters of the question as stated. The following are examples of open-ended questions:

- How might an ideal educational system (or health-care system or university admissions policy, etc.) look if you could help design it?
- How would you structure a workgroup to create greater harmony?
- What are some possible ways for improving interdepartmental communication?

The open-ended question also helps people whose native tongue is in passive languages like Spanish or Arabic to frame questions passively. For example, you could ask, "How might the organization be made more effective by this policy?" rather than, "What do you suggest we do to improve this policy?"

Closed-Ended Questions

The closed-ended question is not designed to explore as much as it is to get very specific answers. The point of closed-ended questions is to narrow the responses and get very concrete. An example might be, "Of the various procurement procedures mentioned, which do you favor and why?" Another might be, "Which information system did you select?"

Speculative Questions

The speculative question asks the interviewee to think about possibilities and show vision. Using the speculative style will give a person the chance to reflect on possibilities that don't currently exist. Realize that though some groups, the Japanese for example, find speculative questions unfathomable, "How" and "What" are useful here. Some sample questions are:

- How might hospital revenues be impacted if there were no more Medi-Cal?
- What future do you envision for our company's global competitiveness if the organization fully employs a diverse workforce? What might happen if it doesn't?

"Tell me..."

The two words "Tell me" are a good starting point because they begin a question disguised as a statement. At the end of a "Tell me" statement is a period, not the traditional question mark. That simple punctuation sets a whole different tone in the request for information. This is a perfect strategy for working with diverse cultures because immigrants often feel defensive when asked questions. In cultures that are more private than U.S.-American culture, this style offers protection from intrusion and still allows you to get the information you need. Here are a few examples:

- Tell me what you liked best about your last job.
- Tell me about the most important accomplishment of your group at Yahoo.
- Tell me what your last boss did to bring out your best.

"Describe......"

The word, or questioning style, "Describe. . ." has the same advantage as "Tell me." It is invaluable because it solicits information without an intrusive style, and in a subtle, non-direct way, it may help define the interviewee and his priorities. The same cultural factors that make "Tell me" effective will also work with "Describe." For example:

- Describe the best company you ever worked for.
- Describe the way you got support for your customer service program.
- Describe an effective quality control system.
- Describe the work environment that brings out the best in you.

TABLE 13.6 | Five Ways To Ask Questions That Set Up Any Candidate for Success

Question-Asking Style	Advantage	Disadvantage
1. Open-ended questions	Designed to explore options or design possibilities. Good at the beginning of discussion process. In passive languages, easy to frame questions.	Time consuming; not designed to give specific information so getting to concrete answers can be a lengthy process.
2. Closed-ended questions	Narrows responses; gets very concrete.	Not designed to let you see the creativity or ability to suggest options that may be a strength in a candidate's thinking.
3. Speculative questions	Designed to encourage vision and reflect on possibilities that don't exist or may seem unlikely; can really showcase creative thinkers.	Some groups, particularly the Japanese, find this style unfathomable—it's not in their thinking style to deal with questions of this nature.
4. "Tell me…"	Because these two words are a question disguised as a statement, it feels less intrusive. It will open people up who may not like to be questioned.	If people are not concise, they can ramble and go off on a tangent.
5. "Describe…"	Like "Tell me . . . ," this also solicits information without seeming intrusive. It will create more openness and less defensiveness.	This also can be time-consuming if people ramble or go off on a tangent.

These five questioning techniques will enable you to get beyond cultural barriers and get information from the people you interview in a nonthreatening way. They provide enough latitude for people to show their industriousness, creativity, and values because questions are posed in a culturally sensitive way. For example, asking someone from either Mexico or Japan to highlight his individual accomplishments would make the candidate uncomfortable. But if you ask a question about the effectiveness and productivity of someone's workgroup and ask a person to discuss that part of the project he was responsible for, you will get the information you seek, and the interviewee will feel comfortable giving it.

Our suggestion is to look at the *Sample Interview Questions* in Activity 13.6. Change any or all of the questions to suit your own style and organizational objectives. Also be sensitive to the cultural norms you have read about in previous chapters. Once you have looked at the list, rephrase five pertinent questions you normally use in interviews along the guidelines offered in each of these suggestions. Pay attention to the cultural implications of asking these questions. Try being less direct and more passive. Avoid asking a lot of questions that will force the individual to look only at individual accomplishment. Frame your questions with a combination of group accomplishment—and the individual's contribution to it—in mind.

We suggest that you take these 12 sample interview questions and get a cultural slant on them from knowledgeable people in your organization. We did by asking a few

Japanese nationals on a tour of duty in the United States. For example, in Japan, question number 3 would not be asked of a new graduate because he is not expected to know about such things. Questions 5, 6, and 11 would rarely be asked because they would put the interviewee in the uncomfortable position of playing boss, and question 8 is unnecessary in Japan because resumes are so detailed. Our Japanese colleagues told us that question number 9 was a Catch-22. If the interviewee enjoyed so much about his or her previous employment, why did he or she leave? And if nothing was enjoyed, what kind of miserable person is this human being? We suggest you seek the various cultural interpretations that reflect your interviewee base. It is indeed interesting and eye-opening.

ACTIVITY 13.6 | Sample Interview Questions

1. What makes this job opening interesting to you?
2. Tell me (or us) why you want to work for this company.
3. What things mean the most to you in any job? In what order of importance?
4. Describe the position as you understand the job. Talk about your experiences in these areas.
5. What qualifications would you look for in a candidate for this job if you were doing the hiring? What attributes do you think would be most essential to job success in this position?
6. How would you distinguish an outstanding employee from a typical one in any job?
7. What have you learned in your past schooling and training that you think would be helpful in the job you are currently applying for?
8. What has your group accomplished in your past position that you feel would be indicative of successful performance in this job? What did your group find most difficult?
9. What did you enjoy most about your previous jobs, co-workers, supervisors, departments, companies, and industries?
10. How did you happen to choose the jobs you have held?
11. Let me describe a situation that we are dealing with in this unit. What are your suggestions for dealing with it?
12. What has your past experience been in dealing with cliques? What has been the biggest impediment to a cohesive work team in your past jobs? How would you change that if you found the same circumstances here?

In the spaces below, rephrase questions you frequently ask so that they are more culturally sensitive. Think about how you could get at the same idea but worded differently.

1. _____

   _____

2. _____

   _____

3. _____

   _____

4. _____

   _____

5. _____

   _____

Rolling Out the Welcome Mat: Using the Interview To Develop Rapport and Sell Your Company

Demonstrating courtesy and warmth is the best way to roll out the welcome mat. There is a good chance that you are an interviewee's first extended contact with a company, so the impression you make will be the definitive view this person has of your company at the beginning. By creating an environment that helps an interviewee feel welcome, he or she will be able to showcase his or her talent, skill, and experience in a way that lets you see his or her strength when he or she is not plagued by nervousness. Furthermore, you will make a good first impression on behalf of your company and increase your chances of attracting the candidate you'd like to hire. Before you can create a "global welcome mat," you need to reflect on your current routine. Does the following scenario look familiar?

1. You extend a warm, solid handshake and a smile. You address the interviewee by first name and say something to the effect of "It is nice to meet you." It is helpful to remember that for religious reasons, devout Jews and Muslims may not shake hands across gender, and while it feels comfortable as a standard business practice in the United States to call someone by their first name, do your homework on the candidate. That informality can be off putting and uncomfortable for some.

2. You direct the interviewee to a seat, and in most cases offer the person coffee, juice, water, or something else to drink.

3. You then make a few minutes of small talk to relax the person, and that conversation usually revolves around weather, traffic, or any local happening that the parties involved may share in common.

4. Sometime during that initial greeting, you make eye contact and smile to extend warmth and put the candidate at ease.

5. After a few minutes of small talk, you give the interviewee the parameters of the interview, including length of time, and a description of the interview process. Then you begin by asking the easiest, least-risky questions first for the best results because the candidate will be able to gain confidence as the interview progresses. You generally start with those that center on the candidate's education and experience. Your tone of voice conveys interest and cordiality.

The following list will give you areas for heightened sensitivity. No culture is monolithic, nor is any race; therefore, assuming that all people from Japan will respond the same to matters of cultural etiquette is a mistake. Nevertheless, knowing cultural norms can be helpful. As you find out about the background of the candidate you are interviewing, you may need to do a little bit of homework to learn about the specific customs of that person's culture. The real skill will come in doing your homework so that you are open to cultural nuances and possibilities while at the same time putting those assumptions on hold till you actually meet the prospective employee in the interview. Muslims look at weather as a gift from God and a blessing, so they don't judge or discuss it. The following caveats and suggestions are a few ways to help people feel comfortable.

1. *Caveat:* Smiles do not mean the same in every culture. Before you rush forward with your "hail-fellow-well-met" smile, check the person's background or face. Your smile may indicate a lack of respect or seriousness.

Suggestion: Temper your warmth and cordiality with an appropriate professional tone.

2. *Caveat:* Most cultures are more formal than the U.S. culture and prefer the use of last names, not first. They may also combine the first name with Mr., Ms., Miss, or Mrs., for example, as in Miss Susan or Mr. Juan.

    Suggestion: You will provide greater comfort for most interviewees who are of immigrant backgrounds if you use your last name when you introduce yourself and use their last name in addressing them.

3. *Caveat:* The firmness of a handshake differs by culture. Germans have the firmest grip, while people from the Asian Pacific have a soft handshake. A sturdy American grip will do just fine with the Germans, and if you can soften yours a little in cultures where the handshake is less pronounced, you'll do just fine.

    Suggestion: There are two important things to remember about handshakes, and all the symbols of etiquette we are mentioning. If you can match the interviewee's, do so. It will help him feel comfortable, and it will show your sensitivity and openness to differences. Also avoid making assumptions about a person's competence based on his or her handshake.

4. *Caveat:* Eye contact varies by culture. Of all the cultural differences immigrants bring to this country, lack of eye contact is probably one of the most well known. But knowing it doesn't mean that we don't still judge people negatively when their eyes don't meet ours. You may know that the interview candidate from Taiwan may have been "programmed" to avert your gaze as a sign of respect, but your own programming tells you that eye avoidance is an indicator of having something to hide. Remembering all of these differences and factoring them into your assessment is easier said than done, but your adaptation is critical to your company's success in the marketplace.

    Suggestion: Remind yourself that someone from the Asian Pacific who will not look you in the eye is most likely engaging in the behavior he was taught, rather than being underconfident or dishonest.

Most important of all, remember that in a high-stress situation, both you and the job candidate will fall back on knee-jerk responses, regardless of how much you know and how hard you try to overcome your programming. Stress makes us reactive. Remembering that will enable you to be more compassionate and less intimidating as your probe for the information you need in getting the best candidate for the job.

Remember that the spirit of goodwill you exhibit in an interview will be more important than any question you ask or any norm you observe. People can feel when they are treated with dignity and respect. Ultimately, your behavior and tone are the most important allies you have in rolling out a welcome mat.

Checking Your Own Biases at the Interview Door

We've talked about a lot of factors involved in the effective interviewing, hiring, and recruiting of employees from diverse backgrounds. We have looked at ways to neutralize the application process and have given you suggestions for networking creatively. We have talked about how to ask questions and have even given you sample questions to ask.

We've looked at the impact of culture on an interviewee's behavior and suggested that you not determine someone is incompetent because he or she is operating under different cultural rules. What we haven't done is really ask you to acknowledge your own biases and check them at the door. It is important to do that now because all our other suggestions will be for naught if you don't come to terms with your own preferences first. The purpose of this reckoning is not to accuse you or point a finger at you for having preferences. We all have them. Once you identify yours, they will be less likely to limit your perceptions of others. Ask yourself the questions in Activity 13.7.

In order to locate and hire top talent, an organization needs to demonstrate its commitment to searching out talented people with varied backgrounds, beliefs, and behaviors. Dedication to accomplishing this goal is essential from the top of the organization on down if you are going to create a truly open, welcoming company that retains recruits.

Beyond that commitment from the top of the organization, people whose responsibility it is to recruit and hire need to have knowledge about different cultural norms, an open mind about those differences, and the energy to cultivate the relationships that pay off long-term. If you have the commitment to use some of the many strategies you just read about throughout this chapter, there is no doubt you will be a formidable competitor in the marketplace of top talent.

Years ago, we heard Dave Grant, a seminar speaker, talk about what he called the law of the radiator. The essence of that law is very simple. What you radiate is what you attract. This law has significant implications regarding recruitment.

In the end, effectively recruiting and hiring a diverse workforce combines old techniques with new. Cultivating relationships, being open, and gaining cultural knowledge and sensitivity never go out of style. At the same time, while old-style relationship-building always matters, there is an important place for technology with social networking tools like LinkedIn and Facebook or organizations like Monster.com. Using all the avenues available will help your organization get good talent, as will having the wisdom to invest in the process of doing so even in the midst of a recession. Attracting and getting good people at every level of the organization is a process and there is no time like the present to begin.

ACTIVITY 13.7 | Interviewing Assumptions and Biases

Directions: Answer the following five questions. The more candid you are, the more helpful this information will be.

1. What behaviors do I currently expect from someone I interview or hire? Consider the following areas specifically:

    - Language skills/usage

      _____

      _____

    - Communication style (verbal and nonverbal)

      _____

      _____

    - Etiquette (involves social norms such as handshakes, how people are introduced, and distance between people)

      _____

      _____

    - Social values (egalitarianism vs. hierarchical structure)

      _____

      _____

      _____

2. What assumptions do I make about potential interviewees and their competence when I see different behaviors than I want or am used to?

    - Language:_____

      _____

    - Communication:_____

      _____

    - Etiquette: _____

      _____

    - Values: _____

      _____

3. What differences are easy for me to handle? _____

    _____

    _____

4. What differences are a problem?_____

    _____

    _____

5. What does this suggest I need to do differently to be more sensitive and open when I interview people different from me in a whole variety of ways? _____

    _____

    _____

Suggestions for Using
"Interviewing Assumptions and Biases"

Objectives:

- Identify biases or assumptions in areas of language, communication, style, etiquette, and social values that impact the interviewing and selection process
- Determine where biases can sabotage hiring and recruitment efforts

Intended Audience:

- HR professional or affirmative action officer in charge of recruiting
- Manager in charge of recruiting
- Work team that hires its own team members
- Vice president of HR who wants to coach particular managers

Processing the Activity:

- This can be used with teams who hire their co-workers or by HR professionals who want to coach a manager one-on-one. In either case, it needs to be filled out first.
- If a team uses this to broaden its awareness of biases, a facilitator would ask team members to share in pairs first, then discuss as a whole group.
- A group discussion would follow.

Questions for Discussion:

- Use the five questions in the questionnaire to guide your discussion, focusing on four areas: (1) language, (2) communication style, (3) etiquette, and (4) social values.
- All five questions are important, but ultimately, numbers 4 and 5 need to be discussed fully: What differences are a problem? What does this mean I (we) need to do differently?

Caveats, Considerations, and Variations:

- Like all the tools in this chapter, this can be used with a group, but it can also be very helpful in coaching managers one-on-one.

CHAPTER 14.

Promoting, Coaching, and Career Development To Engage the Talent of Everyone

• •

This chapter will provide you with:

- An awareness of the subtle assumptions that sabotage your diversity promotion efforts

- Considerations about how globalization shapes criteria for successful leadership and management

- A model of career development

- Skills necessary for being promoted

- Suggestions for effective coaching and mentoring

- An assessment that measures your organization's openness to promoting candidates of many different backgrounds

> *The most exciting thing about women's liberation is that this century will be able to take advantage of talent and potential genius that have been wasted because of taboos.*
>
> —HELEN REDDY

Helen Reddy was a visionary when she made the above statement about the 20th century many years before the current demographic revolution. Today, if we substitute the word *people's* for women's, the quote would be equally appropriate or relevant. As we enter the second decade of the 21st century, the new workforce is already upon us, while the new management and leadership to match are still in metamorphosis. We are reminded of two co-existing truths as we explore leadership at this time in history: progress has certainly been made in expanding who sits at the top of organizations. On the other hand, statistics about who sits on corporate boards and who gets leadership or management positions show us that we have a long way to go. According to R. Roosevelt Thomas, Jr., "Women and minorities no longer need a boarding pass, they need an upgrade. The problem is not getting them in at the entry level; the problem is making better use of their potential at every level, especially in middle-management and leadership positions. This is no longer simply a question of common decency, it is a question of business survival."[1] Recognizing the need for upgrades is a first step. Many variables impact full utilization of employee potential at every level of an organization but most certainly at the top and in the middle.

Quality vs. Diversity: Not an Either-or Proposition

The subtle message historically delivered by most corporations at mid-level management and above has been that Euro-American males are the "A Team." When necessity demanded, the thought was that real talent might have to be diluted just a bit in deference to politics, demographics, or affirmative action. For a variety of reasons, and through many experiences, people in organizations today are coming to the realization that predominantly white-male leadership or management teams must change. While there is recognition of rich talent among white males, there is also awareness that talent does not reside solely in them. The talent pool of people from different racial, ethnic, geographic, and generational groups is wide and deep. Forward-thinking organizations know this and their leadership choices reflects this knowledge. Changes are occurring but some attitudes linger. In many cases, the perception still remains that selecting pluralistic management teams for reasons of equity and justice will most assuredly mean sacrificing quality.

We witnessed this perception firsthand when we worked with one of our clients, a team of 48 managers struggling with the question of how to widen the ethnic, racial, and gender composition of their team. While white males were the dominant group in positional power and numbers, the team was diverse. Most ethnic groups, including Native Americans, were represented on the team, which was committed to the cause of diversity and to achieving parity at top echelons of the division. Even so, with all their awareness, commitment, and desire to move forward, when it came time to look at the valued management characteristics they promote or hire, the intensity of discussion on this issue showed how deep, subtle, and difficult the resistance is. They had a hard time getting beyond the idea residing somewhere deep down that quality really would suffer if accommodations were made to promote diverse candidates, in spite of high regard for colleagues from a variety of backgrounds. The socialization is very deep and often subliminal or unconscious.

Incorrect Assumptions That Sabotage Your Diversity Promotion Efforts

Part of what makes the quality vs. diversity issue a difficult one is that human beings attach certain beliefs to the worth, talent, or performance abilities of certain individuals or groups. These assumptions are based on direct and indirect experiences such as the teaching we have received from our parents and the attitudes that permeated the environment in which we were reared. Societal influences may incorrectly indicate what certain groups of people are capable of or where they should be slotted professionally. For example, Asians are often seen as superior performers in the area of quantitative analysis. The stereotypes come not only from those outside the community, but inside as well. We remember very well the senior high school student of Japanese ancestry who was utterly gifted and brilliant in math. She likes math, but her real passion was calligraphy. Neither her parents nor her teachers could see that as a valid area of study or interest, regardless of her talent and passion for it. The suggested limitations placed on her came from adults in many parts of her life and of varied backgrounds. Does that mean someone of Asian background is always expected to go into computer science or engineering? Carrying this assumption or belief further, does it mean she could be seen as too technical to be good with people in a managerial role? What makes these thoughts dangerous is not only that they are limiting but also that they are unconsciously absorbed through osmosis. Assumptions are part of the air you breathe and they are just as hard to get hold of. The problem is not only that they are inaccurate, but also that they exert a powerful influence. Think about the following four assumptions. Do you hold any of these yourself? Identify those that operate at your company because until they are acknowledged, their negative impact can't be minimized and efforts toward building a truly diverse management team will be impeded.

Women and people of color, gays and lesbians, or any people who come under the classification of affirmative action face perceptions of only getting their jobs because they fill a slot.

It is not uncommon for people of color to feel like token appointments. The false assumption still exists in some places that a diverse promotion is a less-qualified promotion. One can hope that because Barack Obama is president of the United States and his cabinet posts are wide and diverse by gender, ethnicity, race, and other factors, that over time, the same osmosis that got us stuck in our long-held assumptions can also unstick us and make us more open. Tiger Woods changed our perception about not only who plays golf, but what excellence in golf means. In truth, individuals of every race, religion, or nationality are qualified in some areas and not in others. The determiner of qualification is a coalescing of many factors—experience, innate talent, a passion to do the job, intelligence, developed skills and competencies, raw potential, and so on. Diversity-related promotions can be as good a fit and as right (or as bad a fit and as wrong) as any other promotion.

The best way to get beyond this obstacle is to pick people with excellent track records who are ready for increased responsibility and who have been coached. Furthermore, the organization only does part of its job when it picks a diverse candidate for the upward climb. The other part is to offer continued support, technically and emotionally. In that way, new managers can be set up for success.

Merit and competence in very specific areas are the only salient qualifications.

Sometimes only certain job skills are emphasized as necessary when, in fact, the role requires multifaceted skills. For example, lifeguards have traditionally been selected on the basis of athletic performance. While no one disputes the importance of being a superb swimmer in order to rescue people, the job also necessitates being able to resolve conflict, solve problems, and communicate with the diverse public that uses the beaches. Swimming competence is only one part of the job. In some circumstances, resolving conflict and dealing effectively with different people may be even more critical. These skills also need to be factored into the job description and given some weight.

A diverse management team is a weaker team than an all-white male group.

No intelligent person would openly admit to this theory, but the battles for equity are fought and won in the deep recesses of our mind, not out in the open. Homogeneity may be comfortable, but it is no longer reality in the United States. It is also no guarantee of an effective team. Both homogeneous and heterogeneous teams can be effective and ineffective, depending on management's ability to tap the skills and commitment of the group as well as the innate talent on board. The obstacle arises when white males (or any other homogeneous team) who have the power to open up the management team buy in to this assumption. The time is right for the leadership to realize that talent and tenacity come in both genders plus a variety of sizes, shapes, and colors.

Women, people of color, those with physical disabilities, or any person of the nondominant culture must sell out in order to make it.

The perception exists that the elevator to the top floor leaves a good part of a person's integrity behind as he or she travels upward. Questions abound: "Did this individual sell out in order to make it? Can he or she be an authentic self and survive?" For example, we have had smart, dedicated students in parts of some African-American communities tell us when they do well, they are accused of being "too white." We heard the First Lady, Michelle Obama, talk to kids in a Washington D.C. school and she told them that because being smart and learning have always mattered to her, she dealt with that very same accusation. But she didn't care. Excellence and knowledge acquisition were very important priorities, even as a teenager, so she let the rejection and criticism from peers roll off.

Questions about authenticity dealt with by students in teenage years morph into similar questions in adult life. One executive recently told us a story that illustrates the need for simultaneous and evolutionary change as we build cultures that value people for who they are. She was at a meeting with her executive management team when her secretary came in and announced that she needed to take a phone call right then from her child's school. She took the call in the meeting. As she recounted this story, one of our colleagues asked her why she didn't take the call elsewhere. Her response was both quick and clear. It was important to her that her colleagues redefine their image of an executive to include being a nurturer. She is unwilling to deny that part of her and feels strongly that her male colleagues need to come to terms with both her maternal role outside of work as well as her executive role at the office. Meeting these issues head on is the only way society will change. What's more, in that way she can be her authentic self, not someone else's picture of whom she should be.

Unconscious Factors That Influence Promotions

A critical beginning step in making room at the top for diverse talent is to realize how the subconscious thinking of all parties sabotages the diversity promotion efforts and results. When assessing your company's progress at mid-level and above, some important questions need to be asked. What elements influence promotion decisions? How subtle or overt are the selection criteria? Which ones can be measured and verified? Once you address these questions, there are four unconscious decision factors that strongly influence promotion decisions. They are simply another variable that sways candidate selection. They deserve some thought and attention as they rattle around your subconscious because they are influential by virtue of their being unrecognized or unarticulated. As you read these unconscious factors, note any that influence promotional outcomes in your organization.

The Clone Effect

It is predictable and natural for human beings to value and appreciate those people who are most like them. When promotion time rolls around, appointing a carbon copy might feel like the most natural thing to do if you don't force yourself to think about the pros and cons of anointing your double. In countries with homogeneous populations, the issue of racial or ethnic clones is less salient than in our immigrant nation. With Euro-American males holding most of the power positions in American businesses, promotions have traditionally gone to other white males, and without some emphasis on the need to build a multitalented management team from different backgrounds, that reality won't change. When promoting people, be aware of the pitfalls of appointing someone just like you, not only in appearance and background, but values and thinking styles as well. There is strength in differences. We remember a few years ago when the vice president of operations for Pepsi-Cola, said, after a three-and-a-half-day diversity training course, "A year ago, I might have automatically hired somebody who thought like me. Now I am much more likely to hire someone with a different point of view."[2] As you deal with the natural tendency to hire clones, consider looking for similarities between you and potential promotees in less obvious ways than that of skin color and ethnic background.

Comfort Level

One reason why there is a tendency for individuals to promote or select "clones" is that we are most comfortable with people like us. When executives or managers add new players to their team, among the factors they consider are their own comfort and trust levels with those they're bringing on board. Jack Gibb, a management consultant, said, years ago when talking about trust, "I like the me in you." There is safety in the familiar reflection. Trust is often a function of how similarly people see things. Because we feel safer in the company of those whose values, looks, traditions, or habits are like ours, we keep adding them to our executive staffs. In this way, the clone effect and comfort level are tied together. Replicating yourself feels safe, but it doesn't necessarily produce the strongest management team. Since comfort is an important component of a high-trust management team, find commonality in less superficial ways. Instead, focus on values, habits, hobbies, skills, and just plain human preferences. The trick is to expand areas of comfort way beyond what you used to look for.

Expectations and Socialization

One of the most harmful saboteurs of equal opportunity promotion has to do with our unconscious expectations and the prejudices we have about other groups of people. Most of us became acquainted with the self-fulfilling prophecy, or the "Pygmalion effect," years ago in some educational classroom. It is the idea that we live up to or down to the expectations others have for us. But in reality, we have lived its effects all our lives from the teachings of the parents who reared us, the schools that educated us, and the communities that encultur-ated us. Over a lifetime, our brains have collected pictures and ideas about the capabilities of various groups and individuals. Through print and media, these ideas have been reinforced. The end result: Labeling individuals from various groups based on these ideas. The labeling often occurs in subtle ways, which can be helpful or harmful, depending on the level of expectations we set for others. The good news is that we can unlearn our harmful thoughts.

When we mention the subtle power of expectations and socialization in workshops, participants often deny being affected by them. But we equate expectations from stereotypes to secondhand smoke. Most managers don't set out to put limiting expectations on their staffs, but they sometimes do so without being aware. Do you ever catch yourself expecting the women to be the nurturing part of your organization's climate? What about the idea of Mexicans or Central Americans mopping floors and cleaning rooms? If so, what effect might such thinking have on promotions for people around gender or ethnicity? If you do find these expectations on automatic pilot, it is time to reprogram the software.

Double Standard

Gloria Steinem once said that we'll know women have made progress in our society when they can be as mediocre as men. The idea that women, or other members of the non-dominant culture, have to perform stunningly to pass muster when those in the dominant group can get by doing less has not gone unnoticed. You can look at most organizations in this country and find an example of a woman or person of color who has to jump through more hoops, win more battles, and prove themselves in more arenas than those in power to even be considered for a promotion.

Deborah Tannen speaks eloquently and humorously about the double standard and miscommunication between men and women. She cites the example of women speaking up in mixed-sex groups being harshly described as "overbearing" or "hard-edged." On the other hand, when women are not aggressive in presenting their ideas, they are viewed as "push-overs." Tannen makes the point about women's double bind: "If they speak in ways expected of women, they are seen as inadequate leaders. If they speak in ways expected of leaders, then they are seen as inadequate women. The road to authority is tough for women, and once they get there it's a bed of thorns."[3] In a broader but equally relevant arena, Latinos and African Americans are often considered passive if they don't speak up, but militant if they do.

On more occasions than we care to recount, even when the objective performance is stellar, due to factors like the clone effect and comfort level, diverse employees frequently lose out, or worse still, are simply ignored. Their behaviors and performances are interpreted or defined differently from that of white males. By helping those who have the power to promote become increasingly aware of these unconscious factors, they will have less influence on promotional decisions in your organization.

New Competencies for Managers and Leaders in a Global World

This book was first published in 1993 and we revised it in 1998. Our third revision is being written in 2009-10. You can do the math, but just counting the number of years can't fully explain the huge change in what constitutes effective leadership. The definition of what effective management and leadership looks like is among the biggest changes experienced in the life of this desk reference. In the past, U.S.-American models in particular, and Western models in general, were the standards of effective leadership. The articles, models, research came mostly out of the United States in the last part of the 20th century. While the world was changing in response to globalization, with emerging economies rapidly growing in countries like Brazil and India, the developed world of Europe and the United States were still dominant leadership models. That is no longer true. A one-size-fits-all model of leadership is obsolete. Instead of having strictly defined leadership characteristics in our very fluid world, effective leaders any place will need to be adaptable, knowledgeable about cross-cultural norms, and bring a global mind-set to the table.

Even if you work primarily in the United States, you will need intercultural literacy because the demographic richness and complexity within our own borders demand it for effectiveness. The most difficult adaptation from the previous leadership model to a more fluid one will probably be felt in the United States. Other countries and leaders were always adapting to our norms and preferences. The fact that the model of effectiveness is now more multi-faceted will take some getting used to, not only by those in the power positions or striving for them, but also in the minds of the followers they lead. Conversations and collaborations rather than edicts certainly played some part of past leadership styles, but even those conversations began with an unconsciously ethnocentric frame of reference. The result was that even if you were open and a good listener, you still heard with a culturally biased ear. It was difficult to do otherwise at that time.

The need for leaders to have high levels of Cultural Intelligence (CQ) is illustrated in a quote by D.C. Thomas and K. Inkson: "The idea of great individuals such as Gandhi,

Abraham Lincoln and Joan of Arc is one that has had a great deal of influence on how we think about leadership."[4]

Their question, both incisive and relevant for anyone looking at leadership and management today hits the bulls-eye. "Would these people have been great leaders at another time, in another place, or indeed in another culture? Would these people have been great leaders with different followers, particularly followers who were culturally different from them?" What a great question. Leadership has historically been quantified by looking at leadership traits in conjunction with the time, historical events, and charisma of the leader. It looked at the relationship between those doing the leading, and those being led. Being culturally competent, knowledgeable, and having a global mind-set have not been not front-and-center qualities for most of the 20th century, but they are today. When borders were less porous, a global mind-set and CQ mattered less. Today this competency is not a luxury. Adaptability rules—the ability to handle ambiguity and complexity amid vast cultural differences is primary.

So if it is increasingly clear that a one-size-fits-all leadership model is no longer effective, what is? Our own experience validates the work of many thinkers in this field, thinkers and writers like Janet Bennett, Fons Trompenaars, and Peter Woolleams.

Critical Leadership Competences in a Global World

Awareness of a Global Reality

There is a vast difference between rationally knowing that the world has changed and experiencing it in your gut. If you read Thomas Friedman's book, *The World Is Flat,* you have seen literally hundreds of examples of a vastly changing world.[5] Through news delivered via TV, technology or print media, you can't miss the change. However, there is a big difference between seeing the movie *Slumdog Millionaire* and actually going to India and seeing how that very complex country works. What protocols, sensitivities, and norms would you have to pay attention to if you worked there? Can you legitimately assume that all or most of your employees want you to delegate so they can take initiative and shape direction in their workgroup? No, we don't think so. Can you rightly assume employees around the world want freedom and autonomy to make their own decisions rather than tight structure and hierarchy? No, again. It means starting with the acknowledgement that a person's worldview, belief, and behaviors can be truly different from yours; therefore, your leadership or management must be as well. Sometimes the old rules may apply but, just as often, they won't—and effective leadership today does not assume they will.

Cultural Competence

Cultural competence, metaphorically, gives you the figurative map. It tells you the behavioral highways and byways that will enable you to get things accomplished as you build effective relationships whether teams are on-site or virtual. In the age of shorthand that uses IQ and EQ to help see how adept we are dealing with our reasoning and our emotions, some people talk about CQ, cultural quotient, to describe how knowledgeable we are about understanding different cultural norms. The good news about gaining cultural competence is that there are many primers that give you both general and specific cultural information. Intercultural Press, for example, is a good resource for this kind of information. But equally important is your openness to learning, observing, paying attention and developing relationships so you can ask people from various cultural backgrounds for the clues and help you need. In our latest work that combines Emotional Intelligence and Diversity (EID), one of our four concepts, Social Architecting, talks about the need to become a cultural interpreter. If you can provide know-how for others, it is a great gift, but if you can't, then find cultural interpreters you can count on and trust. They can help you and others read the maps.

Respecting Different Norms

Our emotions don't lie. We are not saying that managing all of these differences is easy, because it isn't. One of the most challenging aspects for U.S. employees is managing differences in time orientation. Think about someone you work with who is pretty exact regarding time. Meetings called for 9 a.m. should start at that time. Others may be much more flexible and getting to a 9 a.m. meeting at 9:15 a.m. is not an affront or a problem to that person … it is just how the schedule worked out. The differences in how people see and experience time are real, and working out these different views matters. They test your ability to really understand the underlying values of others and to respect their patterns and beliefs. Demonstrating acceptance of and appreciation for these differences can pay very big dividends. Recognize that it is valuable and potentially satisfying to spend time cultivating a relationship even though the schedule can suffer. Keeping your eye on the big picture, that of building trust and relationship, can help you reframe your thinking and actually welcome the chance to grow and adapt as you also grow your business. This is one of the reasons why our work on emotional intelligence and diversity has been helpful to our clients, or others who do straight EQ work; it has the capacity to help people reframe their current reality and become much better at dealing with ambiguity and cultural dilemmas. Step one is getting to the point where you truly understand the core values of a norm you find difficult. Doing that makes it easier to identify its benefits for you so that you can be genuinely gracious in navigating the relentless differences you face. One last note on this—differences don't have to be global or cultural. They can be as plain as the personality differences among those of you on a team reared in the same place, who have known each other and worked together for a long time.

Adaptability and Openness

Once you have seen your role as leader or manager through a cultural lens and you start to really see how pervasive the influence of culture is, you also begin to understand what is required in negotiating all these differences to get the job done. It helps to know that the cultural rules play out differently across countries, regions, and departments. It is probable that the way respect and harmony, which are so critical in Asia, Arab, and African countries, are demonstrated, may mean that offering a different idea than yours would be very difficult for an employee.

If harmony or conformity, loyalty or face-saving are prime values, how can you ask for what you want from others anchored in those values?

We have said that leadership is different as we enter the second decade of the 21st century. What is the same is that respect, relationships, being part of a team, and getting work done in a humane, safe environment still matter. Paying attention to people, being respectful, the need to get work done has not changed but doing all that through the primary lens of culture is different. Doing so requires a multicultural lens.

New Management: Expanding the Mix

Part of the responsibility for being promotable falls on the shoulders of any candidate who wants a new, better, or different job. Part of the responsibility also falls on the organization. The problem is that, in far too many cases, the overwhelming responsibility for promotion has been borne by the candidate, and the results are not heartening for diverse candidates. In an unyielding system, where one type of management characteristic is valued to the exclusion of others, you have high turnover and diminished credibility with a diverse population. To be successful in making room for nondominant-culture promotions, the model of what constitutes successful and effective management must grow beyond the traditional assumptions of leadership. Cracks are starting to appear in some ceilings. The question is, "Are they big enough to squeeze through?" You can ponder that question by reflecting on your own company. What traits are currently being promoted in your organization? Considering the changing nature of leadership, what traits should be valued? Start by looking at this issue broadly and considering what constitutes effective leadership in your organization (see Activity 14.1)

Determining what is rewarded and promoted in your company is the first step increasing the structure and articulating what moves people up or holds them back. But genuinely opening up the organization is a system-wide challenge that looks at many things: power shifts, utilization of resources, and alterations in the reward structure, to name a few. It requires analyzing policies, practices, and procedures to see where comprehensive change can begin. Take the questionnaire *What Does Your Company Do To Increase Promotions of Its Diverse Employees?* (Activity 14.2) to see how promotion-friendly your company is to employees from a wide variety of backgrounds.

Having a system for implementing these strategies is necessary but not sufficient to build the promotability of diverse candidates. For that, mentoring is a helpful approach.

ACTIVITY 14.1 | Valued Management Competencies for Success in a Global World: What Is and What Might Be

In the first column, list 10 important traits your company looks for in someone it promotes to a leadership position. In the second column, list competencies it should look for in today's global business environment. You are looking for a gap between what qualities you currently reward and what this era demands. There may be overlap, but identify any necessary competencies that are missing.

Currently valued traits and competencies we select for:	Traits and competencies we should also select for:
1. _____	_____
2. _____	_____
3. _____	_____
4. _____	_____
5. _____	_____
6. _____	_____
7. _____	_____
8. _____	_____
9. _____	_____
10 _____	_____

Now go back and place a check by any of these traits that you have, in either of the two columns. Do these traits desired in the first column disadvantage or advantage any particular group(s)? Explain, for example, that it is very important to speak out at meetings and offer suggestions but our colleagues from Thailand have a hard time doing this.

What can the organization do to make certain that particular populations of employees are not disadvantaged or unconsciously ignored?

_____

_____

What traits do you see that currently hold people back, creating barriers to promotion?

_____

_____

What are the advantages in these traits? In other words, what is the flip side and what do these traits offer our organization or team?

_____

_____

Who in the organization needs to think about a more expanded set of competences?

_____

_____

Suggestions for Using
"Valued Management Competencies for Success in a Global World: What Is and What Might Be"

Objectives:

- Identify management traits that are rewarded and promoted in your organization
- See how frequently you and other managers or executives already have the traits that are valued
- Identify traits you are overlooking for success in a global world
- Consider how difficult it might be for diverse candidates to succeed and be promoted in your organization
- Get a sense that other cultures have traits we can learn from

Intended Audience

- Facilitator, consultant, or HR professional working with a middle-management group to help look at opening their promotion process
- Affirmative action officer or vice president of HR who wants to help an executive staff understand current promotability with an eye toward opening up the system

Processing the Activity:

- Ask participants to fill out the worksheet. When working with an executive staff, discuss responses among the whole group. For a middle-management group, break up into small groups first, then process with the entire group.
- Chart the list of competencies on an easel in front of the group. Put checks by them every time they are mentioned. You can also place a check when the word might not be exactly the same but the concept is. For example, being honest and having integrity are the same meaning.

Questions for Discussion:

- Discuss each of the questions with the biggest focus on what qualities are being promoted?
- How does this model of promotability hold a diverse candidate back?
- What can we do about it?
- Where is the opportunity for the organization to expand the list of qualities needed and rewarded?
- What are the consequences for the organization if nothing changes?

Caveats and Considerations:

- Do not even begin the analyses of valued management traits unless you are willing to do something about broadening the criteria. Looking at the issue will raise expectations, but doing nothing will create cynicism and hopelessness.

ACTIVITY 14.2 | What Does Your Company Do To Increase Promotion of Its Diverse Employees?

Directions: With your organization in mind, respond to the following questions by putting a check in the appropriate column.

Questions	Yes	No
1. Top management uses formal processes to meet with and encourage top talent from diverse backgrounds.		
2. Teaching potential "stars" the rules for success is a top priority.		
3. A balanced life is compatible with the demanding workload of those who move up.		
4. Our company is attractive to diverse employees because we are flexible enough to accommodate differences.		
5. Our company models change by welcoming diversity at all levels of the organization.		
6. A formal mentoring system exists to nurture top talent.		
7. The golf course is the best place to tap into the informal pipeline.		
8. Taking parental leave is possible but frowned upon.		
9. Our organization can sell itself to diverse employees by pointing out that a large percentage of top management are currently women and people of color.		
10. Involvement in change is pushed to the lowest level of the organization.		
11. Top management seeks advice from and contact with employees from all backgrounds.		
12. Our organization reaches out to and is knowledgeable about the populations we have and want to develop.		
13. A reward structure exists to accommodate the different employee motivations.		
14. Our company has an excellent reputation for retaining top talent because of our child- and elder-care policies and other benefits.		
15. The flexibility to work from home (as long as deadlines are met) is available to employees.		

Scoring: Items number 7 and 8 should be *no* answers and all the rest should be *yes* if your organization promotes advancement of diverse individuals. Here are the concepts being measured:

Items 1, 6, 11 — *Building connections:* Helps employees develop and maintain relationships that are sturdy and enhancing at all levels of the organization.

Items 2, 7, 12: — *Political savvy:* Helps employees make use of the informal organization and pick up the unstated clues.

Items 3, 8, 13: — *Dealing with multiple motivations:* Demonstrates a willingness to be flexible with today's workforce, realizing that different employees are motivated by different things.

Items 4, 9, 14: — *Positioning:* Indicates the organization's ability to make itself attractive by presenting outcomes in a value base employees respect and respond to.

Items 5, 10, 15: — *Mastering change:* Attests to an organization's openness to new people, ideas, and systems.

Suggestions for Using
"What Does Your Company Do To Increase Promotion of Its Diverse Employees?"

Objectives:
- Assess your organization's openness to promoting diverse employees
- Identify areas that could be developed to enhance promotion of diverse employees

Intended Audience:
- Executive staff who want to see how open they perceive the organization to be and where they can be more so
- Middle management to give executive staff feedback about openness as they see it
- Employees seeking promotion who want to give the organization feedback

Processing the Activity:
- Have each participant take and score the questionnaire.
- In executive staff, discuss as a whole group; for mid-level management and employees, break into small groups first.
- Collate results from mid-level management and feed upward.

Questions for Discussion:
- What item number and category do you see as this organization's greatest strength in opening up the system?
- What are its greatest weaknesses?
- What, according to the data, needs to be done in order to expand the promotional system?

Caveats and Considerations:
- Use this as a feedback tool with mid-level managers or employees where executives are open to the feedback and to opening the system. This tool offers a look at important skills that can be taught, coached, mentored, and developed. Willing executives could make a very positive difference if they actually used this tool as a framework.

Opening the Promotional System

Beyond developing individuals, organizations that want to access the talent and ability of all must also look at their promotional system. These practices and policies may be inadvertently sabotaging your efforts. To overcome these barriers, organizations have taken the following steps.

1. Review of job postings and requirements: R. Roosevelt Thomas, Jr., makes a distinction between preferences and requirements, advising that it is the preferences that are not only nonessential, but that prevent organizations from considering a wider range of promotees. How essential is an MBA? Does the person really need experience on Wall Street, in construction or in agriculture?

2. Review of job descriptions for cultural bias: Taking initiative and being a self-starter is not universally valued. Though you may want this quality you may be filtering out a terrific team player.

3. Diverse promotion panels: Promotion decisions made by a diverse panel of employees who bring a wider set of perspectives to the experience help reduce the chance that unconscious biases will influence the selection.

4. Diversity training for managers and hiring-panel members: Those who have a decision-making role in promotions need training to recognize and manage their own biases and assumptions, and to understand the cultural influences that may be operating in the promotional process.

Mentoring: A Proven Way To Groom and Grow Talent

While coaching helps an organization grow talent through good one-on-one development, support and feedback, mentoring can be counted on to provide the role modeling and career counseling. By definition, mentoring is the sponsoring or guiding of another person; it resembles the apprenticeship idea from days of old. The best mentoring takes place within a formal system in the organization even though the relationship itself can have an informal style or feel to it. While conclusive evidence on the value of mentors is still scant, Jerry Wilbur, vice president of Service Master Company states, "For females and members of minority groups entering management, the chances for career success improve when these individuals obtain mentoring."[6] However, we believe that mentoring should be open to the whole range of probable candidates in an organization, including white males. Any talent developed helps not only the person being groomed, but also those people who come in contact with the mentee and the organization as a whole.

Mentoring is usually a less-structured, less-formal relationship than coaching. It is most successful when mentors act as a career counselor, while at the same time they are advocates who increase a protégé's visibility, accessibility, and promotability. The higher up a mentor is, the better, because he or she can do some PR work for the protégé and the advocacy will carry more influence. When interesting assignments come up, the mentor can throw out a suggested name. When a new job opportunity is in the offing, a mentor can guide a protégé through the process of meeting influential people, accumulating the right skills and experiences, or handling oneself in appropriate and positive ways. A mentor can be the magnet that helps pull a protégé upward. And this relationship is not an all-give-and-no-take experience. The mentor garners loyal support that can increase his or her power base, as well as increase access to feedback and information through the lower-level pipeline. It provides an opportunity for the mentor to grow by polishing and refining some of his or her own skills.[7] The value to the organization increases when relationships between mentor and mentee cross lines of difference.

All in all, mentoring can be a winning strategy for everyone. If a company is serious about developing and retaining diverse talent, we suggest a few essential steps that can add some substance and structure to a mentoring program. It is based on a process used years ago in working with the Council of Mexican-American Administrators, a group of educators in the Los Angeles Unified School District. There were two clear purposes, the first of which was to teach and groom those already functioning as administrators to be mentors so they could help other Hispanics be promoted. The other purpose was to design a program that would build the skill and confidence of the potential administrators they were trying to promote. To meet both goals, we did the following:

1. Consulted with the leadership of the organization to determine concrete outcomes they wanted from the mentoring program. This was helpful in forming the content and nature of the training.

2. Designed the training content to clearly differentiate the roles of the mentors from those of the protégés. Each role had different responsibilities. It was important to clarify expectations so accountability and success could occur. The training content was set up to increase self-confidence and performance by teaching specific skills such as risk-taking, self-reliance, dealing with conflict, and giving feedback effectively. While all the administrators in our program were Latino, they were either born in the United States or had been here so long that their acculturation into the norms and expectations for students and teachers in a major U.S. school district populated with mostly Latino students was not in question.

3. Mentors were paired with specific protégés in formal relationships. Mentors sought answers to specific questions from those at the top of the organization in order to provide necessary and useful information without raising false hopes. Some of them may be pertinent to your organization:

   • How do you make sure there is opportunity for mentees to have both line and staff experiences as you try to groom candidates?

   • Are you trying to build general skills? Skills for specialists? Operational skills? How can you build and provide experiences in all of them?

   • Both mentors and protégés need to be evaluated. What are some good ways to track performances for both? How long is the mentoring process and where are the evaluation points? How intermittent?

   • What feedback do we need from each part of the pair to assess the program's structure and its effectiveness? Are there parts they evaluate together? Some they do alone?

These are but a few of the questions that need to be addressed if an organization is going to use mentoring as more than a token tool to increase promotability and retention of minority candidates. Tracking the results is absolutely critical in order to find out what parts of the program are working and what needs to be improved. We expect that the dynamics between mentors and mentees will offer useful information in designing a continuously evolving program that increases chances of success. As you start your process, or consider doing so, look at the Table 14.1. The questions raised here are the ones that need answers if you expect worthwhile outcomes.

TABLE 14.1 | Mentoring-Process Guide: Steps To Ensure Success

Directions: Before you engage in any mentoring process, be sure you can have a sentence or two that clarifies each part of the process and what you expect from each as it is implemented.

- **Purpose and Objectives**
  What clear goals are we hoping to accomplish with our mentoring process?

- **Selection of Participants**
  How do we select participants from all backgrounds, units, and parts of the organization so that every group is reflected? What are the overall criteria and under what circumstances should there be flexibility?

- **Clarification of Roles/Expectations**
  What is expected of the mentor? List as many duties and responsibilities/ opportunities as possible. What is expected of the mentee? Make a similar list.

- **Training**
  Who is doing the training? Who are the trainers? (Internal, external or a mix?) What are the advantages and disadvantages of each? Is training conducted one-on-one or in groups?

- **Process/Mechanism**
  What are the different parts of the process? What are the measures for success? How much of the process is about upward mobility? How realistic is this? How much is about skill development and polish? Exposure? What is the length of the formal process?

- **Follow-up**
  When the formal process is over, how does the organization keep tracking progress and results?

- **Evaluation**
  What measures indicate success?

Cross-Cultural Coaching for Top Performance

Our guess is that if you did "Man on the Street" interviews and asked randomly selected people for examples of great coaches, most names would come from the ranks of competitive athletics. In the basketball world, John Wooden and Phil Jackson immediately come to mind. They stand out in part because of their winning records and championships, and in the case of John Wooden, UCLA's legendary icon, because he took teenage boys and helped guide them into becoming remarkable men. While athletic coaches provide us with some of the most visible models of excellence in coaching, they are by no means the only, or even the dominant model, as we apply coaching to the business world. A coach is the equivalent of a private tutor or personal trainer. Applied to a company's diversity effort, it entails a demonstrable commitment to the growth and grooming of employees who, like diamonds, will benefit from some polish. If done effectively, there is the chance that an employee can flourish as he or she moves up rather than washes out.

The Hows and Whys of Cross-Cultural Coaching

Whether an executive or mid-level employee is a potential star that could benefit from a little polishing, or someone who is already in a job and seems to leave havoc in his or her wake, coaching is a tool that, with an open and willing participant, can build insight, develop an awareness of one's impact on others, clarify the norms and expectations set by the organization, and provide the opportunity for a journey toward self improvement and increased effectiveness. Key factors that determine chances of success are the dynamics of and chemistry between the relationship of coach and client (or coachee). There is a much greater chance of achieving good results where there is competence by both parties and trust in the coaching relationship. And, as already mentioned, there is no substitute for being open to feedback and actually using some of it.

In implementing an individual plan for each employee, a coach needs many skills. The particulars can change and adapt, but four skills would be critical:

1. **Being a third-ear listener.** This means that a coach hears not only the words the client is telling you, but also the meaning behind the things a coachee or client cannot or does not say. A person's fears or feelings of inadequacy are difficult to talk about but a good coach might pick those feelings up. It means being able to anticipate questions that someone is unable to articulate. Sometimes these clues come from body language. Sometimes it is as simple as a statement to a coachee who heaves a deep sigh, which can be very telling: "Boy, that was a big sigh. What is that all about?" is a good example of third-ear listening.

2. **Being a good questioner.** This is one of the most critical skills in life, not just in coaching. One has to balance the need and desire to know more against the need to give the coachee space so you don't come across as too intrusive. There is the appropriate balance between asking open- and closed-ended questions. When do you want your client to explore different options? When you do, some open-ended question beginning with, "How might it ...? What if ... What possibilities could ...?" are great openers.

    On the other hand, there are times as a coach when a simple "yes" or "no," or some direct, explicit answer, is also important. "Was that strategy effective enough that you would use it again tomorrow if you could?" The "yes" or "no" follow-up to the direct question is, "Tell me why," which works with both the "yes" and the "no" answer.

3. **Having a cross-cultural lens.** For example, Japanese culture is no fan of hypothetical questions. U.S.-American culture is more direct than most so issues of time will be important in how you deliver questions to people reared elsewhere. You can ask direct questions with a tone that is soft and does not feel rushed, combative or urgent. Tone is a factor in communicating everywhere but being mindful of it in cross-cultural surroundings is even more essential.

4. **Attending to tone.** The importance of tone can be seen in feedback, which is a critical component of coaching. It is important to always give it in a helpful and tactful manner, but tact becomes even more critical when you give it to employees whose culture has norms around saving face. Depending on the coachee, a coach has to have a broad repertoire of ways to deliver an observation. One example of a direct statement is "From what you are telling me, it seems like you continually move your deadlines so urgent issues are placed at the top of the list but that makes it difficult to be seen as trustworthy and accountable when you are always changing priorities and people can't predict your delivery."

In a culture, or with a person who can't hear the directness, try this example: "If I hear you right, deadlines for reports due at the beginning of the month were not met. Is this true? How might your bosses or colleagues interpret this? What is the cost to you in regard to future career opportunities because usually, there will be a consequence?"

Every person you coach is different but the skills of being able to listen, ask good questions, and give feedback so one can actively hear it, are essential. Beyond these skills, it never hurts to be empathetic and really hear a client's pain or frustration, and it is invaluable to check your assumptions at the door (see Activity 14.3). The latest rage on the Internet is Susan Boyle, a singer discovered on the British version of *America's Got Talent*. This 47-year-old woman with huge aspirations to be a remarkable singer had people rolling their eyes and laughing at her huge ambition set against what was perceived to be an ordinary appearance. Then she started to sing and all the laughing and the assumptions stopped. It was a global reminder to not prejudge and assume … coaches have to be very mindful of this too, because they are human and it would be easy to do. As you work with the coachee over time and actually get to know the person better, the chance of assumptions coloring what you see and how you interpret behavior can lessen but they can also get locked in. Hold yourself accountable for an open point of view.

Finally, combining EQ and CQ are a winning combination for a coach. It will enable you to put that cultural lens on so that you can work with people in a way that is effective as you manage your own feelings and frustrations, while avoiding too much projecting about your own experiences as you work with coachees. Every good coach guards against such projection but there will be days, even for the most enlightened, when not projecting is difficult to accomplish. During moments such as these, give yourself permission to experience those feelings and insights without putting them on your coachee.

Activity 14.4 offers sample questions. What else you choose to ask will depend on the norms you are trying to teach. These norms will vary from one organization to another, but the key to the success of this undertaking remains teaching any unwritten rules that could sabotage the success of your protégé. Working with an attentive coach can help a potential promotee learn to be observant so he or she can continue the learning process.

Activity 14.5, *Coaching for Promotion*, is designed to help coaches uncover any biases or hidden expectations they may have about certain groups. This learning exercise needs to be conducted in a group setting. Divide people into small groups. Based on the background of the candidate, each group determines a coaching strategy. It is not until groups report on their respective strategies that participants realize that their strategies unconsciously influenced by the diversity factors suggested by the name, background, and ethnicity of the coachee. How would you coach a person who is Latino? What differences would it make if that person with the same qualifications were gay? In a wheel chair? An elder worker? In terms of opening up the system, it is important to see if expectations influence coaching. When each group reports its coaching strategy, you may not notice any differences between groups at all, but if different strategies do exist, they may provide good opportunity for discussion. What does this tell you about the coaching, inclusivity, and openness of this organization? A good facilitator will help you maximize the learning and determine any accommodations that need to be made.

The candidate we have used in the sample is Maryann Ransom, a lesbian who is a member of the Gay and Lesbian Rights Association. We suggest a few other examples, such as Roberta Rothstein, a Jewish woman who is active in the American Jewish

Federation; Luis Hernandez, a Latino active in the Mexican American Legal Defense Fund; and LaVerne Johnson, an African American who gives her time to the NAACP. Make up candidates pertinent to your employee population. Only the names, extracurricular organizations, and backgrounds change. All professional experiences and qualifications are the same. Therein lies the learning.

Implementing system-wide career development across cultures calls for nothing less than a paradigm shift in how career development is conducted. The very idea of career development—with its ladder stretching upward and its assumption that you reward individuals who like recognition and take responsibility for their own life and career—flies in the face of many of the cross-cultural norms we have discussed throughout this book. Furthermore, the focus on individual growth and rewarding the self for accomplishment is foreign to many cultures. By looking at values cross-culturally (see Activity 14.6), you will increase your understanding of their impact and be able to use organizational systems to enhance career opportunities for all. Beyond understanding cultural realities, it is also important to understand economic ones. With a very fragile economy and vulnerability in hanging on to jobs, this is not a time for a high amount of promotions, but there will be some and the economy will eventually rebound. This information is valid and may be more useful in post-recession days.

ACTIVITY 14.3 | Tips for Effective Cross-Cultural Coaching

As you read these tips, place a checkmark by any that you do regularly.

_____ 1. **Have an Appreciation for Different Cultures.** Select a coach who does not have an ax to grind about globalization, immigration, the younger generation, or any label or category. A coach has to be apprecia-tive of and accepting of all backgrounds to even begin the coaching process.

_____ 2. **Provide Support.** It is important to encourage risk-taking, assertiveness, and the ability to sell oneself or one's ideas if you coach people who want to succeed in U.S. businesses. By offering support and encouragement, as well as a good explanation about why this matters through values the coachee un-derstands, you can help increase a person's confidence, visibility, and, ultimately, promotability. It is also important to note that being supportive means that you have an ethical responsibility to ask some tough questions. Support means holding your client accountable and, on occasion, being a full-length mirror. Balancing empathy and honesty are doable and both are aspects of support.

_____ 3. **Give Helpful and Usable Feedback.** Imagine that, as a coach, you function like a digital camera taking pictures frequently. You make it your business to give your coachee usable information based on behav-iors you see firsthand. These behaviors focus on skills such as giving presentations, leading meetings, or representing the company at a public function. But the feedback doesn't have to be only skill-based. You may also give the coachee useful information about cultural norms that he violated or common organiza-tional practices that are career derailers if broken. Be careful of how you give the feedback. Chapter 6 gives you hints on how to do so effectively.

_____ 4. **Teach the Importance of Cause and Effect.** Doing this makes accountability both real and practical. In cultures where external locus of control is a strong concept, it is more difficult to teach the idea that what you do has consequences and your behavior triggers them. It is helpful not only to teach cause and effect, but also to help create more options so people rarely feel backed into corners and almost always see alternatives. In terms of professional growth and maturation, always looking for options is a critical concept.

_____ 5. **Point Out the Big (or Whole) Picture.** Perspective is a healthy coping strategy. The coaching journey should help coachees see that taking a risk may not always work out as initially imagined, and that's all right; gains can always be had from the learning and the results. Helping the coachee keep an eye on the big picture fosters a method of thinking that will serve an employee well over the long haul. While the details of each task or job responsibility matter, so does the learning gained and applied from every experience.

_____ 6. **Tailor the Teaching of Promotable Skills.** A topnotch coach is primarily an excellent teacher, and as with any good teaching, excellent coaching necessitates understanding the learner. People in different cultures and with different personalities and abilities think and learn differently. Is one culture's learning style more didactic? Is another's more hands-on? How much participation might an employee be used to? The sensitivity required in teaching skills needed, both individually and culturally, includes knowledge of cultural norms and customs, and also an understanding of the subtle but significant nuances of the protégé's acculturation. How much adaptation would be required to get this individual ready to make a presentation? What might be a comfortable way for her to present ideas by herself when all the work she has ever done has been as a team member? Where might the self-advocacy required for promotion cross the line and become personally and culturally diminishing?

_____ 7. **Create a Collaborative Partnership.** As a coach, you can be a person's professional confidante. As a partner or collaborator, you can help an employee define his or her goals. If he or she wants to become a mid-level manager, start pointing out how mid-level managers dress. Ask him or her to look at differences in dress at each level of the organization. Focus on certain behaviors and customs such as how people introduce one another, or whether first names or surnames are used when addressing colleagues. The learning exercise in Activity 14.5 is an example of the kind of worksheet you can give your apprentice as you try to coach him or her up the organization. It's sort of an "everything you wanted to know about promotion in this organization but were afraid to ask." Give the employee you are coaching worksheets like these, focusing on all the norms the protégé needs to learn. Set up appointments to discuss any observations and what the learning means to your particular student.

ACTIVITY 14.4 | Norms: The Unwritten Rules of This Organization

Directions: Take a few days to consciously observe behavior throughout the organization and then fill in your answers. Be prepared to discuss with your coach

Dress

What is the organizational uniform? How do people dress? Who wears suits? At what level are jackets required? Do women wear pants?

	Men	Women
Top executives		
Senior management		
Middle management		
Supervisors		
Firstline staff		
Other		

Communicating and Addressing

How are people addressed? (First name, title, etc.) How are people contacted?
(Phone call, e-mail, BlackBerry, memo, texting, etc.)

	Men	Women
Top executives		
Senior management		
Middle management		
Supervisors		
Firstline staff		
Other		

Employee Gatherings/Interacting

Who interacts with whom? If there are interaction taboos, what are they? Who invites whom? How much time is spent? Is promptness valued/expected?

	Format (Where, When, Interaction)	Participants (Who, Roles)
Meetings		
Breaks		
Lunch		
After work		

Suggestions for Using
"Norms: The Unwritten Rules of This Organization"

Objectives:

- Help potential managers learn the unwritten rules of behavior in your company

Intended Audience:

- Coaches working with potential promotees so they can teach them the "rules"
- Coachees attempting to learn the unwritten rules

Processing the Activity:

- Coachee uses the worksheet to make notes about observations.
- One-on-one discussion between coach and promotee.

Questions for Discussion:

- Use questions on the worksheet and whatever other questions the coach suggests.

Caveats and Considerations:

- It is possible for a trainer to bring coaches together and use a seminar format to collectively determine what the norms are so that all coaches in a given organization teach and reinforce the same ones.

ACTIVITY 14.5 | Coaching for Promotion

As a unit manager in systems planning, Maryann Ransom, a lesbian, has just come to work for you. She has a B.A. from a state university and graduated in the top third of the class. Her first job out of business school was as a management trainee at Merck, where she received excellent training in basic supervisory skills and computer programming. Working with you, her job duties will involve budget planning and analysis, project management, and supervision of a small group of data processors. References indicate good peer relationships, initiative, creativity, and great promise. Maryann is also an active member of the Gay and Lesbian Rights Association.

The quality of her work has been excellent; however, she has had little experience in some key areas required for the new job, such as personnel relations, EEOC and affirmative action guidelines, and hiring and interviewing skills.

1.   What are Maryann's greatest assets? In what areas does she need the most development?

2.   What would you do to help groom Maryann for promotion?

3.   How would you coach her to develop the skills and experiences necessary to move up in the organization?

4.   List 10 steps you would take or suggest to enhance Maryann's development and career success.

Suggestions for Using
"Coaching for Promotion"

Objectives:

- Determine whether people are coached differently because of ethnicity, race, gender, or other dimensions of diversity
- Detect any biases in who is promoted and how people are coached

Intended Audience:

- Facilitator, consultant, HR professional, or trainer charged with the task of helping mid- and upper-level management personnel examine biases in how people are coached

Processing the Activity:

- Use the worksheet, changing only the name and background of the person, and keeping the criteria the same and creating a number of different individual profiles.
- Divide people into small groups. Have them discuss coaching strategy and then report back to the entire group about their strategy.
- Write strategies on chart paper.
- After each group reports its coaching strategy, discuss what differences emerge based on background.

Questions for Discussion:

- What differences in coaching exist?
- Depending on what factors? How can they be minimized?

Caveats and Considerations:

- Make certain that the different employee populations in your geographic area are represented in the profiles.
- Don't let participants know that candidate names are different but qualities are the same for all profiles.

ACTIVITY 14.6 | Impact of Values on Career Expectations and Performance

Point of Contact	Mainstream Culture	Other Cultures
Interview	I need to showcase my experience, skills, and talents.	My track record and seniority speak for themselves. I need to establish a relationship and get comfortable with the other person first.
Performance review	I need feedback so I can do a better job.	Criticism could cause me to lose face and feel shame.
Meetings	Making suggestions and actively participating show I am motivated and take the initiative.	Contributing my ideas, asking questions, voicing complaints, or making suggestions look like I am showing off and may make my boss lose face. Besides, ideas and suggestions need to come from the leader.
Socializing/networking	I'm going to these events because you never know who will be there. The visibility can't hurt my career.	I will go to this event because my boss asked me to and I wouldn't let her down.
Mentoring	I'd like the CEO to be my mentor because he has the clout in this organization. If he's in my corner, it will certainly help.	I like my boss, Miss Shirley. She is a very nice person who treats me with respect.
Self-promotion	Expected and rewarded; to paraphrase American Express, "Don't expect a promotion without it."	Very difficult for other cultures; it would be embarrassing and a violation of some of the most sacrosanct norms to toot your own horn.
Forming alliances	Pragmatic in the dominant culture; people and organizations are political. This is a survival skill.	Inclusion in the group and relationships are critical. They are formed because of personal loyalty and affection, not because of position in the organization.
Social skills; ice breaking; establishing rapport	The dominant culture is short on social lubrication, long on getting right to the point. Self-introduction is accepted and sometimes expected.	This skill could be a natural ally for most other cultures where far more time is invested in relationships. Formal introductions are expected. Individuals may be reluctant to establish relationships outside of their own group.
Giving and getting feedback	Needed and expected skills for one's growth; "If you don't give me feedback, how can I know what I need to do differently or better?" Done in the good old American way—directly. Separation of the behavior from the worth of a person makes it more objective and less personal.	This is very delicate in other cultures. Loss-of-face warrants shame. People have left jobs because of negative feedback and the perception of disgrace. Feedback is often taken personally and seen as a personal affront.
Tapping the grapevine	Skeptical of informal communication. There is a tendency to believe what is in print and official.	Those out of power generally make the greatest use of the grapevine and are often skeptical of official information channels.
Scheduling/goal-setting	Task and time consciousness, coupled with linear thinking and planning matter. Anything can be done or accomplished if the individual works hard enough. Each person is responsible for his or her own success or failure.	Time is relative and the accomplishment of tasks depends on more than the individual alone. Other priorities often change schedules and plans. Fate and the will of God play a part.

HR departments responsible for career development and promotion of diverse employees need to look at the formal systems such as performance review, interviewing, recruiting, and mentoring, as well as the informal systems such as socializing, networking, and support groups. For a career development system to work, it has to be both top down and bottom up. The *Career Development Framework* in Table 14.2 shows some of the major pieces needed.

TABLE 14.2 | Career Development Framework

1. **Top down:** Build career development through all the systems. Some examples are:
   - Performance review
   - Recruitment/hiring/promotion
   - Accountability
   - Training

2. **Bottom up:** Conduct skill training for managers and employees in various diversity-related areas. Some examples are:
   Managers:
   - Giving performance reviews in culturally sensitive ways
   - Handling intercultural conflict
   - Running effective meetings in a diverse environment
   - Conducting interviews in culturally appropriate ways
   - Building effective multicultural work teams
   - Recognizing cultural biases in making promotions
   - Expanding the list of valued management characteristics

   Employees:
   - Building connections
   - Becoming politically savvy
   - Learning to position ideas effectively
   - Managing and becoming comfortable with change
   - Becoming comfortably assertive
   - Gaining self-promotion skills

The importance of this model is in the realization that making room at the top involves not only systems changes with leadership and buy-in at the highest levels but also training for managers and entry-level employees. Managers used to dealing with a homogeneous workforce need new skills and information, and employees from all over need to be more fluent with different behavior and norms worldwide. Attracting, developing, and maintaining the top talent requires nothing less than an open attitude, flexibility, and recognition of the world's pluralism. The payoff will be worth it. What Stephen M. Wolfe of United Airlines said about women is applicable to all employees in an organization that makes room for diverse talent at all levels: "Fortunately, U.S. society is learning that not only can women succeed in just about any arena, but the qualities they bring to the competition raise the level of the entire playing field."[8]

In terms of long-term organizational effectiveness and success, probably nothing is more critical to an organization than how it builds, uses, nurtures, and develops its people. This chapter has given you information and raises questions for you to consider about how you manage and develop your talent. While we offer suggestions, we cannot provide magic. The magic takes place between the people engaged in these development relationships, and in the organization's intention and commitment to making it happen in both good and tough times.

CHAPTER 15.

Evaluation and Measurement: Tracking the Effects of Diversity Initiatives

• •

This chapter will provide you with:

- Guidelines for designing an evaluation strategy
- Methods of measurement and sources of hard and soft data for tracking diversity initiatives
- A model of the five levels of evaluation and their purposes in measurement
- Samples of typical diversity-and-inclusion metrics

How to measure the results of diversity initiatives is one of the most frequently asked questions as well as one of the most difficult aspects to address in implementing diversity and inclusion. Complicating the issue is that diversity interventions don't take place in a vacuum. Rather, there are always confounding variables, a variety of other events, changes, and factors in the external environment, in the organization, and in the lives of employees that may impact the results of any diversity changes. How much of the reduction in employee turnover is due to the newly instituted mentoring and flextime programs and how much to an economic slump and higher unemployment? What part of the increase in discrimination complaints and suits is due to the ineffectiveness of diversity programs, and what part is due to the recent downsizing with its accompanying lay-offs?

Another factor that often makes evaluation difficult is that too often it begins toward the end of the change process rather than being built in from the beginning. Finally, the target objectives of diversity initiatives are often unclear or poorly defined so that evaluation efforts can't be accurately targeted.

Measurement is an essential component of any change process for a number of reasons. As the saying goes, "What gets measured, gets done," and measuring results increases the chances that progress will be made. Measuring also provides feedback that helps an organization learn. It generates information that keeps the process on target, eliminating ineffective aspects and helping to refine what is working well. It also supplies data that can be used to demonstrate the effectiveness of the effort to decision-makers and potential cynics, thereby building support and reducing doubt about the initiative's value to the organization. Measurement also demands a discipline and rigorousness that helps build a strategic, targeted, and efficient process. Finally, evaluation that demonstrates results energizes and motivates those involved in implementing the initiative. Seeing clearly their accomplishment through measurable data is an esteem and energy boost for them.

Gathering Baseline Data

Measurement is essentially a comparative process. Gathering data with nothing to compare them to gives you little evaluative information. Therefore, measurement requires both baseline data (what are conditions before we start?) as well as clear criteria against which to measure any change (what do we want to achieve or gain in this process?)

The first step in measurement, then, is to gather baseline data about current conditions. Relevant information can be collected from a number of sources.

Existing Organizational Data

Reports and computers in your organization contain valuable information that describes current conditions. Affirmative action plans, EEO complaints, and grievances, as well as turnover and absenteeism statistics, present pieces of the total picture. Existing employee satisfaction survey results also shed light on factors relevant to diversity. These data provide even more insight when statistics are compared by group. For example, is there higher turnover among females than males? What is the dollar cost of turnover to your organization? Is there a higher percentage of EEO complaints in less-diverse divisions? Is there a greater rate of absenteeism among a specific group of employees? Is there a significant difference in satisfaction levels of employees by ethnicity, job classification, or gender? What do customer satisfaction ratings show?

Diversity Surveys

Many organizations get additional baseline information by conducting a diversity survey. This can be done using a random sample or by asking all employees to respond to an electronic or paper-and-pencil survey. It is important that the tool used is carefully tailored and constructed to provide the information you need. It should also supply enough demographic data about informants to help you pinpoint issues and problems. It is critical that the format encourages employees to participate. In one client organization, a one-page, 10-item team-development scale was used because leaders knew that rough-and-ready field staff would not spend time on a lengthy questionnaire. Other organizations have considered using a telephone survey response system to overcome the resistance to paper-and-pencil and online instruments. Such a survey, which is frequently used in the assessment phase of data gathering, can become the pretest against which post-test results can be compared.

Focus Groups

Having employees, in groups of eight to 12 people, discuss their perceptions of obstacles, issues, and conditions is another way to obtain pertinent information. Discussions need to be led by skilled facilitators who keep the group on track and make sure data are captured either by taking notes or taping the discussions.

The baseline data collected then give you information that can help set the objectives for interventions as well as a picture of existing conditions against which you can measure the results of any changes. They can also provide statistics to bolster the business rationale for your initiative.

Setting Clear Criteria Up Front

When asked how they would know that the desired culture change had been accomplished, a team at one organization responded enthusiastically, "Rest rooms!" Expanding on their answer, team members explained that tidy rest rooms with no graffiti on walls or trash on floors would be a sign of commitment and belonging by all employees. This refreshingly unusual approach to setting clear and measurable criteria is creative, tangible, and powerful. However, most organizations would require additional measures that tie to organizational objectives. Criteria such as these are examples:

* Reduction of turnover of female sales representatives by 25 percent
* Increased satisfaction of all employees by 10 percent and reduced satisfaction disparities between groups by 50 percent
* Demographics of management-level employees more closely matched to that of our total workforce
* Reduction of the number of customer complaints by 25 percent

Allstate Insurance Company, having what has been called a "world-class diversity program," set these four clear criteria:[1]

- Our process must be "best in class."
- We must attract and retain customers at the highest rate in the industry.
- We must provide our shareholders with a superior rate of return.
- Our employees must be able to say that they are personally fulfilled and proud to work here.

To assess progress toward meeting these criteria, Allstate instituted a measurement system that would track objectives for employees, shareholders, and customers. For example, employees' effectiveness measures include a diversity index, a leadership index, and an education index.[2]

To be helpful in evaluation, criteria need to be specific and measurable. While creating a more inclusive environment, a more tolerant workplace, or an organization where differences are valued and leveraged may be laudable goals of a diversity change process, they are too diffuse to be accurately measured. Evaluation criteria need to specify, for example, the concrete signs of an inclusive environment, tolerant workplace, or the valuing and leveraging of diversity. Fewer complaints and grievances related to specific diversity dimensions such as age, gender, race, sexual orientation, ethnicity, or religion might be an indication of increased tolerance. Another might be more mixed seating in the cafeteria.

Criteria also need to be outcomes that can realistically be expected from a particular intervention. For example, while culture change may be the long-term goal, awareness training cannot legitimately be expected to accomplish that feat. It can, however, be expected to reduce the number of e-mail jokes and slurs targeted at particular groups.

Focusing Measurement: What to Evaluate

Most diversity initiatives are multifaceted with a variety of activities, interventions, and processes implemented simultaneously. Robert Hayles and Armida Mendez Russell in their book, *The Diversity Directive*,[3] suggest the following six key areas for measurement.

1. *Program evaluation.* Diversity events and activities such as training sessions, mentoring programs, celebrations, or pay equity analyses should be evaluated.
2. *Representation.* The demographic composition and changes regarding the flow in, up, and out of the organization should be measured with an aim toward equity of representation.
3. *Workplace climate.* Measuring the quality of work life, especially across groups in the organization, also aims at equability.
4. *Benchmarks and best practices.* Comparing the organization to exemplary organizations provides another measure.
5. *External recognition.* Gaining some award as the best in a particular arena is still another form of evaluation. Being listed as one of the best organizations for working mothers or "minorities" would be an example of such recognition.
6. *Relating diversity to overall performance.* Connecting diversity work to the attainment of key organizational objectives is the final area of measurement.

The Conference Board report *Corporate Practices in Diversity Measurement*[4] also suggests six areas in which to focus evaluation efforts:

1. Demographics
2. Organizational culture
3. Productivity, growth, and profitability
4. Benchmarking
5. Programmatic measures
6. Accountability

While the first five are similar to the Hayles-Russell list, the last one, accountability, expands the focus to include the use of review processes such as 360° feedback and peer review as well as tying diversity-related objectives to incentives and bonuses. "Management Diversity Commitment and Guidelines for Specific Actions"[5] demonstrates Aetna's accountability measures, which specify management actions in four areas: leadership, awareness, integration, and performance. For example, two leadership actions suggested are making diversity a periodic agenda item for staff meetings and mentoring a woman or person of color. An awareness action suggested is to tap employee diversity networks as a resource for marketing and customer service. These specific actions translate diversity objectives into measurable accountabilities.

Wherever the focus, evaluation efforts fall into two categories: process and results. In the realm of process, the questions center around:

- Did we do what we set out to do?
- How well did we do it?
- What needs to be changed to do it better?

In the results domain, the key questions are:

- Did it make a difference?
- What is the impact on organizational objectives?
- What improvements can be seen resulting from this?
- Did it achieve the results set out in the organization's criteria?

While both are important to measure, it is critical that the two not be confused in the strategy. Each answers different questions and calls for different methods and measures. The following model of the levels of evaluation offers guidance in measuring both process and results.

A Diversity-and-Inclusion Scorecard

Many organizations have developed a scorecard of diversity-and-inclusion metrics that is used to assess progress and hold leaders accountable. Table 15.1 is an example of metrics that are commonly used.

TABLE 15.1 | Examples of Diversity-and-Inclusion Metrics

Representation
- Workforce count by business unit, location related to level/status, race/ethnicity, gender, age, job classification, etc.

- Percentage of minorities and women in executive and other leadership positions (e.g., director, manager, and supervisor)

Talent Management
- Percentage of minorities in candidate pools

- Turnover (voluntary and involuntary) by business unit/department regarding race/ethnicity, gender, age, and job classification

- Applicants, transfers, and new hires by business unit/department regarding race/ethnicity, gender, age, and job classification

- Promotions by business unit/department regarding race/ethnicity, gender, age, and job classification

- Dollars spent per employee on training and education

- Number and/or percentage of leadership (executive to supervisor) attending diversity training

- Number and/or percentage of managers and professional staff attending diversity training

- Overall number and/or percentage of workforce attending diversity training

- Number of and dollars spent on diversity-related conferences/seminars/events

- Employee satisfaction scores by business unit/department regarding race/ethnicity, gender, age, position, seniority, and other relevant categories

---

Customer Satisfaction
- Customer satisfaction scores by race/ethnicity, gender, age compared to population

- Customer satisfaction scores related to business units/departments

- Percentage of returns of Customer Satisfaction Survey by race/ethnicity, gender, and age

---

Supply Chain Management
- Number of diverse suppliers (MBE, WBE, VET, SBE) by business unit/department
- Number of bid packages that contained diverse suppliers
- Spending with diverse supplier by business unit/department
- Spending with premier diverse supplier by business unit/department
- Percentage of overall spending with diverse suppliers
- Percent increase of diversity spending from prior year
- Dollars spent with direct second-tier suppliers and contractors

---

Five Levels of Evaluation

Marsha Mondschein of MEASURIT, a consulting organization specializing in tracking training impact, offers guidance in evaluating diversity initiatives at various stages through the following Five-Level Tracking Model (see Figure 15.1). Since not all levels need to be tackled for each aspect of diversity implementation, this model helps clarify which are the most appropriate questions to be asked and what kinds of measures need to be used for different interventions.

FIGURE 15.1 The Five-Level Tracking Model

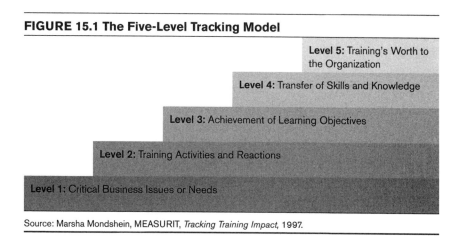

Level 5: Training's Worth to the Organization

Level 4: Transfer of Skills and Knowledge

Level 3: Achievement of Learning Objectives

Level 2: Training Activities and Reactions

Level 1: Critical Business Issues or Needs

Source: Marsha Mondshein, MEASURIT, *Tracking Training Impact,* 1997.

Level 1, Critical Business Issues or Needs, centers around determining what the important issues, problems, or obstacles are that indicate a need to take action. These are best determined by working in partnership with those who own the problem and who care about its solution. Your initial audit-assessment process undoubtedly uncovered these obstacles and problems, and their connection to the bottom line was probably part of the business case made to decision-makers early in your diversity strategic planning. Are you missing out of gaining a share of an expanding market? Are diversity obstacles hampering teamwork and productivity? Are you losing the retention war? The more clearly these barriers and problems are defined, the easier will be the ultimate evaluation at Level 5.

At Level 2, Training Activities and Reactions, measurement focuses on participation in and reaction to diversity events, programs, and initiatives. How many employees took part in your diversity day celebration and how did they rate the experience? What is the number of mentor-protégé pairs in your mentoring program and how do they evaluate the process? What suggestions would they make for improvement? This kind of measurement is often referred to as the "smile sheet" evaluation because of the reaction rating sheets that are usually collected at the end of training seminars.

At Level 3, Achievement of Learning Objectives, measurement begins to track results. Were the objectives of the intervention achieved? Did the establishment of on-site day care reduce absenteeism of working parents? Did the addition of flexible benefits attract a wider range of recruits? Did the mentoring program result in any promotions or a higher degree of retention? Did trainees demonstrate a mastery of concepts and skills learned in the workshop?

At Level 4, Transfer of Skills and Knowledge, application on the job is the focus. How are trainees using skills learned when they interact with customers of different backgrounds?

What new markets or deeper inroads into less-tapped markets have been made? How much natural mentoring with direct reports is now being done by former official program mentors? How much voluntary diversity recruitment is now being done by managers without asking human resources for a slate of candidates?

Finally, at Level 5, Training's Worth to the Organization, the evaluation measures what difference the intervention makes to the organization. What are the cost savings in reduced absenteeism of working parents or lowered turnover? What is the benefit to the organization in a more diverse management team? What is the return on investment (ROI)? One company could attribute the gain of a new client organization to the diversity of its project team. Demonstrating their own diversity to the potential client organization got them the business. American Express Financial Advisors and St. Paul Companies connect their success in expanding markets to diversity.[6] Avon and Pillsbury[7] attribute their increasing share of ethnic and Hispanic markets respectively to recruitment, development, and retention of staff with diversity knowledge and skills.

Even "soft" interventions such as training can have results measurable at Level 5. Allstate Insurance Company used a simple but relevant method. To measure the effect of their diversity awareness training, they simply added one question to the regularly administered satisfaction survey. By asking respondents to indicate whether or not they had attended diversity training, they could compare survey results of those who had and hadn't participated. The results were dramatic: Those who had attended showed a significantly higher level of satisfaction in general and higher scores on many of the other relevant measures. The case was made that the training did have a positive impact on employee performance. While there may be no hard data to compute the exact dollar amount of this return, there was an intuitive understanding that more satisfied employees were also more productive ones.

A powerful aspect of measurement at Level 5 is demonstrating ROI, return on investment, in financial terms. This dollars-and-cents analysis tells the organization not just what was saved or gained by a particular program, but what its return was in relation to resources expended. It requires keen financial analysis to quantify the costs necessary to the computation. Both direct and indirect costs, such as the hidden cost of employee time away from regular duties, are needed. However, it can be computed by using the following formula:

$$\text{Computing ROI}$$
$$\text{ROI (\%)} = \frac{\text{Gross Benefits or Savings} - \text{Program Costs}}{\text{Program Costs}} \times 100$$

All program costs are subtracted from gross benefits or savings to determine the net return of the program. This figure is then divided by the program costs (the investment) and multiplied by 100 to calculate the percentage of return on investment. If the reduced turnover resulting from a flextime program saved the organization $150,000 in recruiting and training outlays and cost the organization $50,000 in extra benefits, the ROI would be 200 percent. For every dollar spent, the organization received two.

$$\text{ROI (\%)} \quad \frac{\$150{,}000 - \$50{,}000}{\$50{,}000} \times 100 = 200\%$$

Once you have determined what part of your diversity strategy you are measuring and what levels of evaluation you will be tracking, you are ready to select the appropriate data to use. Table 15.2 provides some examples of the types of "hard" and "soft" data that can be gathered for use in measurement. Hard data come in the form of statistics that can be analyzed and compared. Soft data, on the other hand, are more phenomenological, giving the perceptions and opinions of respondents. Rather than quantitative, they are more qualitative in content.

A diversity council or action team working on a particular intervention can help in planning the evaluation strategy. Activity 15.1 might stimulate the generation of potential sources of data to be used in tracking results.

TABLE 15.2 | Examples of Sources of Data for Measurement/Evaluation

Hard Data	Soft Data
• Demographic representation	• Diversity audit
• EEO grievances and complaints	• Employee satisfaction surveys
• EEO and AA statistics	• Customer satisfaction surveys
• Lawsuits and settlements	• Focus group reports
• Promotions	• Testimonial data
• Turnover and retention rates	• Performance appraisal ratings
• Accidents	• Use of
• Safety violations	• Use of suggestion box, input system
• Absenteeism	• Exit interviews
• Languages spoken	• On-the-job observation
• Productivity measures (e.g., output, money collected, forms processed, defective products, customers visited, units assembled)	• Program evaluations
• Recruiting costs	
• Sales figures	
• Workers' compensation claims	
• Response time	
• Overtime utilization	
• Market share	
• Return from leave rates	
• Utilization of benefits	
• Training costs	

ACTIVITY 15.1 | Data Sources for Evaluation and Measurement in Your Organization

	Hard Data	Soft Data
Existing		
Need to Collect		

Suggestions for Using
"Evaluation and Measurement of Data Sources in Your Organization"

Objectives:

- Identify data sources for use in measurement and evaluation
- Generate discussion about and creativity in tapping data sources

Intended Audience:

- Diversity council or task force members designing evaluation strategy
- Leaders and managers giving input to evaluation strategy

Processing the Activity:

- Facilitator leads a discussion of evaluation levels and purposes, as well as hard and soft data.
- Participants working individually fill out the chart listing sources of data.
- Participants form small groups, pooling their information, charting, and then reporting collected responses.
- Facilitator leads total-group discussion of prime sources and methods for gathering needed data.

Questions for Discussion:

- Where do we have the most data already?
- What would we need to do with existing data to make them useful?
- What data do we still need?
- What are the best ways to get them?

Caveats, Considerations, and Variations:

- The organization needs to be prepared for and willing to deal with any data that are collected.
- There may be confidentiality issues and personnel policies governing the use of some sources.

Guidelines for Effective Evaluation

Maximize the use of existing data and processes.

Using existing sources or processes as much as possible reduces resistance because it is less disruptive and more integrated into regular operations. Adding questions or demographic categories to an existing survey rather than creating an additional one can be more effective with a "surveyed out" staff. Adding a short checklist to the exit interview process can capture data you might not otherwise obtain.

Select the appropriate level of measurement and data source for the question you want to answer.

Pre- and post-tests will show knowledge gained in training (Level 3), but not whether or how well that knowledge is applied on the job (Level 4) or whether it resulted in a higher volume of sales (Level 5). Comparing the demographic composition of management staff before and after the mentoring program may tell you if you reached the objective of diversifying management (Level 3), but not what worked and didn't (Level 2) so you can improve the process. Neither can it show how a more diverse group of managers benefits the organization (Level 5).

Allow a reasonable time interval between pre- and post-report assessments.

When aiming at behavior change or skill acquisition, measurement expert Marsha Mondschein advises a minimum of three months and a maximum of six months as an appropriate interval between pre- and post-testing to obtain a meaningful assessment.

Make the evaluation strategy an integral part of each intervention's plan as well as the overall diversity process.

Identifying specific measurement criteria, collecting baseline data at the beginning, and planning to gather appropriate tracking data will give you the most accurate evaluation and prevent you from overlooking important findings. These processes need to be made part of each diversity intervention.

Be prepared for the full spectrum of data—the "good" and the "bad."

While dips in post-test scores or increases in complaints can feel defeating, they are often a sign of progress. Increased awareness often leads to higher expectations and greater sensitivity to problems at initial stages. It does not necessarily mean that things are worse. It may indicate that people are more acutely aware and/or less willing to accept long-standing problems. It may also indicate a greater level of trust and/or a belief that someone is taking input seriously. Assessment data can also tell you where your intervention is veering off target. One organization providing awareness training to all staff received some unexpected but valuable feedback. Opting for a train-the-trainer approach to increase flexibility, relevance, and ownership among staff, they obtained data that indicated staff had different priorities for the training. Participants wanted more consistency of training and suggested that it be provided by a smaller number of facilitators for whom this would be a major job responsibility. Trainers could then offer deeper expertise and greater content knowledge, as well as a more consistent program.

Don't ignore testimonial, soft data.

The human touch of individual stories and quotes can be extremely impactful in evaluating outcomes. Diversity is both a head and a heart issue, and statements such as the following often have a powerful emotional impact:

- "I'm a better person at home as a result of working here. I go home fulfilled."
- "I'm doing things in my community now because of what I've found out through this process."
- "I spoke up about a prejudicial remark I would have previously let pass."
- "I took a risk and learned from someone I would never have spoken to before this."

While such soft data are generally insufficient to demonstrate the full picture of results, they can be an effective complement to the analytical left-brain statistics and graphs, putting a human face on the numbers.

Treat evaluation and measurement as a circle, not a line.

Evaluation, like managing diversity and inclusion, is a process rather than an event. It serves the organization best when it is ongoing and self-propelling, continuing to loop back with more data that reshape the initiative and suggest the next phases of growth.

SECTION 3
An External Focus for Diversity

CHAPTER 16.

Corporate Social Responsibility, Sustainability, and Diversity: A Strategic Partnership

· ·

This chapter will provide you with:

- An understanding of the connection between corporate social responsibility, sustainability, and diversity

- Questions to consider in creating a partnership between your CSR, sustainability, and diversity processes

- Several examples of ways organizations are using these three pillars to make a difference beyond their walls

- Ways to integrate supplier diversity into this process

When we try to pick out anything
by itself ... we will find it hitched to
everything else in the universe.

—JOHN MUIR

The first time we heard of corporate social responsibility (CSR), it was in the mid-1990s and we were working in London with British Telecom. It was common for some European corporations to make their business decisions based in part by how those decisions impacted the larger community they served and in which they operated. In those days, there was little conversation about global warming or of being green, and the discussion of carbon footprints was almost nonexistent. What's more, a focus on intentionally being a good corporate citizen in the local and global community was not yet a major part of the conversation in the United States. The idea was inspiring, and we wished that somehow, even in our Wall Street-driven short-term culture, there would be room for these conversations. Since then, the coming together of this critical need, increased awareness about the health of the planet, and the desire to behave differently have made CSR something that is part of the conversation in corporations and organizations in the United States and around the world. There is a new ethos, visible and growing, that being good stewards of our planet and being good members in a global community matter. It is about survival, it is about responsibility, and, at a practical level, it is about branding and polishing corporate image. If you can do well and do good at the same time, everybody wins. Examples of good work and promising results are numerous. We'll share just a few.

Walmart, in its *2007-2008 Sustainability Progress Report*, cites some moving and inspiring examples of its commitment.[1] The company begins by saying that since it operates in 14 countries with close to 2 million associates, it knows that its carbon footprint is huge. From aspects as concrete as the vast transportation system that trucks their goods to the amount of waste from the packaging of all their products, this corporation knows it can, and believes it must, make a difference on the sustainability front. It is capitalizing on the necessity of being a responsible global citizen to increase its impact in a positive way wherever it operates in communities worldwide. According to the *Sustainability Report*, Walmart's global impact encompasses creating jobs in the same communities where shoppers can save money buying necessary goods while also generating tax revenues to help the local tax base. In one Mexican community, they support the handiwork of local artists. They sell crafts made by local women in Superana and Sam's Club locations, giving 100 percent of the proceeds directly back to the communities where the crafts are made.

Walmart is not alone. Target is also a major contributor when it comes to CSR. Giving money to local schools to enhance learning and to the Los Angeles Police Department to develop an automated Citywide Crime and Resources Dashboard to make the community safer are just two of the many ways that the company improves local communities and life for the people who live in them. Target has been a pioneer, annually dedicating 5 percent of its income to making positive changes in the community since 1962, long before it was fashionable. On average, this retailer and its employees give $3 million a week plus countless volunteer hours.[2]

CSR has become almost a public relations necessity in the business world, so what is it? According to *Source Watch*, it is defined by advocates as "aligning a company's activities with the social, economic, and environmental expectations of its stakeholders."[3] While there are no regulations in the CSR field, it is a tool used by many large organizations to polish, promote or improve their public image while they also try to make a positive difference to consumers in their local and global communities. They can score PR points for their brand if they commit to and actually achieve some worthy goals such as investing in better education in their own neighborhoods, helping fund research in health care and the environment, or creating jobs in communities that need the tax base and resources.

In the process of doing research on the connection between CSR, sustainability, and diversity, we interviewed Shaheen Husain, the Executive Director of Corporate Relations and Business Development at the Paul Merage School of Business, University of California, Irvine. Because we believe that the field of diversity is moving in a direction that will take the connection between CSR, diversity, and sustainability, and integrate it into business strategies, we asked Husain to share her thoughts on what considerations and knowledge would be critical for diversity directors or OD practitioners to help move this process forward.

Truisms about CSR

Support from the Top and Throughout

Husain believes that an initiative of this magnitude needs the clout of an executive who has power, influence, and resources. To have any gravitas in organizations, these three strategic pillars need to be integrated into a core business strategy. The vision, thinking, support, purpose, accountability, and leadership all have to start at the executive level. Since CSR aims at creating partnerships, implementation and application need to be done at all levels and with all groups in the organization. Conversations need to be about priorities, resources, policies, behaviors, and benefits at every level.

There Isn't a Single Approach

CSR cuts through all kinds of companies. Big corporations, small entrepreneurial business, NGOs, in short, any kind of business, institution or foundation can engage in this process, and the impact can go from small and local to big and global. While in the broad sense, CSR expects organizations to form partnerships with constituents in communities to accomplish worthy goals, how this is done differs by industry, geography, goals, resources, and so many other factors.

To Take Root, CSR Needs To Be Integrated Into the Business

It is tied to the vision, mission, and business of the organization. As such it has to be integrated into how business is done and practiced, which requires partnering with diversity and consciously attending to inclusion and exclusion. If it isn't, it won't materialize.

The Accountability Needs Validation

There is story after story and example after example that tout what organizations are doing regarding CSR. The question remains, who is validating these results? Is there an objective, outside party with no vested interest to vouch for the method and results that substantiate the claims? Historically, statistics have been bent to make cases, both good and bad, as a way to influence perception. A great deal of energy and resources are being invested towards doing good work on many fronts with "doing well by doing good" as the goal. PR machines are talented, able mechanisms that can easily publicize goals, values, and objectives. Vigilance is needed to make sure that there is validity both to the work espoused and the results advertised.

The CSR sustainability process is a detailed and demanding one that requires hard work and dogged determination. Consistency and focus are important, but intentionality is equally so. Raising awareness and asking people to purposely make choices that go beyond personal self-interest can engage and capture people's innate quest to make a difference in a way that brings fundamental meaning to work.

FIGURE 16.1 | The CSR Sustainability Process

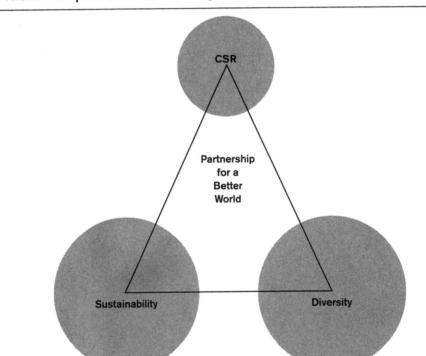

Let's look at Walmart again to see how its process engages employees of all groups and levels, and demonstrates the partnership between CSR, sustainability, and diversity. The Personal Sustainability Project (PSP) is a voluntary project started in 2006. Its emphasis is on helping associates integrate sustainability into their lives every day, starting with small changes. As of September 2007, here are just a few examples of contributions as reported by employees.

They have recycled the following:

- 675,538 pounds of aluminum
- 5,953,357 pounds of paper and cardboard
- 282,476 pounds of glass

At a personal level:

- They have lost combined weight of 184,315 pounds through PSP
- 19,924 have quit or reduced smoking
- Several hundred thousand employees have gotten friends and family involved

What makes this PSP inspiring is that there is room for employees to participate as a group and feel cohesion in ways that are personally meaningful to them, even involving their families. It improves engagement at individual and collective levels, and whether it involves personal health (less smoking) or the collective good of recycling, a positive difference is being made.

This is hard work that takes time. Quick bursts of good PR won't get it done. Bill Gates often speaks about his passion to help eradicate malaria and help lessen the losses and devastation of HIV/AIDS mainly in Africa. What struck us, in addition to his total commitment, is his realistic view that it will probably take 20 years before his goal is achieved.

Supplier Diversity: A Key Element of Inclusion and Corporate Responsibility

While most organizations include supplier diversity in their overall diversity-and-inclusion strategy, there is a critical link between supplier diversity, corporate responsibility, and the organization's diversity-and-inclusion process. Attention to supplier diversity builds the organization's reputation and generates support in the community. It also helps the community increase prosperity and provides jobs, which enhances the economy and stability of the area.

As with other CSR and diversity change initiatives, measurement and accountability are key. As our teacher and mentor, John Jones, used to say, "What gets measured gets done and what gets rewarded gets repeated." Typically, goals and measures for supplier diversity focus on:

- Number of diverse suppliers (MBE, WBE, VET, SBE) by business unit, department, or division.
- Number of bid packages containing diverse suppliers.
- Dollars spent with diverse suppliers overall by business unit, department, or division.
- Dollars spent with a specific diverse supplier by business unit, department, or division.
- Percent increase of dollars spent with diverse suppliers.

Enhancing Supplier Diversity

A number of steps taken to enhance the success of supplier diversity initiatives are used in organizations across the country.

- Supplier diversity mentoring, training, and development are used to support minority suppliers to gain business skills and access to contracts. Diversity Inc's Top 10 Companies for

Supplier Diversity[6] all provide formal mentoring or training for diverse suppliers, and nine of the 10 also provide financial assistance, which usually consists of low-interest loans.

- Report cards, showing dollars spent with diverse suppliers, are shared with CEOs, boards, and government officials, and the media hold organizations publicly accountable for business with all of the community.
- Awards given by specific groups and media outlets further publicize organizations' effectiveness with supplier diversity, either enhancing or detracting from their reputations.
- Communication and outreach through supplier diversity sections on web sites and connection with diverse supplier organizations such as the National Minority Supplier Development Council (NMSDC) help get the word out to diverse vendors. Soliciting information and maintaining lists of diverse suppliers is another helpful strategy organizations use.

The McDonald's diagram in Figure 16.2 provides a look at how the company integrates supplier diversity with CSR and sustainability, and illustrates the interconnection of these processes.[7]

FIGURE 16.2 | McDonald's Priorities: Achieving Sustainable Success

Sustainability

When people hear the term "sustainability," most think of ecology, the natural environment, conservation, and recycling. However, it also pertains to the social environment, how people use resources, and sustain their quality of life. Just as with CSR, there are multiple definitions for sustainability. Mary Francis Winters of the Winters Group, in her March 2009 Linkage presentation cited the definition to members of the World Business Council for Sustainable Development (WBCSD):

> "We believe that the leading global companies of 2020 will be those that provide goods and services and reach new customers in ways that address the world's major challenges—including poverty, climate change, resource depletion, globalization, and demographic shifts."[8]

This definition, clearly showing the link between CSR and sustainability, makes the business case evident.

Another view of the interconnectedness is Toyota's: "Toyota strives to assist the communities where we live and work by supporting local organizations focused on areas of environment, education, and strategy."[9]

The WBCSD is suggesting a window of approximately a decade for companies to distinguish themselves from other organizations and meet the challenges that our natural and social worlds present to us. We live in very complicated times that present both great challenge and great opportunity for organizations. Those that actually put a CSR and sustainability filter on their decision-making lens and are willing to do the hard work can find rich opportunities—not just to achieve noteworthy results, but also to set themselves apart.

Thinking with a sustainability mind-set is a shift in culture and perspective for a U.S. society steeped in consumption. It means developing new attitudes and points of view, and an emphasis on long-term thinking. Do you remember those recruiters we described in previous chapters? They built interest in future employees by starting with young children. With a long-term view they know it is a lengthy challenge but they have to start now. The same is true for sustainability.

While K-12 schools are doing a great deal, universities are probably doing more. Portland State University (PSU) has a particularly interesting program.[10] Its approach is holistic and integrated, focusing not just on sustaining ecosystems in the natural world, but also in the larger community, with a focus jointly on the biological, human, and natural worlds. Jennifer Allen, the acting director of the Center for Sustainable Processes and Practices at PSU, says, "You really need to be taking into account the need for jobs and a solid economic system in order to achieve solid environmental sustainability."[11] PSU's research and its mission regarding sustainability center around four key areas of focus:

1. How the natural environment and human society can be integrated.
2. Ways to create sustainable urban communities.
3. How to implement sustainable strategies into society.
4. Method to measure the efforts of the sustainable practices used.

For example, one project, called the Community Watershed Stewardship Program, has restored more than 2 million square feet of water-adjacent areas.[12] For Allen, it is seeing the interconnectedness between environmental, social, and economic factors that is required. Trying to turn out systems thinkers is absolutely necessary, not just at PSU, but around the country and world if we are to create livable communities.[13]

As Shaheen Husain at UCI said, "This is a holistic movement. It will take being intentional, holistic and long-term thinking if as a species, we are to be successful in this endeavor."[14] PSU is looking at the amounts of locally and organically grown food available to faculty and students, and to the use of renewable energy. By 2010, PSU has a goal of using 100 percent renewable sources, thus cutting greenhouse gas emissions. However, the real goal at PSU, in addition to achieving sustainability, is in creating the complex system thinkers that understand the interconnectedness in the process between equally important but often conflicting systems where needs can be disparate.

As we read much about what PSU and other organizations are doing with water, waste, and CO2, the numbers and statistics become mind numbing. Students at PSU and employees at Walmart demonstrate what can be done, but the commitment to doing this needs to be blessed at the top. Once that commitment is secured, there is opportunity to do work in groups or on teams throughout the organization. The questions really are two-fold around sustainability and diversity. For the diversity manager trying to make this effort work in a meaningful way, what can you do, and whose help do you need? For individuals leading the CSR and sustainability processes, how can you partner with diversity and inclusion? One way to begin is by exploring the following questions.

- What is our mission around CSR, sustainability, and diversity?
- What values drive the connection and our outcomes?
- How do we want to improve our communities? What are the needs and issues?
- How do we want to improve life for our employees? What are their needs and issues?
- Diversity is about using the best of everyone. How is this process helping us do that?
- How can we engage a wider range of employees and community members in this process?

Having conversations around these questions is as starting point. These discussions will hopefully involve others in an energetic, creative dialogue that signals a willingness to tackle this issue. Then your group will be ready for the next step, Activity 16.1.

The purpose of this exercise is to start breaking thinking down into smaller pieces so that people can see the interconnectedness of actions, and how every part is linked together. Decisions cannot be made in isolation if they are to foster healthy communities and organizations. It will mean looking at the impact of decisions you make both inside the organization and out. The ultimate goal is to engage employees in a process of intentionally focusing on taking a systems view and making decisions with a broader lens. An added bonus is that with enough commitment and energy, individuals can also use this process in their own lives on a smaller scale. From a diversity standpoint, employees will start seeing each other more fully. That means acknowledging all the myriad viewpoints, perspectives, and talent that improve decision-making.

ACTIVITY 16.1 | Understanding the Intersection of CSR, Sustainability, and Diversity in Decision-Making

Directions: Identify a key decision or policy change your organization is considering. Then consider the impact in each of the three arenas.

Decision: (*e.g., New headquarters building and location*)

Arena	Considerations/Impact
CSR How will this decision impact the larger community?	• Job creation/loss • Tax base increase/decrease • Support of local business and suppliers
Sustainability How will this decision impact the use of resources, natural and human?	• Fuel consumption • Energy use • Demand on natural resources
Diversity and Inclusion How does this impact employees' lives?	• Transportation means and cost • Travel time • Engagement of staff regarding choice of location, use of space, and facilities planning

Suggestions for Using
"Understanding the Intersection of CSR, Sustainability, and Diversity in Decision-Making"

Objectives:

- Foster conversations that raise insight, consideration of consequences, and good decision-making
- Open people's minds to seeing the impact their decisions have on CSR, sustainability, and diversity
- Understand systems thinking that connects diversity with CSR and sustainability

Intended Audience:

- Any functional work team that makes key decisions about products, resource utilization or overall policy
- An executive staff that needs to clarify thinking before making decisions and explaining them to employees
- An organization intent on becoming a more socially responsible citizen

Materials:

- Copies of the worksheet *Understanding the Intersection of CSR, Sustainability, and Diversity in Decision-Making.*

Processing the Activity:

- Ask people to fill it out the chart and give them 10 or 15 minutes to do so.
- Depending on the number of people, have them get into groups of three or four to discuss and compare perceptions.
- Have the facilitator make a master chart of impact on each of the three arenas.
- Determine what additional information is needed before the decision can be made.

Questions for Discussion:

- What are some words that describe the process of filling this out on your own?
- Give more words that describe the process of your discussion.
- What strikes you based on the conversations you had?
- Where are the areas of greatest agreement? Disagreement?
- Based on what we do in this decision, what do we stand to gain? Lose?
- How does this three-part lens alter how you might have viewed this five years ago? One year ago? Now?
- What is your best learning from this experience?
- Where else can you apply it?

The powerful connection between CSR, sustainability, and diversity is a partnership and a reality that is growing. It forces organizations to ask some very critical questions. The following questions can help to start your conversation. Diversity directors and councils can add critical perspectives to the discussion.

CSR Questions

- What is the impact of our policies and decisions on multiple communities, both inside and outside of these walls?
- How can we be better stewards of our environment and better neighbors to our community?
- What actions could we take that would elevate our community? If we did these things or invested energy/money, what would really happen to our brand?
- What would local and larger communities not have if we weren't here? Look for answers both positive and negative.
- What part of the community are we overlooking in our outreach?

Sustainability Questions

- What natural resources are we using that we could use differently and more efficiently?
- Where can we cut waste?
- What could each department/business unit in this organization do to be 10 percent more eco-friendly?
- How can we demonstrate our commitment to a healthy environment inside our organization and to the larger community?
- How can we teach conservation and environmental stewardship in culturally relevant ways to employees and community members?

Diversity Questions

- How can we make our own diversity process sustainable in our organization so that it has longevity?
- What are some ways to more intentionally use the skills of others?
- What processes could we use to have employees gain more insight about their own previously unutilized skills and the undiscovered skills of others?
- How can we involve a wider range of employees in implementing CSR and sustainability?
- What is one significant gift that diversity can bring to the CSR/sustainability process?
- What are some quality-of-life challenges that employees face?
- How can the Diversity-and-Inclusion Council advise those involved in the CSR and sustainability process?

These questions, and their answers, are just the tip of the iceberg. While the work here is complex, it is also doable with persistence and commitment. We remember years ago seeing that wonderful Chinese proverb which we frequently quote, "May you live in interesting times." No doubt about it. We are!

CHAPTER 17

Diversity and Inclusion Means More Than Equal Employment Opportunity

• •

This chapter will provide you with:

- A brief history of EEO and affirmative action and their relationship to diversity

- A chart that contrasts affirmative action, valuing differences, managing diversity, and inclusion in six dimensions

- An assessment tool to measure your organization's progress in affirmative action, valuing differences, managing diversity, and inclusion

- Tips for getting staff buy-in for diversity and inclusion

If you want to put a match to a powder keg, just utter the words affirmative action in most organizations and you are sure to see an explosion. Often the issues are so politically loaded and the views so polarized that it is difficult to have a rational discussion or reach a clear understanding about these programs and policies. Diversity and inclusion often carry the baggage of their precursors, both equal employment opportunity (EEO) and affirmative action. To understand diversity and inclusion, it is helpful to take a step back and get a historical perspective in order to see this fairly recent concept in an evolutionary light.

EEO Requirements: What the Law Says and Why

At the height of the civil rights movement in the early 1960s, Congress began enacting legislation aimed at eliminating discrimination in the workplace. Recognizing the existence of a long history of exclusion, segregation, and inequality for minorities and women, lawmakers began creating a series of laws that laid the foundation for the EEO requirements and affirmative action programs that exist in most organizations today. The cornerstones of that foundation were the following acts:

- *Title VII of the Civil Rights Act of 1964.* This statute prohibited on-the-job discrimination on the basis of race, color, religion, sex, or national origin and created the Equal Employment Opportunity Commission (EEOC) to enforce this law.
- *The Age Discrimination in Employment Act of 1967.* This piece of legislation prohibits discrimination against employees or job seekers who are aged 40 to 70.
- *The Vietnam Era Veterans Readjustment Assistance Act of 1972.* This law requires companies with government contracts to take affirmative action to hire and promote qualified disabled and Vietnam-era veterans.
- *The Rehabilitation Act of 1973.* This law requires companies with government contracts to accommodate the physical and mental needs of qualified handicapped employees and job seekers.
- *Pregnancy Disability Amendment to Title VII (1978).* This addition to Title VII prohibits the disparate treatment of pregnant women.

All of these laws rest on the premises that society has neither accorded equal treatment nor provided equal opportunity to all, and that inequities in employment continue. Therefore, legislation is required to change conditions that unfairly block certain groups. Their aim is to create a workplace where the only considerations for hiring or promotion are those that pertain to ability to do the job rather than attributes specific to a group (race, color, religion, etc.). The byword of this legislation is nondiscrimination.

Affirmative Action: An Answer to Past Discrimination

In the evolution of workplace equity, affirmative action goes a step further. Its premise is that the elimination of discrimination is not enough to create workplace equity. Because of a long history of discriminatory practices, employers need to make positive efforts to recruit, hire, train, and promote qualified employees of previously excluded groups. Emphasis is placed on reaching parity with local workforce demographics. Generally, organizations either voluntarily or by requirement formulate affirmative action plans that spell out hiring and promotion goals in terms of employee statistics and the method for achieving these objectives. This generally requires some method that gives the advantage to previously disadvantaged groups in order to rectify past and current inequities. Proportionately more women, African-American, or differently-abled individuals, for example, will be moved in and up until parity goals are reached. Affirmative action institutes a temporary imbalance to reach a new balance.

Where Affirmative Action Stops Short

According to Pam Fomalont, former affirmative action administrator at a major Southern California aerospace firm, "Affirmative action is an imperfect system, but it is still the best method we have for getting diverse people into the pipeline. Without affirmative action, there would not be the kind of diverse employee base we have today."[1] One of affirmative action's most often cited limits is that it gets people in but not up. Its programs are generally more successful in getting women and nondominant-group members hired than in getting employees of these groups promoted into middle and upper management.

Another place where affirmative action stops short is in advocating for only a few of the many groups who may be facing discrimination in the workplace. Women and, to a lesser degree, African Americans have historically been the greatest beneficiaries, while Latinos, Asians, and recent immigrants have been less aided by affirmative action programs.

Why the Resistance to EEO and Affirmative Action?

Let's take a look at why there is resistance to EEO and affirmative action programs.

Perceived Restrictions on Individual Freedom

The first and perhaps most powerful reason for resistance is the perception by managers that affirmative action program goals restrict the manager's freedom and limit his or her control in making decisions about whom to hire or promote. The manager may be antagonistic toward affirmative action because he or she perceives it as an infringement on an important managerial prerogative, the freedom to make hiring and promotional decisions. Managers often fear that affirmative action goals may force them to hire or promote someone who is not their first choice.

Perceived Dichotomy Between Diversity and Quality

In many organizations the complaint about affirmative action is that it leads to a lowering of standards, a loss in quality of staff, and hence a loss in quality of output. The underlying assumption is that quality and diversity are on opposite ends of a continuum, that one must be sacrificed for the other. According to this view, choosing the best employee means giving up on increasing the diversity of staff and, conversely, increasing diversity means that a less-qualified person must be chosen. The choice is perceived to be between the most-qualified candidate or a minority candidate. This perception leads to an unwinnable debate over which is most important, a diverse staff or a competent and qualified one. A more helpful way to look at these dimensions is to consider them not as opposite ends of a continuum, but as two independent variables (see Figure 17.1). The organizational goal is to find, develop, hire, and promote individuals who are both high in quality and who increase the diversity of staff—those with the necessary skills, abilities, and experiences, as well as diverse backgrounds, that would enhance the organization.

FIGURE 17.1 | Quality and Diversity: Both-And Not Either-Or

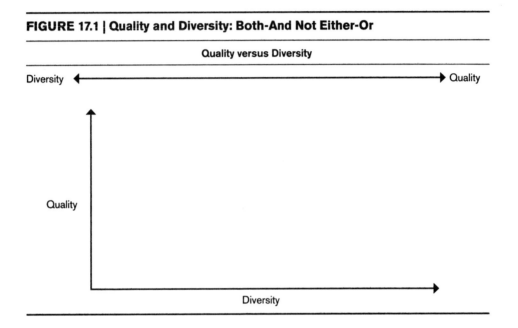

Past Experience

Some employees and managers react negatively to affirmative action because of previous negative experiences with individuals whom they see as affirmative action appointments. If there have been less-than-qualified or undercompetent employees hired under affirmative action's banner, there may be a residue of mistrust and skepticism about future placements.

Supply Shortage

In many organizations the resistance is tied to the difficulty in finding qualified candidates from underrepresented groups. "I just can't find enough candidates," and "There aren't any minorities or women with the experience we need" are examples of the complaints heard. Attending conferences of professional associations such as the National Society of Hispanic MBAs can help change this assumption.

Perception of Unfairness at Being Made To Pay for Past Sins

Some resist because they feel that they are being inconvenienced by requirements and limited by guidelines that are designed to rectify a history of discrimination that they did not create. "It's not my fault. Why should I be the one to pay for it?" is their cry.

The Perception That It Solely Benefits Others

Another source of negative response to affirmative action is the sense that these programs and plans benefit only the targeted groups. In giving this advantage to others, managers as well as other employees may perceive they are putting themselves at a disadvantage. "It doesn't benefit me; it's for them" is sometimes heard.

Reverse Discrimination: A Real or Perceived Fear?

The perception that affirmative action programs, in giving advantage to previously excluded groups, put others at a disadvantage is at the heart of reverse discrimination charges. Those who are passed over when women or nondominant-group members are placed in positions often feel unfairly treated and discriminated against because of their race, gender, or color. Whether it is the cry of white-male managers who have been passed over for promotions to executive ranks or qualified Asian students who are denied admission to universities, members of overrepresented groups who are "held back" to allow others admission often perceive their exclusion as reverse discrimination.

While there has always been hiring and promotion based on factors other than job qualifications (e.g., being the boss's son, a friend's son-in-law, a legacy admission, or a cousin from the old country), there persists a deep U.S.-American faith in meritocracy. We believe the most qualified person should get the job, and feel betrayed when other factors are brought into the decision. It goes against the mainstream value placed on fairness and justice, basic philosophical underpinnings of American society. It is partially from this cultural emphasis on justice that both affirmative action and the charges of reverse discrimination result. Whether allegations of reverse discrimination are upheld or not in the courts is a moot point. What is more germane for today's organization is how to deal with this perceived reality, which creates resistance and undermines the commitment of some "old guard" employees who ought not to be discounted or alienated. In an environment that includes everyone, there is no room for those who perceive themselves to be losers, especially since losers can become powerful organizational saboteurs by withholding commitment and passively resisting.

In dealing with this backlash to affirmative action, organizations have developed some constructive responses. In the public sector, organizations such as school districts and county governments, for example, have instituted systems where promotional selections are made from groupings on a list rather than automatically taking the top-ranking candidate. In this way, managers can choose from among an array of well-qualified candidates; the next five on the list or the top 20 percent of scorers on an exam, for instance. Within this grouping there are undoubtedly candidates from underrepresented groups, so the manager can choose for both quality and diversity.

Embracing Diversity Goes Far Beyond EEO and Affirmative Action

Diversity and inclusion bring with them a paradigm shift, a new way of thinking about differences among people. Rather than arguing about how to cut up the pie and which group gets the largest slice, embracing diversity strives for a workplace where there are not only enough pies but also cakes, churros, and fortune cookies for all. Instead of pitting groups against one another, it works toward recognizing the uniqueness in everyone and valuing the contribution each can make. This concept aims at creating a workplace in which everyone and every group fits, feels accepted, has value, and contributes. Beyond changing numbers, it aims at changing organizational cultures. It is important to remember that the intent of embracing diversity is not to replace affirmative action but to build on the critical foundation laid by workplace equity programs. Affirmative action, valuing differences, managing diversity, and inclusion go hand-in-hand, each reinforcing the gains of the other.

FIGURE 17.2 | A New Way to Think About Differences Among People

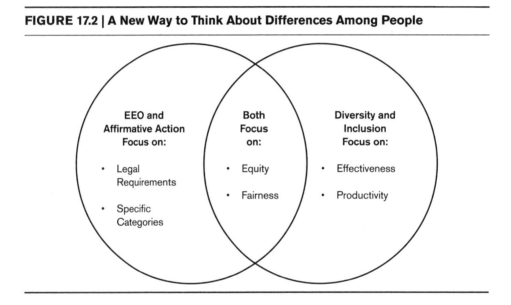

Affirmative Action, Valuing Differences, Managing Diversity, and Inclusion: An Evolution

While there is much overlap both in philosophy and practice, perhaps the easiest way to look at the differences is in the form of a few comparisons (see Table 17.1). In creating an organization that truly leverages diversity, all four of these stages of evolution play an integral part. Without affirmative action's commitment to hiring and promoting diverse employees, having the diversity of staff to reach a stage where differences are valued and diversity effectively managed rarely occurs. Once diverse staff are on board, the organization can focus on creating an inclusive environment where everyone's needs and values are taken into account, where no one is disadvantaged because of his or her differentness, and where organizational policies and management practices work for everyone.

How Does Your Organization/Division/Department Measure Up?

To see how your organization is doing in each of the four areas—affirmative action, valuing differences, managing diversity, and inclusion, respond to the assessment in Activity 17.1.

TABLE 17.1 | Comparing Affirmative Action, Valuing Differences, Managing Diversity, and Inclusion

Affirmative Action	Valuing Differences	Managing Diversity	Inclusion
Quantitative: Emphasizes achieving equality of opportunity in the work environment through the changing of organizational demographics. Monitored by statistical reports and analysis.	*Qualitative:* Emphasizes the appreciation of differences and creating an environment in which everyone feels valued and accepted. Monitored by organizational surveys focused on attitudes and perceptions.	*Behavioral:* Emphasizes the building of specific skills and creating policies which get the best from every employee. Monitored by progress toward achieving goals and objectives.	*Operational:* Emphasizes the design and implementation of systems of operation that include stakeholders in relevant and appropriate ways. Monitored by a wide range of statistics, surveys, and organizational results.
Legally-driven: Written plans and statistical goals for specific group are utilized. Reports are mandated by EEO laws, government contracts, and consent decrees.	*Ethically-driven:* Moral and ethical imperatives drive this culture change. It is the right thing to do.	*Strategically-driven:* Behaviors and policies are seen as contributing to organizational goals and objectives such as profit and productivity and are tied to reward and results.	*Mission-driven:* Strategies build a culture that can fulfill the organization's mission in the current and future business environment.
Remedial: Specific target groups benefit as past and current wrongs are remedied. Previously-excluded groups have an advantage.	*Idealistic:* Everyone benefits. Everyone feels valued and accepted in an inclusive environment.	*Pragmatic:* The organization benefits; morale, profit, and productivity increase.	*Integrated:* The organization sees itself as part of a global community and works to enhance life for employees, customers, the community, and the world.
Assimilation model: Assumes that groups brought into system will adapt to existing organizational norms.	*Diversity model:* Assumes that groups will retain their own characteristics and shape the organization as well as be shaped by it, creating a common set of values.	*Synergy model:* Assumes that diverse groups will create new ways of working together effectively in a pluralistic environment.	*Both/And Thinking:* Rejects either/or thinking, which polarizes and limits options, and assumes an attitude which finds opportunity in differences.
Opens doors: Affects hiring and promotion decisions.	*Opens attitudes, minds, and the culture:* Affects attitudes of employees.	*Opens the system:* Changes policies and practices, which affects engagement and productivity	*Opens the organization:* Affects operations internally and externally as the organization interfaces with the world beyond its walls.
Resistance due to: perceived limits to autonomy in decision-making and perceived fears of reverse discrimination.	*Resistance due to:* fear of change, discomfort with differences, and desire for return to "good old days."	*Resistance due to:* denial of demographic realities, the need for alternative approaches, and the benefits associated with change; also difficulty in learning new skills, altering existing systems, and finding time to work toward synergistic solutions.	*Resistance due to:* insular thinking, refusal to accept new paradigms, and hanging on to existing power alliances.

ACTIVITY 17.1 | How Does Your Organization Measure Up?

Directions: Check off each statement on the list below that describes your organization or department.

Affirmative action is effective when:

_____ There is a good-faith effort to recruit, hire, train, and promote qualified employees from under-represented groups.

_____ The composition of management staff reflects the composition of the workforce in general.

_____ Internal networking surfaces qualified candidates who are from diverse groups.

_____ Mechanisms exist to identify and mentor diverse employees who show promotional potential.

_____ Managers recognize it as their responsibility to make progress in building teams that reflect the composition of the workforce.

_____ There are few gripes about preferential treatment and reverse discrimination.

_____ Diverse individuals who are promoted are accepted in their new positions by the rest of staff.

_____ Managers' pay raises are tied to achieving affirmative action goals.

Differences are valued when:

_____ Turnover among all groups is relatively proportionate.

_____ Employees form friendships across racial, cultural, lifestyle, and gender lines.

_____ Employees talk openly about differences in backgrounds, values, and needs.

_____ No group in the organization is the target of ridicule, jokes, or slurs.

_____ Individuals feel comfortable being themselves at work.

_____ It would not be surprising to employees if the next CEO is not a Euro-American, able-bodied man.

Diversity is being managed effectively when:

_____ Leave, absentee, and holiday policies are flexible enough to suit everyone.

_____ Cultural conflicts are resolved and not allowed to fester and escalate.

_____ Employees of all backgrounds feel free to give input and make requests to management.

_____ Diverse employees take advantage of career enhancement opportunities.

_____ Diverse teams work cooperatively and harmoniously.

_____ Productivity of diverse teams is high.

_____ Managers get commitment and cooperation from their diverse staffs.

_____ Organizational procedures such as performance review and career development have been restructured to suit the diverse needs of employees.

_____ There is diverse staff at all levels.

Inclusion is evident in the organization when:

_____ Diverse representation and viewpoints are routinely sought in decision-making.

_____ The culture continues to evolve to adjust to new groups and issues.

_____ Systems, policies, and practices continue to be reviewed and adjusted to meet the changing needs of staff and customers.

_____ External stakeholders are appropriately included in decision-making.

_____ Task forces, teams, and workgroups are routinely made up of diverse members.

_____ Leaders and managers seek out a variety of opinions and perspectives before making decisions.

_____ All parts of the workforce are involved in continuous self examination and learning.

Suggestions for Using
"How Does Your Organization Measure Up?"

Objectives:

- Assess your organization's effectiveness with regard to affirmative action, valuing differences, managing diversity, and inclusion
- Pinpoint diversity-related issues that need attention
- Give feedback to executive management and HR departments regarding aspects of the development of diversity and inclusion

Intended Audience:

- Managers, supervisors, and other staff members wanting to give feedback to HR departments and executive management
- Executives setting strategic planning goals
- Diversity council members building a diversity-and-inclusion strategy

Materials:

- Copies of the worksheet *How Does Your Organization Measure Up?*

Processing the Activity:

- Individuals respond by checking those statements that describe their organizations or departments.
- Responses are tabulated and data are presented to executive management, HR, diversity council or those in charge of dealing with diversity issues.
- Executive, HR, or other appropriate staff analyze data and identify obstacles to capitalizing on diversity within the organization; they then plan ways to address these barriers.

Caveats, Considerations, and Variations:

- These issues can provoke emotional and heated responses. This assessment activity can best be managed in small groups where venting can take place safely.
- Executives and/or HR professionals on the receiving end of this feedback may react defensively. Help them to see the responses as valid perceptions of respondees so they can use it constructively.
- This assessment can also be used by affirmative action and HR professionals in planning and training.

The more statements you have in each section, the greater your organization's effectiveness in that particular area. It is also important to look at those statements not checked. What obstacles are preventing these conditions from being the norm? What can you do about those obstacles?

A Stark Reality: The Pyramid Narrows at the Top for All

Even with all the predictions about the flattening of the structure in organizations, the typical company is run in a hierarchical fashion, with an organizational chart in the shape of a pyramid. No matter how one cuts it, the number of positions decreases at each higher level. What this means for career plans and promotional aspirations is that competition for positions increases for everyone who aspires to move up the organizational ladder. When promotions are made in companies where there have historically been no minorities or women at upper levels, much attention is focused on who is selected. Previously excluded groups wait to see a sign that the organization is going to come through on its commitment to diversity, while white males who have traditionally been selected often feel they are quite likely to be overlooked.

In one civil service organization, all eyes were on the next promotion. Upper management was entirely white male, and there was a strong affirmative action mandate to increase the diversity within the department, especially at the managerial and executive levels. Only one candidate was not a white male—an African-American veteran of the system with a strong background and ample qualifications who had filed an EEO suit against the department when he was not promoted previously. As can be imagined, the atmosphere was electrically charged in this environment, where resistance to affirmative action was the norm and where allegations of reverse discrimination were common. The department's decision to promote the African-American candidate, who brought both quality and diversity, was met with grudging acceptance by the other candidates for the position. While they understood the reasons, they weren't happy about not getting the promotion themselves.

When the pyramid narrows and there are fewer prizes up the organizational ladder, there will often be more losers than winners. For this reason, it is important to create alternative career paths that allow growth and advancement. One such solution is the creation of career ladders. These are promotional steps based on increased technical competence rather than managerial positional advances. Such systems work especially well in organizations with large professional staffs such as nurses, engineers, or accountants. An employee can advance within the organization, increasing salary and title—for example, engineer level I, II, III or nurse clinician I, II, III—without entering the ranks of management.

The Inclusive Organization: A Model To Strive For

- A pregnant woman is told her position cannot be guaranteed when she returns from maternity leave.
- An Orthodox Jew can never take advantage of the informal mentoring from executive staff, which takes place Saturdays on the golf course.
- An architect who walks on crutches is not hired because it is believed he can't "walk a job" and properly oversee construction.
- A talented young lawyer doesn't take the desired month of parental leave when his first child is born because he's sure if he does he will be eliminated from the partner track.

In each of these situations, both the organization and the individual are losers. When diversity is not capitalized on, the organization loses the full commitment, energy, and capability of the employee, while the individual loses both career opportunities and esteem. In addition, reduced productivity often results from the stress experienced by the employee grappling with these dilemmas. No organization has a utopian environment where magical solutions appear. However, when an organization values differences and effectively manages its diverse workforce, it meets these challenges in a constructive way. First, it sees these kinds of issues as normal challenges of organizational life, not as irritants caused by those who are different. Second, it recognizes the loss to the organization in not finding solutions. Proceeding from a kind of enlightened self-interest, the organization sees benefits in dealing constructively with the diverse needs of staff. Third, the organization responds with creative problem-solving. Rather than complain about, blame, deny, or resist the conflicts between employee needs and existing practices, the organization seeks new ways to satisfy both individual and organizational priorities. In such an organization, the scenarios above might be different.

- The pregnant woman and her boss sit down and discuss both the organization's requirements and the woman's personal and professional priorities. A flexible solution is arrived at that allows the employee various career options depending on when she chooses to return to work. During the leave she will remain in contact with her boss so they can discuss changes as they occur, both in the company and her life, and modify plans as needed. She may opt to work at home with a computer and modem or come back with a flextime schedule for a period.

- Executive staff spend time discussing the effectiveness of their informal mentoring and realize that it nets them a very homogeneous group of executives-in-training. As they examine the informal path to upward mobility in the company, they realize it generally excludes those who are not white, heterosexual, able-bodied males because of the arenas in which the relationships are built. The Saturday golf dates exclude not only Orthodox Jews but also many women and other staff, who are not generally part of the country club set. Realizing this, executives strategize new mentoring methods and venues that are truly inclusive.

- The interviewer feels comfortable enough with the issue of physical disabilities that he is able to "talk straight" with the applicant. He asks him about previous construction projects and inquires about the methods of supervision used. In this way, he gives the candidate a chance to explain how he oversees a project while on crutches. Convinced that the disability will not prevent the applicant from performing required job duties, the interviewer recommends the candidate for the position.

- The law firm spends time with each employee who is going through a major life change such as the birth of a child, marriage, divorce, or death of a spouse, talking about the changes in lifestyle and priorities as well as needs the change may precipitate. The employee has a chance to talk about his or her preferences and discuss the career implications of each. However, because partners in the firm model its values, the young lawyer knows that a few of his colleagues, both male and female, have taken parental leaves and were still made partners. It is clear that while there may be trade-offs, there are no sanctions. The lawyer makes a decision that means he won't have to cheat either of his roles—father or lawyer.

Getting Buy-in for Diversity: What's in It for Staff?

As long as managers and employees see the attention paid to dealing with, managing, and valuing diversity as something that benefits others, there will be resistance among all but the most altruistic. In order to get buy-in, the old WIFM formula—What's in It For Me?—needs to be applied.

When all levels of staff see benefits for themselves, they will be more apt to commit wholeheartedly. Along those lines, organizations need to focus on the following.

Solicit and Pay Attention to the Needs and Priorities of All Employees

In a diverse organization, each employee is a minority of one, with unique preferences, desires, and needs. The most significant experts you need to consult are the employees themselves. Whether through employee surveys, discussions at staff meetings, or focus groups, find out the real issues for employees. You can't eliminate obstacles to employee engagement until you know what they are. You cannot reward appropriately unless you know what staff members want. It is difficult to increase morale if you aren't sure what diminishes job satisfaction for your employees. Ask, then listen, without defensiveness or argument, to what they tell you.

Create Options and Alternatives

Once you have heard the variations in what employees want, formulate systems and policies that give them choices. By making policies flexible enough to suit different priorities, you can best meet everyone's (or almost everyone's) needs. Cafeteria plans for benefits, personal necessity leave days, flextime, insurance plan options, bonus alternatives, and individual discretion about the use of subsidies for child care or elder care are all examples of ways organizations respond to individual needs while making sure policies and benefits are equitable. The element of individual decision-making is critical. A truism of human nature seems to be that people are more committed when they make the choice themselves. Allowing employees to select from an array of alternatives increases buy-in and sends the message that the organization is responding to employees' individual needs.

Focus on the Benefits to Individual Employees

In communicating any changes connected with diversity, emphasize the benefits to each employee. Hiring bilingual customer service representatives may mean less frustration for monolingual customer service staff in communicating with non-English-speaking clientele. Creating an on-site day care center could lower the stress for both male and female employees with children, giving them convenient, accessible, safe, and affordable child care. For managers, it may mean less absenteeism and turnover of staff. Make sure the benefits are brought down to the level of personal relevance for each employee. When these are adhered to, inclusion comes to mean paying attention to each person's unique situation and responding to it in a supportive way. Everyone wins. The organization gets the best in commitment, motivation, and creative thinking from employees who blossom in an environment that demonstrates that the organization truly values them.

CHAPTER 18

Making Diversity Work: Summing It Up

· ·

I am only one; but still I am one. I cannot do everything, but still I can do something; I will not refuse to do the something I can do.

—HELEN KELLER

Our goal in this book has been to help you get hands-on tools, strategies, ideas, and techniques that will enable you to lead productive workgroups and organizations through the massive changes U.S.-American business is undergoing. Specifically, we have discussed the following:

- An inclusive model of diversity.
- Ways to measure and evaluate your diversity processes and initiatives.
- Culture and its pervasive impact on behavior, norms, and values.
- Communication (or miscommunication) in a diverse environment, particularly as it relates to giving feedback and resolving culture clashes.
- Cultural etiquette in a cross-cultural world.
- Globalization as a prominent reality that many U.S. headquarters companies are dealing with.
- How to build cohesive work teams in a cross-cultural environment.
- How to conduct effective performance evaluations with employees of different backgrounds.
- How to create a corporate culture that is inclusive and welcoming to all people.
- Important considerations in determining what kind of audits to conduct and construct in order to assess your organization regarding diversity.
- Ways your organization can increase its chances of recruiting and hiring a pluralistic workforce.
- How to open up promotional, coaching, and career development systems to employees of all groups.
- Ways that corporate social responsibility and sustainability connect to diversity.
- The differences between EEO/affirmative action and managing diversity.
- Diversity-related resources.

This information and these strategies can help leaders and managers develop more inclusive organizations. However, a successful diversity effort rests on more than solid management techniques. It also requires a mind-set that helps you and your organization deal positively with this challenging phenomenon. The battle for effectiveness is waged on two fronts—the individual and the collective, whether that structure is a team, task force, or broader organizational.

The Individual: Ideas Central to a Diversity Mind-Set

"Diversity Is Not about 'Them'; It Is about Us"

When our colleague Terry Owens made the above statement, it had a ring of undeniable truth. First and foremost, diversity is about realizing and accepting your own reactions to differentness and the discomfort it causes. While you do need to learn about the cultural norms, practices, and values of others, those pieces of information are not nearly as important at looking inside and understanding the impact those differences have on you. At its core, diversity asks you to take a look at why holidays, practices, values, or languages different from yours trigger feelings of threat that build walls between you and others. Shirley MacLaine once said something pertinent to this issue: "The more I traveled, the more I realized that fear makes strangers of people who should be friends." Whether or not you choose friendship with those who are different from you, self-comfort is essential. Those who accept themselves are not threatened by the differences they come in contact with. Coming to terms with who you are creates space in your world where these differences can bring enormous gifts and grace.

Face the Fear of Change and the Perceived Losses

The greatest resistance to dealing with the changing workforce comes when we see these changes as taking something away from us. Conscious and subconscious fears abound: "Will my opportunities cease to exist?" "How much adapting will I have to do?" "When I hear co-workers speaking a foreign language, are they talking about me?" Cries of "It's so different since they came" and "I feel like a foreigner in my own community" are common. In the face of these fears, it helps when we understand that all changes are two-sided coins. One eternal truth is that every change has both positives and negatives attached to it. Helping yourself and employees identify the positives is a good starting point. Then encouraging yourself and others to identify the perceived negatives and to problem-solve potential worst-case scenarios is essential to shrinking the losses down to manageable size. If employees don't get beyond the fear, they will never get beyond the resistance. Your diversity effort will be sabotaged and positive results unrealized.

Shed the Predictable Habits and Learn New Behaviors

To be human is to be a creature of habit. All people have patterns of behavior that have become automatic over the years, sort of unconscious rituals. Facing diversity means shaking up some of these habits because many of the old behaviors no longer work in this new environment. Effective management is partially defined by a willingness to forgo the security of a world where everyone responds like clockwork to your tried-and-true techniques. Instead, you are demanding of yourself that you learn or experience a repertoire of new behaviors that offers different responses to the eclectic etiquette and conduct you will continue to face both on the job and in the marketplace.

Get Beyond Ethnocentrism

All of us see the world through our experiences. As a result, our own cultural milieu becomes the yardstick by which all other customs and norms are measured and evaluated.

This practice, though common, can be destructive to your own flexibility and openness, and to an organization's opportunity to grow. Understanding that today's world is not only small and interconnected but also varied makes a strong case for developing both tolerance and appreciation of differences. The recognition that there isn't a right way to greet people, or eat, or bathe, or treat elders—just a lot of different ways that feel comfortable to particular groups of people—goes a long way toward legitimizing variety and creating a positive experience among people of different backgrounds.

Emphasize Common Experiences That Unify Rather than Differences That Divide

If we look at diversity through an anthropological human-behavior lens, what emerges is a picture of humankind that has shared the same basic experiences since time immemorial. While various cultural practices lead to different values, priorities, and behaviors, in truth there are only a few universal life events. Regardless of culture, period of history, race, religion, and a host of other factors, experiences such as birth, growth, marriage, death, the need to feel connected to others, and the desire to engage in meaningful work are shared by people the world over. Once you acknowledge that these milestones and needs are every person's common journey, it is easier to accept that we are more alike than different. We have much to teach, learn from, and share with others on this common journey.

Demonstrate Values Through Actions, Not Words

It is easy to give lip-service commitment to diversity. While this movement has its share of detractors, it is also viewed as being timely and pragmatic. Saying that you value diversity while maintaining the status quo won't cut it. Uttering the right words about inclusion, while conducting business in ways that exclude others, will be self-defeating and will cost you the trust and commitment of employees. Minimizing any serious discussion of legitimate differences in viewpoints, priorities, and norms is insulting and sabotages your attempts at inclusion.

Be Honest with Yourself and Others

The changes we are living through demand the best of us. They require that we stretch, grow, and adapt as we've never done before. In order to make these changes effective, a relentless honesty with the self is a critical starting point. Identifying areas of fear, threat, and discomfort is a must. We all have them. Once we acknowledge them, they are less potent and cease to be a knee-jerk reflex. Honesty can lead to tactful but clear interactions with others that ultimately make a company's diversity results much more positive.

Remember that Diversity Includes Everyone

Much reference has been made throughout this book to the need for white males to help create more open systems, because in most cases they still do hold the power. However, some of the most open and generous people leading the way for change are and have been white males. If we blame and rage against those who have held power, whatever their color, then we miss the point of the diversity movement. If we are to regain the competitive edge and create not only "kinder and gentler" but also more profitable and productive organizations, then it is time to share power. That means representing everyone in the decision-making process. Previously excluded groups who point their fingers and grind their axes move us backward, as do white males who cry reverse discrimination and resist any but token change. Any diversity effort that fails to extend empathy and understanding full circle will end up polarizing people and creating adversaries. We will all lose. Much is being asked of us, but much more will be given. A fuller utilization of all people's talents benefits you as an individual, the company for which you work, and all of us as a nation.

Individuals with open, pliable mind-sets are necessary for a vibrant organization, but unless the organizational systems are in place to support this change, consistency, productivity, and vibrancy won't happen. There are organizational imperatives that will help any willing organization manage a successful change effort. Before you start out on any diversity-related endeavor, consider these organizational "must haves." If they are conspicuous by their absence, do your best to build their presence and make it felt. The success of your organization's venture depends on their full force.

Organizational Imperatives

The following nine factors are indispensable to making diversity work in any organization.

Demonstrate Commitment at the Highest Levels

Without support from the president or CEO on down, any diversity program will always be sandbagged. It's not that individual managers dedicated to this issue couldn't do some good on their own. They can and should wherever possible. But to change the culture of an organization so that it offers genuine opportunity to all people requires not only support from the top but role modeling as well. A CEO who says he is committed to diversity but never expands the composition of the management team when there is an opening indicates lip service, not genuine commitment. At the highest levels, there has to be a willingness to hold people accountable and an unflinching readiness to invest scarce resources in this endeavor. There is nothing complicated about calibrating the commitment; it's either there or it isn't, and like Hansel and Gretel's crumbs, the clues are dropped all along the way in the choices made every day.

Seek Participation and Commitment from the Bottom Up

Starting with entry-level employees, staff members need help in dealing with the frustrations they experience on a regular basis as they come face-to-face with customs foreign to them. Employees will benefit from training that helps create understanding about the impact of language differences, personal biases, cross-cultural norms, and the fears associated with change or feelings of loss. For an organization to prosper amid diversity, getting the involvement and commitment from those at the bottom ranks is just as critical as getting them from those at the top because it is in the day-in and day-out implementation of policy that irritations, prejudices, and lack of patience can sabotage productivity. A three-hour seminar won't do. Engaging in a long-term, reinforced, and sustained effort is the ticket to really changing organizational culture. All of that frustration we have seen, years in the making, resulted in a collaboration between the two of us and our colleague, Dr. Jorge Cherbosque. After years of focusing on awareness, insight, and skills in managing diversity, we still noticed barriers to change at an individual level based on the role emotions play in triggering resistance and hostility to differences. These powerful but often destructive responses often kept may people from moving forward and developing their openness, receptivity, and resilience to a rich but infinitely complicated world. As a result, we created a model of Emotional Intelligence and Diversity that provides a systemic approach combining insight and action so people learn, from the inside out, how to deal with the powerful emotions that emerge when differences meet. Investing in people at every level and helping them through this transition can have high payoff in morale and productivity.

Create a More Fluid Power Structure

The best and most recent example of a fluid power structure was the last presidential election in 2008. This is not about which candidate you favored or who got elected; it was about the democratization of the election process in a way not seen before. Through a combination of the candidates themselves and how they energized people, and through the use of technology, the process has changed. It remains to be seen what difference blogs, town hall meetings, and other means of mass communication actually make in the policy decisions, but the process feels different. Engagement was higher and people were invested. What worked on a national level should certainly have some application to fully investing and engaging people in organizations all over the country, regardless of their size.

Teach a Wide Array of Management Techniques That Work Cross-Culturally

There is a prevailing belief that to be fair means treating all people the same. In truth, being an effective manager today means that you must treat all people with equal dignity, opportunity, and respect, but not necessarily the same. Treating people with equal respect may mean honoring different cultural norms. Managers reared in a homogeneous environment need training about how to deal with these cultural differences on the job. Doing so will impact managerial functions such as performance reviews, interviewing, and building effective teams. An organization that is serious about having a competitive edge has to prepare its managers with the knowledge and information required to do the job. Teaching cross-cultural management tools is a must.

Integrate Diversity into the Fabric of the Organization

Unless valuing diversity is built into the organizational systems, it risks becoming another add-on or being viewed as a fad. If it remains separate from the operational structure, it will be relegated to a token attempt and conveniently ignored. Building diversity into existing systems and procedures in the areas of recruitment, career development, organizational communication, reward, and accountability makes diversity an integral part of the organization.

Expect and Sustain a Long-Term Effort

Changing organizational culture so that it is more fluid, open, and responsive will take patience, perseverance, and vision. Living in a 30-second-sound-bite culture with a proliferation of Twitter, texting, and YouTube makes it impossible to forget that we are used to instant gratification and results. A long-term change venture is counterculture, but it is also necessary. Clarify expectations at the beginning. Tell staff what's in it for them, and then be honest about the time commitment required. Set up benchmarks along the way so that progress can be duly noted and applauded, and then move right back to the fire where you are holding those feet.

Accept the New Demographic Reality

We saw the ultimate denial of the new demographic reality several years ago when a student in a doctoral program was so upset at the projected demographic changes that he walked out of the seminar. Most denial is handled in less overt ways but has just as much frustration attached. Accepting the changes in a world both close to home and far away is a significant first step. Our isolationist days are over. The world is too small and significantly intertwined. Beyond that acknowledgment, what's left is to see this change as offering both great opportunities and stimulating challenges. No one said creating harmony from such an amalgam would be easy, but then neither was crossing the continent, building a railroad, or going to the moon. Being the laboratory for this human experiment is our destiny, and the sooner we welcome that reality, the sooner we can make it work in our favor.

Make Change Your Ally

A familiar saying from the last century is that the only constant is change. If you put that same thought on fast forward, you enter today's world where information explodes and change accelerates so rapidly that everything seems fluid and today's news is old almost as soon as it comes out. As a result, life feels unstable, which is challenging for our species at this stage of evolution. A physiological verity is that human beings favor homeostasis. This desire for stability is equally true in the psychological arena. While there may be a wide variance in how much change people prefer, for the most part, there is a preference for the solid, secure, and predictable. Yet we find our world today in a state of hyper-flux. The organization that is adaptable, flexible, and smart enough to find security in the predictability of change is the organization that will excel and remain healthy, productive, and vital in our swirling world.

Be Willing To Pierce the Power and Work Through the Discomfort

Henri McClenney, who runs the Puget Sound Recruiting Network, advises those who use his services that it is difficult to separate pain from change. Henri knows this because he helps employees from organizations around the Seattle area understand that diversity is about sharing power. It is a gritty, tough issue to deal with. Those who have power want to keep it, while those who don't, want access to it. His viewpoint is that anger and frustration are a natural part of the process. He expects change but knows it will not come easily. He says, with the assurance he could only have gained through his experiences, that there is no remedy where no one pays. Dialogue is the key to getting through the hard times. Shifting authority and making it more diffuse will not appeal to those who hold the reigns. In the short run, there may be some battle scars on both individuals and the organization alike. But in the long run, piercing the power structure is imperative. It is the most far-reaching way we have of fully investing all the players in our society.

Spread Goodwill toward All

As we finish revising this book, we recall past holidays and celebrations. Hanukkah and Christmas come to mind because they happen in close proximity. How to celebrate and not cheapen Christmas without excluding others is an annual question. That time of year, more than any other, seems to evoke memories of that old fashioned but essential concept: goodwill. Our lives would be more mean-spirited and difficult without it. It is the mortar of the diversity movement, even of civilization itself. We think back to the many people we interviewed during the course of writing this book. We recall the countless examples described to us of human difference that could have led to irritating disruptions and painful conflict. What always saved the day, as clearly as any cape-wearing Superman, was generosity of spirit. The bottom line: If you feel warmth and kindness toward people different from you, they will usually feel it and respond in kind. In fact, the Japanese have a proverb, "One kind word can warm three winter months." In the experiences recounted to us, no cultural norm was ever violated that left a harmful residue in the face of goodwill. However, it is not always easy to display respect and charity because it is not always easy to feel. Resources are in short supply, and organizational life can be stressful. The amount of worry about individual job survival and organizational longevity is high, while guarantees and optimism are in short supply. But while the information we have written about in the prior pages can and should be extremely helpful, the ace you always have up your sleeve is a generous heart.

Goodwill alone cannot save us. We believe fervently that our competitive edge as a nation will be found in the advantage we gain from mastering the ability to work and live together in our mosaic-like communities. The change from relative homogeneity to extraordinary pluralism can be fraught with the pain of uncertainty. It can either immobilize us with fear and doubt, or we can work our way through it. Only when the latter occurs can we truly serve as a model for the rest of the world in the most fundamental and critical way. Humankind has no greater experiment at stake. The best of our collective human natures can rise to the challenge and meet it. We will all surely survive better financially, emotionally, psychologically and in every way, if we can see beyond our immediate worries to the major gifts and blessings that come from our sometimes stressful, always intriguing and, most of the time, beneficial and rich differences. Ultimately, we believe they strengthen and elevate us all, and in the most basic way, that adaptability ensures our survival.

Appendix:
Diversity Resources

· ·

General Books About Diversity

Abrams, Bob and George F. Simons, eds. *Cultural Diversity Sourcebook*, Amherst, MA: ODT, 1996. This compilation of articles from a variety of sources gives many views on getting real about diversity.

Aguilar, Leslie. *Ouch! That Stereotype Hurts*. Flower Mound, TX: Walk the Talk, 2006. This practical guidebook gives tools, tips, and techniques for understanding and managing stereotypes in organizations.

Allen, Brenda J. *Difference Matters: Communicating Social Identity*. Long Grove, IL: Waveland Press, Inc., 2004. This book explains how constructions of social identities have impacted members of dominant and nondominant groups.

Allport, Gordon W. *The Nature of Prejudice*. Reading, MA: Addison-Wesley, 1988. The classic study of the roots of discrimination, originally published in 1954, offers important information and insights for those training about or dealing with prejudice and stereotyping.

Arredondo, Patricia. *Successful Diversity Management Initiatives: A Blueprint for Planning and Implementation*. Thousand Oaks, CA: Sage Publications, 1996. Using organizational vignettes, the author explains the steps involved in managing the strategic implementation of diversity.

Baytos, Lawrence M. *Designing and Implementing Successful Diversity Programs*. New York: Prentice Hall and Society for Human Resource Management, 1995. This how-to manual for implementing diversity, identifies and explains each step, giving specific guidelines. From building a business rationale and getting executive commitment to evaluating diversity interventions, the author provides clear, practical information and methods.

Chemers, Martin M., Stuart Oskamp and Mark A. Costanzo, eds. *Diversity in Organization's: New Perspectives for a Changing Workplace*. Thousand Oaks, CA: Sage Publications, 1995. Contributors in this scholarly coverage provide varied perspectives on dealing with the difficulties and reaping the rewards of diversity.

Cox, Taylor, Jr. *Cultural Diversity in Organizations: Theory, Research and Practice*. San Francisco: Berrett-Koehler, 1994. This book provides a conceptual model as well as a comprehensive discussion of cultural diversity and its effects on organizational behavior and performance.

Cox, Taylor, Jr. and Ruby L. Beale. *Developing Competency To Manage Diversity.* San Francisco: Berrett-Koehler, 1997. This resource offers a competency model and three-phase learning process supported by readings, cases, and activities.

Cross, Elsie Y. and Margaret Blackburn White, eds. *The Diversity Factor: Capturing the Competitive Advantage of a Changing Workforce.* Burr Ridge, IL: Irwin Professional Publishing, 1995. This compilation of essays offers theoretical and practical information on managing diversity.

Diversity Best Practices, *The Diversity Officer: A Special Report.* Washington, DC: Diversity Best Practices, 2004. This report presents organizational practices that foster diversity and inclusion.

Dominguez, Cari M. and Jude Sotherlund, *Leading with Your Heart: Diversity and Ganas for Inspired Inclusion.* Alexandria, VA: Society for Human Resource Management, 2010.

Elashmawi, Farid and Philip R. Harris. *Multicultural Management: New Skills for Global Success.* Houston, TX: Gulf Publishing Co. 1993. By contrasting American, Japanese, and Arabian viewpoints on management, this book gives business and community leaders practical strategies and skills for succeeding in the multicultural workforce.

Fernandez, John P. *Managing a Diverse Workforce: Regaining the Competitive Edge.* Lexington, MA: Lexington Books, 1991. Based on a survey of more than 50,000 managers and employees, the author documents the racism, sexism, and ethnocentrism present in organizations across the country. He goes on to highlight the problems and special concerns faced by each group, including white males, and offers steps both individuals and organizations can take to meet these challenges.

Gardenswartz, Lee and Anita Rowe, *Diverse Teams at Work: Capitalizing on the Power of Diversity.* Alexandria, VA: SHRM 2003. This handbook for team-building provides conceptual information, models, techniques, and activities for developing diverse workgroups.

Gardenswartz, Lee and Anita Rowe, *Diversity in Health Care.* San Francisco, CA: Jossey Bass, 1998. Conceptual information and an array of learning activities to help health care providers serve an increasingly diverse patient base, as well as work with diverse staff, is offered in this resource.

Gardenswartz, Lee, Jorge Cherbosque and Anita Rowe. *Emotional Intelligence for Managing Results in a Diverse World.* Mountain View, CA: Davies-Black Publishing, 2008. This practical resource provides information and strategies for developing the emotional intelligence necessary to be effective in today's diverse workplace at the individual, team, and organizational level.

Gardenswartz, Lee, Anita Rowe, Patricia Digh and Martin Bennett. *The Global Diversity Desk Reference.* San Francisco, CA: Pfeiffer, 2003. This resource provides explanations and practical tools for managing the complexity of global diversity.

Gardenswartz, Lee and Anita Rowe, *The Lending and Diversity Handbook.* Burr Ridge, IL: Irwin Professional Publishing, 1996. This book, written for banking and financial services professionals, provides conceptual information and learning activities to increase effectiveness in serving diverse customers. An accompanying trainee workbook is also available.

Good for Business: Making Full Use of the Nation's Human Capital. Washington, D.C.: Federal Glass Ceiling Commission, 1995. This report presents the findings of the Federal Glass Ceiling Commission. It includes an overview of barriers in organizations as well as an extensive table of corporate practices describing a variety of programs and approaches.

Gudykunst, William B. *Bridging Differences: Effective Intergroup Communication.* Newbury Park, CA: Sage, 1991. This book explains the process underlying communication between people of different groups and presents principles for building community with people from diverse backgrounds.

Gudykunst, William B.; Lea P. Stewart; and Stella Ting-Toomey, eds. *Communication, Culture, and Organizational Processes.* Newbury Park, CA: Sage, 1985. This collection of articles weaves theoretical issues with practical organizational concerns such as conflict, negotiation, and decision-making.

Hall, Edward T. *Beyond Culture.* New York: Anchor Books/Doubleday, 1989. This fundamental work on culture gives an in-depth analysis of the culturally determined yet unconscious attitudes that mold our thoughts, feelings, communications, and behavior. It continues from *The Silent Language and The Hidden Dimension* to discuss the covert cultural influences that impact cross-cultural encounters.

Hall, Edward T. *The Hidden Dimension.* New York: Anchor Books/Doubleday, 1969. This book discusses proxemics, the ways humans use space in public and private. It provides insights about how this aspect of culture affects personal and business relations and cross-cultural interactions as well as architecture and urban planning.

Hall, Edward T. *The Silent Language.* New York: Anchor Books/Doubleday, 1973. Insights into the cultural aspects of communication are given in this fundamental work. The author explains how dimensions such as time and space communicate beyond words.

Harris, Philip R., and Robert T. Moran. *Managing Cultural Differences: High Performance Strategies for Today's Global Manager.* Houston, TX: Gulf, 1987. This business-oriented text on diversity gives a comprehensive treatment of cultural differences affecting business, focusing more on international than domestic intercultural issues. It includes questionnaires, surveys, and resources.

Hayles, Robert and Armida Mendez Russell. *The Diversity Directive: Why Some Initiatives Fail and What To Do About It.* Chicago, IL: Irwin Professional Publishing and ASTD, 1997. This guide provides a step-by-step process for helping your organization reach its diversity objectives. It offers models, suggested actions, and real-world applications.

Hepworth, Janice. *Intercultural Communication: Preparing To Function Successfully in the International Environment.* Denver, CO: University Centers, 1991. This self-study guide helps maximize effectiveness in intercultural interactions.

Herbst, Philip H. *The Color of Words: An Encyclopedic Dictionary of Ethnic Bias in the United States.* Yarmouth, ME: Intercultural Press, 1997. This unique resource defines more than 850 controversial and confusing ethnic and racial terms used in the United States.

Hofstede, Geert. *Cultures and Organizations: Software of the Mind.* New York: McGraw-Hill, 1991. In this work, the author shows that effective intercultural cooperation is possible and explains under what circumstances and at what cost this can be done.

Hofstede, Geert. *Culture's Consequences: International Differences in Work-Related Values.* Newbury Park, CA: Sage, 1984. A foundation piece in the literature about culture, this research-based book discusses culturally-based differences in values that impact the workplace. Aspects such as individualism, power distance, masculinity, and uncertainty avoidance are examined.

Hopkins, Willie E. *Ethical Dimensions of Diversity,* Thousand Oaks, CA: Sage Publications, 1997. This work discusses the relationship between ethics and diversity and offers a process model.

James, Muriel. *The Better Boss in Multicultural Organizations: A Guide to Success Using Transactional Analysis.* Walnut Creek, CA: Marshall, 1991. This book aims at helping bosses value themselves and their own cultural diversity as well as that of others. It presents seven skills managers need and explains how to use transactional analysis to increase effectiveness as a boss.

Jamieson, David, and Julie O'Mara. *Managing Workforce 2000: Gaining the Diversity Advantage.* San Francisco: Jossey-Bass, 1991. Built around the authors' six-step flex-management model, this book offers practical strategies to help organizations attract, make the best use of, and retain employees of different groups in order to maintain a competitive advantage.

Jandt, Fred E. and Paul B. Pedersen, eds. *Constructive Conflict Management.* Thousand Oaks, CA: Sage Publications, Inc., 1996. Using 24 cases from Asia and the Pacific Islands, the editors present models for conflict management in a cultural context.

Johnston, William B., and Arnold E. Packer. *Workforce 2000: Work and Workers for the 21st Century.* Indianapolis, IN: Hudson Institute, 1987. Working from census figures and other demographic data, this report from the U.S. Department of Labor delineates workforce trends. The report goes on to discuss the impact of these changes and the challenges they bring.

Judy, Richard W. and Carol D'Amico, *Workforce 2020: Work and Workers in the 21st Century,* Indianapolis, IN: Hudson Institute, 1997. This sequel to the original Hudson Report brings updated information and recommendations for managing the future workforce.

Landis, Dan, Janet M. Bennett and Milton J. Bennett, Eds. *Handbook of Intercultural Training.* Thousand Oaks, CA: Sage, 2004. This text, written by leading authorities, provides information on research, concepts, and methods for intercultural training.

Loden, Marilyn. *Implementing Diversity.* Burr Ridge, IL: Irwin Professional Publishing, 1996. Fourteen principles of effective diversity implementation are explained through short case studies in this book. In addition, a change-management paradigm is delineated and applied to help practitioners implement diversity.

Loden, Marilyn, and Judy B. Rosener, Ph.D. *Workforce America! Managing Employee Diversity as a Vital Resource.* Homewood, IL: Business One Irwin, 1991. This foundation piece in the literature about diversity makes a case for creating an organization that capitalizes on the richness in differences. It offers an insightful look at the issues as well as managerial and organizational strategies to deal with them.

Miller, Frederick A. and Judith H. Katz. *The Inclusion Breakthrough: Unleashing the Real Power of Diversity.* San Francisco: Berrett-Koehler Publishers, Inc., 2002. This resource offers a process for building inclusion into the workplace.

Moodian, Michael A., Ed. *Contemporary Leadership and Intercultural Competence.* Thousand Oaks, CA: Sage, 2009. This text brings together chapters from some of the foremost scholars and practitioners in diversity and intercultural communication, giving conceptual and practical information necessary for leading today's diverse, global organizations.

Morrison, Ann M. *The New Leaders: Guidelines on Leadership Diversity in America.* San Francisco, CA: Jossey-Bass, 1992. This book, written for supervisors, project managers, and CEOs, gives practical advice on how to lead and motivate an increasingly multicultural workforce.

Orey, Maureen. *Successful Staffing in a Diverse Workplace.* Irvine, CA: Richard Chang Associates, 1996. This book provides a five-phase model for diversity staffing, then guides the reader through the stages with examples and worksheets.

Pathways and Progress: Corporate Best Practices To Shatter the Glass Ceiling, Chicago: Chicago Area Partnerships, 1996. (Available from Women Employed, 22 W. Monroe, Suite 1400, Chicago, IL 60603) This product of a collaboration of community, government, and corporate representatives features case studies of eight organizations which have implemented exemplary programs for making progress in breaking through the glass ceiling.

Pedersen, Paul. *A Handbook for Developing Multicultural Awareness.* Alexandria, VA: American Association for Counseling and Development, 1988. While written for counselors, this book also serves as a resource for managers working with staff from other cultures as well as employees working with multicultural co-workers and customers.

Pedersen, Paul B. and Allen Ivey. *Culture Centered Counseling and Interviewing Skills.* New York: Praeger, 1993. This practical guide helps those involved in cross-cultural interviewing and counseling develop the skills to increase their effectiveness.

Ponterotto, Joseph G. and Paul B. Pedersen. *Preventing Prejudice: A Guide for Counselors and Educators.* Thousand Oaks, CA: Sage Publications, Inc. 1993. This relevant and pragmatic book provides information about the nature of prejudice as well as developmentally sequenced exercises for dealing with problems of prejudice.

Ricks, David A. *Blunders in International Business.* Cambridge, MA: Blackwell Publishers, 1993. This book, based on the premise that mistakes often teach more than successes, focuses on examples of blunders that illustrate the cost of not understanding cultural differences in business. It is rich with anecdotes and stories that demonstrate the point.

Rossman, Marlene L. *Multicultural Marketing: Selling to a Diverse America.* New York: Amacom, 1994. In this book, the author describes the $500 billion market represented by America's so-called "minorities," the most important consumer growth area in the United States. She then goes on to explain differences among the segments of this market and how to reach them.

Samovar, Larry A., and Richard E. Porter. *Intercultural Communication: A Reader.* Belmont, CA: Wadsworth, 1976. This anthology provides a series of 44 articles on culture in general as well as on specific cultures and aspects of intercultural communication. Both theoretical and practical information is given.

Shackelford, William G. *Minority Recruiting: Building the Strategies and Relationships for Effective Recruiting.* Dubuque, IA: Kendall/Hunt Publishing, 1996. In this guide for recruiters and HR managers, the author delineates a process for organizations to recruit minority candidates.

Simons, George F., Bob Abramims, L. Ann Hopkins with Diane J. Johnson. *Cultural Diversity Fieldbook.* Amherst, MA: ODT, 1996. This collection of articles and activities offers challenges, insights, and new thoughts about diversity.

Simons, George F., Carmen Vasquez and Philip R. Harris. *Transcultural Leadership: Empowering the Diverse Workforce.* Houston, TX: Gulf Publishing, 1993. This addition to the literature on diversity offers insights into managing and leading diverse employees.

Simons, George F. and Amy J. Zuckerman. *Working Together: Succeeding in a Multicultural Organization.* Los Altos, CA: Crisp Publications, 1994. This short handbook offers exercises and worksheets to help employees understand the basics of diversity.

Tanno, Dolores V. and Alberto Gonzalez, eds. *Communication and Identity Across Cultures.* Thousand Oaks, CA: Sage Publications, Inc., 1997. Seven perspectives of identity in different cultures, along with scholarly discussions about cultural issues in identity, are presented in this book.

Thiederman, Sondra. *Making Diversity Work: 7 Steps for Defeating Bias in the Workplace.* Chicago, IL: Dearborn Trade Publishing, 2003. This book provides leaders and managers with a step-by-step strategy for minimizing bias and maximizing effectiveness in managing diversity.

Thiederman, Sondra, Ph.D. *Bridging Cultural Barriers for Corporate Success: How To Manage the Multicultural Workforce.* Lexington, MA: Lexington Books, 1990. This handbook for cross-cultural communication gives managers and HR professionals practical information about motivating, attracting, interviewing, retaining, and training the multicultural workforce. This reader-friendly book is full of applicable examples, how-to's, and exercises for overcoming obstacles to intercultural communication.

Thiederman, Sondra, Ph.D. *Profiting in America's Multicultural Marketplace: How To Do Business Across Cultural Lines.* Lexington, MA: Lexington Books, 1991. In practical, readable terms, the author explains cultural effects on interpersonal behavior and how to communicate effectively with people of different backgrounds. Included are anecdotes and tests that involve and teach.

Thomas, R. Roosevelt, Jr. *Beyond Race and Gender: Unleashing the Power of Your Total Workforce by Managing Diversity.* New York: Amacom, 1991. This book puts forth a plan for managing diversity coupled with practical examples of how organizations capitalize on their diverse staffs. It includes a strategy for a cultural audit as well as an action plan for change.

Thomas, R. Roosevelt, Jr. *Redefining Diversity.* NY: Amacom, 1996. This book explains the author's "Diversity Paradigm," which forms the basis of a new diversity management approach.

Ting-Toomey, Stella, and Felipe Korzenny, eds. *Cross-Cultural Interpersonal Communication.* Newbury Park, CA: Sage, 1991. This collection of articles provides sources of information about current research and theories in cross-cultural communication.

Trompenaars, Fons, *Riding the Waves of Culture: Understanding Diversity in Global Business.* Burr Ridge, IL: Irwin Professional Publishing, 1993. Based on 30 examples of multinational companies, the author shows how cultural values and beliefs affect business interactions.

Turkewych, Christine and Helen Guerrerro-Klinoroski. *Intercultural Interviewing. The Key to Effective Hiring in a Multicultural Workforce.* Halle, P.Q., Canada: International Briefing Associates, 1992. With guidelines and critical incidents, this manual serves as a resource for managers, HR personnel, and trainees regarding each stage of the interviewing process.

Walton, Sally J. *Cultural Diversity in the Workplace.* Lexington, MA: Lexington, 1994. This reader-friendly handbook provides exercises and worksheets to help managers and supervisors deal with diversity.

Wilson, Trevor. *Diversity at Work: The Business Case for Equity.* Canada: John Wiley & Sons, Canada, Ltd. 1997. This book shows how implementing a successful diversity strategy, where differences are valued, can benefit business.

Wurzel, Jaime B., ed. *Toward Multiculturalism: A Reader in Multicultural Education.* Yarmouth, ME: Intercultural Press, 1988. The purpose of this book is to help the reader develop a multicultural style of thinking, feeling, and self-awareness in order to cope better with change and conflict. The series of articles offers a combination of research studies and accounts of personal experiences with different cultures.

Books About African Americans and Race

Bowser, Benjamin P. and Raymond G. Hunt. *Impacts of Racism on White Americans.* Thousand Oaks, CA: Sage Publications, 1996.This updated version of a 14-year-old book discusses how white Americans act out racism, as well as the advantages and disadvantages of racism to whites.

Chideya, Farai. *Don't Believe the Hype: Fighting Cultural Misinformation about African-Americans.* New York: Penguin Books, 1995. This book offers an array of factual information to refute many common misconceptions and stereotypes about African Americans. It is designed to give readers a chance to question the standard depictions of race in today's news media and popular press.

Davis, George, and Gregg Watson. *Black Life in Corporate America.* Garden City. NY: Anchor Press/Doubleday, 1982. This book sheds light on the impact of American organizational culture on black employees.

Fernandez, John. *Racism and Sexism in Corporate Life.* Lexington, MA: Lexington Books, 1981. This book discusses the findings of a major study of black and white men and women in the workplace, focusing on how racism and sexism affect their work life.

Gary, Lawrence. *Black Men.* Newbury Park, CA: Sage, 1981. This book discusses issues confronting black men in America.

Grier, William H. and Price M. Cobbs. *Black Rage:* New York: Basic Books, 1968. This classic on race offers the views of two black psychiatrists on the inner conflicts and desperation of black life in the United States.

Hacker, Andrew. *Two Nations: Black and White, Separate, Hostile, Unequal.* New York, NY: Scribner's, 1992. This book gives a human analysis of race relations in America, diagnosing the problems though offering no prescription for solutions.

Kivel, Paul. *Uprooting Racism: How White People Can Work for Racial Justice.* Philadelphia: New Society Publishers, 1996. This how-to book provides guidance to whites on taking action to combat racism.

Knowles, Louis, and Kenneth Prewitt. *Institutional Racism in America.* Englewood Cliffs, NJ: Prentice Hall, 1969. This book gives a comprehensive account of the pervasiveness of racism in institutions in this society.

Kochman, Thomas. *Black and White Styles in Conflict.* Chicago, IL: University of Chicago Press, 1981. This study of black culture helps illuminate racial misunderstandings and explain the values and style differences that may be at the heart of problems in interethnic communication.

Moskos, Charles C. and John Sibley Butler. *All That We Can Be: Black Leadership and Racial Integration the Army Way.* New York: Basic Books, 1996. This study of the army's integration process provides insight for other organizations attempting to improve race relations.

Rodgers-Rose, LaFrances. *Black Women.* Newbury Park, CA: Sage, 1983. Issues and conditions confronting black women are discussed in this book.

Rutslein, Nathan and Michael Morgan, Eds. *Healing Racism: Education's Role.* Springfield, MA: Whitcomb Publishing, 1996. This collection of writings from 16 experts focuses on the devastating effects of racism as well as ways to combat these effects through education.

Secundy, Marian Gray, and Lois Lacivita Nixon. *Trials, Tribulations and Celebrations: African-American Perspectives on Health, Illness, Aging and Loss.* Yarmouth, ME: Intercultural Press, 1992. This collection of short stories, narratives, and poems explores aspects of the life cycle from an African-American perspective. It is especially helpful for health care providers, as well as for those living and providing services in a multicultural society.

West, Cornell. *Race Matters.* Boston: Beacon Press, 1993. In this book, the author discusses the dynamics and impact of racism in America.

Williams, Gregory Howard. *Life on the Color Line.* New York: Dutton, 1995. This true story of a white boy who discovered he was black poignantly illustrates the effects of prejudice and discrimination in American life.

Work, John W. *Race, Economics and Corporate America*. Wilmington, DE: Scholarly Resources, 1984. This book explores the socioeconomic factors and racism that impact the status of African Americans.

Books About Latinos

Condon, John C. *Good Neighbors: Communication with the Mexicans*. Yarmouth, MA: Intercultural Press, 1985. In this concise book, the author describes how the culture of the United States and Mexico differ, how Mexicans and North Americans misunderstand each other, and what can be done to bridge the gap. Vital information for those working with Mexicans is provided in a readable, interesting way.

Knouse, Stephen B., Paul Rosenfeld, and Amy Culbertson, eds. *Hispanics in the Workplace*. Newbury Park, CA: Sage, 1992. A comprehensive exploration of Hispanic employment factors, problems at work, support systems, and Hispanic women and work. Contributors deal with specific topics such as recruiting, training, and language barriers.

Kras, Eva S. *Management in Two Cultures: Bridging the Gap Between U.S. and Mexican Managers*. Yarmouth, ME: Intercultural Press, 1989. This book pinpoints the principal differences between Mexican and U.S. cultures and management styles that cause misunderstandings and conflict. Concrete recommendations to both U.S. and Mexican managers for dealing more effectively with each other are given.

Miranda, Alfredo. *The Chicano Experience: An Alternative Perspective*. Notre Dame, ID: University of Notre Dame Press, 1985. The social and economic conditions facing Mexican Americans are explained in this book.

Sharris, Ear. *Latinos: A Biography of the People*. New York: W.W. Norton & Co., 1992. This book offers a deeper understanding of many cultures of Spanish-speaking peoples. The origin of the main groups, their history in the Americas and the United States, and their situation now is told mainly through biographies of individuals and families.

Books About Other Groups

Althen, Gary. *American Ways: A Guide for Foreigners in the United States*. Yarmouth, ME: Intercultural Press, 1988. This books is designed for those wanting to understand the behaviors and values of Americans. In easy-to-understand language and clear examples, the author describes the basic characteristics of American culture and offers suggestions for effective interactions with Americans.

Andres, Tomas. *Understanding Filipino Values: A Management Approach*. Quezon City, Metro Manila, Philippines: New Day, 1981. This book is a resource for understanding Filipino culture and values with an emphasis on management issues.

Barker, Roger G. *Adjustment to Physical Handicap and Illness: A Survey of the Social Psychology of Physique and Disability*. New York: Social Science Research Council, 1953. This book combines a theoretical and a practical discussion of the social psychology of differently-abled people. It also contains a chapter on employment.

Baylan, Esther. *Women and Disability.* London and Atlantic Highlands, NJ: Zed Books, 1991. This book discusses the issues faced by women with disabilities.

Blank, Renee and Sandra Slipp. *Voices of Diversity: Real People Talk About Problems and Solutions in a Workplace Where Everyone Is Not Alike.* New York, NY: American Management Association, 1994. This book provides real discussion from African-American, Asian-American, Latino, immigrant, disabled, gay, lesbian, and white-male and female workers. Scenarios and suggestions are included.

Blumfeld, Warren J., and Deane Raymond. *Looking at Gay and Lesbian Life.* Boston: Beacon Press, 1988. Lesbian and gay lifestyles in the United States are examined and discussed in this book.

Condon, John C. *With Respect to the Japanese: A Guide for Americans.* Yarmouth, MA: Intercultural Press, 1984. In this handbook, the author discusses aspects of Japanese values and behavior that affect communication, business relations, and the management styles. He goes on to make recommendations on how to deal with the Japanese during face-to-face encounters.

Dychtwald, Ken. *Age Power: How the 21st Century Will Be Ruled by the New Old.* New York: Jeremy P. Tarcher/Putnam, 2000. This book explores the impact aging baby boomers will have on the challenges of this millennium.

Fieg, John Paul, and Elizabeth Mortlock. *A Common Core: Thais and Americans.* Yarmouth, ME: Intercultural Press, 1989. Both commonalties and differences between Thai and American cultures are explained in this book. The authors discuss the implication of the differences for those engaged in cross-cultural encounters on and off the job.

Fisher, Glen. *International Negotiations: A Cross-Cultural Perspective.* Yarmouth, ME: Intercultural Press, 1980. By comparing how Japanese, Mexicans, French, and Americans reach agreements, the author demonstrates how culture influences the negotiation process and suggests a useful line of questioning and analysis for intercultural negotiation.

Gochenour, Theodore. *Considering Filipinos.* Yarmouth, ME: Intercultural Press, 1990. This intercultural handbook contrasts the values and perspectives of Filipinos and Americans and offers guidelines for successful interaction between these two groups. It gives suggestions for bridging cultural differences in social and workplace settings as well as case studies showing cross-cultural dynamics in action.

Hankin, Harriet. *The New Workforce: Five Sweeping Trends That Will Shape Your Company's Future.* New York: Amacom, 2005. This book gives you insight into the major trends impacting organizations in this millennium.

Kitano, Harry L., and Roger Daniels. *Asian Americans: Emerging Minorities.* Englewood Cliffs, NJ: Prentice Hall, 1988. This book focuses on the various Asian ethnic groups, discussing their experiences in America.

Lancaster, Lynne C. and David Stillman. *When Generations Collide.* New York: Collins Business, 2002. This book provides information about generation gaps and how to solve generational issues at work.

Lanier, Alison R. *Living in the USA.* Yarmouth, ME: Intercultural Press, 1988. This book is designed to help foreigners and newcomers understand the United States. It provides a guide to customs, courtesies, and caveats, and gives practical advice to anyone coming to the United States.

McLuhan, T.C. *Touch the Earth*. New York: Simon & Schuster, 1971. This book gives a recollection of the Native American way of life and, in contrast, comments on mainstream American society and values.

Mead, Margaret. *Culture and Commitment: A Study of the Generation Gap*. Garden City, NY: Doubleday, 1970. This anthropologist's look at the generation gap explains the differences in views and perspectives between the young and the old.

Nelson, Roberta. *Creating Acceptance for Handicapped People*. Springfield, IL: Charles C. Thomas, 1978. This handbook is designed to teach the community to be supportive and accepting of those with both physical and mental disabilities.

Nydell, Margaret K. *Understanding Arabs: A Guide for Westerners*. Yarmouth, ME: Intercultural Press, 1987. This readable cross-cultural handbook gives a concise and insightful look at Arab culture. It dispels common Western misconceptions regarding Arab behavior and it explains the values, beliefs, and practices of Arabs, particularly in terms of their impact on interactions with Europeans and North Americans.

Raines, Claire. *Connecting Generations: A Sourcebook for a New Workplace*. Crisp Publications, 2003. This resource provides information about four generations and suggestions for mixing and recruiting generations.

Richmond, Yale. *From Nyet to Da: Understanding the Russians*. Yarmouth, ME: Intercultural Press, 1992. This succinctly written book is a cross-cultural guide for dealing with Russians. The author outlines ways of responding most effectively to Russians on a personal level as well as in business.

Root, Maria P.P. *Filipino Americans: Transforming Identity*. Thousand Oaks, CA. Sage Publications, 1997. This collection of articles from historians, social workers, psychologists, educators, and ethnic scholars addresses issues such as ethnic identity, relationships, and mental health.

Sagarin, Edward, ed. *The Other Minorities*. Waltham, MA: Xerox College, 1971. Nonethnic minorities, such as the differently-abled, are the subjects in this collection of articles.

Schroder, Rick. *Finding the Energy: Coming Out in Corporate America*. Dallas, TX: Durban House, 2008. This book tells what it's like to come out as a gay person in a U.S. company.

Shahar, Lucy and David Kurz. *Border Crossings: American Interactions with Israelis*. Yarmouth, ME: Intercultural Press, 1996. In case studies based on real situations, the authors focus on Americans and Israelis attempting to communicate across cultural barriers. They also offer coping strategies and exercises that help readers choose the most appropriate responses for their own personal style.

Stewart, Edward C. *American Cultural Patterns: A Cross-Cultural Perspective*. Yarmouth, Me: Intercultural Press, 1972. Using the value-orientation framework of Kluckholn and Strodtbeck, the author examines American patterns of thinking and behaving. He goes on to analyze the assumptions about human nature and the physical world that underlie these values, and to compare and contrast them with those of other cultures.

Wenzhong, Hu, and Cornelius L. Grove. *Encountering the Chinese: A Guide for Americans.* Yarmouth, ME: Intercultural Press, 1991. This useful book goes beyond description to explain Chinese behavior. It provides a cross-cultural analysis that can guide Westerners toward more effective relationships with the Chinese.

Winfield, Liz, and Susan Spielman. *Straight Talk about Gays in the Workplace: Creating an Inclusive Environment for Everyone in Your Organization.* New York: American Management Association, 1995. This candid book brings the myths and facts about gays out into the open and offers a clear look at how companies can include sexual orientation in their nondiscrimination and diversity management programs.

Zemke, Ron, Claire Raines and Bob Filipczak. *Generations at Work: Managing the Clash of Veterans, Boomers, Xers and Nexters in Your Workplace.* New York: Amacon, 2000. This resource provides profiles of four generations in the workplace and suggestions for managing them effectively.

Books About Men, Women, and Gender Differences

Astrachan, Anthony. *How Men Feel.* New York: Anchor, 1988. How men feel about women is the topic of this book, which contains a number of chapters focusing on work relationships.

Cheng, Cliff, ed. *Masculinities in Organizations,* Thousand Oaks, CA: Sage Publications, 1996. This collection of essays offers research about and discussions of male norms and behaviors in legal, governmental, business, and other settings.

Collins, David L. and Jeff Hearn, *Men as Managers, Managers as Men,* Thousand Oaks, CA: Sage Publications, 1997. Drawing on both theoretical and empirical contributions, this book explores the relationship between men, masculinity, and management, and examines gender inequality in organizations.

Farrell, Warren. *Why Men Are the Way They Are.* New York: McGraw-Hill, 1986. This book offers insights and understanding, not only about male behavior but also about male-female relationships.

Gardenswartz, Lee, and Anita Rowe. *What It Takes: Good News from 100 of America's Top Professional and Business Women.* New York: Doubleday, 1987. From interviews with 100 of America's top-achieving women, the authors distill five critical factors shared by all. This book dispels the myths about successful women and offers a guide for women wanting to create their own brand of success.

Gilligan, Carol. *In a Different Voice: Psychological Theory and Women's Development.* Cambridge, MA: Harvard University Press, 1962. This book presents a seminal discussion of gender differences in moral/ethical development and the implications for the workplace.

Gray, John. *Men Are From Mars, Women Are From Venus: A Practical Guide for Improving Communication and Getting What You Want in Your Relationships.* New York: Harper Collins, 1992. This look at male-female differences argues that communication problems between the sexes are rooted in gender-related values differences.

Gutek, Barbara A. *Sex and the Workplace.* San Francisco, CA: Jossey-Bass, 1985. This book examines a critical aspect of male-female interaction on the job—the impact of sexual behavior and harassment on women, men, and organizations. The issue is looked at from managerial, legal, psychological, and social perspectives.

Heim, Pat and Susan Galant. *Hardball for Women: Winning at the Game of Business.* Los Angeles, CA: Lowell House, 1992. Differences in male and female leadership skills are the subject of this book. Tracing gender differences to the play of boys and girls, the authors apply these preferences to adult behaviors in the workplace.

Higginbotham, Elizabeth and Mary Romero, eds. *Women and Work: Exploring Race, Ethnicity and Class,* Thousand Oaks, CA: Sage Publications, 1997. This collection of original research articles explore women's working conditions, wages, and perceptions about their options. Much attention is paid to women of color, noncitizens, and working-class women.

Landrine, Hope and Elizabeth A. Klonoff. *Discrimination Against Women: Prevalence, Consequences and Remedies.* Thousand Oaks, CA. Sage Publications, 1997. The authors offer an empirically-validated scale for measuring the health effects of sexism and report their findings on the mental and physical health impact of discrimination.

Lipman-Blumen, Jean. *Gender Roles and Power.* Englewood Cliffs, NJ: Prentice Hall, 1984. This book explains the way in which the gender system is a foundation for all other power relationships.

Loden, Marilyn. *Feminine Leadership: Or How To Succeed in Business Without Being One of the Boys.* New York: Times Books, 1985. This book delineates differences in male and female leadership styles, making implications for enhancing the workplace.

Milwid, Beth, Ph.D. *Working with Men: Professional Women Talk about Power, Sexuality, and Ethics.* Hillsboro, OR: Beyond Words, 1990. Interviews with 125 professional women provide a look at what it's like for women in the workplace. This book gives an insider's look at the pressures, problems, and hopes of women in the work world.

Morrison, Ann M.; Randall P. White; and Ellen van Velson. *Breaking the Glass Ceiling.* Reading, MA: Addison-Wesley, 1987. Based on a study of executives, this book examines the factors that determine the success and failure of women in corporate America.

Pearson, Judy C. *Gender and Communication.* Dubuque, IA: William C. Brown, 1985. This book focuses on the gender gap's effect on interactions, discussing the difficulties and differences in communication between men and women.

Powell, Gary. *Women and Men in Management: The Dynamics of Interaction.* Thousand Oaks, CA: Sage Publications, Inc., 1993. In this book about gender differences, the author downplays the importance of male-female differences.

Rosener, Judy B. *America's Competitive Secret: Utilizing Women as a Management Strategy.* New York: Oxford University Press, 1995. This book describes the unique contribution of female professionals and explains why men and women are perceived and evaluated differently at work. It helps both men and women understand the economic, social, and psychological impact of women and men interacting as peers and competitors.

Sargent, Alice G. *Beyond Sex Roles.* St. Paul, MN: West, 1977. Through exercises and narrative explanations, the author and other contributors teach, raise awareness, and prod self-exploration about sex roles and change regarding those roles.

Simons, George, F., and G. Deborah Weissman. *Men and Women: Partners at Work.* Los Altos, CA: Crisp Publications, 1990. The objective of this book is to help men and women approach each other openly, creatively, and with effective communication tools. Exercises and worksheets help readers identify and resolve gender issues that inhibit productivity and understanding.

Smith, Dayle M. *Kincare and the American Corporation: Solving the Work/Family Dilemma.* Homewood, IL: Business One Irwin, 1991. This book addresses child and elder care as business survival for working parents.

Tannen, Deborah. *You Just Don't Understand: Women and Men in Conversion.* New York: William Morrow, 1991. In a down-to-earth, reader-friendly style, the author explains gender differences in communication that produce obstacles. Recognizing and understanding these differences can be a help in avoiding barriers to clear communication between men and women.

Tingley, Judith. *Genderflex: Men and Women Speaking Each Others' Language at Work.* New York: Amacom, 1994. This book gives suggestions about overcoming the gender gap in work communication.

Structured Experiences and Games

Bafa Bafa: Cross-Cultural Orientation. Gary R. Shirts, P.O. Box 910, Del Mar, CA 92014; (619) 755-0272. This experiential activity simulates the contact between two very different cultures, Alpha and Beta. The activity is structured so that participants learn through direct simulated experience and then apply that learning to real-life situations. (*Rafa Rafa,* a simplified version for elementary school children, grades 5–8, is also available.)

Barnga: A Simulation Game on Cultural Clashes. Thiagarajan, Sivasailam, Intercultural Press, P.O. Box 700, Yarmouth, ME 04096; (207) 846-5168. Through playing a simple card game in small groups, participants experience the effect of simulated cultural differences on human interaction. This activity is easy to run in a relatively short time.

The Diversity Game. Quality Educational Development, Inc. 41 Central Park West, New York, NY 10023 (212) 724-3335. This multi-player board game provides insights, raises awareness, and stimulates discussion about diversity issues in the workplace. Questions focus on real workplace issues such as communication, motivation, reward, recognition, respect, and trust in the context of gender, race, and cultural diversity.

Diversophy. Multus, Inc., 46 Treetop Lane, Suite 200, San Mateo, CA 94402-3234 (415) 342-2040. This board game is designed to be played by line managers, supervisors, administrative personnel, sales people, customer service representatives, and senior executives. Easy to play, the game delivers thought-provoking information, deals with critical attitudes, and teaches useful skills for meeting the challenges of diversity.

Ecotonos. Nipporica Associates and Dianne Hofner-Saphiere. Intercultural Press, P.O. Box 700, Yarmouth, ME; (207) 846-5168. This simulation deals with problem-solving and decision-making in multicultural groups.

The Global Diversity Game. Quality Educational Development, Inc. 41 Central Park West, New York, NY 10023 (212) 724-3335. This board game is played by teams answering questions focusing on demographics, jobs, legislation, and society related to the global business environment. Cross-cultural and trans-national information is highlighted, stimulating a dynamic exchange of knowledge and experience between participants.

Redundancia. Dianne Hofner-Saphiere and Nipporica Associates. 10072 Buena Vista Drive, Conifer, CO 80433. (303) 838-1798. This short, effective simulation helps people understand the challenges faced by people attempting to communicate in a second language.

Training Materials

Aguilar, Leslie and Linda Stokes. *Multicultural Customer Service: Providing Outstanding Service Across Cultures.* Burr Ridge, IL: Irwin Professional Publishing, 1995. This skills training handbook provides worksheets, quizzes, and case studies to train customer service staff.

Carnevale, Anthony Patrick and S. Kanu Kagod. *Tools and Activities for a Diverse Workforce.* New York, NY: McGraw-Hill, 1995. This collection of more than 100 training activities and assessment tools from consulting firms and companies provides ready-to-copy handouts.

Deckerson-Jones, Terri. *50 Activities for Managing Cultural Diversity,* Amherst, MA: HRD Press, 1996. This resource provides reproducible activities including notes for the trainer.

Gardenswartz, Lee and Anita Rowe. *Diversity Tool Kit,* Gardenswartz & Rowe 2009, www.gardenswartzrowe.com, (310) 823-2466) This training kit on a CD provides more than 100 diversity training activities in reproducible format with directions for trainers. Exercises designed to build awareness, knowledge, and skills are categorized by topics such as stereotypes and prejudice, culture, communication, and team-building.

Kogod, S. Kanu. *A Workshop for Managing Diversity in the Workplace.* San Diego, CA: Pfeiffer & Company, 1991. This package presents a workshop designed for management training with 18 experiential activities as well as lectures for building awareness and knowledge. It includes three training modules, a trainer's guide, and handouts.

Lambert, Jonamay and Selma Myers. *Customer Relations and the Diversity Challenge: A Trainer's Guide.* Solana Beach, CA: Intercultural Development, 1995. Included in this trainer's guide are 12 activities for developing skills for working with diverse customers.

Lambert, Jonamay and Selma Myers, *50 Activities for Diversity Training.* Amherst, MA: HRD Press, 1995. This resource offers a variety of reproducible interactive learning exercises about gender, communication, and culture in the workplace.

Myers, Selma and Jonamay Lambert. *Diversity Ice Breakers: A Trainer's Guide.* Solana Beach, CA: Intercultural Development, 1994. This collection of 40 icebreakers can be used for introductions, personal awareness, and training about perceptions, strategies, and communication.

Powell, Gary N. *Gender and Diversity in the Workplace: Learning Activities and Exercises.* Thousand Oaks, CA: Sage Publications, 1994. This resource provides individual and group activities, diagnostic instruments, role plays, and simulations to help trainers learn how to deal with gender and diversity issues with integrity.

Rasmussen, Tina, *The ASTD Trainer's Sourcebook: Diversity,* Alexandria, VA: ASTD, 1995. Resources for a one-day, half-day and one-hour workshop are provided in this book, which includes activities, assessments, overheads, and planning tools.

Stringer, Donna and Patricia Cassiday. *52 Activities for Exploring Values Differences.* Yarmouth, MA: Intercultural Press, 2003. This useful resource provides a variety of applicable training activities to engage participants in diversity learning.

DVDs, Videos, and Films

Age and Attitudes. corVision Media, 1359 Barclay Blvd., Buffalo Grove, IL 60089. (800) 537-3138. Produced for ABC News for "Prime Time Live," this video explores discrimination among older workers.

Awesome. Quality Media Resources, (800) 800-5129. www.qmr.com. This two-part series features Gen Ys sharing their perspective and comments from managers on how to help them succeed.

Bill Cosby on Prejudice. Budget Films, 4590 Santa Monica Blvd., Los Angeles, CA 90029; (213) 660-0187. This film presents a monologue by Bill Cosby on prejudice.

Born Free. Educational Equity Act Publishing Center, 55 Chapel Street, Suite 231, Newton, MA 02160. These three half-hour videos feature panel discussions and interviews dealing with sex-role stereotyping.

The Bottom Line. Griggs Productions, 2046 Clement St., San Francisco, CA 94121. (800) 210-4200. This video provides an updated business case for diversity using corporate interviews, narrative, and vignettes.

Brainwaves: Case Studies in Diversity. BNA Communications (800) 233-6067. This six-module video-based program helps trainees build productive relationships with others different from themselves by exploring how perceptions and thinking patterns affect work relationships. Set includes trainer's manuals and participant materials.

Bridges: Skills for Managing a Diverse Workforce. BNA Communications, Inc., 9439 Key West Avenue, Rockville, MD 20850; (800) 253-6067. This eight-module video-based program is designed to train managers and supervisors in managing diverse workers. Both awareness about cultural/racial/gender differences and the skills to deal with them are presented. The series includes manuals for trainers and participants.

Bridging Cultural Barriers: Managing Ethnic Diversity in the Workplace. Barr Films, 12801 Schabarum Ave., P.O. Box 7878, Irwindale, CA 91706-7878; (800) 234-7878. This half-hour film featuring Sondra Thiederman, Ph.D., teaches about effective management of diverse workers through simulated examples of a manager resolving situations with two culturally different staff members. Vignettes are interspersed with lectures by Dr. Thiederman.

Connections: Managing Today's Workforce. BNA Communications, Inc. 9439 Key West Avenue, Rockville, MD 20850; (800) 233-6067. This one-hour video training program gives supervisors and managers an understanding of how EEO, diversity, and good management fit together in selecting and managing employees for maximum performance.

The Cost of Intolerance. BNA Communications, 9439 Key West Ave., Rockville, MD 20850-3396, (800) 233-6067. This six-unit video program helps employees improve customer service and increase sales by valuing diverse customers. Issues such as handling customers who speak with heavy accents and overcoming subtle biases and stereotypes are dealt with through realistic vignettes.

Dealing with Diversity. American Media Incorporated, 4900 University Ave., West Des Moines, IA 50266-6769, (800) 262-2557. This video training program helps employees deal with diversity by understanding how others want to be treated. It focuses on understanding and respecting individual differences, and improving communication by asking questions and listening.

Dialogue: New York Talking! Quality Media Resources. (800) 800-5129. www.qmr.com. This four-program series uses a scenario to demonstrate how to build bridges across differences such as generation-using dialogue.

Dialogue on Diversity: Straight White Men Speak Out. Loden, Marilyn, Loden & Associates, 1996. This video features seven white men grappling with fundamental diversity issues such as being inclusive, communicating across cultural barriers, and building trust. A facilitation guide is included.

Diverse Teams at Work. corVision, 1339 Barclay Blvd., Buffalo Grove, IL 60089, (800) 537-3130. This video, based on the book of the same title, demonstrates the impact of the many dimensions of diversity on the interactions of a work team. Understanding these differences is developed as a critical step toward building respect between people of different backgrounds.

Diversity Management: A Business Necessity! American Media, 4900 University Ave, West Des Moines, IA 50266, (800) 262-2557. This video, featuring R. Roosevelt Thomas, Jr., provides the business case for managing diversity.

Diversity Management: An Individual Perspective. American Media, 4900 University Ave, West Des Moines, IA 50266, (800) 262-2557. This video, featuring R. Roosevelt Thomas, Jr., promotes ongoing self-evaluation which leads to personal and professional growth.

Diversity: The Competitive Advantage. BNA Communications (800) 233-6067. This four-part video-based program focuses on the business case for diversity, intergroup barriers, the connection between diversity and empowerment, and the impact of differences on teams. Set includes a facilitator's kit.

Faces. Salinger Films, 1635 12th Street, Santa Monica, CA 90404; (310) 450-1300. This one-minute, non-narrated video shows a kaleidoscope of human faces of different sexes, races, and ages merging and complementing each other to form an integrative whole. By showing the individual worth of each face as well as its contribution to the total picture, the video demonstrates that we are all unique, yet we share a common bond.

The F.A.I.R. Way To Manage Diversity. American Media, 4900 University Ave, West Des Moines, IA 50266, (800) 262-2557. This video helps employees acknowledge cultural and job-related differences and work toward common ground.

Getting Along: Words of Encouragement. Cross Cultural Communications, 4585 48th St., San Diego, CA 92114, (800) 858-4478. In four-and-a-half minutes of printed messages and music, this video reminds people to work and live together with open hearts and open minds.

Let's Talk Diversity. American Media Incorporated, 4900 University Ave., West Des Moines, IA 50266-6769, (800) 262-2557. This video training program helps all employees understand how values, attitudes, and behaviors affect others. It also helps them recognize biases and stereotypes based on gender, race, religion, age, culture, disability, and lifestyle.

Living and Working in America. Via Press, Inc., 400 E. Evergreen Blvd., Suite 314, Vancouver, WA 98660; (800) 944-8421. A comprehensive three-volume audiovisual series for training non-native speakers of English in communication skills needed for supervisory/management positions in the multicultural workforce. Includes video scenes, textbook, audiotapes, and an instructor's manual with experiential learning activities.

Managing Diversity. CRM Films, 2233 Faraday Avenue, Carlsbad, CA 92008; (800) 421-0833. This film combines dramatizations of information from experts in the field to focus on diversity issues such as stereotyping and communication as well as differences in perception regarding teamwork, power, and authority. It ends with a useful list of things people can do to improve communication in a diverse environment. A guide is included.

Managing a Multicultural Workforce: The Mosaic Workplace. Films for the Humanities and Sciences, P.O. Box 2053, Princeton, NJ 08543-2053; (800) 257-5126. This video training program consists of 10 videos addressing the issues of the diverse workplace. It covers topics such as understanding different cultural values and styles, men and women working together, and success strategies for minorities.

The Multicultural Customer. Salinger Films, 1635 12th Street, Santa Monica, CA 90404; (310) 450-1300. This video helps customer service staff understand the dynamics of cross-cultural communication and get beyond barriers to establishing positive relationships with diverse customers. Vignettes of typical customer/staff interactions are shown, and tips for providing top-notch service to a diverse population are given.

Ouch! That Stereotype Hurts and Ouch! Your Silence Hurts. International Training and Development, LLC, P.O.Box 592562, Orlando, FL. www.OuchThatStereotypeHurts. com and www.OuchYourSilenceHurts.com.

Partners in Change. American Association of Retired Persons (AARP), Program Resources Department, P.O. Box 51040, Washington, D.C. 22091. This 17-minute video demonstrates how a business can benefit from hiring the mature woman. It discusses the skills that displaced homemakers can transfer to a job as well as the commitment and stability they can bring to an organization.

Racism didn't end .... Elsie Cross. corVision Media, 1359 Barclay Blvd. Buffalo Grove, IL 60089. (800) 537-3130.1996. In this video narrated by Elsie Cross, U.S. leaders of color candidly tell their own stories and experiences with racism.

Sandcastle: A Film about Teamwork and Diversity. Salinger Films, 1635 12th Street, Santa Monica, CA 90404; (310) 450-1300. Teamwork and the unique contribution of each diverse team member is illustrated in this Academy Award-winning, non-narrated 13-minute video. Through a unique story about the building of a sandcastle, the film demonstrates the value of diversity.

Serving Customers with Disabilities. Salinger Films, 1635 12th St., Santa Monica, CA 90404, (310) 450-1300. The film offers etiquette and customer service skills to help employees serve customers with disabilities more effectively.

A Tale of "O." Goodmeasure, Inc., P.O. Box 3004, Cambridge, MA 02139. This film/ video focuses on the insider/outsider dynamic by showing how a few O's learn to function in organizations made up of X's.

True Colors. Coronet/MTI Film and Video, 420 Academy Drive, Northbrook, IL 60062, (800) 777-2400. In this provocative edition of ABC's "Prime Time," host Diane Sawyer follows two college-educated men in their mid-thirties, one black, one white, as they involve themselves in a variety of everyday situations to test levels of prejudice based on skin color. The results are startling and unsettling.

Valuing Diversity. Copeland Griggs Productions, 302 23rd Ave., San Francisco, CA 94121, (415) 668-4200. This seven-part film/video series for managers and other employees focuses on the advantages inherent in diversity. Segments deal with issues such as managing/supervising differences, upward mobility in a multicultural organization, and communicating across cultures. The series includes users' guides.

West Meets East in Japan. Pyramid Film and Video, Box 1048, Santa Monica, CA 90406; (800) 421-2304. This culture-specific video lets you experience Japanese culture from the point of view of an outsider learning the norms of Japanese etiquette. A study guide is included.

Why Do We Kick a Brother or a Sister When They're Down? The Riverbend Press, P.O. Box 586, Concord, MA 01742; (508) 371-2664. This powerful videotape is the true story of childhood friends and the destructive influences of classism and other prejudices. The training tool about human relations is especially useful in dealing with valuing differences.

A Winning Balance. BNA Communications, Inc., 9439 Key West Avenue, Rockville, MD 20850; (800) 233-6067. Using five dramatic segments on video, this program addresses questions such as what is diversity and why should I care. It goes beyond understanding to give employees the skills to be diversity change agents. The set includes a facilitator's kit.

Working Together: Managing Cultural Diversity. Crisp Publications, 95 First Street, Los Altos, CA 94022-9803; (800) 442-7477. This video-book program teaches how to work productively in a multicultural environment. Users learn how to manage their attitudes and communication in interactions with people from other cultures. The kit includes a leader's guide.

A World of Difference. corVision Media, 1359 Barclay Blvd. Buffalo Grove, IL 60089. (800) 537-3130. This animated 10-minute video conveys the message that living in a diverse world is a benefit rather than a threat.

Assessment Tools and Instruments

Bennett, Milton J. and Mitchell R. Hammer. *The Intercultural Development Inventory.* Hammer Consulting Group, LLC, dihammer@msn.com, (301) 330-5589. This valid and reliable instrument based on the Developmental Model of Intercultural Sensitivity, can be used for team development, coaching, organizational assessment, and training needs analysis.

Crabtree, Kristen M. and Cresencio Torres. *Intrapersonal Diversity Awareness Profile.* Amherst, MA: HRD Press, (800) 822-2801. This instrument assesses an individual's awareness on a continuum from naivete to internalization focusing on diversity awareness from within the individual.

Grote, Karen. *Diversity Awareness Profile and Diversity Awareness Profile, Manager's Version.* San Diego, CA: Pfeiffer & Company (619) 578-2042. This is a 40-item questionnaire that places individuals in one of five categories on the "Diversity Awareness Spectrum." It also suggests action steps and includes notes for trainers.

Halverson, Claire B., Ph.D. *Cultural Context Work Style Inventory.* Brattleboro, VT: School for International Training, Experiment in International Living, (802) 254-6098. This self-scored, 20-item questionnaire is designed for self-understanding based on the high-low context framework of Edward Hall. It includes background information, charts, and a bibliography.

Hammer, Mitchell R. *The Intercultural Conflict Style Inventory.* Hammer Consulting Group, LLC, dihammer@msn.com, (301) 330-5589. This instrument, based on a four-quadrant intercultural conflict style model, can be used for identifying approaches for resolving conflict across cultural and ethnic differences.

Kelley, Colleen, and Judith Meyers. *The Cross-Cultural Adaptability Inventory.* 2500 Torey Pines Road, La Jolla, CA 92037; (619) 453-8165. This self-scoring instrument is designed to help those planning to work and live abroad. It measures four critical dimensions of cross-cultural adaptability. A trainee's manual is included.

Overseas Assignment Inventory. (OAI). Moran, Stahl & Boyer, International Division, 900 28th Street, Boulder, CO 80303; (303) 449-8440. This self-response questionnaire measures 15 attitudes and attributes important to cross-cultural adjustment. Resulting in a profile of cross-cultural adaptability, this standardized and normed instrument can be applied in selection, placement, counseling, workforce planning, career development, and self-selection.

Simons, George. *The Questions of Diversity: Assessment Tools for Organizations and Individuals.* Amherst, MA: ODT (800) 736-1293. This resource contains nine surveys that assess personal and organizational issues of diversity in the workplace. These instruments are intended as learning tools.

Torres, Cresencio, *The Diversity Management Survey.* Amherst, MA: HRD Press (800) 822-2801. This 21-question survey gives respondents the opportunity to evaluate seven variables contributing to organizational effectiveness: strategies, structures, systems, style, skills, staffing, and shared values.

Periodicals, Journals, Newsletters, Web Sites, and Other Resources

Cultural Diversity Hotwire. http://www.diversityhotwire.com. This web site of the *Cultural Diversity at Work* newsletter provides an article of the month, abstracts of newsletter articles, a catalogue of books, videos, and back issues, as well as a networking/learning events calendar.

Diversity Inc. A daily newsletter and magazine with topical information about diversity issues. www.diversityinc.com.

Diversity Matters. This web Talk Radio program provides a forum for weekly conversations about issues of diversity and inclusiveness with thought leaders and practitioners in the field. www.diversitymatters.info.

Inter-Face International. http://www.cmihub.com/†/InterFaceInt.htm. This web site offers a listing of diversity products and services for the health care field.

Managing Diversity. Jamestown Area Labor Management Committee, Inc. P.O. Box 819, Jamestown, NY 14702–0819 (716) 665-3654. This monthly newsletter directed at business leaders and managers offers a series of articles on pertinent issues faced in leading and managing diversity organizations. It challenges and educates the reader through thoughtful articles and practical approaches.

Multicultural Calendar. Creative Cultural Communications, 12300 Contra Costa Blvd., Suite 270, Pleasant Hill, CA 94523. (800) 883-4072. This wall calendar, with 12 original ethnic artworks, lists holidays and cultural events of a wide variety of religions and cultures.

Multicultural Resource Calendar. Amherst Educational Publishing, 30 Blue Hills Rd., Amherst, MA 01002. (800) 865-5549. This award-winning calendar educates staff by increasing awareness about the contributions of people of more than 35 different backgrounds, and holidays of more than 35 groups.

National Multicultural Institute. http:www.nmci.org/nmci/links.htm. This site provides many "multicultural web links.

Society for Human Resource Management. www.shrm.org.

Endnotes

• •

Chapter 1

[1] Milton J. Bennett, "Toward Ethnorelativism: A Development Model of Intercultural Sensitivity" in Michael Paige, ed., *Cross-Cultural Orientation: New Conceptualizations and Applications* (New York: University Press of America, 1986), p. 27.

Chapter 2

[1] Richard Judy and Carol D'Amico, *Workforce 2020: Work and Workers in the 21st Century* (Washington, D.C.: Hudson Institute, 1997).

[2] Ibid.

[3] Bob Abramms and George F. Simons, "Getting Real!: Where Are We, Where Are We Going," in Bob Abramms and George F. Simons, *Cultural Diversity Sourcebook* (Amherst, Mass.: HRD Press, 1995).

Chapter 3

[1] Marilyn Loden, and Judy B. Rosener, *Workforce America! Managing Employee Diversity as a Vital Resource* (Homewood, Ill.: Business One Irwin, 1991).

[2] *Good for Business: Making Full Use of the Nation's Human Capital* (Washington, D.C.: Federal Glass Ceiling Commission, March 1995), pp. iii-iv. Available at www.dol.gov/ oasam/programs/history/reich/reports/ceiling.pdf.

[3] *Los Angeles Times*, poll taken July 23-24, 1994.

[4] Natasha Josefowitz, *Is This Where I Was Going?* (New York: Ballantine Books, 1983).

[5] Deborah Tannen, *You Just Don't Understand: Women and Men in Conversation* (New York: Ballantine, 1991), p. 244.

[6] Cornell West, *Race Matters* (Boston: Beacon Press, 1993).

[7] Janet Elsea, *The Four Minute Sell* (New York: Simon & Schuster, 1984).

[8] Farai Chideya, *Don't Believe the Hype: Fighting the Cultural Misinformation About African Americans* (New York: Penguin Group, 1995).

[9] Alicia H. Minnell, et al, "Mortgage Lending in Boston: Interpreting HMDA Data." Unpublished report. (Boston: Federal Reserve Bank of Boston, 1992).

[10] Marilyn Aquirre-Molina and Carlos W. Molina, "Ethnic/Racial Populations and Worksite Health Promotion," *Occupational Medicine: State of the Art Reviews*, Vol. 5, No. 4, October-December 1990.

11 Good for Business (March 1995).

12 Marlene Rossman, *Multicultural Marketing: Selling to a Diverse America* (New York: Amacom, 1994).

13 Jon Meacham, "The End of Christian America," *Newsweek*, April 13, 2009.

Chapter 4

1 Lee Gardenswartz, Anita Rowe, Patricia Digh, and Martin F. Bennett, *The Global Diversity Desk Reference* (San Francisco: Pfeiffer, 2003).

2 Melissa Lamson, "What Matters Where," *Communication Director*, March 2007.

3 Diversity Best Practices, Washington, D.C., 2004.

4 Jennifer Palthe, "Global Human Resource Management" in *Contemporary Leadership and Intercultural Competence*, Michael Moodian, ed., (Thousand Oaks, CA: Sage, 2009).

5 *The Global Diversity Desk Reference* (2003).

Chapter 5

1 Geert Hofstede, "National Cultures and Corporate Cultures," in Larry A. Samovar and Richard E. Porter (eds.), Communication Between Cultures (Belmont, CA: Wadsworth, 1984).

2 Nancy J. Adler, and Moses K. Kiggunder, "Awareness at the Crossroad: Designing Translator-Based Training Programs." In Don Landes and Richard Breslin, eds., *Handbook of Intercultural Training*, Vol. II. (New York: Pergamon, 1983).

3 Sondra Thiederman, *Bridging Cultural Barriers for Corporate Success* (Lexington, Mass.: Lexington Books, 1990), p. 12.

4 Robert Fulghum, *All I Really Need To Know I Learned In Kindergarten: Uncommon Thoughts on Common Things* (New York: Villard Books, 1988).

5 Philip R. Harris, and Robert T. Moran, *Managing Cultural Differences* (Houston, Tex.: Gulf Publishing Co., 1979), pp. 190-195.

6 Edward T. Hall, *The Hidden Dimension*. New York: Doubleday, 1966, p. 49.

7 Ibid.

8 Peter Farb, "Man at the Mercy of Language." In Jaime S. Wurzel, ed., *Toward Multiculturalism: A Reader in Multicultural Education* (Yarmouth, Me.: Intercultural Press, 1988), p. 194.

9 Harris and Moran (1979).

10 *How to Communicate Better with Clients, Customers and Workers Whose English Is Limited* (Los Angeles County Commission on Human Relations). Available at http://humanrelations.co.la.ca.us/publications/docs/CommBrochure.pdf.

11 Melanie Tervalon and Jon Murray Garcia, "Cultural Humility Versus Cultural Competence; A Critical Distinction in Defining Physician Training Outcomes in Multicultural Education," *Journal of Health Care for the Poor and Underserved*. May 1998.

12 Gary Althen, *American Ways: A Guide for Foreigners in the United States* (Yarmouth, Me.: Intercultural Press, 1988).

Chapter 6

[1] Patti Watts, "Bias Busting: Diversity Training in the Workplace," *Management Review*, December 1987, pp. 51054.

[2] *How to Communicate Better with Clients, Customers and Workers Whose English Is Limited* (Los Angeles County Commission on Human Relations). Available at http://humanrelations.co.la.ca.us/publications/docs/CommBrochure.pdf.

[3] Nancy J. Adler, "Cultural Synergy: Managing the Impact of Cultural Diversity," *The 1986 Annual: Developing Human Resources* (San Diego: University Associates, 1986).

Chapter 7

[1] Gordon W. Allport, *The Nature of Prejudice* (Reading, Mass.: AddisonWesley, 1959).

[2] Leon Festinger, *A Theory of Cognitive Dissonance* (Stanford, Calif.: Stanford University, 1957).

[3] Liz Winfeld and Susan Spielman, *Straight Talk About Gays in the Workplace: Creating An Inclusive, Productive Environment For Everyone In Your Organization* (New York: AMACOM, 1995).

[4] Allport (1959).

[5] Leslie Aguilar, *Ouch! That Stereotype Hurts* (Flower Mound, Tex.: Walk the Talk Books, 2008).

[6] Thomas F. Pettigrew and Linda R. Tropp, "A Meta-Analytic Test of Intergroup Contact Theory," *Journal of Personality and Social Psychology*, 2006, Vol. 90, Nos. pp 751-787.

Chapter 8

[1] John C. Condon, *With Respect to the Japanese: A Guide for Americans* (Yarmouth, Me.: Intercultural Press, 1984).

[2] Malcolm Gladwell, *Outliers: The Story of Success* (New York: Little Brown, 2008).

[3] In a discussion with the authors.

[4] Sondra Thiederman, *Bridging Cultural Barriers for Corporate Success* (Lexington, Mass.: Lexington Books, 1990), p. 12.

[5] Natasha Josefowitz, *Paths to Power: A Woman's Guide from First Job to Top Executive* (Reading, Mass.: Addison-Wesley, 1980).

[6] Gardenswartz, L., Anita Rowe, Patricia Digh, Martin Bennett, *Global Diversity Desk Reference: Managing an International Workforce*. San Francisco, Pfeiffer, 2003.

[7] Jack Gibb, *Trust: A New View of Personal and Organizational Development* (Los Angeles: The Guild of Tutors Press, 1978), pp. 16-17.

Chapter 10

[1] William Bridges, *Surviving Corporate Transition* (New York: Doubleday, 1988).

[2] Ibid.

[3] Cyndia Wahlen, "Choosing alternatives to layoffs," *Los Angeles Times*, April 21, 2009, B8. Available at http://articles.latimes.com/2009/apr/21/business/fi-smallbiz21.

Chapter 11

[1] Michael Wheeler, *Diversity: Business Rationale and Strategies. A Research Report* (New York: The Conference Board, 1995), pp. 11, 14.

[2] Densford, Lynn E. "Studies Make Economic Case for Diversity." *Workforce Training News*, Vol. 3, No. 5, June 1995, pp. 1, 6.

[3] "Multicultural Marketing, Sales, Advertising and the Diversity Officer: Overview; *Diversity Best Practices*, 2004, p. 196.

[4] Thomas Kochan et al, "The Effects of Diversity on Business Performance: Report of the Diversity Research Network," *Human Resource Management*, Spring 2003, Vol. 42, No 1, pp. 3–21.

[5] *BusinessWeek*, August 2, 1989.

[6] Ibid.

[7] Ibid.

[8] Ibid.

[9] Ibid.

[10] Ibid.

[11] Ibid.

[12] Ibid.

[13] Judy Rosener, "Greater Oversight, Profits Come With Women on Board," *Los Angeles Business Journal*, July 21, 2003.

[14] *Wall Street Journal*, May 4, 1993.

[15] *BusinessWeek*, August 2, 1989.

[16] U.S. Department of Labor. *Opportunity 2000: Creative Affirmative Action Strategies for a Changing Workforce*. Washington, D.C.: U.S. Government Printing Office, 1988.

[17] Richard W. Judy and Carol D'Amico, *Workforce 2020. Work and Workers in the 21st Century* (Indianapolis, Ind.: Hudson Institute, 1997), pp. xiv, 22-26, 53, 64, 92, 107, 110, 122.

[18] Amy E. Kahn and Steve Gomez, *Challenging Diversity: Taking the Next Step*, Amy E. Kahn, www.culture-link.com.

[19] Marilyn Loden, *Implementing Diversity* (Burr Ridge, Ill.: Irwin Professional Publishing, 1996).

[20] R. Roosevelt Thomas Jr. Diversity Symposium, Washington, D.C., 1997.

[21] Taylor Cox Jr., *Cultural Diversity in Organizations: Theory, Research and Practice* (San Francisco: Berrett-Koehler, 1993).

[22] John E. Jones, "The Organizational Universe," in William Pfeiffer and John E. Jones, eds., *The 1981 Annual Handbook for Group Facilitators* (San Diego: University Associates, 1981).

[23] "Domestic Health Care," *USA Today*, October 8, 1997.

Chapter 12

[1] Badi G. Foster, et al, "Workforce Diversity and Business," *Training and Development Journal*, April 1988, pp. 38-42.

[2] In a conversation with the authors.

Chapter 13

1. Mary Cook, "The Workforce of the Year 2000," *Management Review*, August 1989, pp. 5, 34.
2. Ibid.
3. Estella Romero, "Reaching Out to the Hispanic Immigrant Workforce, "in *Interchange*. Los Angeles: Association of Training and Development, July 1989.
4. John Forsythe, *Boston Globe Magazine*, special advertising section, September 7, 2003.

Chapter 14

1. R. Roosevelt Thomas Jr., "From Affirmative Action to Affirming Diversity," *Harvard Business Review*, March/April 1990, p. 108.
2. Laura London, "Understanding Female Diversity." A document for the Pepsi-Cola Company, November 1991, p. 14.
3. Deborah Tannen, *You Just Don't Understand: Women and Men in Conversation* (New York: Ballantine, 1991), p. 244.
4. *Contemporary Leadership and Intercultural Competence*, Michael Moodian, editor. Fischer, Charles M., "Assessing Leadership Behavior as it Relates to Cultural Competence," Sage, Los Angeles, 2009.
5. Thomas L. Friedman, *The World Is Flat: A Brief History of the Twenty-first Century* (New York: Farrar, Straus and Giroux, 2005).
6. Jerry Willbur, "Does Mentoring Breed Success?" *Training and Development Journal*, November 1987, p. 38.
7. Michael G. Zey, "A Mentor for All Reasons," *Personnel Journal*, January 1988, pp. 46-51.
8. Stephen M. Wolfe, "A New Perspective," *Via a Vis*, June 1991, p. 12.

Chapter 15

1. "Allstate: Creating a World-Class Diversity Program," *BNC Communicator*, Vol. 15, No. 3, Fall 1997, pp. 1, 6.
2. Ibid.
3. Robert Hayles and Armida Mendez Russell, *The Diversity Directive* (Chicago: Irwin Professional Publishing, 1997), pp. 89-90.
4. Michael Wheeler, *Corporate Practices in Diversity Measurement* (Report No. 1164-96-RR). (New York: The Conference Board, 1996), pp. 7, 8, 15.
5. Ibid.
6. Ibid.
7. Hayles and Russell (1997).

Chapter 16

1. *Sustainability Progress Report to Date, 2007-2008: We're Making Sustainability Our Business*. www.walmartstores.com/sustainability.

2   *Target Corporate Responsibility Report.* http://sites.target.com.

3   Source Watch, *Corporate Social Responsibility*, January 22, 2010.

4   Conversation with the authors.

5   Ibid.

6   Barbara Frankel, "The Diversity Inc Top 10 Companies for Supplier Diversity," *Diversity Inc.* March 30, 2009.

7   McDonald's Corporation, 2009, *Worldwide Corporate Responsibility Online Report: The Values We Bring to the Table.*

8   Mary Francis Winters, "The Triple Bottom Line: Sustainability and Diversity: The New Business Case," Linkage Diversity Conference, March 16-18, 2009, The Writers Group.

9   Toyota in the Community. www.toyota.com/about/philanthropy/community.

10 Paul Clarke, "Green Degrees," *Alaska Airlines Magazine*, Feb. 2009.

11 Ibid.

12 Ibid.

13 Ibid.

14 Conversation with the authors.

Chapter 17

1   Conversation with the authors.

Index

Activities, worksheets, figures, tables, and charts are indicated by *italic* page numbers.

About the Authors

. . . .

Lee Gardenswartz, Ph.D., and Anita Rowe, Ph.D., began helping organizations with diversity in 1977. Since that time they have specialized in the "human side of management" for a variety of regional and national clients, helping them manage change, leverage diversity, build productive and cohesive work teams, and create inter-cultural understanding and harmony in the workplace.

In addition to direct client relationships, they have co-authored a series of books on diversity: *Managing Diversity: A Complete Desk Reference and Planning Guide* (1993), *The Managing Diversity Survival Guide* (1994), *The Diversity Tool Kit* (1994), *Diverse Teams at Work* (1995), *Managing Diversity in Health Care* (1998), *Managing Diversity in Health Care Manual* (1998), and *The Global Diversity Desk Reference* (2003). Their most recent publication is *Emotional Intelligence for Managing Results in a Diverse World* (2008.)

Among Gardenswartz & Rowe's clients are Harvard Medical School, Cox Communications, Starbucks, Equity Residential, Ohio State University, Shands Hospital at the University of Florida, Sempra Energy, IRS, Kaiser Permanente, Blue Cross Blue Shield of Florida, ABC, UCLA Medical Center, Boeing Aircraft Group, Walt Disney World, Shell Oil Company, and Progress Energy. Anita and Lee have lectured widely, giving keynote speeches, facilitating team building retreats, and teaching seminars across the country. Gardenswartz & Rowe's principals also continue to teach about diversity, not only through training in client organizations, but also through institutions such as the Intercultural Communication Institute in Portland, Oregon and the Emotional Intelligence and Diversity Institute.

For more information, see their two web sites:
www.eidi-results.org and wwwgardenswartzrowe.com.

Book + cd